Building Object
Applications That Work

Managing Object Technology Series

Charles F. Bowman
Series Editor
and
President
SoftWright Solutions,
Suffern, New York

1. What Every Software Manager Must Know to Succeed with Object Technology, *John D. Williams*

2. Managing Your Move to Object Technology: Guidelines and Strategies for a Smooth Transition, *Barry McGibbon*

3. The Object Primer: Application Developer's Guide to Object-Orientation, *Scott W. Ambler*

4. Getting Results with the Object-Oriented Enterprise Model, *Thornton Gale and James Eldred*

5. Deploying Distributed Business Software, *Ted Lewis, Ph.D.*

6. The Blueprint for Business Objects, *Peter Fingar*

7. Object Technology Strategies and Tactics, *Gilbert Singer*

8. Upgrading Relational Databases with Objects, *Robert Vermeulen*

9. Building Object Applications That Work: Your Step-by-Step Handbook for Developing Robust Systems with Object Technology, *Scott W. Ambler*

10. CUC96: Component-Based Software Engineering, *Collected and Introduced by Thomas Jell*

11. Developing Business Objects, *Edited by Andy Carmichael*

12. Component-Based Development for Enterprise Systems: Applying the SELECT Perspective™, *Paul Allen and Stuart Frost*

Additional Volumes in Preparation

Building Object Applications That Work

Your Step-by-Step Handbook for Developing Robust Systems with Object Technology

SCOTT W. AMBLER

 CAMBRIDGE
UNIVERSITY PRESS

 SIGS
BOOKS

PUBLISHED BY THE PRESS SYNDICATE OF THE UNIVERSITY OF CAMBRIDGE
The Pitt Building, Trumpington Street, Cambridge, United Kingdom

CAMBRIDGE UNIVERSITY PRESS
The Edinburgh Building, Cambridge CB2 2RU, UK   www.cup.cam.ac.uk
40 West 20th Street, New York, NY 10011-4211, USA   www.cup.org
10 Stamford Road, Oakleigh, Melbourne 3166, Australia
Ruiz de Alarcón 13, 28014 Madrid, Spain

Published in association with SIGS Books & Multimedia

First published 1998
Reprinted 2000

Composition by Doric Lay Publishers
Cover design by Brian Griesbaum

Printed in the United States of America

Typeset in Stone Serif

A catalog record for this book is available from the British Library

Library of Congress Cataloging in Publication Data is available

ISBN 0 521 64826 2 paperback

To

Rick Berman, Jeri Taylor, and Michael Piller

*Because I really, really, really want a walk-on part on
Star Trek Voyager*

Contents

About the Author, xix

Foreword, xxi

Preface, xxiii

Acknowledgments, xxix

Part I
INTRODUCTION TO BUILDING OBJECT APPLICATIONS

Chapter 1   Where We've Been Before—Object-Oriented
Concepts and Techniques, 3

1.1   Object-Oriented Concepts—A Really Quick Recap, 4

    1.1.1   Objects and Classes, 5

    1.1.2   Attributes and Methods, 6

    1.1.3   Abstraction, Encapsulation, and Information
Hiding, 6

Contents

1.1.4   Inheritance, 8

1.1.5   Persistence, 9

1.1.6   Instance Relationships, 10

1.1.7   Aggregation, 11

1.1.8   Collaboration, 12

1.1.9   Coupling and Cohesion, 12

1.1.10 Polymorphism, 13

1.2   Object-Oriented Analysis and Design Techniques—
A Really Quick Recap, 14

1.2.1   CRC Modeling, 14

1.2.2   Use-Case Scenario Testing, 20

1.2.3   Class Diagramming, 25

1.3   Iterative Object-Oriented Development—The Pinball
System Development Life Cycle (SDLC), 27

1.3.1   The Pinball Metaphor, 28

1.3.2   The Steps of the Pinball SDLC, 30

1.4   What We Missed in *The Object Primer*, 33

1.4.1   The Difference Between Class and Instance
Attributes, 33

1.4.2   The Difference Between Class and Instance
Methods, 35

1.4.3   The Implications of Class Attributes and
Methods, 37

1.4.4   What We Mean When We Say "Attribute" or
"Method," 40

1.4.5   The Ambler Class Diagram Notation v2.0, 40

1.4.6   The Unified Modeling Language Class-Diagram
Notation (Simplified), 41

1.5   Just in Case You've Forgotten—The Bank Case Study, 42

1.5.1   The ABC Case Study, 42

1.6   Where We're Going in This Book, 45

Contents

$\lfloor$ *ix* $\rfloor$

Part II
OBJECT-ORIENTED ANALYSIS, DESIGN, AND ARCHITECTURE

Chapter 2   Bubbles and Lines—Useful Diagrams for Object-Oriented Analysis and Design, 49

2.1 The Importance of Bubbles and Lines, 50

    2.1.1   Making Your Diagrams Look Good, 50

2.2 Other People's Notations—Understanding Class Diagrams, 54

2.3 Use-Case Diagrams—Understanding Use Cases, 57

    2.3.1   Drawing Use-Case Diagrams, 58

    2.3.2   Why and When Should We Create Use-Case Diagrams?, 59

2.4 Sequence Diagrams—Understanding Use Cases Even Better, 60

    2.4.1   How to Draw Sequence Diagrams, 62

    2.4.2   Why and When Should We Draw Sequence Diagrams?, 63

2.5 State Diagrams—Understanding Complicated Classes, 63

    2.5.1   How to Draw a State Diagram, 66

    2.5.2   Taking State Diagramming a Bit Further, 67

    2.5.3   When and Why Should We Draw State Diagrams?, 68

2.6 Collaboration Diagrams, 69

    2.6.1   Drawing Collaboration Diagrams, 69

    2.6.2   Why and When Should We Draw Collaboration Diagrams?, 70

2.7 Process Models—Understanding What's Currently Going On, 70

    2.7.1   Drawing Process Models, 72

    2.7.2   Why and When Should We Draw Process Models?, 74

2.8 Interface-Flow Diagrams—Understanding the User Interface, 74

2.8.1 Drawing Interface-Flow Diagrams, 75

2.8.2 Why and When Should We Draw Interface-Flow Diagrams?, 76

2.9 Data Models—Modeling Your Database Design, 77

2.9.1 Drawing Data Models, 78

2.9.2 Why and When Should We Draw Data Models?, 79

2.10 An Overall Analysis and Design Strategy, 79

2.11 What We've Learned, 81

Chapter 3 Improving Your Design—A Class-Type Architecture, 85

3.1 Why Do We Need a Class-Type Architecture?, 87

3.2 Building Up to a Class-Type Architecture, 87

3.2.1 A Two-Layer Class-Type Architecture, 88

3.2.2 A Three-Layer Class-Type Architecture, 90

3.2.3 A Four-Layer Class Architecture, 93

3.2.4 A Five-Layer Class-Type Architecture, 97

3.3 A Detailed Look at the Various Class Types, 98

3.3.1 Interface Classes, 98

3.3.2 Business Classes, 101

3.3.3 Persistence Classes, 102

3.3.4 System Classes, 105

3.4 Issues with the Five-Layer Class-Type Architecture, 106

3.4.1 To Which Layer Does This Class Belong?, 106

3.4.2 Can I Buy Some of These Classes?, 107

3.4.3 What Are the Implications for Project Management?, 109

3.4.4 What Are the Implications for Development?, 110

3.4.5 Is This Enough?, 113

3.4.6   What Are the Advantages and Disadvantages?, 114

3.5 What We've Learned, 114

Chapter 4   Reusing Your Development Efforts—Object-Oriented Patterns, 117

4.1 Design Patterns, 119

4.1.1   Singleton, 119

4.1.2   Proxy, 120

4.1.3   Roles Played (State), 122

4.2 Analysis Patterns, 125

4.2.1   Item-Item Description, 126

4.2.2   Business Entity, 128

4.2.3   Contact Point, 128

4.2.4   Shipping/Billing, 130

4.2.5   Place, 131

4.3 How to Use Patterns Effectively, 132

4.4 How to Discover New Patterns, 133

4.5 The Advantages and Disadvantages of Patterns, 134

4.5.1   Advantages, 134

4.5.2   Disadvantages, 135

4.6 What We've Learned, 136

Chapter 5   Development in the 90s and Beyond—Designing Distributed Object-Oriented Applications, 139

5.1 Centralized Mainframes, 141

5.2 Client/Server, 142

5.2.1   Two-Tier Client/Server, 144

5.2.2   Three-Tier Client/Server, 146

5.3 Distributed Classes, 148

    5.3.1   "Traditional" Client/Server Using Object Technology, 149

    5.3.2   Taking a Peer-to-Peer Approach—Object-Oriented Client/Server, 149

    5.3.3   Applets, 160

5.4 Distributed Objects, 161

    5.4.1   Common Object Request Broker Architecture, 163

5.5 What We've Learned, 167

Part III

OBJECT-ORIENTED CONSTRUCTION

Chapter 6   Measuring and Improving the Quality of Your Work—Object-Oriented Metrics, 171

6.1 What Are Metrics and What Can They Do for/to Me?, 172

6.2 Estimating Projects, 173

    6.2.1   Number of Key Classes, 174

    6.2.2   Person Days per Class, 174

    6.2.3   Classes per Developer, 175

    6.2.4   Number of Reused Classes, 176

    6.2.5   Function and Feature Points, 177

6.3 Improving Your Development Efforts, 178

    6.3.1   Analysis Metrics, 179

    6.3.2   Design Metrics, 180

    6.3.3   Construction Metrics, 185

    6.3.4   Testing Metrics, 189

6.4 Choosing the Right Tools, 190

    6.4.1   Comments per Method and Percentage of Commented Methods, 190

Contents

$$|xiii|$$

6.5 Improving Your Development Approach, 191

6.6 Metrics Success Factors, 191

6.7 What We've Learned, 194

Chapter 7   Choosing an Object-Oriented Language—
                Comparing the Leading Languages, 197

7.1 What to Look For in an OO Language, 198

7.2 The Leading OO Languages, 202

    7.2.1   C++, 202

    7.2.2   Java, 203

    7.2.3   ObjectCOBOL, 205

    7.2.4   Smalltalk, 207

    7.2.5   Comparing the Leading OO Languages, 207

7.3 Understanding Electronic Commerce on the Internet, 207

    7.3.1   An Architecture for Supporting Electronic
           Commerce, 209

    7.3.2   Payment Processing on the Internet, 210

    7.3.3   It's the WORLD Wide Web—International Issues, 211

    7.3.4   You Can Sell Both Physical and Virtual Products
           Internationally, 212

    7.3.5   Don't Forget Taxes, 212

    7.3.6   Using Smalltalk/ObjectCOBOL and Java to Develop
           Electronic Commerce Applications, 213

7.4 Beyond Programming Languages—Other Development Tools,
    216

7.5 What We've Learned, 218

Chapter 8   Building Your Application—Effective Object-
                Oriented Construction Techniques, 221

8.1 Attitude Is Everything, 222

    8.1.1   There's More to Development Than Just Coding, 222

Contents

$\boxed{xiv}$

8.1.2　There's More to Development Than Just Develop ment, 223

8.1.3　You Need to Get the Design Right First, 224

8.1.4　You Need to Develop in Small Steps, 225

8.1.5　You Need to Work Closely with Your Users, 226

8.2　Working with Attributes Effectively, 226

8.2.1　Naming Attributes, 226

8.2.2　Accessor Methods, 229

8.3　Writing High-Quality Methods, 237

8.3.1　Naming Methods, 237

8.3.2　Documenting Methods, 237

8.3.3　Paragraphing Your Code, 241

8.3.4　Methods Should Always Do Something, 242

8.3.5　Methods Should Do One Thing Only, 243

8.3.6　Do One Thing per Line, 244

8.3.7　The 30-Second Rule, 245

8.3.8　Specify Order of Message Sends, 245

8.3.9　Polymorphism the Right Way—Avoiding Case Statements, 246

8.4　Creating Maintainable Classes, 247

8.4.1　The Law of Demeter, 247

8.5　Programming Techniques and Approaches, 249

8.5.1　Implementing Instance Relationships, 249

8.5.2　Error Handling, 251

8.5.3　Callback Methods and Message Dispatchers, 253

8.6　Organizing Construction Around the Class-Type Architecture, 255

8.7　What We've Learned, 256

Contents

$$\boxed{xv}$$

Chapter 9   Making Your Applications Usable—Object-Oriented User Interface Design, 261

9.1   What Are Object-Oriented User Interfaces?, 262

    9.1.1   An OO Bank Teller Application, 264

    9.1.2   Why OOUIs Are Different but the Same, 268

9.2   Designing Effective User Interfaces, 269

    9.2.1   Human Factors, the Study of People Using Machines, 269

    9.2.2   Enough User Interface Design Tips to Sink a Ship, and Then Some, 273

9.3   Developing Effective Object-Oriented User Interfaces, 278

    9.3.1   Applications Are No More, Just Objects, 278

    9.3.2   You're Working with Objects Too, Not Just Windows, 280

    9.3.3   Modeling Object-Oriented User Interfaces, 281

    9.3.4   Prototyping Object-Oriented User Interfaces, 282

9.4   What We've Learned, 287

Chapter 10   Making Your Objects Persistent—Object-Orientation and Databases, 291

10.1   Getting Started—Some Common Terminology, 292

10.2   Saving Your Objects into Flat Files, 295

    10.2.1   An Approach to Mapping Objects to Flat Files, 295

10.3   The Current Reality—Relational Technology and OO Applications, 298

    10.3.1   Normalization, 299

    10.3.2   Overcoming the Object/Relational Impedance Mismatch, 311

    10.3.3   An Approach for Mapping Objects to Relational Databases, 326

    10.3.4   The Seven Commandments for Mapping Objects to Relational Databases, 332

10.3.5 Looking into My Crystal Ball—OO and RDB in the Future, 334

10.4 Persistence on the Leading Edge—Object-Oriented Databases, 334

10.4.1 What to Look For in an OODBMS, 335

10.4.2 Debunking the Myths of Object Databases, 338

10.5 Taking a Hybrid Approach—Object/Relational Databases, 339

10.6 What We've Learned, 341

Chapter 11 Integrating Legacy Code—Wrapping, 343

11.1 Why Wrap?, 344

11.2 Approaches to Wrapping, 346

11.2.1 Leaving Things Well Enough Alone, 347

11.2.2 Wrapping Only Hardware and Operating System Calls, 347

11.2.3 Scaffolding Legacy Applications, 347

11.3 Wrapping Technologies, 348

11.3.1 Wrapping Hardware and Operating-System Calls, 348

11.3.2 Wrapping Legacy Applications, 351

11.3.3 Comparing Wrapping Technologies—When to Use Each One, 355

11.4 The Advantages and Disadvantages of Wrapping, 357

11.5 What We've Learned, 358

Part IV
OBJECT-ORIENTED TESTING

Chapter 12 Making Sure Your Applications Work—Full Life-Cycle Object-Oriented Testing (FLOOT), 363

Contents

$\boxed{xvii}$

12.1 Why FLOOT?, 365

12.2 Testing Your Previous Efforts—Regression Testing, 367

12.3 Testing Your Analysis, 369

    12.3.1 Use-Case Scenario Testing, 370

    12.3.2 Prototype Walkthroughs, 370

    12.3.3 User-Requirement Reviews, 371

12.4 Testing Your Design, 372

    12.4.1 Technical-Design Reviews, 372

    12.4.2 Requirement-Verification Matrices, 379

12.5 Testing Your Program Code, 380

    12.5.1 Code Reviews, 382

    12.5.2 Traditional Testing Methods, 383

    12.5.3 New Testing Techniques for OO Program Code, 388

    12.5.4 Language-Specific Testing Issues, 398

    12.5.5 Implementing Program Code Test Cases, 398

    12.5.6 A Process for Successfully Testing Your Code, 401

    12.5.7 The Strengths of Each Program Code Testing Technique, 402

12.6 Testing Your Application As a Whole, 403

    12.6.1 System Testing, 403

    12.6.2 User-Acceptance Testing, 407

    12.6.3 Alpha, Beta, and Pilot Testing, 409

12.7 Software Quality Assurance and ISO 9000, 410

12.8 Testing Tips and Techniques, 412

12.9 Full Life-Cycle Object-Oriented Testing Overview, 414

12.10 What We've Learned, 415

Contents

$\boxed{xviii}$

Part V
CONCLUSION

Chapter 13 Where to Go from Here—Personal Success Strategies, 419

13.1 Advice for Overcoming the OO Learning Curve, 420

13.2 What We Learned in This Book, 422

13.3 Parting Words, 424

APPENDICES

Appendix A Notation Summary, 427

A.1 The Ambler Class Diagramming Notation, v2.0, 427

A.2 The Unified Modeling Language Class-Diagramming Notation v1.0 (Simplified), 428

Appendix B Visual Glossary, 429

Index, 457

About the Author

ScottAmbler IS AN INSTANCE of an **SeniorOOConsultant** with ambySoftInc based in Sharon, Ontario (http://www.ambysoft.com). Messages can be sent to him via the electronic mail facade scott@ambysoft.com.

scottAmbler is a very versatile object that will change type in order to meet the needs of his clients. For example, he often takes on the role of **OOMentor, OOTrainer, OOProcessExpert,** or **OODeveloper.** Scott has been an instance of an OOConsultant since 1991. ScottAmbler has instantiated the books *The Object Primer* (sigsBooksCambridgeUniversityPress, nyCity, 1995), *Building Object Applications That Work* (sigsBooksCambridgeUniversityPress, nyCity 1998), and *Process Patterns* (sigsBooksCambridgeUniversityPress, nyCity 1998). He holds the roles of contributingEditor with SoftwareDevelopment (millerFreemanPress), columnist with *ObjectMagazine* (sigsPublications), columnist with *ComputingCanada* (plesmanPublications). **scottAmbler** is an avid watcher of **StarTrekEpisodes,** and intends to one day do his doctorate degree at **starFleetAcademy.**

About the Author

| xx |

scottAmbler used to be a MastersStudent object, having received a InformationScienceDegree from the UniversityOfToronto. As a MastersStudent, scottAmbler did a lot of work in OO CASE and instantiated a ThesisPaper object in computer-supported co-operative work (an academic alias for groupware). Before being a MastersStudent, he was an instance of a TechnicalSystemAnalyst at RoyalBankOfCanada where he originally became interested in object-orientation.

Foreword

AS A BROAD-FACED INTRODUCTION to object-oriented (OO) technology, this is one of the best books that I have read. It is well written, employing a style that makes it enjoyable to read and easy to understand. Although it covers a diverse range of topics, the coverage is balanced and the topic selection is well chosen.

Topics that usually receive only passing mention in other texts of this kind are included. The first part of the book looks at where we have been in the field and lays a foundation for the rest of the text by introducing general concepts. The second part focuses on architectural issues, and the subjects of object-oriented analysis, design, and patterns are introduced. The author chooses to feature UML notation in the short examples that are presented. The third part introduces OO matrics, user interface design, and OO databases and presents a brief survey of some OO languages. The fourth part of the book focuses on OO testing. All these subjects are covered in much greater detail in more specialized books—but that is to be expected in a book of this kind. Experienced practitioners may object to the omission of important topics and incomplete coverage of some subject areas, but this book is not meant to be a rigorous treatise on object technology; rather, it is a compelling early read for those interested in this area of software development.

I recommend this book to programmers and managers who are relatively new to the field of object technology.

Richard Wiener
Editor, JOOP
Associate Professor of Computer Science,
University of Colorado at Colorado Springs

Preface

THIS BOOK is about:

- The Unified Modeling Language (UML), and how to use it effectively
- Architecting your applications so that they're maintainable and extensible
- Analysis, so you know what you have to build
- Design techniques, so that you know how you're going to build your application
- Creating applications for stand-alone, client/server, and distributed environments
- Using both relational and object-oriented (OO) databases to make your objects persistent
- Collecting the right metrics to improve your development approach
- Applying OO patterns to improve the quality of your applications
- Testing approaches to ensure that your applications work

- User interface design, so your users can actually work with the systems that you build

This book is about object-oriented development.

- Coding applications in a way that makes them maintainable and extensible

Welcome to *Building Object Applications*. To make this book easier to work with it is divided into the following five parts:

Part I   Introduction

Chapter 1   Where We've Been Before—Object-Oriented Concepts and Techniques

Part II   Object-Oriented Analysis, Design, and Architecture

Chapter 2   Bubbles and Lines—Useful Diagrams for Object-Oriented Analysis and Design

Chapter 3   Improving Your Design—A Class-Type Architecture

Chapter 4   Reusing Your Development Efforts—Object-Oriented Patterns

Chapter 5   Development in the 90s and Beyond—Designing Distributed Object-Oriented Applications

Part III   Object-Oriented Construction

Chapter 6   Measuring and Improving the Quality of Your Work—Object-Oriented Metrics

Chapter 7   Choosing an Object-Oriented Language—Comparing the Leading Languages

Chapter 8   Building Your Application—Effective Object-Oriented Construction Techniques

Chapter 9   Making Your Applications Usable—Object-Oriented User Interface Design

Chapter 10   Making Your Objects Persistent—Object-Orientation and Databases

Chapter 11   Integrating Legacy Code—Wrapping

Part IV   Object-Oriented Testing

Chapter 12   Making Sure Your Applications Work—Full Life-Cycle Object-Oriented Testing

Part V   Conclusion

Chapter 13 Where to Go from Here—Personal Success
Strategies

Introduction to Building Object Applications

This volume starts where *The Object Primer* left off—OO design. Well, actually it starts with a review of, and a few improvements to *The Object Primer*. To keep things simple I purposely left out a few things in the first volume, specifically class methods and class attributes. These two concepts are just too darn confusing for OO beginners, so I skipped them until this book. Besides, I wanted to make sure there was enough new stuff in the first chapter to make reading it worthwhile.

Object-Oriented Analysis, Design, and Architecture

In the second chapter we'll discuss several diagramming techniques that we didn't cover in the first book. We'll also learn some really good tips and techniques to make your diagrams look better, as well as how to convert back and forth from an Ambler Class Model to the notations of the other leading OO methodologies.

Chapter 3 introduces us to an OO class architecture. We'll propose a four-level architecture that actually has five and maybe even six levels, but who's counting? We then get into OO patterns in chapter 4. You've heard a lot about them, you've seen the huge tomes, now it's time to actually find out what this stuff is really all about. Because the proof is always in the pudding, but never in the jelly (for some reason) we'll look at several patterns that are being used in live applications today.

In chapter 5 we'll delve into distributed OO architectures. Because the client/server (C/S) architecture is currently the dominant approach to systems development, I figured we'd better show you how to design for C/S. We'll discuss the seven steps for creating an object-oriented client/server (OOCS) design. C/S can be very complex, and experience has shown that OO is the surest way to guarantee success in a C/S environment. We'll also discuss how OOCS leads to distributed objects, an architecture that is quickly catching on and that is most likely in your future.

Object-Oriented Construction

Chapter 6 covers object-oriented metrics that you can use both to estimate the size of a project and to evaluate how well you are doing. The design and coding implications that they make are what makes metrics important for developers. Understanding the basis for metrics will help you to improve your development skills.

We're going to spend a fair bit of time talking about OO languages and OO construction issues in chapters 7 and 8, so all you programmers out there might want to skip immediately to those chapters. Although there are a fair number of OO programming languages, we're going to concentrate on Smalltalk, C++, Java, and ObjectCOBOL. We're going to cover a lot of programming tips in these chapters, so I think that you'll really like it.

Chapter 9 covers interface design because it's critical that we design applications that are user-friendly. I begin by arguing that just because you use a graphical-user interface (GUI) it isn't necessarily OO. We'll see designs for both a standard GUI interface for the bank and an object-oriented user interface (OOUI) for it. When you see the difference you'll be astounded.

As saving objects is a reasonably common thing to do, we're going to cover this topic in detail in chapter 10. Relational technology is the reality out there, not object databases, so for most of the chapter I'll assume you're trying to store your objects in a relational database (DB). Unfortunately, this is easier said than done. We're going to discuss issues like OO normalization, converting objects to relational records, inheritance issues, and design issues when using a relational DB to store objects. The chapter ends with a discussion of both object/relational and object databases, what they're all about and where they're going. The bottom line is that object databases are an important topic that must be covered.

Chapter 11 discusses wrapping, which is a technique for getting a few more miles out of your legacy applications. If the legacy applications were horses we would have shot them long ago, but unfortunately we've made a huge investment in them that we'd prefer not to lose.

Object-Oriented Testing

As testing is always left to the very end of application development, that's exactly where we've put the testing chapter, at the back of the book. Until now, OO testing hasn't been well covered by the mainstream OO methodologies, and that's a problem we want to address. Users really like it when their application works, so it's not a bad idea to test your application before you release it. The bad news is that traditional testing techniques don't always work for OO applications. The good news is that chapter 12 describes several OO testing methods that are quite effective.

Conclusion

In chapter 13 we'll wrap up the book with a few pointers on how to succeed at learning object-oriented development techniques. They might seem obvious, but considering how many people have run into trouble learning this stuff, I highly suggest that you follow the advice in this chapter.

Who Should Read *Building Object Applications*?

For the most part, this book is geared toward designers, programmers, and testers. Analysts will find this material useful for filling out their knowledge of OO, but probably won't find it directly applicable to their daily jobs. Project managers of OO development teams should definitely read this book to gain a better understanding of what their people are doing.

Why the Unified Modeling Language?

In this book I've decided to move away from my original modeling notation to the Unified Modeling Language (UML), the notation that is quickly becoming the industry standard. I wanted to keep this book as simple as possible to communicate the fundamentals of OO development. I also wanted to do so in a manner that the knowledge you gain is directly applicable on your job. This is why I've adopted the UML, and why I hope that your organization adopts the UML as its standard notation as well. If you've read *The Object Primer* and have learned my notation, you don't have to worry; in chapters 1 and 2 we'll transition from the Ambler Notation to the UML very smoothly.

Acknowledgments

S PECIAL THANKS GO TO my friends at Mark Winter and Associates, who provided both excellent input and sounding boards for many of the concepts presented in this book. I'd also like to thank the friends that I have made at several client organizations while writing this book (although I can't reveal the organizations due to confidentiality issues, they were in Toronto, Rio, Buffalo, and Anchorage, so you folks know who you are). All of you helped to shape the experiences on which this book is based and I greatly appreciate it.

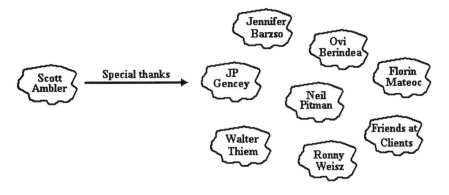

Part I

Introduction to Building Object Applications

Chapters

1 • Where We've Been Before — Object-Oriented Concepts and Techniques

Chapter 1

Where We've Been Before — Object-Oriented Concepts and Techniques

What We'll Learn in This Chapter

Object-oriented concepts, including a few that we missed in The Object Primer.

Modeling techniques like class responsibility collaborator (CRC) modeling, use-case scenario testing, and class diagramming.

An iterative development life cycle called "The Pinball System Development Life Cycle (SDLC)."

What this book is all about.

Unless you're reading The Object Primer *and* Building Object Applications That Work *back to back you're going to need a quick refresher. Furthermore, there's some new material in this chapter starting in section 1.3 (hey, like we'd want you to skip an entire chapter).*
Until the release of this book, The Object Primer *was the greatest thing since time-sliced bread. Now we have* Building Object Applications, *a book that is*

even more spectacular than its predecessor. In The Object Primer *we covered analysis techniques such as class responsibility collaborator (CRC) modeling and use-case scenario testing. We also introduced several object-oriented (OO) concepts and showed you how to model them using class diagrams. We finally put all this into the context of the Pinball System Development Life cycle (SDLC), an iterative and incremental approach to OO systems development.*

1.1 Object-Oriented Concepts — A Really Quick Recap

In *The Object Primer* we introduced you to several concepts that are critical to understanding the OO development process. Let's invest a few minutes reviewing the following object-oriented concepts:

- Objects
- Classes
- Attributes
- Methods
- Abstraction
- Encapsulation
- Information hiding
- Inheritance
- Persistence
- Instance relationships
- Aggregation
- Collaboration
- Coupling
- Cohesion
- Polymorphism

1.1.1 Objects and Classes

An *object* is any person, place, event, thing, screen, report, or concept that is applicable to the system. In a university system, Arthur Dent is a student object, he attends several seminar objects, and he is working on a degree object. In a banking system, Arthur is a customer object, and he has a checking account object from which he bounces rubber check objects. Consider an object-oriented inventory control system: every inventory item is an object, every delivery is an object, and every customer is an object. Things, events, and people are all objects in an OO inventory control system (actually everything is an object, I just like being specific sometimes).

An object is any person, place, thing, event, concept, screen, or report.

Objects are often similar to other kinds of objects. Students share similar characteristics (they do the same sort of things, they are described in the same sort of way), courses share similar characteristics, inventory items share similar characteristics, bank accounts share similar characteristics, and so on. Although we could model (and program) each and every object individually, that's a lot of work. We would prefer to define what it is to be a student once, define courses once, define inventory items once, define bank accounts once, and so on. That's why we need the concept of a *class* of objects.

A class is a blueprint from which objects are created.

When an OO program is running, objects are *instantiated* (created/defined) from classes. In other words a class is effectively a blueprint from which objects are created. We say that an object is an *instance* of a class, and that we *instantiate* objects from classes.

Objects are instances of a class.

DEFINITIONS

Object—Any person, place, thing, event, screen, report, or concept that is applicable to the design of the system. Objects have both data and functionality that define their behavior.

Class—A category of similar objects. A class is effectively a blueprint from which objects are created.

Instance—Another word for object. We say that an object is an *instance* of a class.

Instantiate—To create an instance. When we create an object we say that we *instantiate* it from a class.

1.1.2 Attributes and Methods

The basis of the object-oriented paradigm is the concept that systems should be built out of objects, and that objects have both data and functionality. *Attributes* define the data, whereas *methods* define the functionality.

DEFINITIONS

Attribute—Something that an object or class knows. An attribute is basically a single piece of data or information. Attributes can be simple, like a string or integer, or they can be a complex object, like an address or customer.

Method—Something that an object or class does. A method is similar to a function or procedure in structured programming.

Member function—This is the C++ term for method.

1.1.3 Abstraction, Encapsulation, and Information Hiding

When we determine what a class knows and does, we say that we abstracted the interface of the class. When we hide how the class will accomplish these things, we say that we *encapsulated* them. When we design the class well by restricting access to its attributes, we say that we've hidden their information.

The world is a complicated place. In order to deal with that complexity, we form generalizations, or *abstractions* of the things in it. For example, consider the abstraction of a person. A university needs to know a person's name, address, phone number, social security number, and educational background. A police department needs to know a person's name, address, phone number, weight, height, hair color, eye color, and so on. It's still the same person, just a different abstraction depending on the application at hand.

We abstract, or define, the interface of an object.

Although the act of abstraction tells us that we need to store a student's name and address, as well as be able to enroll students in seminars, it doesn't tell us how we are going to do this. *Encapsulation* deals with the issue of how do we intend to modularize the features of a system. In an object-oriented world we modularize systems into classes, which in turn are modularized into methods and attributes.

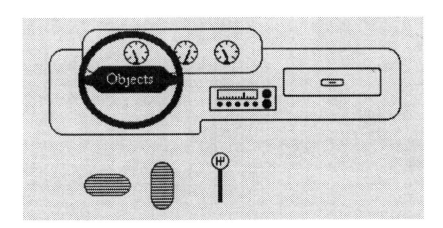

Figure 1.1.
The driver's interface for a car.

We say that we *encapsulate* behavior into a class, or that we *encapsulate* functionality into a method.

We encapsulate, or build, behavior into a class.

In order to make our applications maintainable we want to restrict access to data attributes and some methods. The basic idea is this—if one class wants information or services from another class, it should have to ask for it instead of take it. When you think about it, this is exactly the way that the real world works. If you want to find out somebody's name what would you do? Would you ask them their name or would you steal their wallet and look at their ID? By restricting access to attributes, which we call *information hiding,* we prevent programmers from writing highly coupled code. When code is highly coupled, a change in one part of the code forces us to make a change in another, and then another, and so on. We'll discuss coupling in detail later in this chapter.

Information hiding is the restriction of access to attributes.

In Figure 1.1, the abstraction is how we work with the wheel, pedals, and gear shift to drive a car. Encapsulation allows the different carmakers to provide a consistent interface, even though each make of car is built differently. Information hiding is represented by the fact that although there is a certain amount of oil in the engine, the driver doesn't know exactly what it is (well, at least I don't). In other words, information about the oil is hidden from the user.

DEFINITIONS

Interface—The set of messages an object or class will respond to.

continued

> **DEFINITIONS**
>
> *continued*
>
> **Abstraction**—The definition of the interface of a class (what it knows and does).
>
> **Encapsulation**—The hiding of the implementation of what a class/object knows or does, without telling anyone how it's done.
>
> **Information hiding**—The restriction of access to attributes.

1.1.4 Inheritance

There are often similarities between different classes. Very often two or more classes will share the same attributes and/or the same methods. Because we don't want to have to write the same code over and over and over and over and over we need a mechanism that takes advantages of these similarities. Inheritance is that mechanism. *Inheritance* models "is-a" and "is-like" relationships, allowing us to reuse existing data and code.

There are often similarities between classes. For example, students have names, addresses, and phone numbers, and they drive vehicles. At the same time, professors also have names, addresses, and phone numbers, and they drive vehicles. Without a doubt, we could develop the classes for student and professor, and get them both running. In fact, we could even develop the class **Student** first, and once it is running make a copy of it, call it **Professor**, and make the necessary modifications. Although this is fairly straightforward to do, it isn't perfect. What if there was an error in the original code for **Student**? Now we'd have to fix it in two places which is twice the work. What would happen if we needed to change the way we handled names (say we go from a length of 30 to a length of 40)? Now we'd have to make the same change in two places again. That's a lot of dull, boring, tedious work.

Inheritance models "is-a" and "is-like" relationships.

Wouldn't it be nice if somehow we could only have one copy of the code to develop and maintain? That's what inheritance is all about. Inheritance allows us to take advantage of similarities between classes and develop the code for them only once. In fact, you could say that inheritance goes hand in hand with abstraction: you abstract out the similarities and use inheritance to take advantage of them.

DEFINITIONS

Inheritance—This allows us to take advantage of similarities between classes by representing "is-a" and "is-like" relationships.

Superclass—If class "B" inherits from class "A," then we say that "A" is a superclass of "B."

Subclass—If class "B" inherits from class "A," then we say that "B" is a subclass of "A."

Single inheritance—When a class directly inherits from only one class, we say that we have single inheritance.

Multiple inheritance—When a class directly inherits from more than one class, we say that we have multiple inheritance. Note that not all OO languages support multiple inheritance.

Concrete class—A class that has objects instantiated (created) from it.

Abstract class—A class that does not have objects instantiated from it, but will provide functionality inherited by its subclasses.

Override—A term used to indicate that we redefine attributes and/or methods in subclasses to provide slightly or completely different behavior.

Overload—See override.

Class hierarchy—A set of classes that are related through inheritance.

Root—The topmost class in a class hierarchy.

1.1.5 Persistence

Persistence describes the issue of how to save objects to permanent storage. To make an object persistent you must save the values of its attributes to storage (onto disk), as well as any information needed to maintain the relationships (both aggregation and instance relationships) that it is involved with. Persistence allows objects to exist between executions of the system. A *persistent object* should be able to be recreated exactly at a future time.

Persistent objects are saved to permanent storage and transitory objects aren't.

From a development point of view, there are two types of objects: persistent objects that stick around and transitory objects that don't. For example, a customer is a persistent object. You want to save customer objects into permanent storage so that you can work with them again in the future. A customer editing screen, however, is a *transitory* object. Your application creates the customer editing screen object, displays it, then gets rid of it once the user is done editing the data for the customer with whom they are currently working. A common use for transitory objects is to manipulate data for a short period of time and then be discarded. In chapter 10 we will cover persistence in detail.

DEFINITIONS

Persistence—The issue of how objects are permanently stored.

Persistent object—An object that is saved to permanent storage, making it retrievable for future use.

Transitory object—An object that is not persistent.

Transient object—See transitory object.

Persistent memory—Main memory plus all available storage space on the network.

1.1.6 Instance Relationships

Objects are associated with, or are related to, one another. For example, students TAKE courses, professors TEACH courses, criminals ROB banks, politicians KISS babies, and captains COMMAND starships. Take, teach, rob, kiss, and command are all verbs that define relationships between objects. We want to identify and document these relationships so that we can gain a better understanding as to how objects interact with one another. An *instance relationship* is the same concept as a relationship in an entity-relationship (ER) diagram or a data model.

Not only must we identify what the relationship(s) are between objects, we must also describe the relationship. For example, it isn't enough to know that students take courses. How many courses do students take? None, one, or several? Furthermore, relationships are two-way streets: not only do students take courses, but courses are taken by students. This leads to questions like: how many students can be enrolled in any given course and is it possible to have a course with no one in it? We also need to identify the *cardinality* and *optionality* of the relationship. Cardinality tells you how many objects are involved in an instance relationship, whereas optionality indicates whether or not you have to do it.

Cardinality indicates how many objects are involved in a relationship, optionality indicates whether or not there have to be any objects involved.

DEFINITIONS

Instance relationship—There are relationships, or associations, between objects. For example, customers BUY products.

Association—Another term for instance relationship.

Cardinality—Indicates how many objects are involved in a relationship.

Optionality—Indicates whether or not it is mandatory that other objects are involved in a relationship.

1.1.7 Aggregation

Sometimes an object is made up of other objects. For example, an airplane is made up of a fuselage, wings, engines, landing gear, flaps, and so on. A delivery shipment is made up of one or more packages. A team consists of two or more employees. These are all examples of the concept of *aggregation*, which represents "is-part-of" relationships. An engine is part of a plane, a package is part of a shipment, and an employee is part of a team. Aggregation allows us to model these "part-of" relationships.

Aggregation models "is-part-of" relationships.

DEFINITION

Aggregation—Represents "is-part-of" relationships.

1.1.8 Collaboration

Objects collaborate (work together) by sending messages to other objects.

In order to get the job done, objects often need to *collaborate* (work) with other objects. For example, an airplane collaborates with its engines so that it can fly. In order for the plane to go faster, the engines must go faster. When the plane needs to slow down, the engines must slow down. If the airplane didn't collaborate with its engines effectively, it wouldn't be able to fly. Objects collaborate with one another by sending each other *messages*.

DEFINITIONS

Collaboration—Classes/objects work together (collaborate) to get things done.

Message—A message is either a request for information or a request to do something.

Messaging—In order to collaborate, classes send messages to each other.

1.1.9 Coupling and Cohesion

Coupling and *cohesion* may be the two most important principles to come out of the discipline of software engineering. To develop a system that is easy and inexpensive to maintain you want to develop classes that are loosely coupled and highly cohesive.

Coupling measures how interconnected two things are.

Coupling is a measure of how much two program modules, or in our case, classes or methods, are interconnected. When one class relies on another class, we say that they are coupled. When one class interacts with another class, but does not know any of the implementation details of the other class, we say that they are loosely coupled. When one class relies on the implementation (i.e., it directly accesses the data attributes of the other), we say that they are tightly coupled.

Cohesion measures how much something makes sense.

Cohesion is a measure of how much a class or method makes sense. A good measure of the cohesiveness of something is how long it takes to describe it in one sentence—the longer it takes, the less cohesive it is. We want to design methods and classes that are highly cohesive. In other words, it should be very clear to us what a method or class is all about. In chapter 3 we will discuss a class-type architecture that reduces the coupling between classes while at the same time increases their cohesion, which is exactly what we want.

DEFINITIONS

Coupling—A measure of how connected two classes are.

Cohesion—A measure of how much a method or class makes sense.

1.1.10 Polymorphism

Any individual object may be one of several types. For example, a "Ford Prefect" object may be a student, a registrar, or even a professor. Should it matter to other objects in the system what type of person Ford is? It would significantly reduce the development effort if other objects in the system could treat people objects the same way, and not have to have separate sections of code for each type. The concept of *polymorphism* says that you can treat instances of various classes the same way within your system.

TIP

Set Naming Conventions for Methods

Because polymorphism allows you to treat objects in similar ways, it is important to make sure that similar objects respond to the same types of messages to take advantage of this. For example, if you want a collection of objects to be able to output themselves to the printer, you should decide what you wish to call the method that will do this, perhaps **print** or **output**. If some classes implement the method as **print**, and others as **output**, then they really aren't polymorphic (they respond to different messages).

DEFINITIONS

Polymorphism—Polymorphism says that an object can take any of several forms, and that other objects can interact with the object without having to know what specific form it takes.

Polymorphic—Two classes are polymorphic when they exhibit the same public interface.

1.2 Object-Oriented Analysis and Design Techniques — A Really Quick Recap

It's all right to review the concepts we learned previously, but how do we apply them? In this section we'll briefly overview the three analysis-and-design techniques that we covered in *The Object Primer*. Hold onto your seats, this is going to be quick.

In *The Object Primer* we covered three main analysis-and-design techniques:

1. CRC modeling

2. Use-case scenario testing

3. Class diagramming

1.2.1 CRC Modeling

The first step of systems development is to gather user requirements. You can't build a system if you don't know what it should do. *CRC (class responsibility collaborator) modeling* provides a simple yet effective technique for working with your users to determine their needs.

CRC modeling is an analysis technique in which users form most of the modeling team.

CRC modeling is a process in which a group of *business domain experts (BDEs)* analyze their own needs for a system. CRC modeling sessions typically start with brainstorming, a technique in which people suggest whatever ideas come into their heads (the topic under discussion is the system at hand). Brainstorming allows people to get loosened up, as well as to gain a better understanding of where the other BDEs are coming from. After the brainstorming is finished the group produces a CRC model together, which describes the requirements for the system.

A *CRC model* (Ambler, 1995; Beck & Cunningham, 1989; Wirfs-Brock, Wilkerson, and Wiener, 1990; Jacobson, 1992) is a collection CRC cards, standard index cards (usually 5"x7") that have been divided into three sections as shown in Figure 1.2.

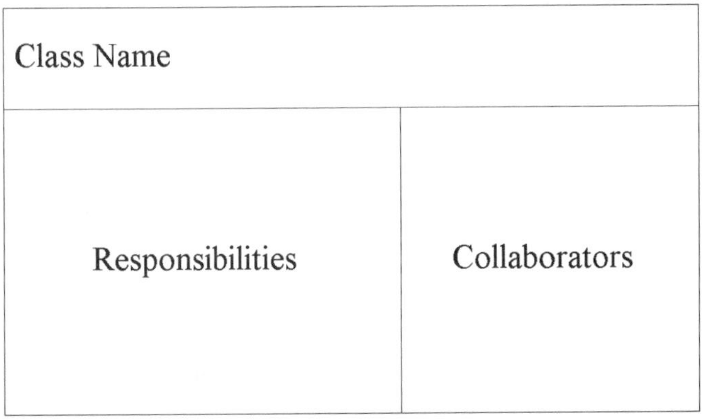

Class Name	
Responsibilities	Collaborators

Figure 1.2.
CRC card layout.

DEFINITIONS

CRC card—A standard index card divided into three sections showing the name of the class, the responsibilities of the class, and the collaborators of the class.

CRC model—A collection of CRC cards that describe the classes that make up a system or a component of a system.

CRC modeling—The act of creating a CRC model.

Business domain expert (BDE)—Someone with intimate knowledge of all or a portion of the problem domain that you are modeling.

Class—A class represents a collection of similar objects. An object is a person, place, thing, event, or concept that is relevant to the system at hand. For example, in a university system there would be **Student**, **Professor**, and **Course** classes. The name of the class appears across the top of the card.

Responsibility—A responsibility is anything that a class/object knows or does. For example, students have names, addresses, and phone numbers. These are the things that a student knows. Students also enroll in seminars (I realize that the term "class" is more common than "seminar," but because we are already using the term "class" to mean something else, "seminar" is more appropriate), drop seminars, and request transcripts. These are the things that students do. *continued*

The things that a class knows and does constitute its responsibilities. *Important:* A class/object is able to change the values of the things that it knows, but it is not able to directly change the values of what other classes know. In other words, classes update their own attributes, and nobody else's.

Collaborator—Sometimes a class/object will have a responsibility to fulfill, but will not have enough information to do it alone. For example we see in Figure 1.3 that students sign up for seminars. To do this, a student needs to know if there is a spot available in the seminar, and if so he then needs to be added to the seminar. Students only have information about themselves (their name, . . .), however, and not about seminars. What the student needs to do is collaborate (work with) the card labeled **"Seminar"** in order to sign up for the seminar. Collaboration will take on one of two forms: a request for information (in this case the card **"Student"** requests an indication from the card **"Seminar"** whether or not there is a space available) or a request to do something (in this case **"Student"** will then request to be added to the **"Seminar"** if there is a seat available).

Figure 1.3.
An example of a
CRC card.

Student	
Student number	Seminar
Name	
Address	
Phone	
Enrol in a seminar	
Drop a seminar	
Request transcripts	

1.2.1.1 CRC Modeling in a Nutshell

There are two main steps to CRC modeling: you must first plan the session, and then you must facilitate it. For the most part, the planning process is determining who to get into the CRC modeling room —you'd like to have business domain experts (BDEs) who know the business well. The facilitation process is a little more complicated, and is made up of the following steps:

1. Brainstorm.

2. Explain the CRC modeling technique.

3. Iteratively perform the following modeling steps:
   - Find classes
   - Find responsibilities
   - Define collaborators
   - Define use cases
   - Rearrange the cards
   - Prototype

4. Perform use-case scenario testing (covered in the next section)

1.2.1.1.1 Brainstorming Pointers

- All ideas are good—they aren't judged by the group.

- All ideas are owned by the group, not the individual.

- All ideas immediately become public property, anybody is allowed to expand on them.

1.2.1.1.2 Explaining How to CRC Model

- Walk through some sample cards.

- Suggest a few classes to start them out (such as "Customer").

1.2.1.1.3 Finding Classes

- Look for anything that interacts with the system or is part of the system.
- Ask yourself, "Is there a customer?"
- Follow the money and/or workflow.
- Look for reports generated by the system.
- Look for any screens used in the system.
- Immediately prototype interface and report classes.
- Look for the three to five main classes right away.
- Create a new card for a class immediately.
- Use one or two words to describe the class.
- Class names are singular.

1.2.1.1.4 Finding Responsibilities

- Ask yourself what the class knows.
- Ask yourself what the class does.
- If you've identified a responsibility, ask yourself what class it belongs to.
- Sometimes we identify responsibilities that we won't implement, and that's OK.
- Classes will collaborate to fulfill many of their responsibilities.

1.2.1.1.5 Defining Collaborators

- Collaboration occurs when a class needs information that it doesn't have.
- Collaboration occurs when a class needs to modify information that it doesn't have.

- There will always be at least one initiator of any given collaboration.

- Sometimes the collaborator does the bulk of the work.

- Don't pass the buck.

- New responsibilities may be created to fulfill the collaboration.

1.2.1.1.6 Defining Use Cases

- The BDEs will identify use cases as responsibilities of actor classes.

- Do some brainstorming.

- Transcribe the scenarios onto cards.

1.2.1.1.7 Moving the Cards Around

- Cards that collaborate with each other should be close to one another on the desk.

- The more that two cards collaborate, the closer they should be on the desk.

- Expect to move the cards around a lot at the beginning.

- Put "busy" cards toward the center of the table.

- Actually move them around.

- People will identify business relationships between classes as they move them around.

1.2.1.1.8 Prototyping

- Do it right away.

- Tape the prototypes on the wall for everyone to see.

- Ask yourself what functionality the prototype represents.

1.2.1.2 Advantages and Disadvantages of CRC Modeling

In Table 1.1 we see a summary of the advantages and disadvantages of CRC modeling (Ambler, 1995).

Table 1.1. THE ADVANTAGES AND DISADVANTAGES OF CRC MODELING

Advantages	Disadvantages
The subject-matter experts do the analysis	CRC modeling is threatening to developers
User participation increases	It's hard to get users together
It breaks down communication barriers	CRC cards are limited
It's simple and straightforward	You still need class diagramming
It's nonthreatening to users	You need management support
It's inexpensive and portable	Doesn't collect all user requirements
It goes hand in hand with prototyping	
It provides a good system overview	
It leads directly into class diagramming	
It is an effective method to gather detailed user requirements	
It allows you to deal with system complexity one class at a time	

1.2.2 Use-Case Scenario Testing

Use-case scenario testing is an integral part of the object-oriented development life cycle. It is performed immediately after CRC modeling by the same group of people who created the CRC model. In fact, many people consider use-case scenario testing as simply an extension of CRC modeling. Basically, use-case scenario testing is a technique that helps to ensure that your analysis, in this case your CRC model, accurately reflects the aspect of the real-world business that you are modeling. In short, it helps you to find errors in your analysis.

Use-case scenario testing helps you to verify your CRC model.

1.2.2.1 What Is a Use-Case Scenario?

A *use-case scenario* or *use case* is a description of a potential business situation that users of a system may face. For example, the following would be considered use-case scenarios for a university information system:

- A student wishes to enroll in a course, but he doesn't have the prerequisites for it.

- A professor requests a seminar list for every course that she teaches.

- A student wants to drop a seminar the day before the drop date.

- A student requests a printed copy of his transcript so that he may include copies of it with his resume.

In short, a use case describes a way in which a real-world actor interacts with the system.

1.2.2.2 Why Are Use-Cases Important?

Use cases help us to gain a better understanding of how the system will be, or perhaps won't be, used. By acting them out on our CRC model, we are able to detect analysis errors when they are easiest to fix—during analysis.

> **DEFINITION**
>
> *Analysis error*—An analysis error occurs when:
> - A user requirement is missing.
> - A user requirement is misunderstood.
> - A user requirement is ambiguous.

There are several problems endemic to the testing of systems (described below). Use-case scenario testing is one approach that attempts to address these issues by performing tests at the beginning of the system development process.

INTERESTING ISSUES IN TESTING

- The most significant mistakes are those made during analysis.
- The cost of fixing errors increases the later they are detected in the development life cycle.
- Developers don't like to test their systems.
- When left to the end of the life cycle, testing is often left out.
- Testing should done throughout the entire development process.
- We test systems the way we think they are supposed to be used, not the way they actually get used.
- Users lower their resistance to change when they are involved in the testing process.

1.2.2.3 How to Perform Use-Case Scenario Testing

1. *Perform CRC modeling.* See previous section. Use-case scenario testing is performed as either a part of CRC modeling (this is usually the way to go) or is performed as a separate task immediately following CRC modeling (you could then argue that it is still part of the CRC modeling process).

2. *Create the use-case scenarios.* A use-case scenario describes a particular situation that your system may or may not be expected to handle. Although many scenarios were created during CRC modeling, we'll see in the next section that some new ones will still need to created. You'll typically start by having the business domain experts brainstorm some scenarios. The scenarios are then transcribed onto index cards. We'll discuss this process in greater detail in the next section.

3. *Distribute the CRC cards among the BDEs.* The CRC cards need to be distributed evenly among the BDEs. Each BDE should have roughly the same amount of processing in their hands. This means that some BDEs will have one or two busy cards, whereas others may have numerous not-so-busy cards. The main goal here is to spread the functionality of the system evenly among BDEs. Additionally, it is very important that you DO NOT give two cards that collaborate to the same person. The reason for this will become apparent when we discuss acting out the scenarios.

4. *Describe how to act out a scenario.* The majority of effort in use-case scenario testing is the acting out of scenarios. Just like you needed to explain CRC modeling to your BDEs, you must also describe how to act out scenarios. The best way to do this is to first describe the process, and then to walk through one or two scenarios with them.

5. *Act the scenarios out.* As a group, the facilitator leads the BDEs through the process of acting out the scenarios. The basic idea is that the BDEs take on the roles of the cards that they were given, describing the business logic of the responsibilities that support each use-case scenario. To indicate which card is currently doing "processing," a soft, spongy ball is held by the person with that card. Whenever a card has to collaborate with another one, the user holding the card throws the ball to the holder of the second card. The ball helps the group to keep track of who is currently describing the business logic, and also helps to make the entire process a little more interesting. We want to act the scenarios out so that we gain a better understanding of the business rules/logic of the system (the scribes write this information down as the BDEs describe it), and find missing or misunderstood responsibilities and classes. Because some scenarios are fairly straightforward, you may choose not to act those ones out at all. This process is summarized below in Figure 1.4.

6. *Update the CRC model.* As the BDEs are working through the scenarios, they'll discover that they are missing some responsibilities, and sometimes even some classes. Great, that's why we're acting out the scenarios in the first place. When the group discovers that the CRC model is missing some information, the model should be updated immediately. As a result, once all of the scenarios have been acted out the group ends up with a fairly bullet-proof model. There is very little chance of missing information (assuming you generated a complete set of use-case scenarios) or of misunderstood information (the group has acted out the scenarios, describing the exact business logic in detail).

7. *Save the scenarios.* Don't throw the scenarios away once you are finished acting them out. The stack of scenario cards is a really good start at your user acceptance test plan, so keep the cards. We'll use them later for system maintenance, documentation, and enhancement.

Figure 1.4.
A flow chart
describing how to
act out scenarios.

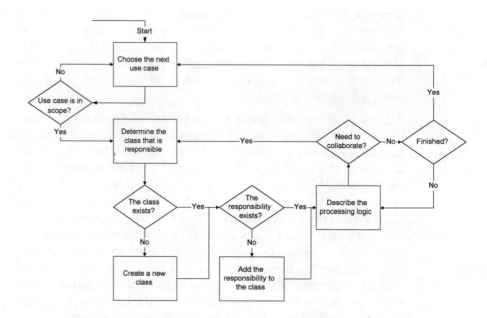

Table 1.2. The Advantages and Disadvantages of Use-Case Scenario Testing

Advantages	Disadvantages
It helps you to find and fix analysis errors	Your BDEs must make the time to do it
It provides you with a detailed description of the business logic of the system	It's low tech—developers are often skeptical
It's simple and it works	People often feel "real" work isn't accomplished

> **DEFINITIONS**
>
> *Use case*—A description of a real-world scenario that a system may or may not be able to handle.
>
> *Use-case scenario testing*—The process of having a group of BDEs act out use-case scenarios to ensure that their CRC model handles the use cases correctly.

1.2.3 Class Diagramming

Class diagrams are the mainstay of OO analysis-and-design.

Class diagrams, often called *object models*, show the classes of the system, their inter-relationships (including inheritance, aggregation, and instance relationships), and the collaborations (interactions) between those classes. Class diagrams are the mainstay of object-oriented analysis-and-design. We use them to show both what the system should be able to do (analysis), and how we're going to do it (design).

1.2.3.1 The Steps of Class Diagramming

Because class diagramming is used for both object-oriented analysis-and-design, there are naturally both analysis-and-design steps in the class-modeling process. In fact, in this chapter we'll see that all of the steps of class diagramming have both analysis-and-design aspects to them. It needs to be noted, however, that for the most part the "Find" steps are analysis, and the "Define" steps are design. The steps of class diagramming are as follows:

- Find classes
- Find attributes
- Find methods
- Find relationships
- Define inheritance
- Define collaborations
- Define aggregation

*CRC modeling
and class
diagramming go
hand-in-hand!*

As you can see there is a fair bit of overlap between CRC modeling and class diagramming. For example, both techniques include the steps "find classes" and "define collaborations." Additionally, the CRC modeling step "find responsibilities" is covered by the steps "find attributes" and "find methods" (remember, responsibilities are the things that a class knows [its attributes], and the things that a class does [its methods]). It is this overlap in modeling steps that allows us to take our CRC model and convert it into a class diagram.

GREAT MOMENTS IN OO ANALYSIS

As I was writing this book I was involved in the analysis-and-design of a new billing system, and three weeks into the project I was reasonably convinced that we had a handle on what we were doing. I was watching TV one night and an advertisement for the client came on. Being the dedicated consultant that I am, I paid close attention to the ad, especially because I knew I really hadn't seen a lot of their ads. Part way through the ad they started talking about a new promotion that I hadn't heard about yet, but would soon have to bill for. A brand-new user requirement, and I didn't even need to lift a finger. Yet another great moment in object development.

1.2.3.2 How Class Diagramming Fits In

Although both CRC modeling and use-case scenario testing are incredibly effective, the main problem with them is that we really can't justify handing off a stack of index cards to upper management as our analysis document. They just won't go for it. Additionally, although a CRC model provides an excellent overview of a system it doesn't show the details that we need to build the system—that's why we have scribes to take down the business logic during CRC modeling. As shown in Figure 1.5, we use our CRC model as a base and fill in the details required in a class diagram from the scribe's notes.

CRC models show the initial classes of a system, their responsibilities, and the basic relationships (in the form of a list of collaborators) between those classes. Although our CRC model of user requirements provides an excellent overview of a system, it does not provide the details needed to actually build the system. Luckily, those details have been captured in the notes taken down by the scribe(s) during CRC modeling. We use the CRC model and the detailed notes

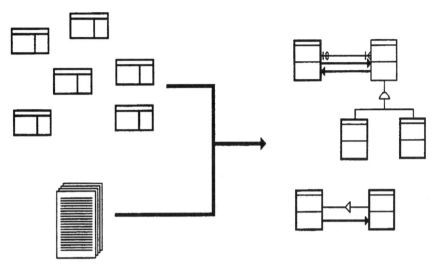

Figure 1.5.
Your CRC model and the scribe's notes are used as input for your class diagram.

as input for our class diagram. The main goal in class diagramming is to "flesh out" our CRC model, and naturally make improvements to it, in order to document the results of our analysis-and-design in a manner that developers can use to construct a system.

Class diagrams show greater detail than CRC models.

DEFINITION

Class diagram—Class diagrams show the classes of the system, their interrelationships, and the collaborations between those classes.

1.3 Iterative Object-Oriented Development—The Pinball System Development Life Cycle (SDLC)

Experience shows us that an iterative approach to systems development improves our chances for successfully developing OO applications. The Pinball System Development Life Cycle (SDLC) (Ambler 1994, Ambler 1995) of Figure 1.6 is an iterative Object-Oriented System Development Life Cycle (OOSDLC). The basic idea is that the game of pinball is an excellent metaphor for systems development.

Figure 1.6.
The Pinball SDLC.

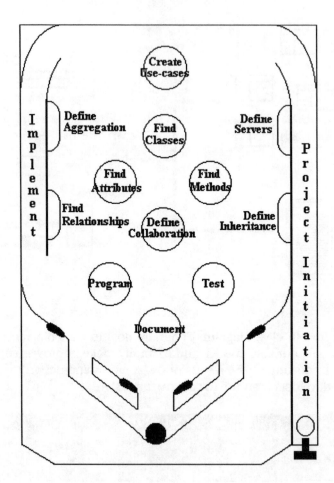

1.3.1 The Pinball Metaphor

1. *The ball.* The ball represents the current version of the application or system under development.

2. *The bumpers.* The bumpers represent the steps of OO systems development. Unlike structured development, which for the most part is serial in nature, OO development is an iterative process. Instead of performing analysis, then design, then programming, then testing, with OO development you may do a little bit of analysis, then some design and programming, then back to

analysis. Although you perform the same OO development tasks over and over again, the order in which you do them is never quite the same. It's exactly the same when you are playing pinball. The ball is constantly bouncing off the same set of bumpers, yet doing so in a different order each game.

3. *The points.* The points scored during the game represent the benefits achieved by the project. When the ball bounces off a bumper, the player scores some points. When the project goes through a development step, some benefits are derived for the company (one hopes).

4. *The player.* The player represents the project manager. Just like the player guides the ball through the game, the project manager guides the project through development. The better the player, the more points that can be scored. The better the project manager, the more benefits she will achieve for her company.

5. *The machine.* The pinball machine represents the way in which an organization develops systems. Just like every pinball machine is similar yet different, so is the way that every organization develops systems.

6. *The paddles.* The paddles represent project resources. A pinball player uses the paddles to keep the ball bouncing between bumpers, whereas a project manager commits resources such as money, time, and people to keep a project going.

7. *The hole.* The hole represents a major transition point in the life of a project. During play the ball sometimes goes down the hole. When this happens, either the ball is put back into play, or the game ends. Every so often throughout the life of a project, development work stops on it. At this point one of two things will happen—either development begins on a new version (the ball is put back into play) or the project is finished (the game is over).

8. *The quarter.* Putting the quarter in represents the project feasibility study. Sometimes you put a quarter in a pinball machine and the game is activated, and sometimes the machine just eats your quarter. It's exactly the same with project feasibility studies: sometimes the project is a good idea and you get approval for it, sometimes you don't. In both cases you've invested something—either a quarter or your time and effort. Additionally, in both cases you may or may not get to play the game.

9. ***The plunger.*** The plunger represents management approval to begin the project. The player pulls on the plunger to get the ball rolling, and management gives its approval to get the project going.

1.3.2 *The Steps of the Pinball SDLC*

The bumpers of the pinball machine represent the iterative steps of object-oriented development. In this section we describe the various steps that are taken during OO systems development.

1.3.2.1 *Project Initiation*

Project initiation doesn't change under the OO paradigm. We still need to do a feasibility study. Feasibility studies address the issue of whether or not your organization should go ahead with a project. A feasibility report will include a cost/benefit analysis indicating whether a project is economically viable, an indication of whether the project is operationally viable, and an indication of whether it is currently possible to build the project.

The one main difference is that for your first OO project you will likely need to sell the concept of the OO paradigm to upper management during the project initiation phase. This means you will have to consider training/retooling issues, language issues, methodology issues, and so on. The third volume in this book series will discuss this issue in detail.

1.3.2.2 *Create Use Cases*

Use cases are created during analysis, usually during interviews, brainstorming sessions, or CRC modeling sessions. Business domain experts are the best, and arguably the only valid source, of use cases. A use case should describe a business scenario that the system may or may not be able to handle. It is also important to determine how important the use case is, that is, is it a must have or a nice to have?

1.3.2.3 *Find Classes*

A class is any person, place, thing, event, concept, screen, or report that is applicable to the application being developed. If you think that you've identified a potential class, try to find either attributes or methods for it. If you can, chances are exceptionally good that you've found a class.

1.3.2.4 Find Attributes

To find attributes you need to ask yourself what information you need to store about this class. For example, we need to store the balance and account number for bank accounts, as well as the name and address of customers.

1.3.2.5 Find Methods

To find methods you need to ask yourself what does this class do (or what is it asked to do by other classes?). For example, bank accounts need to be able to deposit to and withdraw from themselves.

1.3.2.6 Find Relationships

There are often associations between objects, and even between classes and objects. For example, customers HAVE accounts and students TAKE courses. You'll find relationships during CRC modeling when your BDEs describe the application. You'll also find relationships when you define collaborations (see below) as you need a relationship between two objects before they can communicate.

1.3.2.7 Define Inheritance

Inheritance describes "is-a" and "is-like" relationships—it models similarities between classes. When you notice that two or more classes have similar attributes and/or methods you have a potential opportunity for inheritance. The key to determining whether or not inheritance is applicable is that the following sentence should make sense: "An object A is (like) an object B." For example, the sentence "a student is a person" makes sense, but "a student is a vehicle" doesn't. Therefore the class Student can potentially inherit from Person, but not from Vehicle.

1.3.2.8 Define Collaborations

Objects collaborate (work with) one another to get tasks done. Collaboration occurs in one of two ways: an object requests another object to do something for it, or an object requests information from another object.

1.3.2.9 Define Aggregation

Aggregation models "is-part-of" relationships. Just like with inheritance, the following sentence must make sense: "An object A is part of an object B." For example, it makes sense to say "a person is part of a team" or "an engine is part of an airplane." It doesn't make sense to say "a person is part of an airplane."

1.3.2.10 Programming

With the OO approach, programming should be only 10% to 15% of the entire development effort. As we'll see througout this book, the majority of the OO development process is concentrated on analysis-and-design. One of the advantages of object orientation is that very little effort is needed to go from design to programming. The reason for this is simple—both OO programming and OO design are based on the same principle, to build systems out of reusable components called objects. When you are coding in an OO environment, you are basically filling in the details for a class. Chapters 6 and 7 cover object-oriented construction in detail.

1.3.2.11 Testing

We still need to verify that our system works. On the one hand object-oriented testing is similar to structured testing in that both white/clear box and black box testing is applicable. On the other hand it is different from structured testing because instead of unit and integration testing, we now have method, class, and integration testing. Chapter 12 covers OO testing in detail.

1.3.2.12 Document

In *The Object Primer* we talked about how to properly document class diagrams, and in this book we'll continue to discuss documentation issues. As I've said before, there's a fine line between overdocumenting a system and underdocumenting it. Only through experience, and reading this book series of course, can you learn how to properly document your development efforts.

1.3.2.13 Implementation

Implementation of an OO project should be little different than what your organization has done in the past. When and what you implement might change, however. Because you are developing the system in an iterative manner, you may be in a position to implement small parts of the system at a time. This enables you to get functionality out into the hands of your users quickly, and at the same time make it obvious that you are doing some work. Implementing in small steps is often radically different than what many developers are currently used to. With the ever-changing business environment, gone are the days of the multiyear project. We need to be able to give systems to our users quickly. That means quick releases, and one way to do that is implementing in small steps, a process called incremental development.

1.3.2.14 Define Servers

Part of object-oriented development is the process of mapping your design to your hardware architecture. As we'll see in chapter 5, defining servers is a large part of this process as we discuss how to map an OO design onto an OO client/server architecture. It is during this process that we separate our classes among one or more servers.

1.4 What We Missed in *The Object Primer*

You had enough to learn in the first book without the addition of several often-confusing concepts. Actually, confusing isn't the correct term—perhaps "not so critical for the purposes of analysis" is a better one. So, I made an executive decision and purposefully left out two concepts from *The Object Primer*: class attributes and class methods.

1.4.1 *The Difference Between Class and Instance Attributes*

Instance attributes, usually referred to simply as "attributes," are chunks of information that are applicable to a single object (instance). *Class attributes*, on the other hand, are chunks of information that are applicable to a class as a whole. In other words, class attributes describe information that is common to a collection of

A class attribute describes information that is applicable to all instances of a class.

Figure 1.7.
Adding class
attributes to
accounts.

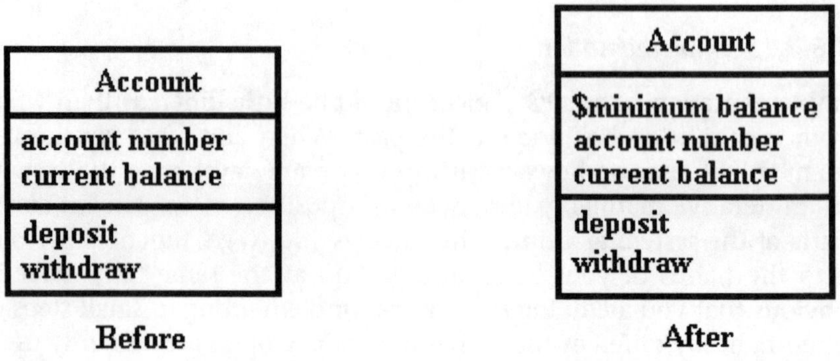

Account
account number current balance
deposit withdraw

Before

Account
$minimum balance account number current balance
deposit withdraw

After

similar objects. Think of it like this—a class attribute is a variable that is visible to all instances of a class.

Consider bank accounts. Accounts have account numbers and current balances. Account numbers and current balances obviously are applicable to individual accounts. Because the values of the account number and the current balance are different for each account we say that they are instance attributes. As instance attributes they define information that is specific to a single object.

Accounts also have minimum-deposit levels. If your balance dips below that level you don't receive any interest. Suppose the minimum-deposit level is $500 and it is the same for all accounts. If we make the minimum-deposit level an instance attribute it will be maintained for each and every account, potentially in millions of places. This doesn't make sense. A better solution is to store it once as a class attribute.

Figure 1.7 shows a before and after picture of the class **Account**. The before picture shows only the instance attributes whereas the after picture includes class attributes as well. Notice how we add a dollar sign ($) onto the beginning of the attribute name to denote class attributes. Also notice how we listed class attributes first, a habit that I've found to be quite effective.

Class attributes appear first and are preceded by a dollar sign.

The dollar sign is the notation proposed in the *Unified Modeling Language (UML)* (Booch, Jacobson, Rumbaugh, 1997), the OO modeling notation that is quickly becoming the industry standard. In this book we will use a subset of the UML for all of our diagrams, moving away from my original approach, The Ambler Notation (Ambler, 1995). Don't worry, as I promised in *The Object Primer* (Ambler, 1995) it isn't very hard to move from my notation to another one. At the end of this chapter we will present an updated version of The Ambler Notation as well as a summary of the class-diagram notation from the UML. In chapter 2 we will explore many of the diagrams from the UML, using them throughout the rest of the book where appropriate.

DEFINITIONS

Instance attribute—Information that is specific to a single object.

Class attribute—Information that is applicable to an entire class of objects.

Unified Modeling Language (UML)—The industry standard OO modeling notation proposed by Grady Booch, James Rumbaugh, and Ivar Jacobson. At the time of this writing the UML is being considered by the OMG to make it the OMG standard.

1.4.1.1 A Thought-Provoking Question

How should interest rates be stored? As an instance attribute of account, as a class attribute of account, or as an object in their own right?

The answer depends on how complex interest calculations are at the bank. If all accounts receive the same rate of interest, say 5% annually, then make the interest rate a class attribute. Even if the interest rate is different for each kind of class, you can always have a different value for each subclass. However, if interest calculations are complex then you should probably make interest rate a class in its own right. See section 1.4.3.3 for this solution.

1.4.2 The Difference Between Class and Instance Methods

Just like there is a need to distinguish between the two different types of attributes, we must also distinguish between two different types of methods. *Instance methods* are applicable to individual objects, modifying and accessing instance attributes. *Class methods*, as you would expect, are applicable to classes.

Class methods are applicable to a single class, not to a single object.

Once again, consider accounts. You can deposit and withdraw to/from accounts. The "deposit" method adds money to your balance, while the "withdraw" method subtracts money from your balance. Because these methods are applicable to an individual account, we say

Figure 1.8.
Accounts with
class methods
added.

Figure 1.8.
Accounts with
class methods
added.

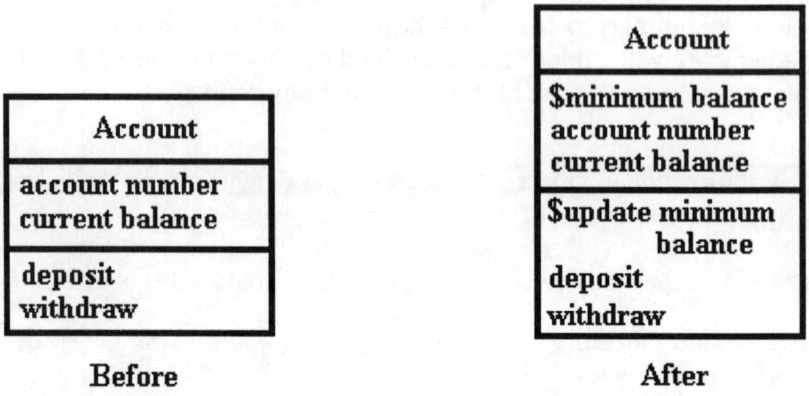

they are instance methods. Due to the competitive pressures of the marketplace the bank often finds that it needs to change the minimum balance depending on the time of year. As a result, it needs a method to update the value of the minimum balance. Because it applies to the class as a whole, we say this is a class method. In Figure 1.8 we see that we precede class methods with dollar signs ($).

Other common class methods are constructors and destructors. A constructor is a class method whose sole purpose is to allocate the memory required for a new object of that class. A destructor is the exact opposite of a constructor as it de-allocates the memory used by an object, effectively destroying it.

It is very common to see class methods that do things such as searching for and listing objects. For example, you might decide to write a class method that lists all of the accounts that haven't had any transactions performed on them for a certain period of time. Or perhaps even a class method that simply gives you a list of all instances of that class.

DEFINITIONS

Instance method—
A method that operates on an individual object.

Class method—
A method that operates on a class.

IMPORTANT DESIGN ISSUE

Class methods often become dumping grounds for behavior, so you want to use them sparingly. A good rule of thumb is that a class should have at most three or four class methods—if it has more then you should ask yourself whether or not some of them are really more applicable to a single instance of a class as opposed to all instances of a class.

1.4.3 The Implications of Class Attributes and Methods

How does the addition of class attributes and class methods affect and/or relate to our current repertoire of OO knowledge? To answer this question, let's consider several of our original OO concepts—inheritance, collaboration, relationships, and aggregation—in light of class attributes and methods.

1.4.3.1 Inheritance of Class Methods and Attributes

Inheritance of class methods and class attributes? Sure, why not? Both class methods and class attributes are inherited directly, although the value of class attributes will often be different for subclasses. For example, consider the minimum-deposit level for accounts. Although each type of account has a minimum balance, it is likely to be different for each type of account. The bank may require a minimum balance of $500 for savings accounts, but only $250 for checking accounts. The concept is still the same, it's just that the amount has changed.

The values of class attributes will often be different for subclasses.

Now consider the search methods for accounts that we defined earlier. It makes sense that if we send the message **Search For** to the class **Account** that it should answer (return) a list of all accounts, no matter what their type, that match the given criteria. It also makes sense that if we send the same message to **Savings Account** that it would answer a list of all savings accounts (as well as any instances of subclasses of **Savings Account**) that meet the criteria.

In first example the subclasses of **Account** inherit the class attribute **Minimum Balance**, so therefore they should be able to set the value of the minimum balance to whatever they want. This is similar in concept to the fact that an object can set the value of its attributes to anything that it wants. For example one customer object can set the value of its first name attribute to "Jake" whereas another customer object might set the value of its name to "Elwood." Just like an instance attribute a specific instance, a class attribute applies to a specific class.

You inherit both class methods and class attributes.

1.4.3.2 Sending Messages to Classes

Of course we can send messages to classes. Remember, an instance method is invoked whenever we send a message to an object. It makes sense that we should be able to send a message to a class to invoke a

Figure 1.9.
Sending a
message to a
class.

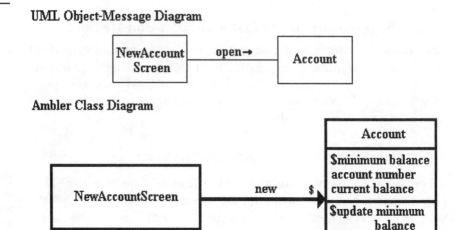

UML Object-Message Diagram

Ambler Class Diagram

*You send
messages to
classes just like
you send
messages to
objects.*

class method. For example, in Figure 1.9, we have an example of a UML *collaboration diagram* and the equivalent Ambler class diagram. We see that the class **NewAccountScreen** sends the message **open** to the class **Account** in order to get a new account object created. In a collaboration diagram classes/objects are represented as rectangles, relationships are represented as straight lines, and messages are represented by labels with arrows indicating the direction of the message flow.

UML—COLLABORATION DIAGRAMS

The only significant different between the UML class diagram and the Ambler class model/diagram is the fact that the UML class diagram doesn't include messages. Instead, they are shown on an alternate diagram called a "collaboration diagram." Collaboration diagrams show the message flow between objects and classes and imply the basic relationships between classes. The advantage of this approach is that your class diagrams become less cluttered; the disadvantage is that you have one diagram showing state, the class diagram, and one diagram showing behavior, the collaboration diagram. We'll cover collaboration diagrams in greater detail in chapter 2.

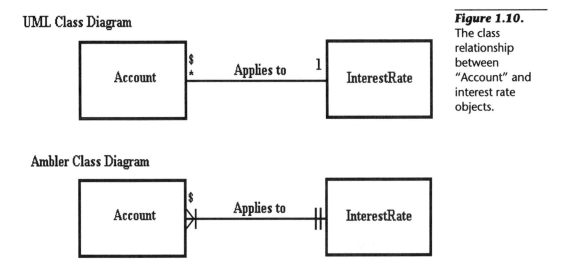

UML Class Diagram

Ambler Class Diagram

Figure 1.10.
The class relationship between "Account" and interest rate objects.

1.4.3.3 Class Relationships and Class Aggregation

We know that the combination of instance attributes and instance methods is used to define instance relationships. It seems reasonable that the combination of class attributes and class methods could also be used to define *class relationships* and *class aggregation*. A class relationship (or class aggregation) occurs when a class is involved in some sort of association with either another class or an object.

Consider interest rates. Although in a simple world with just one way to calculate interest we could have interest rate as a class attribute of **Account**. Realistically, however, we probably need an interest-rate class. Interest rates are typically calculated on a sliding scale which means that the more money you have in your account the better the rate you get. Interest can also be calculated over different time periods (daily, weekly, monthly, ...). Furthermore, to stay competitive the bank may decide to add new ways to calculate interest in the near future. The implication is that because interest rate calculations are complicated and prone to change it makes a lot of sense to have a class called **InterestRate**, which would encapsulate all of the processing required to calculate interest rates based on various formulas. Because each subclass of account has a different interest rate associated with it, there must be a class relationship between **Account** and **InterestRate**—each account class is associated with one interest rate object. Figure 1.10 shows how

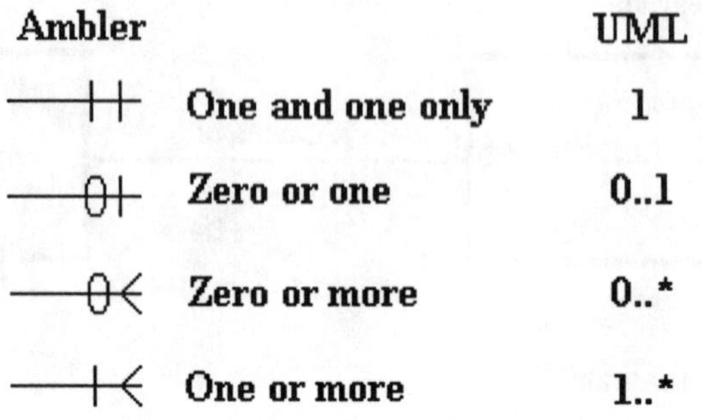

Figure 1.11.
Showing cardinality and optionality on class diagrams.

Ambler		UML
——++	One and one only	1
——0+	Zero or one	0..1
——0<	Zero or more	0..*
——+<	One or more	1..*

we would model this relationship using both the UML notation and the Ambler notation. Notice how with the Ambler notation we have a dollar sign beside the **Account** class to denote the fact that the relationship is with the class **Account** and not with account objects, although we don't have the same concept for UML. Don't worry, I'll put in a proposal to have the UML updated to include this.

On UML class diagrams optionality and cardinality are shown together, with the notation being placed above the association line. As with the Ambler class diagram notation, the UML notation uses the same symbols for both association and for aggregation. Figure 1.11 shows how to convert back and forth between the two notations.

1.4.4 What We Mean When We Say "Attribute" or "Method"

Throughout this book, whenever we say attribute we really mean instance attribute. Whenever we say method we really mean instance method. The bottom line is that we'll say class attribute and class method only when we're talking about class attributes and methods.

1.4.5 The Ambler Class Diagram Notation v2.0

A couple of new concepts and suddenly our modeling notation needs to be updated. Here it is, the new and improved Ambler Notation in Figure 1.12:

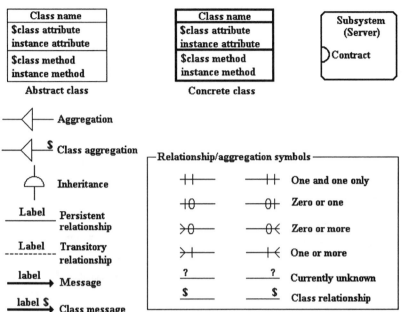

Figure 1.12.
The Ambler
Notation v2.0.

1.4.6 The Unified Modeling Language Class-Diagram Notation (Simplified)

For the rest of this book we will use the notation of the Unified Modeling Language (Booch, Jacobson, Rumbaugh, 1997). Figure 1.13 presents a simplified version of the UML notation for drawing class diagrams. I say simplified because I don't intend to show all of the parameters passed to methods in the diagrams presented in this book, nor do I intend to use all of the esoteric details for associations (relationships). These things are more suitable for an advanced book on OO modeling.

It's interesting to note that UML has added the concept of "navigation direction" to associations/relationships. The basic idea is that sometime relationships are in fact unidirectional, in other words are traversed in only one direction. To model this, the arrow head symbol has been added to show the direction of the relationship. Note that we still need to identify the optionality and cardinality for both ends of the relationship.

Figure 1.13.
A simplified UML
class-diagram
notation.

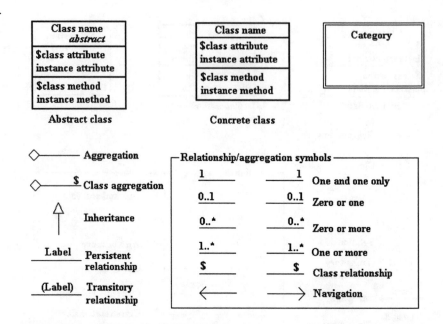

Important: The Relationship/aggregation symbols for class relationship are only proposed.

1.5 Just in Case You've Forgotten — The Bank Case Study

I'll be referring to this case study throughout the book, so I thought that I should repeat it here for your convenience.

1.5.1 The ABC Case Study

The Archon Bank of Cardassia (ABC) would like to develop an information system for handling accounts. The following is a summary of interviews with employees and customers of the bank.

The bank has many different types of accounts. The basic type of account is called a savings account. Savings account customers do not get a monthly account statement. Instead, they have a passbook that gets updated when they come in. Each passbook page has enough room to have up to ten transactions, and everytime the book is updated the next transaction is printed immediately after the last one printed in the book. The bank already has the passbook printers and printing software in place (bought from a third-party vendor).

Customers are able to open and close accounts. They can withdraw, deposit money, or get the current balance. The current balance is displayed on an account update screen, which will be part of the teller's information system. This screen displays the account number, the customer's name, and the current balance of the account. An account is associated with a specific branch. Although we now support multi-branch banking, every account is still assumed to have a "home" branch.

A checking account is just like a savings account, except customers can also write checks on it. We sell a box of 100 checks for $30. Once a customer uses 75 checks, or check #90 comes in, we send the customer a notice in the mail asking if they want to purchase more checks. Account statements are sent out every month. Checking accounts do not have passbooks, and savings accounts do not have account statements.

There is a $1,200-a-year fee for private banking accounts (PBAs). PBAs are just like checking accounts. PBAs entitle customers to investment counselling services, as well as other services not available to other clients. A PBA account can be held by only one customer, although a customer may have more than one PBA account. This is exactly like a savings account. Checking accounts, however, can be joint. This means that a checking account can be accessed by one or more customers (perhaps a husband and wife).

A current account is for our corporate customers. It works like a checking account, with a few extra features. For example, there is a quarterly account statement (which is exactly the same as a monthly account statement, except it is done for an entire quarter) sent out, in addition to the regular monthly statements. The quarterly statement is sent in the same envelope as the statement for that month. Corporate customers also get to choose the number of checks they can order (100, 250, 500, or 1000) at a time. Current accounts are not joint, nor can they be accessed through an automated teller machine (ATM). Furthermore, because of the different service needs of our corporate customers, we deal with them at special branches called "corporate branches." Corporate branches serve only corporate customers, and do not serve our retail (normal) customers. Corporate customers can be served at "retail branches," although they rarely are because the tellers in a retail branch do not have the necessary background to meet their special needs.

There can be more than one account accessible from a bank card. We currently give cards out to any customer who wants them. Customers access their accounts using two different methods—an ATM or at a bank branch. ATMs allow customers to deposit to, withdraw from, and get balances from their accounts. They can also pay bills (this is basically a withdrawal) and transfer money between accounts (this is basically withdrawing from one account and depositing into another).

Everything that can be done at a bank machine can also be done by a teller in a branch. The teller information system provides the screens to perform these functions. Additionally, tellers can also help customers to open and close their accounts, as well as print out account statements for the customer. The account statements are just like the monthly/quarterly statements, except they can be for any time period. For example, a customer could request a statement from the 15th of August to the 23rd of September, and we should be able to print that out on the spot.

Monthly and quarterly account statements are normally printed out on the first Saturday of the following month. This is done by an automated batch job.

Because we have started to put ATMs into variety stores and restaurants (in the past we only had ATMs at branch locations) we now consider each and every ATM, including those in our "brick-and-mortar" branches, to be a branch as well. That means that ATMs have branch IDs and addresses, just like a normal branch.

To manage the bank effectively, we split it up into collections of branches called "areas." An area is a group of between 10 and 30 branches. A branch is part of only one area, and all branches are in an area. Each area has a unique name, and is managed by an "area manager." Area managers receive weekly transaction summary reports every Monday morning before 9 a.m. This report summarizes the number and total amounts of all withdrawals, deposits, and bill payments performed at each branch (including ATMs) for the previous week. For brick-and-mortar branches, there is also an indication of how many accounts in total were at that branch at the beginning of the week, how many accounts were opened during the week, and how many accounts were closed during the week, and how many accounts there are in total. Finally, all of these figures are summarized and output for the entire area.

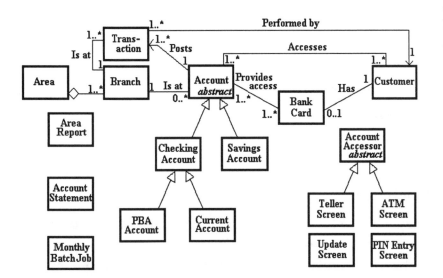

Figure 1.14.
The class diagram for the ABC case study from *The Object Primer.*

A class diagram, using the UML notation, for the ABC case study is presented in Figure 1.14.

1.6 Where We're Going in This Book

Building Object Applications is a continuation of *The Object Primer.* In this book we're going to look at OO design in greater detail, as well as OO construction and testing. The two volumes combined provide a complete description of the object-oriented system development life cycle.

This book has it all:

- A class-type architecture

- Object-oriented metrics

- Patterns

- Class message-trace diagrams

- Object-oriented state diagramming

- Object-oriented client/server modeling

- The trade-offs of the leading object-oriented languages

- Object-oriented programming tips (and even a few techniques)
- Object-oriented user interface design
- Object-oriented databases
- Accessing relational databases
- Wrapping
- Object-oriented testing

References

Ambler, S.W. (1994). "In search of a generic SDLC for object systems," *Object Magazine* 4(6), 76–78.

Ambler, S.W. (1995). *The Object Primer: The Application Developer's Guide to Object-Orientation*. New York: SIGS Books.

Beck, K. & Cunningham, W. (1989). "A laboratory for teaching object-oriented thinking," *Proceedings OOPSLA'89*, 1–6.

Booch, G., Jacobson, I., & Rumbaugh, J. (1997). *The Unified Modeling Language for Object-Oriented Development Documentation, Set v1.0*. Monterey, CA: Rational Software Corp.

Jacobson, I., Christerson, M., Jonsson, P., & Overgaard, G. (1992). *Object-Oriented Software Engineering—A Use-Case-Driven Approach*. ACM Press.

Wirfs-Brock, R., Wilkerson, B., & Wiener, L. (1990). *Designing Object-Oriented Software*. Englewood Cliffs, NJ: Prentice-Hall.

Part II

Object-Oriented Analysis, Design, and Architecture

Chapters

2 • Bubbles and Lines—Useful Diagrams for OO Analysis and Design
3 • Improving Your Design—A Class-Type Architecture
4 • Reusing Your Development Efforts—OO Patterns
5 • Development in the 90s and Beyond—
Designing Distributed OO Applications

Chapter 2

Bubbles and Lines — Useful Diagrams for Object-Oriented Analysis and Design

What We'll Learn in This Chapter

Why we need each type of diagram.

How to draw each type of diagram.

How to read class diagrams drawn in other modeling notations.

*How and when to use use-case diagrams, sequence diagrams, state diagrams,
process models, data models, collaboration diagrams,
and interface-flow diagrams.*

This book is an extension of The Object Primer *and in this chapter we'll extend
our knowledge of object-oriented analysis-and-design techniques. This chapter is
perfect for people who wish to gain a broad understanding of the analysis-and-
design options that are open to them when developing a system.*

There's more to object-oriented (OO) development than CRC (Class Responsibility Collaborator) models, use cases, and class diagrams. Although all three techniques are useful, they don't give you the whole picture. In this chapter we'll see several types of diagrams that help to fill in the blanks: use-case diagrams, sequence diagrams, state diagrams, interface-flow diagrams, data models, collaboration diagrams, and process diagrams. We're also going to compare the Ambler notation with other leading notations to help you understand the class diagrams that you see in other OO development books.

2.1 The Importance of Bubbles and Lines

Management is constantly talking about deliverables. These are usually, but not always, physical by-products of your development effort. Although the ultimate deliverable should be a fully functioning application that has been successfully installed and accepted by the user, interim deliverables often include project plans, analysis documents, design documents, test plans, and so on. The point that I want to make is that the deliverable for your analysis-and-design efforts is usually one or more diagrams supported by detailed written documentation. For the most part these diagrams are a collection of bubbles connected by lines.

The problem is that most developers are coders by nature, and coders typically don't want to invest their time drawing diagrams describing what they're going to do. They'd rather just do it. Although this attitude was predominant in the Dark Ages (1990 and earlier) we can no longer afford to think like this. Far too many systems have failed because we didn't do adequate analysis-and-design. It is obvious now that we must repent our sins and start doing a mature development job. This means we're going to do analysis-and-design. This means we're going to draw bubbles connected by lines. This means we're going to document what those bubbles and lines mean. Before we begin discussing the various types of diagrams that are used for OO development, I would like to describe a few drawing tips that will help to make your diagrams look crisp, clean, and professional.

2.1.1 Making Your Diagrams Look Good

In this section I'll pass on to you several important diagramming techniques that will help to distinguish you from your peers. This simple,

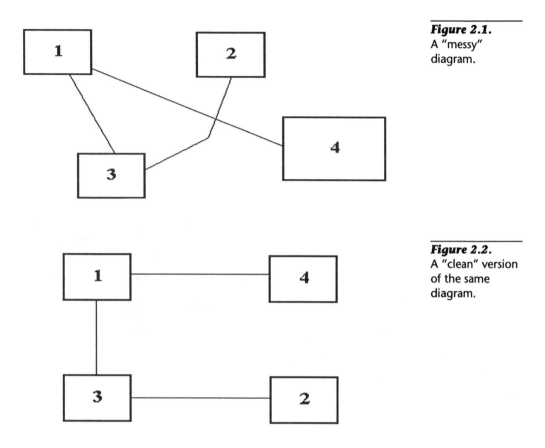

Figure 2.1.
A "messy" diagram.

Figure 2.2.
A "clean" version of the same diagram.

yet critical, advice is applicable to all kinds of diagrams and not just class diagrams. In Figures 2.1 and 2.2 we see a diagram drawn using two different styles. The first one is complex and disorganized whereas the second is simple and well organized, albeit a little boring. Which one looks like a better design to you? The second looks better because it's laid out in a cleaner way, although the fact is that both designs are functionally identical. The rules of thumb that I'm about to share with you will help you to make your diagrams look better.

Knowing how to simplify/complicate your diagrams often comes in handy.

2.1.1.1 Avoid Crossing Lines

In Figure 2.1 we have two lines that cross each other. By moving a few bubbles around we can quickly avoid having the two lines cross. Although you can't always avoid crossing lines, as we see in Figure

2.3, where we try to fully connect five bubbles, we should at least strive to minimize how many crossings we have. I really like the way crossing lines are shown on electrical-wiring diagrams: one line is drawn hopping over another one, as we can see in Figure 2.4. The advantage of hopping is that it is clear that the lines are only crossing on your diagram, they don't connect in any way.

2.1.1.2 Avoid Curved and Diagonal Lines

Curved and diagonal lines should be avoided if possible. People like straight lines that are either vertical or horizontal. If you place your

---

TIPS

Tips for Creating Clean-Looking Models

- Avoid crossing lines
- Avoid curved lines
- Avoid diagonal lines
- Avoid different size bubbles
- Avoid cluttered diagrams
- Avoid too much detail
- Avoid wasting too much time making your diagrams look pretty.

Figure 2.3.
How do you connect 3 and 5 without crossing a line?

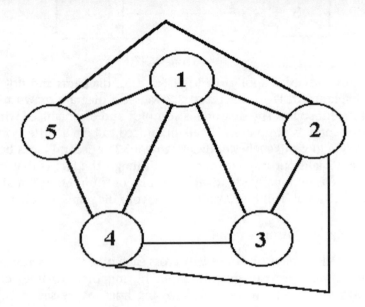

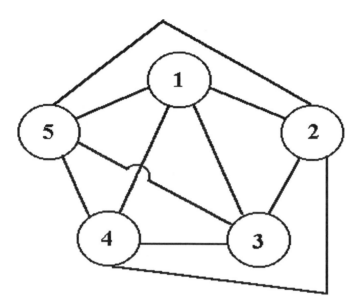

Figure 2.4.
One line "jumps"
over another.

bubbles on your diagram as if they are centered on a grid point of a graph (this is actually a built-in feature of many computer-aided system engineering (CASE) tools) then you make it easier to connect your bubbles by only using horizontal and vertical lines.

2.1.1.3 Avoid Different Size Bubbles

Another problem in Figure 2.1 is that bubble #4 was larger than the others, making it look more important. If that's the effect that you want then go for it, otherwise you should strive to make your bubbles of uniform size.

2.1.1.4 Avoid Cluttered/Complex Diagrams

Diagrams that show too many details, or that appear cluttered don't look good. It is better to have several diagrams showing various degrees of detail than one complex diagram that shows everything (which sort of shoots down some of my class-diagramming notation, but ...). Also, one diagram spread out over several pages is better than a diagram with everything smushed in just so it'll print onto one page. Take as much space as you need.

2.1.1.5 Avoid Wasting Too Much Time Making Your Diagrams Look Pretty

Leave making your diagrams look good until the end of modeling.

Although these rules of thumb work very well, there is always the danger of adding hours onto your modeling efforts tweaking the way your diagrams look. One approach is to try to get your diagrams looking good in a rough sort of way—it doesn't have to be perfect while you're working on it. Once you're satisfied that your diagram models the application the way that you want it to, then begin moving bubbles around to avoid crossing lines and improve its understandability. Your main goal is to model the system, not to produce a pretty diagram.

Your real goal is to produce a great model that also looks great.

Although on the topic of pretty diagrams, it is important to point out that you can use these rules of thumb to make a bad design look good. Instead what you really want to do is make a great design look spectacular. This is what is described in rest of this book.

2.2 Other People's Notations — Understanding Class Diagrams

The methodology is the approach. The notation is the collection of symbols.

There are a lot of object-oriented development methodologies out there, and just as many notations. Notice how I distinguish between methodologies and notations—a methodology is the approach that you take to develop systems, whereas a notation is the collection of symbols you use to document your work. Note the difference. It is a mistake to confuse the two concepts.

Which notation should you use? Who cares. Notations are only a bunch of bubbles and lines. What's important is how you use them to describe your modeling efforts and not what they look like. You

---

DEFINITIONS

Notation—The set of symbols that is used to document the analysis/design of a system.

Methodology—In the context of systems development, it is the collection of techniques and approaches that you take when creating systems.

CASE—Computer-aided system engineering.

should choose the notation that you're the most comfortable with to draw your models and get on with the real work, that of system development. Too many people waste time trying to choose the right notation and not get down and do the actual work that they're being paid to perform.

Meanwhile, Back in Reality

Although it's easy to say that you shouldn't worry about what notation to use it is actually a very important issue. You want to ensure that everyone in your organization is using the same notation, preferably one that is well-documented and easy to understand. Furthermore, you want to have a CASE (computer-aided system engineering) tool that supports your notation.

Because I want to keep this book as simple as possible to communicate the fundamentals of OO development, and because I want to do so in a manner that the knowledge you gain is directly applicable on your job, I've decided to use a simplified version of the Unified Modeling Language (Booch, Jacobson, Rumbaugh, 1997).

In Figure 2.5 we see a comparison of several of the leading class-diagramming notations. This comparison is from my point of view—I'm taking all of the concepts supported by my class diagramming notation and seeing how other notations support them. What I'm not doing is the same thing in reverse. For example, Booch (1994) and Object Modeling Technique (OMT) (Rumbaugh, Blaha, Premerlani, Eddy, & Lorenson, 1991) support symbols for some very specific needs. Although you could argue that this is a good thing, and it probably is, I believe that both the Booch and OMT notations are far too complex for people who are just getting into objects. Figure 2.5 will prove useful to you for comparing the leading class diagramming notations.

Notice how the Ambler notation is reasonably similar to both the Coad & Yourdon (1991) and the OMT notation. That's because when I was creating the Ambler notation I didn't want to reinvent the wheel so I took the best of breed wherever I could find it and used that. Although I couldn't find one notation that was just right for novice OO developers, and believe me I looked, I was able to find a lot of really good ideas here and there.

The Ambler class notation is based on the best of breed, just like UML.

If one notation is going to come out on top it will be the Unified notation, which I why I've decided to move from my notation presented in *The Object Primer* (Ambler, 1995) to it. It's not because

Figure 2.5.
The leading class diagramming notations.

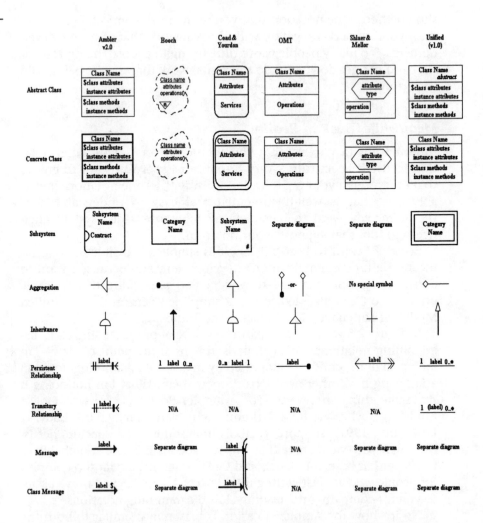

We're transitioning from the Ambler notation to the Unified notation.

Unified is better than any of the others, instead it's because of where Unified is coming from. Some of the best minds in the industry—Booch, Rumbaugh, and Jacobson—have come together to produce this notation. These three already have a significant following, and I believe that the OO market will rally behind this notation.

Finally, it should be clear that it really isn't all that hard to move back and forth between notations. In this book we're transitioning from the Ambler class-diagramming notation to the Unified notation, a transition that will prove to be easy.

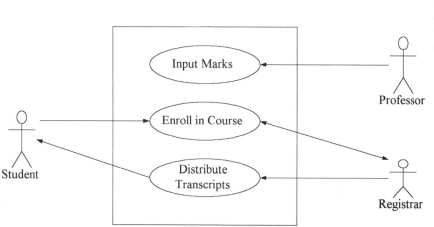

Figure 2.6.
A use-case diagram for a simple university.

Although class diagrams are the mainstay of OO development there are several other diagrams that are used in conjunction with class diagrams. The reason for this is simple—these diagrams model various aspects of a system that class diagrams don't do as well. The end result is that you often need to use several different types of techniques to model your applications, so let's invest some time discussing them.

2.3 Use-Case Diagrams — Understanding Use Cases

One problem with our current approach to use cases is that it is fairly basic—we have a collection of use cases, each of which is documented on an index card. Although this approach is fine, we may find that we want to take a more organized approach to documenting use cases. One such approach is the *use-case diagram* (Booch, Jacobson, Rumbaugh, 1997; Jacobson, Christerson, Jonsson, Overgaard, 1992), an example of which is shown in Figure 2.6.

Use-case diagrams are straightforward, showing the *actors*, the use cases they are involved with, and the system itself. Actors are shown as stick figures, use cases are shown as ovals, and the system is shown

Use-case diagrams put use cases into context.

as a box. The arrows indicate which actor is involved in which use cases, and the direction of the arrow indicates flow of information (in the UML indicating the flow is optional, although I highly suggest it). In this example, students are enrolling in courses via the help of registrars. Professors input and read marks, and registrars give the OK to send out transcripts (report cards) to students. Note how for some use cases there is more than one actor involved, and that sometimes the flow of information is in only one direction.

We've seen what a use-case diagram is, now let's talk about how to draw them.

DEFINITIONS

Use case—A use case describes a real-world scenario that a system may or may not be able to handle.

Actor—A person, organization, or external system that interacts with the application that we are currently developing.

Use-case diagram—A diagram that shows the use cases and actors for the application that we are developing.

Use-case "uses" relationship—A use-case "uses" relationship indicates that one use case invokes another use case to fulfill its behavior.

2.3.1 Drawing Use-Case Diagrams

Once you have your use cases identified (Ambler, 1995) it is fairly straightforward to draw a use-case diagram. First identify the actors, which are the people, organizations, or external systems that interact with your system. Second, draw ovals for each use case. Third, connect the actors with the use cases that they are involved with. If they supply information or simply initiate the use case then make sure that there is an arrowhead pointing from the actor to the use case. If the actor receives any information as a result of the use-case, even if it is only a simple acknowledgment that the use-case scenario happened, then there should be an arrowhead pointing from the use-case to the actor.

The value of use-case diagrams comes in with *use-case "uses" relationships*—a use-case "uses" relationship indicates that one use case invokes another use case to fulfill its behavior. An example is shown in

Drawing use-case diagrams is easy, identifying use cases is the hard part.

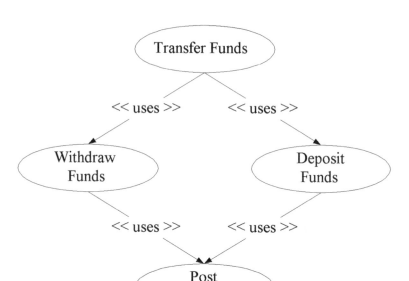

Figure 2.7.
Use cases can be invoked by other use cases.

Figure 2.7 which describes how the use cases for depositing funds and withdrawing funds are invoked by the funds transfer use-case. This makes sense, as a transfer is simply a withdrawal from one account and a deposit into another. Figure 2.7 also shows how the post transaction use-case is invoked both the deposit funds and withdraw funds use cases. The advantage of the "uses" concept is it allows you to take advantage of similarities between use cases, in other words you can reuse use cases.

Use-case "uses" relationships indicate opportunities for re-use.

2.3.2 Why and When Should We Create Use-Case Diagrams?

We should create use-case diagrams whenever we need to "properly" document use-case scenarios, as opposed to just maintaining them using a word processor. There are several CASE tools available now that support this kind of diagram, so if you really have to draw a use-case diagram then you should consider purchasing one. I'm not saying that you should go out and buy a CASE tool that just does this, but if you can find one that supports it in addition to other modeling diagrams then you should consider it an extra bonus.

Use-case diagrams can be used to communicate use cases to upper

management, although you should avoid showing the "uses" relationships as they can be confusing. However, if you want to show that
you're going to get a lot of reuse in your application then I suggest
showing them.

Another way to document use cases is to use sequence diagrams.

2.4 Sequence Diagrams — Understanding Use Cases Even Better

When we covered use-case scenario testing in *The Object Primer* (Ambler, 1995) we saw that part of the process was to get the business
domain experts (BDEs) to work through the basic logic of a use case.
This helped to test and verify that our analysis, in the form of a CRC
model, was correct. At the same time we also recorded the basic business logic, typically as point-form notes, so that we wouldn't lose the
important knowledge we had gained. Although there is nothing wrong
with point-form notes, we often need a more rigorous way to document the logic for a use case. One such technique is to create a *sequence
diagram* (Booch, Jacobson, Rumbaugh 1997; Jacobson, Christerson,
Jonsson, Overgaard, 1992) for each use case (or at least the complex
ones). Sequence diagrams are often referred to as interaction diagrams
or message-trace diagrams.

A sequence diagram, see Figure 2.8 for an example, shows the types
of objects involved in the use case, the messages that they send each
other, and any return values associated with the messages. The basic
idea is that a sequence diagram shows the flow of logic of a use case
in a visual manner, allowing you to both document and reality-check
your application design at the same time.

DEFINITIONS

Sequence diagram—A diagram that shows the types of objects involved in a
scenario, including the messages they send to one another and the values that
they return.

Message-invocation box—The long, thin, vertical boxes that appear on sequence diagrams which represent a method invocation within an object.

OOD—Object-oriented design.

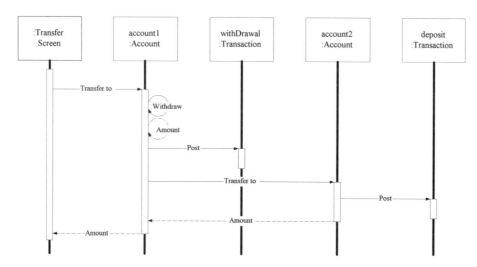

Figure 2.8.
A sequence diagram for transferring funds from one account to another.

In the sequence diagram above we see the five objects, each shown as vertical lines, that are involved in transferring money from one account to another. The first object is a transfer screen, either implemented as part of a teller workbench or as part of an automated-teller-machine (ATM) interface. The screen sends a message, represented as a solid arrow, to the first account telling it to transfer money into another one. The first account withdraws the requisite money (another arrow pointing back to itself), returns the amount withdrawn (an arrow pointing back to itself), and then posts a transaction. The money is then deposited into the second account, which also posts a transaction. This account returns the amount that was deposited, which is shown as an arrow with a dotted line going back to the first account. The first account then returns the amount that was transferred back to the screen, which would presumably display it to the user.

The boxes on the vertical lines are called *method-invocation boxes*. These represent the running of a method in that object. Notice in Figure

2.8 that the method to deposit money in account number two runs for a short time, during which the post method is run for a transaction.

2.4.1 How to Draw Sequence Diagrams

Drawing sequence diagrams can be hard because you're often doing a lot of design work when you're drawing them.

Although sequence diagrams look fairly straightforward they can often be difficult to draw. The problem is that when you are drawing sequence diagrams you are often making some significant design decisions. For example, in Figure 2.8 we could easily have decided to put the business logic for doing a transfer of funds in the transfer screen instead of putting it into the **Account** class. Taking this approach, the transfer screen would have sent the withdraw message to **Account 1** and then the deposit message to **Account 2**. A seemingly small design decision, yet it would greatly impact the extensibility of the banking application (it's a bad idea to put business logic in an interface class, an issue that we'll discuss in detail in the next chapter). The point that I'm trying to make is that people can have a really rough go when they draw sequence diagrams for the first few times, especially when they are new to object-oriented design (OOD).

The first step in drawing a sequence diagram is to identify the class in which the use-case scenario starts, which will almost always be some sort of interface class. You then want to walk through the process logic for the scenario, identifying each message that needs to be sent and to which object it gets sent to. Every time you identify a new object, add a new vertical line. Note that although all of the messages went from left to right in Figure 2.8, that isn't always the case.

Whenever a method is run in an object add a method-invocation box. At the very top of the method-invocation box will be a message that initiated the method coming from another object. From the box there may be messages sent to other objects that in turn invoke methods within those objects. Finally the method will end, and it may return a value to the object that sent the original message that invoked the method.

The important thing when you're drawing sequence diagrams is to get the logic right. If you send messages to several objects of the same type (in Figure 2.8 we sent messages to two different account objects) then have a vertical line for each instance. If an object sends a message to itself, don't forget to show it.

2.4.2 Why and When Should We Draw Sequence Diagrams?

You want to draw sequence diagrams for several reasons. First and foremost they're a great way to test your design, as they are a more formalized approach than use-case scenario testing (Ambler, 1995). Second, they're a great way to document your design, at least from the point of view of use cases. Third, they're a great mechanism for detecting bottlenecks in your design. By looking at what messages are being sent to an object, and by looking at roughly how long it takes to run the invoked method, you quickly get an understanding of where you need to change your design to even out the load within your system.

Sequence diagrams are used to test your design and to document use cases.

Another advantage of sequence diagrams is that they often give you a feel for which classes in your application are going to be complex, which is often an indication that you need to draw state diagrams for those classes.

2.5 State Diagrams — Understanding Complicated Classes

People like to say that objects have both behavior and state. In other words they do things and they know things. Some objects do and know more things, or at least more complicated things, than other objects. Some objects are incredibly complex, so complex that we have difficulties understanding them. To better understand complex classes we often draw a state diagram (Booch, Jacobson, Rumbaugh, 1997; Booch 1994; Rumbaugh, Blaha, Premerlani, Eddy, & Lorenson, 1991; Shlaer & Mellor 1992) describing how it works.

Many methodologies support state diagrams, although they'll call them by different names. For example, OMT (Rumbaugh, Blaha, Premerlani, Eddy, & Lorenson, 1991) calls them *dynamic models* and Booch (1994) calls them *state-transition models*. The term dynamic model makes sense because we're modeling the dynamic nature of an object, the term state-transition (ST) model also makes sense because that's really what we're drawing (ST models are very popular for development of real-time systems). I'm going to use the term state diagram because it's short and sweet, and it appears to be the term that is most widely accepted.

> **DEFINITIONS**
>
> *State*—A state represents a stage in the behaviour pattern of an object. A state can also be said to represent a condition of an object to which a defined set of policies, regulations, and physical laws apply. On state diagrams a state is shown as a horizontal rectangle.
>
> *Transition*—A transition is a progression from one state to another. A transition will be triggered by an event (either internal or external to the object). A transition is shown on a state diagram as an arrow leading from one state to another.
>
> *State diagram*—A model which describes the states that an object may be in, as well as the transitions between states.
>
> *Initial state*—The state in which an object is in when it is first created. All objects have an initial state.
>
> *Final state*—A state from which no transitions lead out of. Objects will have zero or more final states.
>
> *Recursive transition*—A transition is considered recursive when it leads into the same state that it originated.

Let's do an example. In Figure 2.9 we see the state diagram for a bank account. The rectangles represent *states*, which are a stage in the behavior of an object. We see that an account can be in one of five states: active, overdrawn, updating, querying, or closed. The arrows represent *transitions*, which are progressions from one state to another. When an account is active we see that we can withdraw from it, deposit to it, query it, and close it.

States are represented by attribute values.

States are represented by the values of the attributes of an object. For example, an account is active if the current balance is greater than or equal to zero, it isn't currently being updated or queried, and it isn't closed. An account is being updated when a deposit or withdrawal is occurring (some sort of flag would be set to true while this is happening).

Transitions are represented by the invocation of a method, although not all methods are represented as transitions (for example,

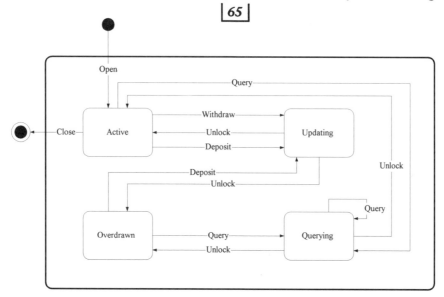

Figure 2.9.
A state diagram
for a bank
account.

we don't see a "post transaction" transition for accounts). Transitions also are a reflection of our business rules. For example, we see that we can withdraw from an account that is active, but not one that is overdrawn. We also see that we can query an account when it is active, overdrawn, or being queried. The query transition when an account is being queried is called a *recursive transition*, which is a transition that starts and ends in the same state.

Transitions are represented by methods, often reflecting business rules.

Taking a look at our diagram, we see two unusual states. The first one is the active state, which has an open transition coming into it

INHERITANCE ISSUES

Although it would be very nice to be able to inherit state diagrams, it is extremely unlikely that it will happen. The definition of inheritance says that although the subclass is similar to the superclass, it is still different. The behavior of the subclass is usually different than that of the superclass. This means that you will need to reconsider the state diagram when you inherit from a class with one. The one good thing is that many of the states and transitions are reusable. You'll probably find that you will either add new states and transitions, or be redefining some.

A good test as to whether or not you have pure inheritance (the subclass inherits everything from the superclass) is that the state diagram of the subclass should at most add new states and transitions and shouldn't remove any existing ones.

from nowhere. Active is considered an initial state—once an account is opened it becomes active. In other words "Active" is the first state that an account goes into. Furthermore the closed state is called a final state, which is a state from which there are no transitions leaving from it. The implication is that once an account is closed there will be no more transactions on it.

Objects are always in one and only one state. Transitions are considered instantaneous.

For the sake of convention we say that an object is always in one and one only state, implying that transitions are instantaneous. Although we know that this isn't completely true (every method is going to take some time to run) it makes life a lot easier for us to assume that transitions take no time to complete.

We've seen what state diagrams are, now let's talk about how to draw them.

2.5.1 How to Draw a State Diagram

Drawing a state diagram is fairly straightforward, and can be described in the following five easy steps:

1. Identify the creation state.

2. Identify the final state(s) if any.

3. Identify as many other applicable, "real-world" states as possible.

4. To identify transitions, for each state, ask yourself how does the object leave this state.

5. For each transition, ask yourself what state does the object go to.

You can find states by looking at the boundary values of your attributes.

The first thing that you want to do is identify the creation state and whether or not there are any final states. In other words you basically want to identify both the start and the end of an object's life. After you've done this, ask yourself what other states or stages in the life of an object does it pass through? You can often find states by looking at the boundary values of your attributes. For example, when the current balance of a bank account goes below zero it becomes overdrawn. Overdrawn is a valid state because different rules apply to an account when it is overdrawn (you can't withdraw anymore).

Try to identify as many states as possible first, and then look for transitions.

Once you've identified as many states as you can, start looking for transitions. For each state, ask yourself how the object can get out of it, if possible. This will give you a transition. Because all transitions lead from one state to another, ask yourself what new state the transition leads you to (don't forget about recursive transitions that lead to the same state). You should also look at the methods you identified in your class diagram—some of them will correspond to a transition in your state diagram.

HINT SUMMARY

- States are represented by the values of certain attributes. Consider the "boundary values" for each attribute, as this may indicate the difference between two or more states.

- Your business rules will often define different states of an object.

- Look at your class diagram for methods that change the values of one or more attributes. These methods may represent a transition.

DEFINITIONS

Substate—A specific state that is part of a more generalized superstate.

Superstate—A general state that is decomposed into several substates.

State precondition—A condition that must be met before a state can be entered.

pre/—A keyword used on a state diagram to document state preconditions.

do/—A keyword used on a state diagram to document actions taken by an object while in a state.

2.5.2 Taking State Diagramming a Bit Further

The style of state diagramming proposed up to this point is fairly basic, it depicts the main states and the transitions between states. There are a lot of other issues that can be considered when you are drawing state diagrams. First of all you have to take into consideration *superstates* and *substates*. Superstates are collections of two or more specific substates. You define superstates when you recognize that you have a cluster of related states that form their own subsystem.

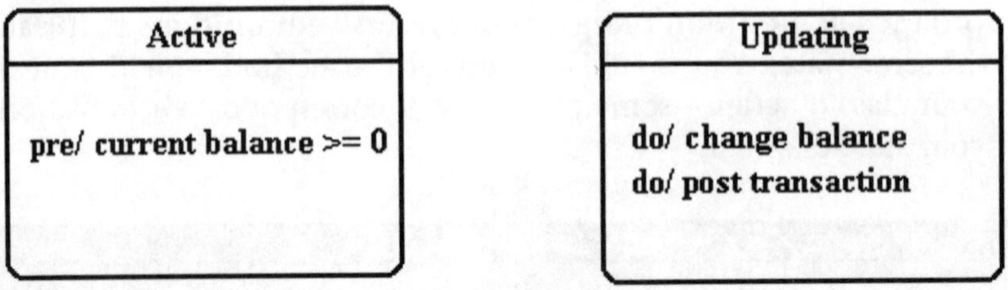

Figure 2.10.
Extending states
on a state
diagram.

```
┌─────────────────────────┐        ┌─────────────────────────┐
│         Active          │        │        Updating         │
├─────────────────────────┤        ├─────────────────────────┤
│                         │        │                         │
│ pre/ current balance >= 0│       │  do/ change balance     │
│                         │        │  do/ post transaction   │
│                         │        │                         │
└─────────────────────────┘        └─────────────────────────┘
```

Second, you could also consider identifying the state preconditions that must be met before the state is entered. For example, a state precondition for the **Active** state is that the current balance must be zero or more. In Figure 2.10 we see that we use the **pre/** keyword to document state preconditions.

Third, you might also want to document what actions should be taken when in a state. For example, in Figure 2.10 we see that when we are in the updating state we should change the balance and post a transaction. We indicate the actions that should be taken with the **do/** keyword.

You can make state diagrams as complicated as you like, but personally I'm a big fan of keeping them as simple as possible. If you find that you are working with very complex classes then you should consider going even more complex. I suggest looking at OMT (Rumbaugh, Blaha, Premerlani, Eddy, & Lorenson, 1991) and the Shlaer and Mellor methodology (1992) for more complicated approaches to state diagramming.

2.5.3 When and Why Should We Draw State Diagrams?

State diagrams are used to document complex classes, often in real-time systems.

A state diagram should be drawn for a class whenever it exhibits complex behavior that is often, but not always, dependent on asynchronous activity. State diagrams are also very useful in real-time environments (which are typically complex). If an object displays significantly different behavior depending on its state, then you should draw a state diagram to help you understand the differences. For example you can withdraw from bank accounts when they are active but not overdrawn.

2.6 Collaboration Diagrams

The Ambler class diagramming (Ambler, 1995) approach shows both state and behavior on class diagrams, the UML, however, doesn't. The UML only shows state on class diagrams and separates out behavior into *collaboration diagrams* (Booch, Jacobson, Rumbaugh, 1997). The basic difference between the two approaches is that the Ambler class diagram includes messages whereas the UML class diagram doesn't. Collaboration diagrams have also been referred to as object-message diagrams and simply as object diagrams.

DEFINITION

Collaboration diagram—A diagram that shows the message flow between objects/classes and implies the basic relationships between classes.

Collaboration diagrams show the message flow between objects in an OO application, and also imply the basic associations (relationships) between classes. Figure 2.11 presents a simplified collaboration diagram for a university application. The rectangles represent the various classes that make up the application, and the lines between the classes represent the relationships/associations between them. Messages are shown as a label followed by an arrow indicating the flow of the message and return values are shown as labels with arrow-circles beside them. In Figure 2.11 **Seminar** and **Enrolment** are both classes, **open** and **display info** are both messages, and **seats** is a return value (presumably the result of sending the message **max seats** to **Course**).

2.6.1 Drawing Collaboration Diagrams

Collaboration diagrams are usually drawn in parallel with class diagrams and sequence diagrams. Class diagrams provide input into the basic relationships between objects, and sequence diagrams provide an indication of the message flow between objects. The basic idea is that you identify the objects, the associations between the objects, and the messages that are passed between the objects.

The main difference between collaboration diagrams and sequence diagrams is that sequence diagrams show the objects and messages

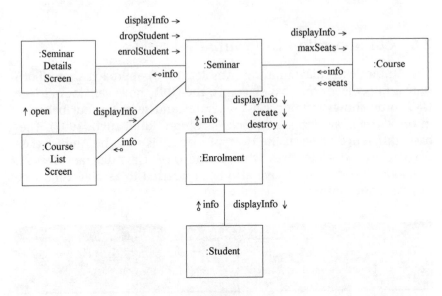

Figure 2.11.
A collaboration diagram for a simple university.

involved, as well as the appropriate order for message invocations, for a single use case. Collaboration diagrams, on the other hand, are used to get a big picture outlook for the system, incorporating the message flow of many use cases. Collaboration diagrams do not indicate the order of message invocations.

2.6.2 Why and When Should We Draw Collaboration Diagrams?

Collaboration diagrams should be drawn whenever you want to fully understand the behavior of an OO application as the show the objects that make up the application and the message flow between them. If you want to see the data flow, instead of the message flow, between the portions of a system then you should consider drawing a process model.

2.7 Process Models — Understanding What's Currently Going On

When you first start a project the current system is complex and convoluted and it's your job to understand it. You could draw a class diagram to represent the existing system, but it just doesn't seem to represent the system completely. What are you going to do?

DEFINITIONS

DFD—Data-flow diagram.

Process model—A diagram that shows the movement of data within a system. Similar in concept to a DFD but not as rigid and documentation-heavy.

External entity—In a process model it is the source or destination of data that is external to the system being modeled. In a class diagram we would call this an actor class.

Process—In a process model a process takes some data as input, does something to it, and then outputs it.

Data flow—In a process model a data flow represents the movement of information, either physical or electronic, from one source to another.

Data store—In a process model it is a place where information is stored, such as a database or filing cabinet.

In the late 1970s (Gane & Sarson, 1979) *data-flow diagrams* (DFDs) were introduced and popularized (actually, they're still popular today). DFDs showed the flow of data from external entities into the system, showed how the data moved from one process to another, as well as its logical storage. In Figure 2.12 we see an example of a DFD using the Gane and Sarson notation. Notice how there are only four symbols: a square representing *external entities*, rounded rectangles representing *processes*, arrows representing the *data flows*, and open-ended rectangles representing *data stores*.

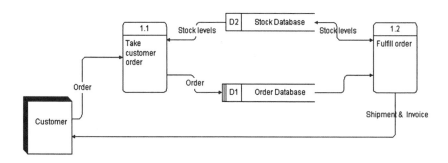

Figure 2.12.
A DFD for a very simple order-entry system.

The basic idea behind DFDs was that you create sets of diagrams that show varying levels of detail. In the "official" methodology you would create five sets of diagrams: context, current physical, current logical, proposed logical, and proposed physical. Realistically at most you'd create two sets, one for the current system and one for the new system.

The DFD technique helped to improve the analysis-and-design process by providing a reasonably simple mechanism for modeling the movement of information within a system. Unfortunately it had its problems. First of all drawing and documenting DFDs proved to be a long and drawn-out process. Second, a simple change in business rules would often result in significant changes to the DFDs. Third, there was little if any correlation between the model and the code, the end result being that the code would quickly get out of synch with the model. To be fair, there are several CASE tools available on the market today that reduce the impact of these problems, although there really isn't a tool that completely solves these difficulties.

We still need to model the flow of information in a system.

Many people like to deride DFDs, telling you that you don't need them to model a system. Pure hogwash. I have never seen anyone model a reasonably complex application without having to resort to drawing some sort of DFD at some point. The technique may have been flawed, but the ability to represent the flow of information within a system is still required. The end result is that we need to model the processing of objects.

A process model is a DFD on a smaller scale.

One of the best approaches to meeting this need is presented by OMT (Rumbaugh, Blaha, Premerlani, Eddy, & Lorenson, 1991) in the form of a *process model*. A process model is basically a scaled-down version of a DFD—you draw a simple diagram showing the data flow for one small section of a system. You're not trying to model an entire system, just the part that you are currently interested in.

2.7.1 Drawing Process Models

The best way to draw a process model is to model the "real-world" flow of information from an actor (external entity) into the system. Then ask how that information is processed and how it is stored. Is any information sent back to an actor, or perhaps to another actor? If so then model it. Let's work through a simple example: a customer wants to purchase gas at a fully automated gas station. To do so she inserts her credit card into the gas pump and inputs her PIN (personal identification number). The PIN is verified with an online credit

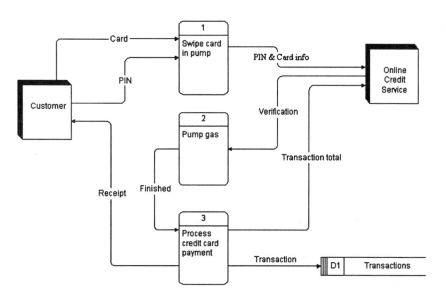

Figure 2.13.
The gasoline
process model.

service and if it is accepted the gas pump is activated. Once the pump is activated she takes the nozzle and pumps the gas into her vehicle, puts the nozzle back into the pump and then picks up the printed receipt from the pump. The transaction is processed by the online credit service and is also recorded for reporting purposes in a database connected to the gas pumps.

To draw Figure 2.13 we basically follow the data throughout the process. The customer and the online credit service both get modeled as external entities (actors) because they are outside the scope of our control. They interact with the system but we don't have any real control over them. The swiping of the customer's card and the inputting of the PIN is modeled as both a data flow and a process. The data flow represents the fact that the customer has given us information, her card and her PIN (note how some information, the card, was physical). The process represents the fact that we create a data packet that gets transmitted to the online credit service so that we can get the card validated. The verification comes back, a data flow, and the customer can begin pumping gas. Once she's done she puts the nozzle back on the pump, indicating that she's finished (another data flow). Once finished the card payment is processed with the online credit service and the transaction gets recorded in the database (which is modeled as a data store). A receipt is printed and given to the customer.

2.7.2 Why and When Should We Draw Process Models?

Process models allow us to describe the often complicated flow of data within a system. Whenever you find that you need to understand the flow of data then you should draw a quick process model describing what you are interested in. Note that you may or may not decide to make an "official" process model that you include in the system documentation. The point to be made is that most of the process models that I draw fit on a small whiteboard and never make it off the board, and that's OK. The concept of data-flow diagrams was valid, it's just that we went a little too far with them.

Process models are a valid OO diagramming technique, just don't go too far.

TIPS

Important Tips for Process Modeling

1. **Keep your process models small.** Notice how I drew a process model for just a single process, that of buying gasoline via a credit card. We didn't draw a huge model showing every possible thing that could happen in a gasoline station: that's what DFDs were all about and it didn't work that well. Draw process models ONLY for a small part of a system, not the entire thing.

2. **You don't need to make process models look pretty.** I often draw process models by hand but don't bother to clean them up using a CASE tool or drawing package. In other words, I use process models to help me gain a better understanding of a system, but I often don't include them in my official documentation. If they're important, then I clean the diagrams up and put them in my documentation, otherwise I don't bother.

2.8 Interface-Flow Diagrams — Understanding the User Interface

To your users the user interface is the system. It's as simple as that. Doesn't it make sense that you should have some sort of mechanism to help you design a user interface? Prototypes are one means of describing your user interface, although with prototypes you can often get bogged down in the details of how the interface will actually work. As a result you often miss high-level relationships and interactions between the interface objects (usually screens) of your application. *Interface-flow diagrams* (Page-Jones, 1995) allow you to model these high-level relationships. Interface-flow diagrams are also referred to as storyboards. At the time of this writing, the UML doesn't support interface-flow diagrams.

Interface-flow diagrams, also called story-boards, allow you to separate the user interface forest from the widget trees.

DEFINITIONS

Interface-flow diagram—A diagram which models the interface objects of your system and the relationships between them. Also referred to as story-boards.

Interface classes—These are classes that provide the ability for users to interact with the system. Interface classes typically define a graphical user interface (GUI) for an application, although other interface styles, such as voice command or handwritten input, are also implemented via interface classes.

Interface object—An instance of an interface class.

In Figure 2.14 we see an example of an interface-flow diagram for an order-entry system. The boxes represent interface objects, in this case screens, whereas the arrows represent the possible flow between screens. For example, when you are on the main menu screen you can go to either the customer search screen or to the order-entry screen. Once you're on the order-entry screen you can go to the product search screen or to the customer order list. Interface-flow diagrams allow you to easily gain a high-level overview of the interface for your application.

Interface-flow diagrams show a high-level overview of your application's interface.

2.8.1 Drawing Interface-Flow Diagrams

As you can see, drawing interface-flow diagrams is very easy. You merely draw a box for each interface object and then connect them by arrows whenever you can reach/call/instantiate one interface object from another. It's that simple.

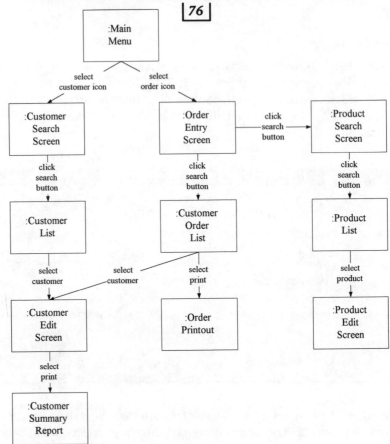

Figure 2.14.
An interface flow
diagram for an
order-entry
system.

2.8.2 Why and When Should We Draw Interface-Flow Diagrams?

If interface-flow diagrams are so simple then why bother? Good question. Because interface-flow diagrams offer a high-level view of the interface of a system you can quickly gain an understanding of how the system is expected to work. It puts you into a position where you can easily do some reality checking. For example, does the screen flow described in Figure 2.14 make sense? I'm not so sure. Why can't I get from the customer edit screen to the customer order list, which is a list of all the orders that a customer has ever made. Furthermore, why can't I get the same sort of list from the point of view of a product? In some cases it might be interesting to find out which orders include a certain product, especially when the product is back-ordered or no longer available.

*Interface-flow
diagrams allow
you to quickly
reality-check your
interface design.*

The questions mentioned previously are all very interesting, and are all very obvious once we've drawn the interface flow diagram. I prefer to include these new requirements in my design up front, rather than to have a user come to me once the system is in place and say, "Oh, by the way, could you just add ...."

2.9 Data Models — Modeling Your Database Design

As we'll see in chapter 10, relational databases are often used as the mechanism to make your objects persistent. Because relational databases don't completely support object-oriented concepts (don't worry, we'll learn how to deal with this issue in chapter 10), the design of your database is often different than the design of your class diagram. Data models, also called entity-relationship (ER) diagrams, are used to communicate the design of a database, usually a relational database, to both your users and to other developers. At the time of this writing, the UML doesn't support data models.

DEFINITIONS

Data model—A diagram used to communicate the design of a (typically relational) database. Data models are often referred to as entity-relationship (ER) diagrams.

Data entity—A person, place, thing, event, or concept. Data entities are similar to classes with the exception that they have data attributes but do not have functionality (methods).

Key—A data attribute, or collection of data attributes, that uniquely describes a data entity.

In Figure 2.15 we see an example of a data model for the design of a simple human resources system. In the data model we have four data entities—**Position**, **Employee**, **Task**, and **Benefit**—which in many ways are simply classes that have data but no functionality. The entities are connected by relationships. Relationships in a data model are identical in concept to instance relationships in a class diagram. One interesting thing to note is the concept of a key: a key is one or more attributes that uniquely identifies a data entity. On data models keys are indicated by underlining the attribute(s) that define them. In our data model in Figure 2.14 the attribute **EmployeeNo** is the key of the **Employee** data entity.

Figure 2.15.
A data model for
a simple human
resources
database.

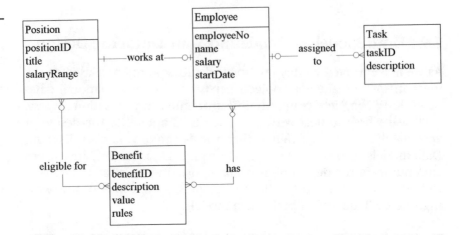

2.9.1 Drawing Data Models

Drawing data models is very straightforward and like class diagramming is often an iterative process. There are four steps to drawing data models.

1. **Identify data entities.** Look for any person, place, thing, event, or concept that you are interested in storing data about. If you have a class diagram, and we'll see in chapter 10 that your class diagram should drive the design of your data model, then your concrete business classes map directly to corresponding data entities.

2. **Identify data attributes.** What information do you want/ need to store about each data entity? Just like concrete classes map directly to data entities, the attributes of classes map directly to attributes of data entities.

3. **Identify the key attribute(s).** Ask yourself if there is one or more data attributes that can be used in combination to identify an occurrence (instance) of a data entity. Often you have several choices for your key forcing you to choose one, and sometimes you don't have any attributes that can be used for a key, forcing you to introduce a new attribute to act as the key.

4. **Identify relationships between data entities.** Identifying relationships between data entities is identical to identifying instance relationships between classes.

2.9.2 Why and When Should We Draw Data Models?

Data models are used to document the design of a database. You typically need to draw a data model whenever you are using a relational database to store your objects in. The strength of data models is that data entities are conceptually the same as the tables of a relational database and that attributes are the same as table columns. We'll see in chapter 10 that with a little bit of work you can modify your data model to give you a direct one-to-one mapping between your model and the design of your database (you basically need to make a few modifications to handle the relationships between data entities).

Data models are used to document the design of a database.

Although often tempted to use data models to drive the development of class diagrams, I tend to shy away from this approach unless I know the data model is designed very well, that is, the data model is highly normalized. We'll discuss normalization in greater detail in chapter 10. It is my experience that to successfully use relational technology on object-oriented applications you should let your class diagram drive the design of your data model. In other words create the class diagram that is right for your application and then use it to derive the data base design for that application.

Your class diagram should drive the design of your data model, not the other way around.

2.10 An Overall Analysis and Design Strategy

Between *The Object Primer* and this chapter we've discussed a lot of approaches for analyzing and designing an object-oriented application. In this section we put everything into context, explaining how all the models and diagrams fit together.

Before explaining Figure 2.16, it should be made clear that this IS NOT another type of model. We've seen enough bubbles connected by lines to last us a lifetime. The boxes in Figure 2.16 represent each one of our analysis-and-design techniques. In the bottom corner is an indication of what development stage the technique is applicable for, an A represents analysis and a D represents design. The arrows represent a "drives relationship." For example, we use a CRC model to drive the development of a class diagram as well as the development of use cases. Use cases are used to drive the development of a CRC model.

Some models act as input for others, and vice versa.

Figure 2.16.
How all the modeling approaches fit together.

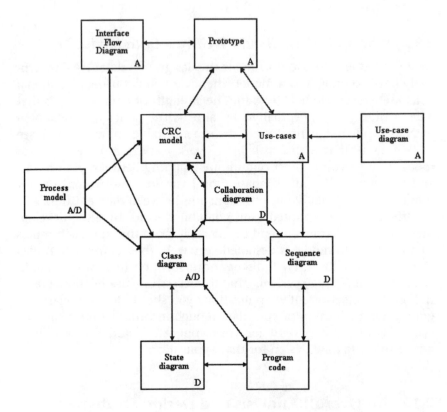

Comments:

1. **This reflects one development style.** This diagram is based on my experience and the experience of many other well-respected OO developers. The techniques presented in this book series are proven and they work well. Don't expect everyone to completely agree with this approach however. For example, CRC cards are typically only used for analysis although they can be used effectively for design.

2. **It's mostly an iterative process.** Although many of the techniques drive each other (for example, CRC modeling, use cases, and prototyping) there is still at least a rough order in which things are done. The analysis models will be done for the most part before the analysis-and-design models, which in

turn are typically done before the pure design models. It's still iterative in the small, but in the large it's only semi-iterative.

3. **There's a lot to OO analysis-and-design.** Everybody keeps telling you that OO development is mostly analysis-and-design, now I'm showing you that it is in fact true.

4. **Don't go nuts.** Just because you have a wide selection of modeling techniques doesn't mean you have to use them all. Sometimes it's appropriate to prototype and sometimes it isn't. Sometimes you need to develop a process model and sometimes you don't. Furthermore, just because you draw a model doesn't mean you have to make it look pretty. Or document it.

5. **Your deliverables are defined for you.** Large OO development projects tend to take more of a waterfall (serial) approach to development. In other words you do analysis, then design, then programming, then testing. Figure 2.16 provides a general indication of the order in which the models, or in this the deliverables, need to be developed. It also shows what diagrams can be done in parallel, indicating opportunities to distribute the work across multiple teams.

2.11 What We've Learned

In this chapter we saw that the class-diagramming notations being used in other methodologies map easily to the one presented in this book series. Don't get hung up on what your bubbles and lines look like, the important thing is how good your models are. We also saw that there are several techniques that you can use that make your diagrams look better. Simply moving a few bubbles around can work wonders on a diagram. Finally, we discussed several diagrams, summarized in Table 2.1, which can be used together with techniques discussed in chapter 1 to document your modeling efforts.

Table 2.1. OBJECT-ORIENTED MODELING TECHNIQUES PRESENTED IN
THE OBJECT PRIMER SERIES

Technique	Description	When to Use
Collaboration diagram	An approach in which you model the classes/objects of an application and the message flow between them	Whenever you need to understand the overall behavior of an OO application
CRC modeling	An approach in which you use index cards to analyze and document the user requirements of a system	When you need to analyze the user requirements for a system
Class diagramming	An approach in which you model the classes of a system and their relationships	When you need to document in detail your analysis-and-design of an OO application
Data modeling	An approach in which you model the data entities of a system and the relationships between those entities	When you need to document the design of a (typically relational) database
Interface-flow diagramming	An approach in which you model the interface objects of your system and the relationships between them	When you want a bird's-eye view of the user interface and the relationships between screens
Process modeling	An approach in which you model the movement of data within a system	When you need to understand information flow
Prototyping	An approach in which you iteratively analyze and design the user interface of an application with your users	When you need to determine what your user interface will look like
State diagramming	An approach in which you model the states that an object may be in, as well as the transitions between states	When you need to understand or document a complex class

continued

Table 2.1 (*continued*)

Technique	Description	When to Use
Sequence diagramming	An approach in which you model the types of objects involved in a scenario, including the messages they send to one another and the values that they return	When you want to document critical use cases or when you want to verify your design
Use-case diagramming	An approach in which you model the use cases and actors for the application you are developing	When you need an overview of how people interact with the system
Use-case scenarios	An approach in which you identify and document common scenarios, or use cases that a system may or may not be able to perform	When you want to understand the interactions of people with the system
Use-case scenario testing	An approach in which your business domain experts act out use-case scenarios in order to verify their CRC model	When you want to verify that your analysis is correct

References

Ambler, S.W. (1995). *The Object Primer: The Application Developer's Guide to Object-Orientation.* New York: SIGS Books.

Booch, G. (1994). *Object-Oriented Analysis and Design with Applications, 2nd edition.* Redwood City, CA: Benjamin/Cummings.

Booch, G., Jacobson, I., & Rumbaugh, J. (1997). *The Unified Modeling Language for Object-Oriented Development Documentation, Set v1.0.* Monterey, CA: Rational Software Corp.

Coad, P., & Yourdon, E. (1991). *Object-Oriented Analysis, 2nd edition.* Englewood Cliffs, NJ: Yourdon Press.

Gane, C., & Sarson, T. (1978). *Structured Systems Analysis: Tools and Techniques*. Englewood Cliffs, NJ: Prentice-Hall.

Jacobson, I., Christerson, M., Jonsson, P., & Overgaard, G. (1992). *Object-Oriented Software Engineering: A Use-Case-Driven Approach*. ACM Press.

Page-Jones, M. (1995). *What Every Programmer Should Know About Object-Oriented Design*. New York: Dorset-House.

Rumbaugh, J., Blaha, M., Premerlani, W., Eddy, F., & Lorensen, W. (1991). *Object-Oriented Modeling and Design*. Englewood Cliffs, NJ: Prentice-Hall.

Shlaer, S., & Mellor, S. (1992). *Object Life Cycles: Modeling the World in States*. Englewood Cliffs, NJ: Yourdon.

Chapter 3

Improving Your Design — A Class-Type Architecture

What We'll Learn in This Chapter

Why we need a class-type architecture, and more to the point, why we need a five-layer class-type architecture.

The implications of the architecture for both system development and for project management.

What each layer is really all about and how it fits in with the other layers.

Users want systems that are better, faster, and cheaper. Not only do they want new systems that conform to these requirements, they also want systems that are adaptable and modifiable. You might get lucky and get new requirements that are easy to meet, but I wouldn't want to count on it. Without a well-thought-out architecture in place you will probably not be able to develop applications in a timely and efficient manner that meet the demands of your users. The class-type architecture presented in this chapter meets these goals.

As an object-oriented developer you need to have an overall game plan as to how you intend to design your system. The class-type architecture described in this chapter provides you with an excellent strategy for organizing the classes of your application to increase both its extensibility and maintainability. I don't claim that this architecture is detailed enough for the needs of your organization. I do claim, however, that it does provide an approach to partitioning your applications that leads to a significantly better design.

A class-type architecture provides a strategy for how to distribute the functionality of an application among classes. Furthermore, class-type architectures provide guidance as to what other types of classes a given type of class will interact with, and how that interaction will occur. This will increase the *extensibility*, *maintainability*, and *portability* of the systems that we create.

What are the qualities that make up good *layers*? First, it seems reasonable that we should be able to make modifications to any given layer without affecting any other layers. This will help to make our

---

DEFINITIONS

Class-type architecture—The classes of an application are organized into well-encapsulated layers according to their general properties. The interaction between classes is often restricted based on the layer they belong to.

Extensibility—A measure of how easy it is to add new features to a system. The easier it is to add new features, the more extensible we say the system is.

Layer—A layer encapsulates the broad functionality of a collection of classes that exhibit similar behaviors. Layers help us to identify, define, and potentially restrict how classes interact with one another.

Maintainability—A measure of how easy it is to add, remove, or modify existing features of a system. The easier a system is to change the more maintainable that system is.

Portability—A measure of how easy it is to move an application to another environment. Application environments may vary by the configuration of both their software and hardware. The easier it is to move an application to another environment the more portable we say that application is.

system easy to extend and to maintain. Second, it also seems reasonable that we should be able to completely replace a layer, and as long as the new version presents the same interface as the old version did then the other layers shouldn't be affected. This will help to make our system portable.

A good class architecture leads to systems that are extensible and portable.

What I'm getting at here is that layers should be well modularized. We should be able to either rewrite a layer or simply replace it, and as long as the interface remains the same the rest of the system shouldn't be affected. In other words, what we're looking for are well-encapsulated layers in our architecture.

3.1 Why Do We Need a Class-Type Architecture?

Legacy applications are the bane of IS (information system) departments. An application is considered a legacy if it is difficult, if not impossible, to maintain and enhance. Just because something runs on a mainframe it doesn't mean it's a legacy application. By the same token, just because an application runs on a PC doesn't mean that it isn't. The short story is that there are a lot of developers out their right now who are creating tomorrow's legacy applications. The reason why this is happening is because they haven't taken the time to develop an overall approach to the way that they design their system. This chapter presents a *class-type architecture* that promises to avoid the development of new and improved legacy applications.

OO legacy applications may be avoided via a class-type architecture.

> **DEFINITION**
>
> *Legacy application*—Any application or system that is difficult, if not impossible, to maintain and enhance.

3.2 Building Up to a Class-Type Architecture

Throughout this book I will use a five-layer architecture that I am about to gradually build up to in the next four sections. Although you can skip to section 3.2.4 and just read about the final recommended architecture, I highly suggest that you don't. There's a lot of really good material in all four sections, and frankly a three-layer or four-layer architecture might work fine for your organization. (Yes, I'm implying that the two-layer architecture presented below is too simplistic.)

3.2.1 A Two-Layer Class-Type Architecture

Let's start with a simple architecture based on what as covered in *The Object Primer* (Ambler, 1995). Taking a look at our banking information system in Figure 3.1, we see that we could easily separate our system into different class types. There are a lot of business domain classes, such as **Account**, **Branch**, **Area**, and **Customer**. We'll refer to them as *business classes*, although *business domain classes* or *analysis classes* are other possible terms that we could use. There are also two reporting classes, **Area Report** and **Account Statement**, as well as several classes representing screens, such as **Teller Screen** and **ATM Screen**. Reporting classes and screen classes are concerned with I/O—input and output. They form the access points with which users interact with the system. Because they help to form the system's interface, we'll call them *interface classes*. We'll discuss these class types in gory detail later on in this chapter.

With the exception of the class **Monthly Batch Job**, which we'll leave until section 3.2.4, all of the classes that we modeled in *The Object Primer* (Ambler, 1995) can be categorized as either interface classes or business classes. This leads us to propose the two layer architecture presented in Figure 3.2, which shows both the layers that make up the architecture and the direction of communication between the layers.

Figure 3.1.
The bank information system.

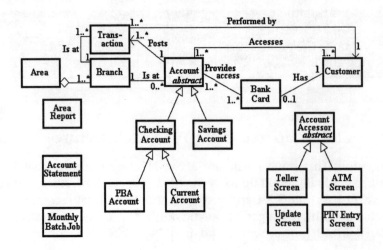

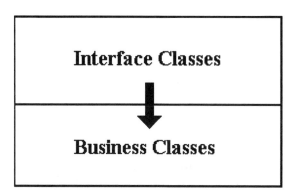

Figure 3.2.
A two-layer class-type architecture.

The first thing that should be pointed out is that within a layer messages can flow freely between classes. Interface classes can send messages to each other, and business classes can send messages to other business classes. However, messages between the layers should be restricted to flow only from the interface classes layer to the business classes layer, but not the other way. We are able to restrict the flow of messages because realistically actions are only initiated by the user interface (this is true 99.99% of the time, so let's go with the flow for now). By restricting the flow of messages to only one direction we dramatically increase the portability of our system by reducing the coupling between classes—the business classes do not rely on the user interface of the system, implying that we can change the interface without affecting the underlying business domain classes.

We only want to restrict message flow between layers, not within layers.

Restricting message flow between layers increases portability by decreasing the coupling between classes.

The second thing that needs to be pointed out is that we have now increased both the maintainability and extensibility of our system. By separating the interface classes from the business classes, we are now

---

DEFINITIONS

Business classes—Business classes model the business domain. Business classes are usually found during the analysis process.

Interface classes—Interface classes provide the ability for users to interact with the system. Interface classes typically define a graphical user interface (GUI) for an application, although other interface styles such as voice command or handwritten input are also implemented via interface classes.

Layering helps to increase system maintainability and extensibility.

in a position to change the interface in any way that we choose. Consider our bank—users currently interact with the system either through the teller screens or through the automated teller machine (ATM) screens. It seems reasonable that people should also be able to do their banking over the phone or over the Internet. To support these new access methods we should only have to add the appropriate interface classes. Although this is a dramatic change in the way that we interact with our customers, *our fundamental business hasn't changed*, therefore we shouldn't have to change our business classes.

On first glance this architecture appears to work. Unfortunately we're missing some significant functionality, such as saving our objects to permanent storage. We talked about persistence in chapter 1 but we really haven't defined how we're actually going to perform this feat. Although chapter 10 covers persistence in great detail, we'll deal with this issue right now through the addition of a persistence layer to our architecture.

3.2.2 A Three-Layer Class-Type Architecture

The persistence layer provides OOCRUD functionality by wrapping access to the persistence mechanism.

In Figure 3.3 we add a persistence layer to our class-type architecture. The persistence layer adds the CRUD (create, retrieve, update, and delete) functionality for objects by wrapping access to the persistence mechanism. The persistence mechanism is the thing that you use for permanent storage, which may be anything from a flat text file to a relational database to a full-fledged object database. In other words, it doesn't really matter where objects are saved to as long as they're saved.

In this architecture messages flow from the business class layer to the persistence class layer. These messages take the form of "create a

Figure 3.3.
A three-layer class-type architecture.

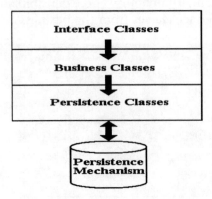

new object," "retrieve this object from the database," "update this object," or "delete this object." Depending on the implementation strategy (see below), these OOCRUD messages may be simple messages such as "create a new savings account" to a complicated SQL (structured query language) or OQL (object query language) statement.

DEFINITIONS

OOCRUD—The object-oriented create, retrieve, update, and delete functionality performed by persistence classes.

Persistence classes—Persistence classes provide the ability to permanently store objects. By encapsulating the storage and retrieval of objects via persistence classes you are able to use various storage technologies interchangeably without affecting your applications.

Persistence mechanism—The permanent storage facility used to store objects, such as a relational database, a flat file, or an object database.

SQL (Structured Query Language)—A standard language used to access and modify data stored in relational databases.

OQL (Object Query Language)—The object-oriented version of SQL that is used to access and modify objects stored in object-oriented databases.

Wrapping—Wrapping is the act of encapsulating non-OO functionality within a class, making it look and feel like any other object within the system.

A key concept here is that the persistence layer only provides access to permanent storage, it isn't the permanent storage mechanism itself. For example, the persistence layer wraps (front-ends) access to a relational database but it isn't the database itself. The goal of the persistence layer is to reduce the maintenance effort that is required whenever changes are made to your database.

You know that your database will be upgraded. You know that tables will be moved from one disk drive/pack to another, or from one server to another. You know that table schemas will be changed. You know that field names will be changed. The implication is clear—because the database is guaranteed to change we need to encapsulate

The persistence layer isolates you from the impact of changes to your storage strategy.

it to protect ourselves from the change. A persistence layer is the best way to do that. Done right, and we'll find out how to do it right in chapter 10, the persistence layer minimizes the effort required to handle changes to the database.

CRITICAL DESIGN ISSUE

Messages should not flow between interface classes and persistence classes

When interface classes send messages directly to persistence classes you effectively couple your interface to your permanent storage mechanism. Although it may be faster to issue SQL statements directly from a dialog box to your database, you quickly find that you pay a very steep maintenance price. When the database changes (tables/fields are renamed, removed, added, or modified), every program that accesses the database must be updated.

Personally, I don't want to have to spend days finding, fixing, and testing sections of code that are affected by a simple database change.

Think of it like this—at the interface level it doesn't matter how objects are stored. Do you know how your bank stores account information? Is it in a relational database? Is it in a network or hierarchical database? On a mainframe? On a personal computer? Is it in a flat file somewhere? You don't know, do you? You just walk up to an automated teller machine, withdraw your money, with luck you don't get robbed, and then walk away. Yesterday your account information could have been stored in a mainframe relational database, and today it's stored in an object database on a PC. It doesn't matter because the ATM still works the same.

There are a lot of development environments out there, including a few versions of Smalltalk that should know better, which allow you to send messages directly from your interface classes to your database. Although this MIGHT be easier to code, you lose the advantage any business logic or functionality provided by your business classes. For example, the class **Person** has a method that computes someone's age by subtracting their birthdate from today's date. You'd have to repeat this functionality for any screen that reads a person's birthdate directly from the database.

At the user interface level, it shouldn't matter how objects are stored.

Although we've improved our architecture, I'm still not convinced that it accurately reflects all of our development needs. Although the

IMPLEMENTING THE PERSISTENCE LAYER

In a pure OO world, this layer would take the form of an object request broker (ORB). In a not-so-pure OO world, the one in which most of us still live, this layer would take the form of an ORB plus a SQL request broker. Both of these strategies are discussed in greater detail in chapter 10.

Access to databases is often performed by wrapping an API (application programming interface), often written in C or C++, with a collection of classes. These classes provide an OO front-end to the database, be it a relational database or an object-oriented database, which allow programmers to send messages to the database requesting it to create, retreive, update, and delete objects. Wrapping is discussed in chapter 11.

persistence layer handles database access via wrapping APIs (see boxed text), what about basic flat-file access via calls to the operating system? Or how about accessing a database server across the network? Don't we have to make system calls for that? And what about that monthly batch job we mentioned earlier that we obviously need to schedule? In the past we were able to register regular batch jobs with the system, so it seems reasonable that we should still be able to do this in the object world. Furthermore, it seems reasonable that we should be able to make calls to the operating system that would take advantage of specific features offered by the platform our system is running on, such as OLE (object linking and embedding) or OpenDoc. It is apparent that we need to add another layer to our architecture that would support these system calls.

3.2.3 A Four-Layer Class Architecture

In Figure 3.4 we see that a fourth layer has been added to support system classes. System classes provide access to system resources, such as hardware components and the operating system itself. On the hardware side system classes can be used to wrap color printers, communication devices, or scanners. On the software side system classes wrap data sharing/conversion capabilities, compound document functionality (such as OLE or OpenDoc), system scheduling features, data communications such as EDI (electronic data interchange), or even other applications residing on the system (such as e-mail and accounting packages).

The system layer provides access to the operating system and non-OO resources.

The key concept here is wrapping. System classes for the most part encapsulate non OO functionality that we need to make accessible to objects within an application. It is quite common to wrap a series of related operating system calls so as to provide a related set of functionality. A perfect example would be the file stream classes commonly found in Smalltalk and C++ class libraries (we'll discuss these two languages in detail in chapter 8). When you look into the inner workings of these classes, you find that their methods make specific file handling calls to the operating system just as if you had written the code yourself in a structured development language. The functionality of **File** is provided by wrapping the operating systems file-handling API. Wrapping is covered in greater detail in chapter 11.

DEFINITION

System classes—System classes provide operating-system-specific functionality for your applications, or they wrap functionality provided by other tool/application vendors. System classes isolate you from the operating system (OS), making your application portable between environments, by wrapping OS specific features.

Message flow in this architecture is consistent with that of the three-layer architecture, with the addition of messages flowing from the three previous layers to the system classes. Remember, within a layer messages can flow freely, we only want to restrict message flow between the layers. Let's discuss how messages flow back and forth from the system layer:

1. **Interface to system classes.** Message flow from interface classes to system classes should be rare so as to reduce the coupling between these two layers. One example of when it would be appropriate, however, would be a "Save as" dialog box as it needs to ask the operating system what files reside in the current directory. Either the **File** class or a **FileDirectory** system class would provide that kind of information, both of them being system classes.

2. **Business to system classes.** Message flow from business classes to system classes will occur occasionally. A perfect example would be a check object that needs to electronically ver-

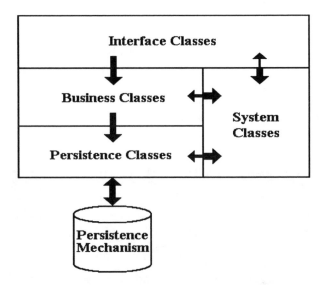

Figure 3.4.
A four-layer class-type architecture.

ify itself via accessing an online check-clearing service. The check is a business class, whereas the check-clearing service is a system class that wraps access to an online service provided by an external vendor. The advantage is that it no longer matters what check-clearing service the bank uses now that we've encapsulated it via a system class. We could change service providers and only need to make a few small changes to the system class.

3. **Persistence to system classes.** Message flow from persistence classes to system classes will occur often. Persistence classes send messages to system classes that provide basic file-handling functionality and to classes that provide network access functionality (perhaps to establish a communication link to a server).

4. **System classes to all others.** Message flow occasionally occurs between system classes and the three other classes, usually through the use of callback methods or message dispatchers (see section 8.6.3 for greater detail). For example, an inventory item object may determine that it is running low on stock and may decide to send out an order request to the

appropriate supplier via an EDI object. The inventory object could request that it be sent a specific message to inform it that the order has been confirmed (this is called a callback method). Assuming the supplier also has an OO system, and what competent supplier wouldn't, when the order comes in (via EDI) the EDI object may decide to pass the request on to a message dispatcher object, which would then pass it on to the appropriate stock object.

DEFINITIONS

Callback methods—When object A communicates with object B, it may request that at some time in the future object B sends message M whenever a certain event happens (such as a process ending). The method that responds to message M is named a callback method.

Message dispatcher—An object that exists solely to pass messages onto other objects. Objects will often register themselves with a message dispatcher to inform it of the events that they are interested in being informed about.

SEMANTICS ISSUE

You could argue that persistence classes are actually system classes, and frankly you'd be right. Persistence classes wrap database management systems, as well as file systems. I believe that persistence classes are significant enough to rate their own layer, however. Furthermore, it is quite possible that you may install a new version of your persistence mechanism without changing the operating system (or vice versa), so why bother coupling them together? Finally, persistence classes should only be sent messages from business classes, whereas systems classes are sent messages from all types of classes.

The only things that are guaranteed are death, taxes, and system upgrades. Spend the extra effort to make your application portable.

From a technical point of view, I think we have a pretty solid architecture. From a mature development point of view, however, our architecture is still missing one critical thing—users.

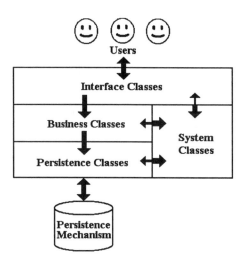

Figure 3.5.
A five-layer class-type architecture.

3.2.4 A Five-Layer Class-Type Architecture

It always shocks me that we leave out the most important component of any system architecture, namely the people who use the applications. We develop systems so that they may be used by real live people who are commonly referred to as users. This group of people is critical to the development of any system as they are the ones who pay the bills. Call me old-fashioned, but I think that it's only natural that the most critical component of a system be included in its architecture. This leads us to our final, five-layer architecture presented in Figure 3.5.

Strategically and politically speaking it's a good idea to include your users.

An important implication of adding users as a fifth layer is that it opens up a few opportunities to relate some analysis concepts to our architecture. First of all it should be clear that we have effectively included the human–computer interaction (HCI) boundary in our architecture. The HCI boundary defines the point at which the outside world interacts with our system, and as we saw in *The Object Primer*, it is described via use-case scenarios. This leads to my second point—with the inclusion of users in our architecture we can now tie in our work with use cases that describe how users work with the systems that we develop.

Use cases describe how users interact with the system.

3.3 A Detailed Look at the Various Class Types

Up to this point we've talked very briefly about several types of classes that you'll work with during the creation of an object-oriented application. Now let's cover them one at a time in detail, discussing why we need them and what factors we need to take into consideration when developing them.

Our four types of classes are

- Interface classes

- Business classes

- Persistence classes

- System classes

3.3.1 Interface Classes

An interface class contains the code for the user interface part of an application. For example, a graphical user interface will be implemented as a collection of menu, editing screen, and report classes. We must not lose sight of the fact, however, that not all applications have GUIs. For example, our banking system accesses account information via automated teller machines, via the telephone, and via the Internet. This is all in addition to the teller information system, which probably would be a GUI. The point to be made here is that the user interface for any given system can possibly take on many forms, even though the underlying business is still the same, in this case banking. The only thing that is changing is the way that you interact with that business functionality.

It is also possible (actually it's almost 100% certain) that users will want modifications made to the user interface in the future. Perhaps they want various views on a single kind of object—different profiles of a single object or perhaps different types of lists of objects. User

> **DEFINITION**
>
> *Interface classes*—Interface classes provide the ability for users to interact with the system. Interface classes typically define a graphical user interface for an application, although other interface styles, such as voice command or handwritten input, are also implemented via interface classes.

interfaces evolve over time and we want to be able to modify them without requiring changes to non interface aspects of our applications.

Additionally, we may need to run the same application on different hardware platforms. At a university it is common to have vastly different hardware configurations within each department, reflecting both the different needs of each department and the different donations of equipment (if any) that each department has received. Even on identical equipment it is possible that users may be running different operating systems. The point to be made is that users will still demand to run the applications that you develop, regardless of their particular computer configuration.

Users want applications to run on multiple platforms. Isn't system development a joy?

From a development point of view, we may want to take advantage of the fact that there are a lot of people out there who now specialize in user interface design. In fact, many organizations have UI specialists who work only on user interface classes. The implication of this is that we need to be able to isolate the user interface code from the rest of the system. By the way, chapter 9 covers OO interface design in detail to give you some of the necessary skills needed to design effective OO applications.

Interface classes isolate your application from changes to the user interface.

In summary, there are several reasons why we need an interface layer:

- We want to access the system via various mechanisms.

- We want to isolate the impact of user interface changes on the system.

- We want to produce applications that run on multiple hardware platforms.

- We want to easily update applications when new versions of operating systems are released.

- We want to leverage UI specialists as user interfaces become more and more complicated.

There are several potential mistakes that developers commonly make when designing interface classes. The first one is to place business logic in the interface and not in business classes where it belongs. For example, we need to implement the fact that only one customer can access any given savings account (in other words savings accounts aren't joint accounts). Although we might decide to build this rule into our interfaces, it probably isn't a good idea. If this business rule

---

INTERFACE CLASSES AND USE CASES

The behaviors of people in the real world are often reflected in the user interface of a system. The same behaviors are documented via use cases. For example, bank customers deposit money into their accounts. This fact is reflected in the user interfaces of the teller application, the ATM application, the phone-access application, and so on. It is also documented in one or more use cases. The point to be made is that because behaviors of people are reflected in both use cases and in the user interface of a system, we are able to claim that use cases indirectly drive the design of a user interface.

Don't put business logic into your interface.

changes and there isn't any reason to believe that it won't, then we'd need to make changes to all interface classes that work with savings accounts (the teller workbench, the ATM interface, ...). This is a lot of work. Instead, we should be able to change the way that we've implemented the instance relationship between customer objects and savings account objects in the business layer and have the user interface take advantage of this expanded functionality automatically.

A second mistake, often fatal for the maintenance efforts of an organization, is to have interface classes communicate with persistence classes. This ignores the concept of encapsulation. The interface classes directly access the data attributes of an object without its knowledge. Talk about the Dark Ages! This approach is unfortunately taken by many fourth-generation languages (4GLs) and object-based languages. It allows you to develop an application faster, but really kills you during maintenance because any change in the database schema requires corresponding changes in any class that accesses the database. The bottom line is that if the way that customer objects are stored in the database changes then at worst I should only have to make changes to a class that fetches objects from the database, not to every interface class that works with customer objects. In chapter 10 when we discuss databases issues we'll see that at most all we should have to change is the data dictionary information that maps our objects into the database.

Don't directly access the database from your interface.

A third mistake is to put system logic in your interface. Even though we might decide to develop an e-mail message input screen, we wouldn't implement the send functionality in the interface class. First of all, this might not be the only place from which we want to send e-mail messages. Second, we may want to be able to use the same screen to front end various e-mail systems. Don't implement system functionality in your user interface. Period.

Don't directly access system resources from your interface.

3.3.2 Business Classes

A business class, also called an analysis or business domain class, is a class that is usually identified during analysis. Your users are often the people who identify these classes, or at least the concrete business classes. To take you on a trip down memory lane, concrete classes are the ones from which you instantiate (create) objects, whereas abstract classes do not have objects instantiated from them.

The business layer allows us to encapsulate the basic business functionality without having to concern ourselves with user interface, data management, or system management issues. This allows us to create classes that we can theoretically port to other environments. I say theoretically because this will work only if the environment you are porting to has a development environment that will accept your code (or if you are using a CASE [computer-aided system engineering] tool you should at least be able to generate the code to this new environment). The moral of the story is that portability is never quite as easy as everybody likes to claim it is.

As with interface classes, there is the potential for putting inappropriate functionality in your business classes. First of all, avoid putting interface functionality in the business layer. For example, even though your business classes may generate error messages, such as you don't have enough money in your account to cover a withdrawal, it isn't their responsibility to display the message. Displaying a message to the user is something that the interface layer should do.

The second common mistake is to put persistence logic in your business classes. For example, one method of the Account class might be to delete a specific account from the database via a hardcoded SQL or OQL statement. The problem with this is that account objects now have knowledge of how they are stored in the database. If you make any changes to the database, it can potentially force you to modify your business classes. Think of it like this—if the business hasn't changed you shouldn't be making modifications to your business classes.

Finally, as you should have guessed by now the third mistake is to put system logic in your business classes. Although a customer object might maintain detailed information about itself in the form of a compound document, perhaps as an OLE or OpenDoc document, it shouldn't know anything about the format of this information. The logic for manipulating the document should reside in a system class due to the

The business layer encapsulates business rules.

Don't display error messages directly in the business layer, instead let the interface layer handle that.

Business classes shouldn't know how they are saved to permanent storage; the persistence layer knows that.

fact that for the most part OLE and OpenDoc are operating system specific. (Actually, at the time of this writing OpenDoc is multiplatform
and OLE is single-platform.) As the OLE and OpenDoc standards evolve,
and you can count on that, all you should need to modify (or perhaps
simply replace via a third-party supplier) are the OLE and OpenDoc system classes. Although the way that the information is manipulated may
change over time, the fundamental business requirement to maintain
that information hasn't changed. Therefore the business layer should-
n't be affected.

Changes to the business are the only valid reasons to require changes in your business layer.

3.3.3 Persistence Classes

The persistence layer provides the infrastructure for the storage and
retrieval of objects. This helps to isolate your application from changes
to the database. You might decide to install the latest and greatest version of your database, change the existing database schema, or even
migrate to a completely new database vendor. Regardless of how your
database changes, your applications shouldn't be affected. The persistence layer, by encapsulating data management functionality, increases
the maintainability, extensibility, and portability of your applications.

It shouldn't mat-ter how you decide to store objects.

In a related topic, ignoring performance issues of course, it shouldn't
matter what mechanism you use to store your objects—flat files, relational databases, and OO databases are all valid candidates. Although
mapping objects to a relational database is fraught with issues (see
chapter 10) relational technology is still a valid alternative for storing
objects. You might decide to use relational technology today with the
intention of migrating to an object database in the future. When you
make this move the only classes that you should have to change are the
ones within the persistence layer, no other classes should be affected.

Furthermore, I never said that you have to use the same mechanism
to store all of your objects. In other words it is a valid design decision
to use a relational database to store some objects and use an object data-

---

DEFINITION

Persistence classes—Persistence classes provide the ability to permanently
store objects. By encapsulating the storage and retrieval of objects via persistence classes you are able to use various storage technologies interchangeably without affecting your applications.

base for others. The beauty of the persistence layer is that it allows you to store objects wherever you want to, regardless of whether or not you are using a homogenous storage approach. There are very few companies that are using one and only one database for all of their storage needs, the implication being that we will probably need to take a flexible approach to the way that we store objects. The persistence layer allows us to do exactly that.

The persistence layer provides flexibility as to how we store objects.

Another data management issue that we face is that we're moving from centralized, single-user stand-alone systems to distributed applications. We need to be able to organize our development efforts in such a way as to allow database experts to concentrate solely on data management issues. In other words, we want to let the database experts do their thing. By encapsulating database functionality in the persistence layer we can do exactly that.

In summary, a persistence layer allows us to do the following:

- Isolate the impact of data management changes on the system.

- Port our relational solution to an OODBMS (object-oriented database management system) solution eventually.

- Evolve over time into distributed applications.

- Let database experts handle the data management aspects of an application.

As with the other types of classes, there is the potential to make mistakes when developing them. The first one is to implement interface logic in persistence classes. A classic mistake is to make your persistence layer responsible for displaying error messages on the screen whenever there is a database problem. Don't get me wrong, the persistence layer should have the ability to detect and report errors, it's just that it isn't responsible for outputting them. Instead, whenever an error is encountered it should simply return an error message object back to the object that made the initial request to access the database. That object should then do whatever is appropriate with the message, potentially passing it onto an interface class so that it can be output to the user. The fundamental issue is that persistence classes shouldn't know how to write to the screen, if only for the simple reason that not all database access is initiated from a screen (nightly batch jobs will often initiate database access).

The persistence layer should return error messages, not display them.

Business rules are implemented in the business layer, not the persistence layer.

A second mistake is to put business logic in your persistence layer. The persistence layer should know how to perform all of the OOCRUD functionality—creating, retrieving, updating, and deleting objects. It shouldn't know, or care, what the objects are or what they do. For example, the persistence layer for an inventory control system shouldn't know anything about the fact that an order is made up of one or more line items. It will provide the required functionality to read and write those objects, and perhaps how to maintain the relationships between them, but that's are far as it goes. The persistence layer doesn't have any knowledge of the business rules that apply to objects.

The persistence layer isn't part of the system layer, although it could be.

You imagine that the third mistake is to put system logic in the persistence layer. When you stop to think about it, however, the persistence layer could easily be considered part of the system layer. The persistence layer collaborates with file- and network-handling classes in the system layer to get its work done. Although the persistence layer obviously provides system type functionality, that of OOCRUD, I am of the belief that persistence is important enough, and complicated enough, to rate its own layer. Furthermore, it is likely that you may change operating systems without changing databases, or vice versa. Chances are pretty good that a separate persistence layer makes sense.

SEMANTICS ISSUE

I would consider a class called **File**, which provides basic open, close, read, and write functionality to be a system class. In fact, I can't imagine an OO language that doesn't support one or more classes that provide this functionality. This is a very basic class that wraps the operating-system-specific features that support file access.

I would consider a class that provided direct-read access and direct-write access, especially of complex objects, into a flat file to be a persistence class, however. This class, call it **ObjectFile**, would work closely with the class File and would provide the extra functionality required to do the reading and writing of objects in a direct-access manner.

The main difference is that **File** provides the basic functionality to read/write characters and strings to a flat file, whereas **ObjectFile** provides the additional ability to (intelligently) write objects to a file. Whew, I thought I'd never be able to figure out a way to explain this difference.

3.3.4 System Classes

Every operating system offers functionality that we want to be able to access in our applications—file handling, multitasking, multithreading, and network access to name a few. Although most operating systems offer these features, they all offer them in slightly different manners. Although many people find this little fact to be worthy of great debate, and perhaps it actually is, the real issue is that the differences between operating systems can make it really tough if you are writing an application that needs to work on many different platforms. We want to wrap the features of an operating system in such a way that when we port an application we only need to modify a minimum number of classes. In other words, we need to create classes that wrap specific features of the operating system.

DEFINITION

System classes—System classes provide operating-system-specific functionality for your applications, or they wrap functionality provided by other tool/application vendors. System classes isolate you from the operating system, making your application portable between environments, by wrapping OS-specific features.

Even if you don't intend to port your applications to other operating systems you still need to consider wrapping system functionality. The reason for this is simple—operating systems constantly get upgraded. Every time there is an upgrade there are always changes to the way that functionality is currently being offered, including issues such as bug fixes and completely new ways to do things. For example, over the last few years operating systems have been improving/redoing the way that they support compound documents. As these "standards" evolve, the **CompoundDocument** class that you wrote to wrap this functionality will need to evolve along with it.

System classes can reduce the impact of change from new versions of the underlying operating system.

I won't go into long-winded detail about the common kind of mistakes that can be made within the system layer. As you'd correctly guess the general problems lie with putting either interface logic or business logic in your system classes. Look at some of the previous sections to get a feel for what I'm talking about.

3.4 Issues with the Five-Layer Class-Type Architecture

I'd like to talk about some of the issues that arise with the class-type architecture presented in this chapter. The issues are as follows:

- How do you decide which layer a class belongs to?
- Can you buy instead of build some of these classes?
- How will this architecture affect project management?
- How will this architecture affect system development?
- What are the advantages and disadvantages of this architecture?

3.4.1 To Which Layer Does This Class Belong?

The following rules of thumb should help you to determine which layer a class belongs to.

3.4.1.1 Interface Classes

- Does this class represent/control a user-interface widget, window, screen, ...?
- Does this class represent a report, either printed or electronically transmitted?
- Does someone or something outside the system directly interact with this class?

3.4.1.2 Business Classes

- Does this class diagram a business concept?
- Was this class described to you by your users?
- Do you need your users to explain some of the finer details of this class's responsibilities?
- Would this class be unaffected if you were to port it to another environment?

3.4.1.3 Persistence Classes

- Does this class provide CRUD access for <u>objects</u> to a file or database?

- Will this class potentially need to change if your file system or database is upgraded?

3.4.1.4 System Classes

- Does this class diagram operating-system-specific functionality?

- Does this class wrap access to another system or application?

- Can you develop this class without any input, or at least very little, input from your users?

- Will this class potentially need to change if your operating system is upgraded?

3.4.2 Can I Buy Some of These Classes?

I'm a firm believer in buying as many classes as you possibly can, if only for the simple reason that I don't want to reinvent the wheel. Another thing that I have always believed is that program code is the root of all evil in the system-development world. Think how easy maintenance would be if we didn't have any code. I also realize, realistically, that I'm always going to have to write some code that is specific to the application at hand. So the question now becomes what classes can you reasonably expect to buy and what will you probably need to build yourself:

Program code is evil. Peter Coad is a pretty good guy.

3.4.2.1 Can I Buy Interface Classes?

Although my first reaction is to say "You bet," I'm not so sure that it's that simple. You've already bought very simple interface widgets in the form of button, list box, spreadsheet, and edit field classes that are included in your programming environment's class library. You can also go out and buy endless widget class libraries for a few hundred dollars from advertisements in any OO programming magazines. But are these really interface classes? Well...I suppose so, but frankly I think of interface classes as something a little more complicated.

An interface class to me is a customer-editing screen, a save-as-dialog box, or a student transcript (it's a report). Although some of these classes, specifically the save-as-dialog box, you might be able to buy off-the-shelf, the reality of the situation is that there really isn't a lot of opportunity here. My customer-edit screen is going to be different to your customer screen. My student transcript will be different to your student transcript. Perhaps I'm wrong, but I just don't see a big market for interface classes.

3.4.2.2 Can I Buy Business Classes?

The market for business objects exists, it just might not be as big as everyone thinks.

Business classes are potentially a different story. Although I think that it would be naive to expect to be able to buy a **Customer** class (my customer is different than your customer...), it would be reasonable to be able to buy an **AccountsReceivable** class, or a **CurrencyExchangeRate** class, or a **TaxCalculation** class. All of these business classes are fairly consistent between organizations and it seems to me that there should be a market for these products. The end result is that there will be a market for some types of business classes, but not for all of them.

One of the issues that I see regarding business objects is the need for a detailed understanding of the underlying business functionality that is being wrapped. It's one thing to talk about a class that does tax calculations, it's another to actually build one. Tax laws are constantly changing, and are different between countries, if not between states or provinces. The point to be made is that a set of classes that calculate tax will be very complex. The developers of these classes really need to know their stuff.

3.4.2.3 Can I Buy Persistence Classes?

Buy a persistence layer if you can.

Without a doubt. In fact, although I have built a few myself I really have to question the wisdom of writing your own persistence layer (although in chapter 10 I'll tell you how to do it anyway). The persistence layer is fairly straightforward, and there isn't any reason why you shouldn't be able to buy this stuff. In fact, all you need to do is pick up the latest issue of your favorite database magazine and you should be able to find several vendors offering persistence class libraries for both Smalltalk and C++ applications.

3.4.2.4 Can I Buy System Classes?

Chances are you have already bought several system classes that are included in your programming class library. At the same time, you'll probably also need to buy class libraries that wrap data communication functionality, Internet access, voice-recognition functionality, and printer device drivers. Systems classes will probably be the biggest market for class libraries in the near future, although I suspect that this market will eventually be eclipsed by the market for business class libraries.

There's a market for system classes.

3.4.3 What Are the Implications for Project Management?

There are several interesting project-management implications of the five-layer class-type architecture that is presented in this chapter. First is that it presents an opportunity for your company to organize its development efforts around the architecture. It is very reasonable to have a group of people working on the business domain classes, another group working on the persistence classes, another group on system classes, and finally a fourth group on the interface classes.

PROJECT MANAGEMENT ISSUE

A lot of people like to talk about organizing developers into two groups of people: component builders, and component assemblers. Builders create (or buy) the fundamental base classes needed within your organization, and assemblers put these classes together to form applications. Although this sounds like a good idea, I think that it's a little naive.

What you're really going to have are people who develop and potentially maintain systems classes (system-object engineers), people who develop and maintain persistence classes (persistence-object engineers), people who develop and maintain business classes (business-object developers), and people who develop and maintain interface classes (interface-object developers). You could argue that the people who develop system, persistence, and business classes are all builders, whereas the interface object developers are assemblers. You could also argue that business-object developers are both assemblers and builders at the same time. Or you could argue that everyone is both a builder and an assembler. I'm simply not convinced that it's as simple as people would like to have you think.

Figure 3.6.
The breakdown
of development
effort for systems
classes.

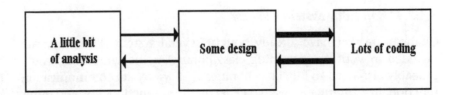

One advantage of the class-type architecture is that you can work on some classes alone. Although you might need to have stubs of some classes available, a stub effectively being a shell of a class, you don't need to have the other layers completed to work on any other layer.

3.4.4 What Are the Implications for Development?

There are some very interesting application development issues that I must make you aware of. For the most part they have to do with the approach that you take to developing them, although there are also a few extra little tips in there that I think you'll like. As we have before, let's take a look at each layer one at a time.

3.4.4.1 System Classes

I want to talk about systems classes first, mostly because they are the easiest to get our mind around. System classes are conceptually very straightforward. For the most part they wrap technical features that are almost always well-defined and clear-cut. As a result, we can take the following approach described in Figure 3.6 to developing systems classes.

You can start coding systems classes reasonably early in the development process.

Figure 3.6 shows the relative breakdown of effort when developing systems classes. Because systems classes are usually straightforward you can often perform analysis very quickly, you simply list the technical requirements that the system class must conform to. Chances are good that you'll have to do a little bit of design to get you going,

> **N O T E**
>
> These development-effort-breakdown diagrams only show the effort spent on analysis, design, and coding. I haven't forgotten about other development steps, such as testing; instead, I've chosen to simplify my diagrams.

but for the most part you can get right in and start coding almost immediately. Although you're coding you'll often discover issues that need to be addressed in design, and every so often you might even find you have to do some more analysis. For the most part, however, you'll probably spend more time on coding than you will on design, and more time on design than on analysis. At least that's the theory.

3.4.4.2 Persistence Classes

As you can see in Figure 3.7, the development effort to create persistence classes is slightly different than for systems classes. Once again analysis is fairly simple, you only have to list the basic technical requirements for the layer. Assuming you're going to actually build the layer yourself (if you're buying the layer then my point is moot), then chances are pretty good that you're going to spend a lot of time designing the persistence layer, but not quite as much coding it. The bottom line is that you'll be spending more time in design than in coding when developing the persistence layer. Then again, we'll see a pretty good design to map objects to a relational database in chapter 9 so perhaps you won't need to do as much design after all.

Get your design right first, then start coding your persistence layer.

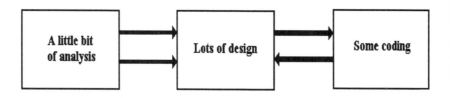

Figure 3.7. The breakdown of development effort for persistence classes.

3.4.4.3 Business Classes

Once again the breakdown of effort changes when we are developing business classes. Figure 3.8 shows that the majority of the effort for developing business classes is spent in analysis. Perhaps you get a 40–30–30% breakdown between analysis, design, and programming. Or maybe a 50–25–25% breakdown, or even a 60–20–20% breakdown. It's always situational. The main point to be made is that you need to get most of your analysis, and even a good chunk of your design done before you begin coding. There's nothing stopping you from coding right from the start, it's just that if you don't know what to code then why are you coding in the first place?

With business classes you need to spend a lot of time with your users analyzing what needs to be done.

CRITICAL DESIGN ISSUE

Systems classes and persistence classes wrap technical functionality provided by the operating system or by tools/applications provided by other vendors. Something can always go wrong—the network doesn't respond, the database is down, the e-mail system is down, too many people are logged in.... The point to be made is that your systems/persistence classes will run into problems that are beyond their control and they need to act intelligently in those situations. My approach has always been to detect the problem and return an intelligent error message describing in proper English the situation and what can possibly be done to correct it. The idea is that this message will eventually be displayed to the user, and then they can react appropriately.

Always return an intelligent message when you run into difficulties.

Figure 3.8.
The breakdown of development effort for business classes.

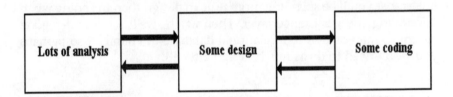

3.4.4.4 Interface Classes

To develop good interface classes you'll spend most of your time prototyping.

Interface classes are different once again. For the most part you'll spend most of your effort prototyping with your users. You'll be designing screens, showing the screens to them, modifying them, showing them again, and so on for quite awhile. As you start to nail down what some of the screens will look like you'll be able to start into design, which for the most part will be determining what business classes you need to interact with to get the job done. Once that's done, coding of interface classes is usually trivial, once again assuming you've done a good analysis-and-design job.

One thing that needs to be pointed out here is that developers of interface classes must have the skill and ability to design good interfaces. Although our discussion of object-oriented user-interface design in chapter 9 is a spectacular extravaganza of tips and techniques, you should really consider taking a 2- or 3-day interface design course. It will be money well spent.

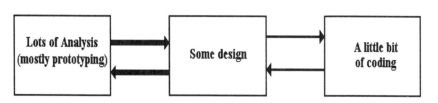

Figure 3.9.
The breakdown of development effort for interface classes.

| Lots of Analysis (mostly prototyping) | Some design | A little bit of coding |

3.4.5 Is This Enough?

Although this architecture presents a good strategy for partitioning your development efforts, it doesn't go into enough detail to specify exactly what needs to be done. How do you handle security issues? Write some system classes. How do you handle interactions with your

ITERATIVE DEVELOPMENT VS. HACKING

I want to step up onto my soapbox for a minute and discuss something that a lot of object developers seem to have missed: the difference between iterative development and hacking. In iterative development you do some analysis, then some design, then some coding, then maybe some more analysis and design and so on until you've developed the system. With hacking you blindly start coding, regardless of whether or not you've done enough analysis and design.

To show you the difference, let's consider the following example. A development team spends half a day doing analysis, a day doing design, and several weeks programming, although they do some design and maybe even some analysis when they find they run into trouble. Is this iterative development or is it hacking? It's iterative development if they're programming systems classes because these types of classes are pretty clear-cut and technical—programmers can figure this stuff out by themselves. It's hacking if this is the approach you took for some business classes—you need to work closely with your users to figure business stuff out; programmers can't go off and do this on their own effectively.

The point to be made is that you need to use the right tool or technique to solve a problem. One size doesn't fit all. Sometimes what we would call iterative development—when we analyze, design, and program for the most part in parallel—works well. Sometimes we need to take more of a waterfall approach and spend some time up front doing analysis, then design, then finally we start programming. Use the right tool for the right job.

The five-layer architecture is a very good start at a more detailed architecture for your organization.

customers? Write some business classes. How are you going to support concurrent access to persistent objects? Put it in the persistence layer. The advice I've given you in this chapter, although solid, merely provides a framework from which you must create an architecture that meets the specific needs of your organization.

3.4.6 What Are the Advantages and Disadvantages?

Although we've hinted at some of the advantages and disadvantages of our class-type architecture, it's worth our while to stop a minute and summarize them here.

3.4.6.1 Advantages

- Increased portability, maintainability, and extensibility

- Provides guidance as to how we should distribute functionality between classes

- Provides guidance as to what classes we can reasonably expect to buy

- Development of classes can be assigned to specialists

- It's simple and it works

- You can organize your development efforts around the class type layers

- It includes the users of the system

3.4.6.2 Disadvantages

- Without a doubt it's a little too simple, but...

3.5 What We've Learned

This chapter presented a five-layer class-type architecture (see Figure 3.10) which promises to avoid the development of OO legacy applications. The architecture provides a strategy for how to distribute the functionality of OO applications among various class types.

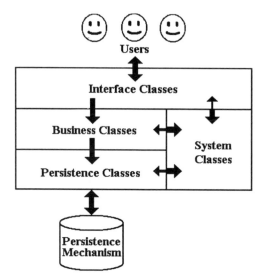

Figure 3.10.
The five-layer
class-type
architecture.

Furthermore, it provides guidance as to what other types of classes a given class will interact with, and how that interaction will occur. This increases the extensibility, maintainability, and portability of the systems that we develop.

Reference

Ambler, S.W. (1995). *The Object Primer: The Application Developer's Guide to Object-Orientation*. New York: SIGS Books.

> *We keep solving the same problems over and over again.*
>
> *There must be a pattern here somewhere.*

Chapter 4

Reusing Your Development Efforts — Object-Oriented Patterns

What We'll Learn in This Chapter

What OO patterns, including both analysis patterns and design patterns, are.

How to use OO patterns effectively in the applications that you create.

How to create new OO patterns.

How to apply OO patterns throughout the life cycle.

What the advantages and disadvantages of OO patterns are.

Considering the number of combinations of operating systems, hardware platforms, and network protocols can you reasonably expect to be able to purchase business objects off the shelf? I'm not so sure. But what I do know is that developers are constantly solving the same problems over and over again. How many of you have been involved with developing inventory-control software? Or human-resource-management software? Or billing software? These problems keep repeating themselves over and over again. Although everyone's inventory-

control system is different, the fact is that there is a lot of similarity between the designs of these systems. Wouldn't it be nice to be able to pick a design up off the shelf that has 80–90% of the thinking done for you already and all you have to do is develop the differences that are unique to your organization? That's what object-oriented (OO) patterns are all about, they're blueprints of generic designs that you can apply to the systems that you develop.

Doesn't it always seem as if you're solving the same problems over and over again? If you personally haven't solved a given problem before, then chances are pretty good you could hunt somebody down who had tackled the same, or at least a similar problem in the past. Sometimes the problem you are working on is simple, sometimes it is complex, but usually it's been worked on before.

Wouldn't it be nice to be able to easily find a solution, or at least a partial solution, to your problem? Think how much time and effort could be saved if you had access to a library of solutions to common system development problems. This is what object-oriented patterns are all about. OO patterns are collections of classes that solve common problems that recur over and over again. To be more accurate, an OO pattern is a model of several classes that work together to solve a common problem in your application's business or technical domain.

DEFINITIONS

OO pattern—A model of several classes that work together to solve a common problem in your application's business or technical domain.

Design pattern—An OO pattern that describes a solution to a design problem.

Analysis pattern—An OO pattern that describes a solution to a business/analysis problem.

There is a lot of exciting work going on right now in patterns. The work done in design patterns (Coad, North, & Mayfield, 1995; Gamma, Helm, Johnson, & Vlissides, 1995) has shown very promising benefits. The patterns described in these books are being used by thousands of developers to improve both their productivity and the quality of the systems that they create. Just as the achievements of great scientists are built on the shoulders of other scientists, the achievements of great developers are being built on the shoulders of other developers.

In this chapter I want to concentrate on two types of patterns: design patterns that solve design problems and analysis patterns that solve business/analysis problems. In the next section we'll discuss several design patterns proposed by other people that I have found very useful in my development endeavors and in the following section we'll cover some really useful analysis patterns that I have used on several projects in various business domains.

4.1 Design Patterns

Design patterns describe a solution to common problems found in the design of systems. Although we won't discuss every design pattern in this section, people are discovering new patterns every day, we will cover several very useful patterns that you should be able to apply immediately to the applications that you are developing.

In this section we will discuss the following three object-oriented design patterns:

1. Singleton

2. Proxy

3. Roles Played/State

4.1.1 Singleton

It is very common to discover classes in your application that should only have one instance. Perhaps there should only be one instance of a certain editing screen open at any given time, perhaps you have configuration information that you want to store in one place only, or perhaps you have one or more constant values that you need to maintain somewhere. In all of these examples you need to have a single instance of the class in question—a single instance of the dialog box, a single instance of the configuration information, and a single instance of the constants.

Singleton (Gamma, Helm, Johnson, & Vlissides, 1995) is a design pattern that shows how to ensure that only one single instance of a

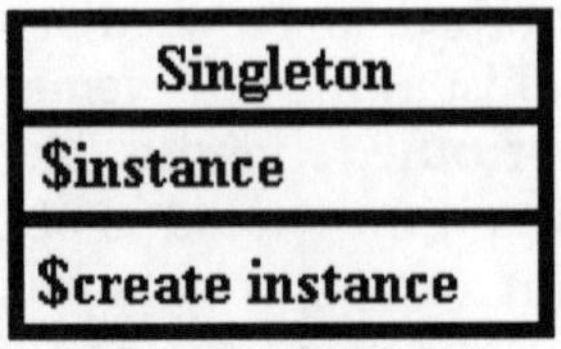

Singleton
$instance
$create instance

Figure 4.1. The Singleton design pattern.

class exists at any one time. In Figure 4.1 we see a class diagram describing the Singleton design pattern. Note that there is a class attribute that keeps track of the single instance, and a class method that creates the instance if it doesn't already exist. Although Singleton is a simple pattern, I suspect that it is one that you will use over and over again when developing OO applications.

In Figure 4.2 we see a common example of how the Singleton pattern is put to good use. In almost every application you need to maintain basic information, such as its name, its version, and the phone number to call if the users need support. The name of the application is used in the titles of message boxes, the version number could be used to automatically determine whether or not the user needs to update his system (a process that you can easily automate in a networked environment), and the support number would displayed in both the about box and with any serious error messages (actually, in a networked environment I always prefer to instantiate "error-transaction" objects that automatically inform support personnel so as to allow them to respond instantly to a problem).

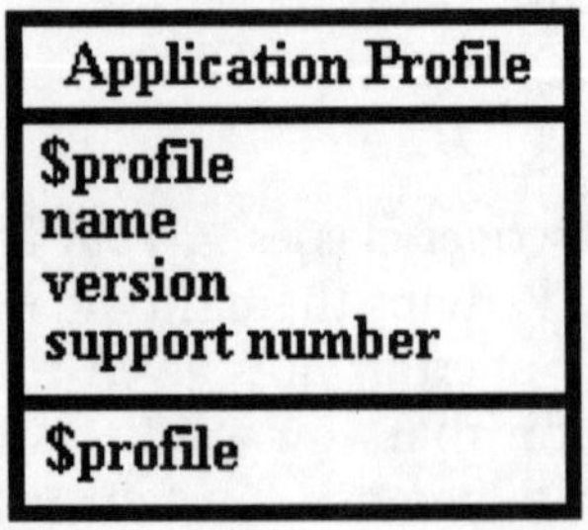

Application Profile
$profile name version support number
$profile

Figure 4.2. An example of the Singleton design pattern.

4.1.2 Proxy

Another common problem faced during design is how to represent objects on a client machine that exist on another machine, perhaps in either a relational or object-oriented database? For example, say

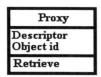 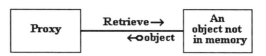

Figure 4.3.
The Proxy design pattern.

you have a customer-search screen from which users are able to define search criteria, press a button, and get a list of customers that meet that criteria. The user then looks at the list, double-clicks on one of the customers, and then edits that customer object. The question is this: Knowing full well that any given search criteria could result in numerous customer objects meeting that criteria, and that the user is typically interested in only one of the customer objects to begin with, what can you do to minimize the amount of information transmitted across the network to the application? One answer to that question is to use proxies.

Proxy (Gamma, Helm, Johnson, & Vlissides, 1995), also called *Proxy-Specific Item* (Coad, North, & Mayfield, 1995), is a design pattern described in Figure 4.3 that shows how to represent an object that is not currently in memory. Note that Figure 4.3 shows both a class diagram and a collaboration diagram so that you can see both the state and behavior of this pattern. When a message is sent to the proxy object, it automatically fetches the real object into memory, passes the original message to the real object, and then the proxy replaces itself with the real object.

The Proxy pattern shows how to represent an object that is not currently in memory.

A proxy object needs enough descriptive information so that users are able to identify it, as well as the *object identifier*, or *OID*, for that object. OIDs are the object-oriented equivalent of keys, attributes that uniquely identify an object. When the real object needs to be retrieved from the other machine, the OID is used to identify and retrieve the right object. In chapter 10 we cover OIDs in more detail in our discussion of database issues.

OIDs are attributes that uniquely identify an object.

Let's do an example. In Figure 4.4 below we see how the Proxy pattern can be applied to our customer-search screen problem. Instead of

Figure 4.4.
An example of
the Proxy design
pattern.

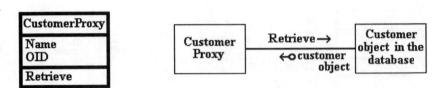

bringing the entire customer object across the network, we instead bring back just enough information so that both our user and the system can identify each customer object. The name of the customer is displayed in the search-results list so that users can distinguish between each customer object, and the OID is used to identify which customer object to retrieve from the database. When our user chooses B. Sisko or K. Janeway the customer proxy object will fetch the corresponding customer object from the database so that it may be displayed on the customer-edit screen.

From the point of view of the class-type architecture presented in chapter 3, the customer-search screen and customer-edit screen are both interface objects, the customer object is a business object, the customer proxy objects are persistence objects, and the network connection is a system object. The reason why the proxy object would be considered a persistence object is because its only purpose is to retrieve business objects from the database.

4.1.3 Roles Played (State)

We've seen that some objects exhibit different behavior depending on the state that they are currently in. For example, you can withdraw from a bank account when it is active but not when it is overdrawn. You can purchase a vehicle from a car dealer when it is on the lot but not when it has been sold or is currently being leased out to another customer. You can promote a person when they are one of your employees but not when they are only your customer. The question is how do you implement an object that changes state and exhibits different behavior in each state?

The Roles Played pattern describes how to design objects that exhibit different behaviors depending on their current state.

The *Roles Played* (Coad 1992), or *State* (Gamma, Helm, Johnson, & Vlissides, 1995) design pattern described below in Figure 4.5 addresses the issue of how to easily implement objects that exhibit different behavior depending on their state. The basic idea is that an object can be built as a collection of one or more state objects that represent the different functionality exhibited by the object for each state that it

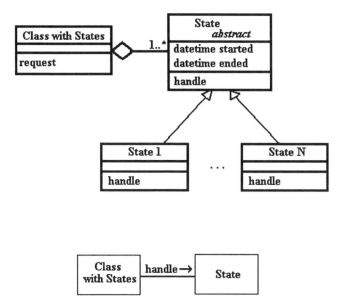

Figure 4.5.
The State design pattern.

can be in. Any behaviors that are affected by the object's state are implemented in the state objects as methods with the original object passing on the appropriate messages to the current state object.

In Figure 4.6 we see an implementation of a **Vehicle** class, presumably for a car lot, that uses the State pattern. From the point of view of a car dealership, vehicles are always in one of three states: on the lot and available to sell, leased out to a customer, or sold to a customer. Because car dealerships want to keep track of the history of a vehicle we've kept the datetimestamps that are common for the State pattern. The three methods in the abstract class **VehicleState** are very sim-

---

TIP

You Need to Choose Between Timestamps and Datetimestamps

The datetime attributes shown in the **State** abstract superclass are sometimes implemented simply as time attributes, and sometimes not implemented at all. The decision that you need to make is whether or not you care when the object entered/left that state. If you're interested, then depending on the length of time that the object will be in that state, then you'll either need to timestamp or datetimestamp the object.

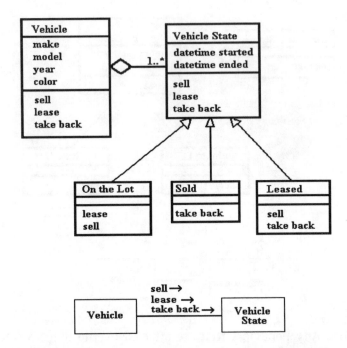

Figure 4.6.
An example of
the State design
pattern.

ple—they return a message in the format: "You cannot lease/sell/take back this vehicle," which would be displayed on the screen to the user when he tries to do these things to the vehicle. The corresponding methods in the subclasses are more complex, as they contain the code needed to actually sell, lease, or take back the vehicle when it is in that state. The advantage of this approach is that regardless of the state the vehicle is currently in, it will always do the appropriate thing. For example, if you try to sell a vehicle that has already been sold a message will be displayed on the screen, although if you try to sell a vehicle that is on the lot the system will do the proper processing.

The Roles Played pattern can be used to simulate multiple inheritance.

A common use for the Roles Played pattern is to simulate multiple inheritance, the ability of classes to directly inherit from more then one superclass, in languages that don't support it. Think of it like this: What's stopping you from allowing an object to have more than one state at any given time? Absolutely nothing. By allowing more than one state at a time you can allow an object to exhibit the functionality of all of its states at one time, which effectively is what multiple inheritance allows you to do. We'll discuss this further in chapter 7 when we cover programming languages.

TIP

If the State Changes Quickly, Don't Use the Roles Played Pattern

Don't use the Roles Played pattern when the object flips back and forth between states quickly. It might be more effective to simply code the state differences in the object itself, at least from a performance point of view. The Roles Played pattern suffers from two problems: you potentially end up with a lot of little state objects, and you have the overhead of passing messages onto these state objects instead of just doing the process in the original object to begin with. The advantage is that it is simpler to code using this pattern, and you are able to simulate multiple inheritance using this approach. As always, you have to make tradeoffs.

In section 4.2.2 we discuss an analysis pattern called *Business Entity*, a very common usage of the Roles Played design pattern.

4.2   Analysis Patterns

Analysis patterns describe a solution to common problems found in the analysis/business domain of an application. Analysis patterns are often a little more specific than design patterns—they describe a solution for a portion of a business domain. This doesn't mean that an analysis pattern is applicable only to a single line of business, although it could be. In this section we'll discuss several analysis patterns that I have used in several business domains and that I believe you will find useful in your organization.

The concept of analysis patterns is fairly new. For the last few years design patterns seem to have dominated the industry. I believe, howev-

---

TIP

How to Use Analysis Patterns Effectively

The real value of analysis patterns is the thinking behind them. A pattern might not be the total solution to your problem, but it might provide enough insight to help save you several hours or days during development. Consider analysis patterns as a good start at solutions.

er, that analysis patterns will prove to be of greatest benefit in the long-term. Don't get me wrong, design patterns are very useful, it's just that analysis patterns provide insight into solutions to business problems. Solving business problems is what systems development is all about.

In this section we will discuss the following five object-oriented analysis patterns:

1. Item-Item Description

2. Business Entity

3. Contact Point

4. Place

5. Shipping/Billing

4.2.1 Item-Item Description

It is quite common to find collections of objects that share the same description, yet are still separate instances. For example, in your organization there might be several employees with the job title "Project Manager" or "Vice President." You might have descriptive information that you maintain about inventory items, or because on an address edit screen you input two-letter codes representing American states so you need to maintain a set of lookup objects with the full name of the state. The point to be made is that because several objects share the same description we should consider creating an object that represents that description.

The Item-Item Description analysis pattern describes how to model objects and their shared descriptions.

The *Item-Item Description* (Coad, 1992) analysis pattern, shown in Figure 4.7, describes how to model objects and their shared descriptions. The basic idea is that **Item** objects are described by **Item Description** objects that hold various pieces of information about the item. Note that the relationship between the two classes is unidirectional: Instances of **Item** know about instances of **Item Description** but not the other way around. For the most part this pat-

Figure 4.7.
The Item-Item Description analysis pattern.

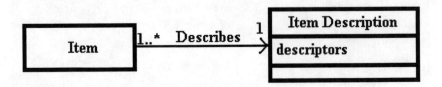

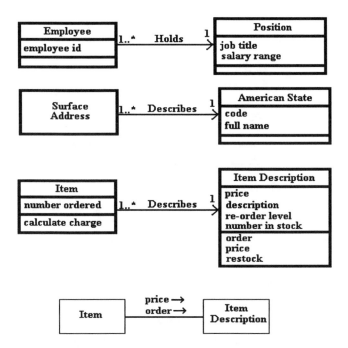

Figure 4.8.
Three examples using the Item-Item Description analysis pattern.

tern models one of the issues that object-oriented normalization addresses: Pulling descriptive information out of an object and creating a new object from it. We cover class normalization in greater detail in chapter 10.

In Figure 4.8 we see three examples that use the Item-Item Description pattern. In the first example we see that employees hold positions. Although it might not be obvious at first, position objects describe the jobs that employees hold. In the second example we see that American state objects describe surface address objects, providing the full name for the state in which an address is in. The third example shows how inventory items are described by item description objects. Note how instances of **Item** collaborate with their corresponding **Item Description** instances to calculate the price that will be charged for them.

Item-Item Description is an incredibly versatile and useful analysis pattern, and I highly suspect that it is the one that you'll use most often in your analysis efforts.

Figure 4.9.
The Business
Entity analysis
pattern.

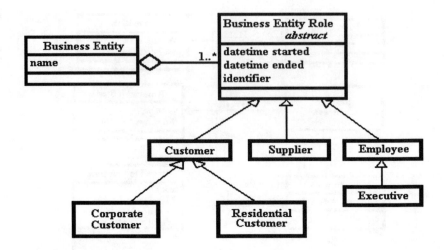

4.2.2 Business Entity

*The Business
Entity analysis
pattern describes
the different
types of people
and organiza-
tions with whom
you interact.*

Every organization has to deal either with other organizations or with people, usually both. As a result, you need to keep track of them. The *Business Entity* analysis pattern that I propose in Figure 4.9 solves this problem nicely. This pattern uses the Roles Played pattern, described in section 4.1.3, to model the different types of organizations and people with whom your company interacts. Please note that the **Identifier** attribute of **Business Entity Role** represents concepts like customer number, employee number, or supplier ID.

*Sometimes it's
the idea behind
a pattern that's
important, not
the details.*

I've left out the description of the Business Entity pattern for one simple reason—because every organization deals with others in a dif-ferent manner they'll create a business entity role hierarchy slightly differently. Some organizations have suppliers, others don't. Some or-ganizations have employees, others don't (virtual organizations are often formed by people who are all considered partners, not employ-ees). Some organizations distinguish among corporate, residential, and governmental customers, others don't. I think that you get the picture. The important implication of all of this is that some patterns are sparse—it's the idea behind them and not the details that count.

4.2.3 Contact Point

Not only do we need to keep track of the business entities that we interact with, we also need to keep track of the ways in which we can

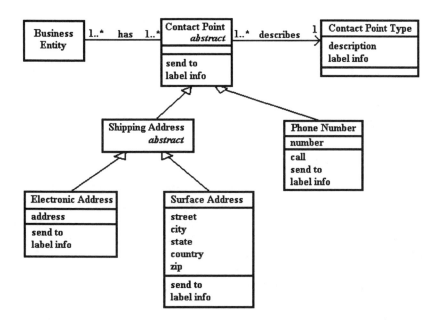

Figure 4.10.
The Contact
Point analysis
pattern.

interact with them. The *Contact Point* analysis pattern shown in Figure 4.10 describes an approach for doing so. Your organization most likely sends letters and bills to, as well as ships products to the surface addresses of your customers. Perhaps it e-mails information to customers and employees, or faxes information to them. It also probably needs to keep track of the contact phone number for anyone it interacts with. The Contact Point pattern models how to do all of these things, enabling you to even automate them.

Note how we've used the Item-Item Description pattern here via the **Contact Point** and **Contact Point Type** classes. The different varieties of contact point types would include things like voice phone line, fax phone line, work address, home address, billing address, and personal e-mail ID. Also, note that we could have added an **American State** instance here, as it is used in Figure 4.8, to describe surface address objects. This points out an important principle of object-oriented patterns—they can be used in combination to solve larger problems.

Subclasses of **Contact Point** need to be able to do at least two things: they need to know how things/information can be sent to them and they need to know how to output their "label info." We can send faxes to phone numbers, e-mail to electronic addresses, and letters and

The Contact Point analysis pattern describes an approach for keeping track of the way your organization interacts with business entities.

You can use patterns together to solve difficult problems.

packages to surface addresses. We also need to be able to print contact point information on labels, letterhead, and reports. To output labels, contact points collaborate with instances of Contact Point Types for descriptor information—for example, we want to output "Fax: (416) 555-1212," not just "(416) 555-1212." Furthermore, the **Phone Number** class should have the ability to be automatically dialed if you need to support that sort of functionality.

4.2.4 Shipping/Billing

The Shipping/ Billing pattern describes how to send and receive both physical and virtual products and information to/from business entities.

Most large organizations need to ship products and information to the business entities that they interact with, as well as send them bills. Because we are now in the electronic age we need to be able to ship/ bill business entities both physically, by sending physical items/ invoices to their surface address, and virtually by sending a stream of information either to their electronic ID or to their fax line. The *Shipping/Billing* analysis pattern shown in Figure 4.11 describes how to do this admirably.

The classes in the **ToFrom** hierarchy basically maintain a relationship between business entities and contact points. They also have the ability to send and receive products and information to/from business entities via contact points. For example, to send a physical product to a business entity a packing list needs to be created that indicates what to send and a mailing label needs to be printed so that we know where

Figure 4.11.
The Shipping/ Billing analysis pattern.

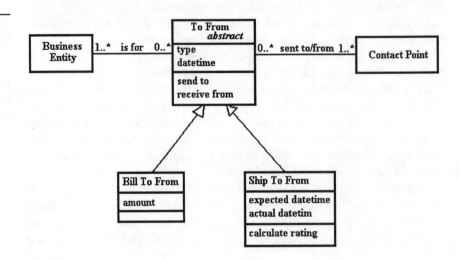

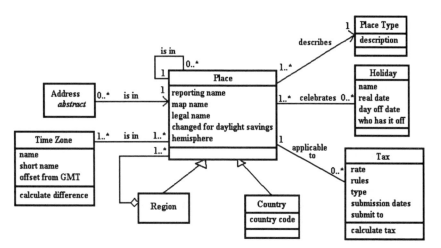

Figure 4.12.
The Place analysis
pattern.

to send the package. To send electronic information we merely have to indicate how we want to send it, either via e-mail or via fax. Actually, now that I think about it you might want to add "teletypewriter" or "Telex" as a contact point type for phones. To receive products and information the process is reversed—you need to redirect what you've received to the proper employee within your organization.

It's worth noting that an instance of **ToFrom** might know about multiple contact points and multiple business entities. Sometimes you might decide to broadcast a message to several business entities. Furthermore, chances are good that you'll want to keep track of both the business entity that sent the product/information and the business entity that received it. Therefore you'll always have at least two sets of business entities and contact points to deal with.

4.2.5 Place

Most organizations need to keep track of the places they do business in. Do you do business in North America? In Europe? In the Canadian province of Ontario? In the town of Hoboken, New Jersey? If you're doing business in numerous places, or perhaps you're a truly international firm, then keeping track of time zones, holidays, and tax laws is probably of interest to you. The *Place* analysis pattern shown in Figure 4.12 describes how to keep track of all this information.

The **Place** class keeps track of basic information such as the various names that a place can have and whether or not the time changes

The Place pattern describes how to keep track of critical information about different places in the world.

in that place when we switch to daylight savings time. It also needs to keep track of which hemisphere the place is in so that when we do change the time for daylight savings it's done correctly (places in the Northern Hemisphere move their clocks ahead in March, whereas places in the Southern Hemisphere move them back an hour).

The **Place Type** class uses the Item-Item Description pattern to describe places. A place might be a city, a country, a town, a hamlet, a continent, a province, ... The **Tax** class also forms an Item-Item Description pattern with **Place** to provide the ability to describe and calculate taxes. The **Country** class maintains information such as the international country code for the phone system in that country. **Region** is a place that is made up of a collection of places. For example, the Golden Horseshoe in Southern Ontario is formed from all of the cities and towns along Lake Ontario between Niagara Falls, Ontario and Pickering, Ontario. Other examples of regions would be the Middle East, Central America, the Wine Region of France, and the East Coast of the United States.

The **Holiday** class defines what holidays are applicable to a place, when they are, and who gets them off. At least in Canada and the United States some holidays are taken only by bankers and government employees, whereas other holidays are taken by everyone. Furthermore, some holidays are taken by people of certain religious backgrounds, whereas others are secular.

4.3 How to Use Patterns Effectively

It's fine and dandy to read about how wonderful OO patterns are, but it's something completely different to use them effectively. The following four easy steps that describe how to use object-oriented patterns:

1. **Study the patterns that you already have access to.** There are a lot of good books out there that describe object-oriented patterns, some interesting WWW (World Wide Web) sites on the Internet, as well as some interesting magazine and journal articles. Go and look at the work that others have done. Study their patterns.

2. **Look for similar underlying concepts.** When you are studying existing object-oriented patterns, ask yourself what underlying concept is being modeled. Then try to find por-

tions of your problem domain that are based on the same underlying concept and match the pattern to the problem.

3. **Apply the pattern.** Once you have identified both a problem and a pattern that are based on the same underlying principle then apply the pattern in your model. Remember that you might have to change the names a bit. Look at the examples for Item-Item Description in Figure 4.8: one used the exact names but two didn't. That's OK, it's more important to use class names that reflect the specific problem domain than to use the often artificial class names that make sense for a generic solution.

4. **Don't expect that everything can be solved by patterns.** The most common mistake that people make when they first start using patterns is that they try to solve all problems with patterns. Unfortunately it doesn't work that way. Although there are lots of common problems between systems, there are also lots of times when portions of them are unique. Patterns model solutions to common problems, not unique problems.

4.4 How to Discover New Patterns

Although there are a lot of well-documented and interesting patterns available to you, there are still many others waiting to be discovered, perhaps by you. The question is how do you discover patterns? Here's some advice.

1. **Can the pattern be used elsewhere?** Every so often as you are modeling you get the suspicion that you've discovered a collection of classes that can be used elsewhere. Whenever this happens, ask yourself where the potential pattern can be used and how it would be used. If you come up with a good answer, or perhaps several good answers to these questions then you should consider discussing your pattern with other people. If you think your pattern could be used to solve a marketing problem, then discuss it with some marketing experts. If you think you've found a solution to a networking problem, discuss your pattern with some networking experts. You don't want to fall

into the trap of assuming that your potential pattern is in fact useful without discussing it with others first.

2. **Use the pattern several times.** The best test to determine if you've discovered a pattern is to actually use it on other projects. A good rule of thumb that we use at my company is that something isn't considered reusable until it's been reused three times, the best situation occurs when it is reviewed by three different development teams on three different projects. By the time the third team has used and potentially modified your pattern you know you have something that's pretty solid.

Something isn't considered reusable until it's been reused at least three times.

3. **Expect to change your class diagram.** As other teams reuse your pattern, chances are very good that they'll change it in the process. That's only natural. Each problem domain has its own set of requirements, some of which will be common and some of which will be unique. You may have left out, or perhaps ignored, something that is critical to another team. If you want to take advantage of the changes that other teams make, or at least remain consistent with them, then you should plan on updating both your class diagram and your source code to reflect those changes.

4.5 The Advantages and Disadvantages of Patterns

There are several advantages and disadvantages to working with object-oriented patterns. They are discussed below.

4.5.1 Advantages

1. **Patterns increase developer productivity.** By documenting solutions to common problems, patterns promote reuse of development efforts, and increased reuse within your organization improves the productivity of your developers.

2. **Patterns increase the consistency between applications.** By using the same patterns over and over again you increase the consistency between applications, making them easier to understand and maintain. When your applications are developed in a consistent manner it makes it that much

easier to do technical walkthroughs that enable you to improve the quality of your development efforts.

3. **Patterns are potentially better than reusable code.** People can talk about reusable code all that they want, but the differences between system platforms makes this dream difficult at best. Patterns on the other hand, because they have a higher level of reuse, can be applied on any system platform as they are not environment specific.

4. **Patterns can be used in combination to solve difficult problems.** We've seen in this chapter that patterns can be used together. For example, we used Item-Item Description in several of our analysis patterns. Business Entity was also as a component used in several other patterns.

5. **There are more and more patterns being developed every day.** There is a lot of exciting work going on in patterns, with new patterns being introduced every day. This allows you to take advantage of the development efforts of thousands of people, often for the mere cost of a book, magazine, or telephone call to link you to the Internet.

4.5.2 Disadvantages

1. **You need to learn a large number of patterns.** Although there is an advantage to having access to a large number of patterns, the disadvantage is that you have to a large number of them, or at least know that they exist. This can be a lot of work.

2. **The NIH (not-invented-here) syndrome can get in the way.** Many developers are unwilling to accept the work of others: if they didn't create it then it isn't any good. Additionally, if a pattern isn't exactly what they need then they might not be willing to use it. Whenever I run into this attitude I always like to point out the versatility of the Item-Item Description pattern, which we've seen used for several different purposes.

3. **Patterns aren't code.** Hard-core techies are often unwilling to accept anything as reusable except code. For some reason they just can't accept that you can reuse analysis-and-design efforts as well as source code.

4. **"Pattern" is quickly becoming a buzzword.** As more and more people realize the value of patterns more and more marketing people will begin to exploit it to increase the sales of whatever product or service they are pushing. Just as in the mid-1990's we saw the term *object-oriented* used as an adjective to describe products that had almost nothing to do with objects, I suspect that we'll see the same sort of thing happen with the term *pattern*.

4.6 What We've Learned

An object-oriented pattern is a model of several classes that work together to solve a common problem. Analysis patterns provide solutions for problems in your analysis/business domain and design patterns provide

Table 4.1. PATTERNS DISCUSSED IN THIS CHAPTER

Pattern	Description
Business Entity	Describes the different types of people and organizations that you interact with
Contact Point	Describes an approach for keeping track of the way your organization interacts with business entities
Item-Item Description	Describes how to model objects and their shared descriptions
Place	Describes how to keep track of critical information about different places in the world
Proxy	Describes how to represent an object that is not currently in memory
Roles Played	Describes how to design objects that exhibit different behaviors depending on their current state
Singleton	Describes how to ensure that only one instance of a class exists at any one time
Shipping/Billing	Describes how to send and receive both physical and virtual products and information to/from business entities

solutions for problems in your design domain. In this chapter we've seen that patterns can be used in combination to solve complex problems. See Table 4.1 for a listing of the patterns explored in this chapter.

References

Coad, P. (1992). "Object-oriented patterns." *Communications of the ACM*, 35(9), 152–159.

Coad, P., North, D., & Mayfield, M. (1995). *Object Models: Strategies, Patterns, and Applications*. Englewood Cliffs, NJ: Yourdon Press.

Gamma, E., Helm, R., Johnson, R., & Vlissides, J. (1995). *Design Patterns—Elements of Reusable Object-Oriented Software*. Reading, MA: Addison-Wesley.

Chapter 5

Development in the 90s and Beyond — Designing Distributed Object-Oriented Applications

What We'll Learn in This Chapter

The various trends and techniques in creating distributed applications.

*How to distribute applications using client/server technology,
taking both a two-tier and three-tier approach.*

*How to distribute the classes of your object-oriented application using traditional
client/server approaches, object-oriented client/server (OOCS), and applets.*

*How to create applications using Common Object Request Broker Architecture
(CORBA), a distributed object standard.*

*The architecture for application development is becoming more and more distributed. We're moving from the centralized mainframe approach popularized in
the 1960s and 1970s through the client/server approach of the 1980s, into the
distributed classes and distributed objects approaches of the 1990s. In this
chapter we will compare and contrast these approaches, concentrating on*

*object-oriented client/server design, a technique for
distributing classes across a network of computers.*

Over the past 15 years we have seen a general migration from high-ly centralized mainframe computers with dumb terminals to more and more decentralized information technologies. In Figure 5.1 we see how information technology is slowly evolving from mainframe technolo-gy to client/server technology to distributed classes and finally to dis-tributed objects. In this chapter we will discuss the merits of all four of these technologies, concentrating on the reality of today and the near future: distributed classes and distributed objects.

Figure 5.1.
A quick history
and future of
distributed
applications.

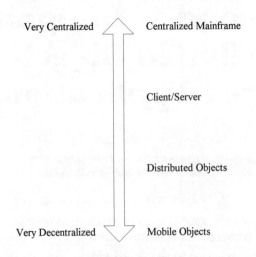

The interesting thing to point out about Figure 5.1 is that within the information industry we can find examples of companies thriving at one or more of these stages of distributing application logic. Although the majority of Information System (IS) departments are working with client/server technology right now, the fact is that the centralized mainframe approach is still being used for many mission-critical appli-cations. Furthermore, many firms are now working with both distrib-uted classes and distributed objects—I highly suspect that object ori-ented client/server (OOCS) will be the reality for most MIS shops for the rest of the 1990s.

*Object-oriented
client/server is
where it is at for
most MIS shops
in the late 1990s.*

T I P

Where You Put the Class Types is Key

In this chapter pay special attention to where we put the logic for each class-type layer, or their non-OO equivalents, as this is indicative of how difficult our applications will be to both develop and maintain. With the exception of centralized mainframes, there is system logic at all layers of each architecture as there will always be at least the need to transmit information/objects between machines—a requirement that is fundamentally a system issue.

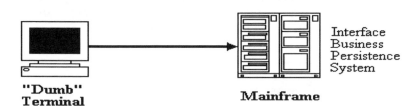

"Dumb" Terminal

Mainframe

Interface
Business
Persistence
System

Figure 5.2.
Centralized mainframes.

5.1 Centralized Mainframes

Dumb terminals connected to a centralized mainframe has been the approach taken by MIS shops to deliver applications to their users for years. As we see in Figure 5.2, the basic idea is that all functionality is provided by the mainframe, a high-powered computer with the ability to accept hundreds and sometimes even thousands of users simultaneously, with access to applications via dumb terminals that provide little or no computing ability. Although this approach is still in use today, and probably will be for some time, it is rarely acceptable to users because of its lack of flexibility and generally poor user interface.

All of the functionality of an application is implemented on the mainframe.

With this architecture the functionality of our four class types—interface, business, persistence, and system—are performed by the mainframe, effectively making it the bottleneck. The main advantage is control: dumb terminals don't provide users with the opportunity to install their own software or to modify the hardware configuration. This is also their greatest weakness because the ability for people to control their own computing environments is usually an important feature to them.

5.2 Client/Server

The functionality of applications is split between two classes of machine: clients and servers.

Client/server (C/S) computing is an environment that satisfies business needs by appropriately allocating application processing between client-and-server processes. A *client*, also commonly referred to as a "front-end," is a single-user PC or workstation that provides presentation services and appropriate computing, connectivity, and interfaces relevant to the business need. A *server*, commonly referred to as a "back-end," is one or more multiuser processors with shared memory that provides computing connectivity, database services, and interfaces relevant to the business need. Clients communicate with servers via middleware, which is the network, its operating system, and any technology needed to connect everything together.

Figure 5.3.
Clients send
requests to
servers.

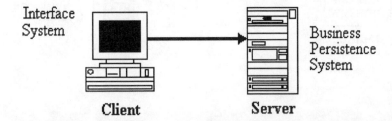

DEFINITIONS

Client—A client is a single-user PC or workstation that provides presentation services and appropriate computing, connectivity, and interfaces relevant to the business need. A client is also commonly referred to as a "front-end."

Server—A server is one or more multiuser processors with shared memory that provides computing connectivity, database services, and interfaces relevant to the business need. A server is also commonly referred to as a "back-end."

Client/server (C/S) computing—An environment that satisfies the business need by appropriately allocating the application processing between the client and the server processes.

Middleware—The technology that allows clients and servers to communicate with one another. This includes the network itself, its operating system, and anything needed to connect computers to the network.

SCOTT'S SOAPBOX

What Makes Up a Good Client/Server Implementation?

Here are the features that I look for in "good" client/server (C/S) implementations:

Good C/S applications:

- Reduce total execution time
- Appropriately offload work to servers
- Minimize network requests (because that's one of your potential bottlenecks)
- Are "user-oriented"

Good clients:

- Provide presentation services (both input and output)
- Have no knowledge of the database environment (it's encapsulated by the persistence layer)
- Have no knowledge of the network environment (it's encapsulated by the system layer)
- Have interfaces that are simple, intuitive, and easy to use
- Potentially encapsulate business knowledge

Good servers:

- Have minimal interfaces
- Are "black boxes" (from the point of view of clients)
- Encapsulate the database environment
- Provide clients with the information that they request but do not hand over raw data (unless otherwise requested)
- Potentially encapsulate business knowledge

"Good" networks

- Are encapsulated at the operating-system level
- Work at a reasonable speed
- Do not hinder the running of applications

As we can see in Figure 5.3 clients send requests to servers via middleware. Because network technology enables this communication, people often describe the network as the computer in client/server computing. It's for this reason that client/server computing is associated with networking instead of development methodologies and I suspect that as a result C/S development techniques have not received the attention that they deserve. Until now.

There are two main approaches to client/server applications, two-tier and three-tier. Both of these approaches are discussed below.

5.2.1 Two-Tier Client/Server

Client machines directly interact with servers.

The basic idea with the *two-tier client/server* (C/S) architecture is that clients and servers communicate with each other in a direct and highly coupled manner—change in one usually implies a change in the other (Fingar, Read, Stikeleather 1996). Clients are able to directly communicate with one or more servers as long as they have knowledge of that server. Two-tier client/server architectures are conceptually simple, but suffer from the fact that when information is needed from several sources the client has to put it together itself. This not only results in additional processing on the client machine it also reflects the fact that there was probably lots of network traffic resulting from the requests for each block of information.

For the most part, the two-tier C/S architecture is a reflection of a hardware downsizing mentality from the mainframe world. There are two main flavors of two-tier architectures—thin client and fat client.

DEFINITIONS

Two-tier client/server—Clients and servers communicate with one another in a direct and highly coupled manner.

Thin-client approach—A two-tier C/S architecture in which the client machines implement only the user interface of an application.

Fat-client approach—A two-tier C/S architecture in which client machines implement both the user interface and the business logic of an application. Servers typically only supply data to client machines with little or no processing done to it.

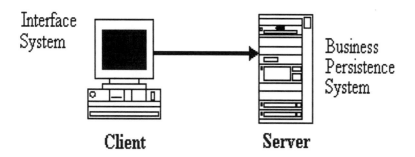

Interface
System

Client

Business
Persistence
System

Server

Figure 5.4.
Two-tier
client/server
taking a "thin"
client approach.

5.2.1.1 The Thin-Client Approach

Figure 5.4 shows that with the thin client approach client machines implement only the interface layer, providing the opportunity for more complex and interesting user interfaces. In many ways this is little different than the centralized mainframe approach, the only difference being that the user interface is (one hopes) better.

Client machines only implement the user interface of an application.

There are several advantages to this approach. First it is reasonably easy to maintain as all the business logic is in the server. Second, it allows you to use low-end client machines, effectively reducing your hardware costs. The disadvantages of this approach are that the client is highly coupled to the server and that the server is still the bottleneck for an application.

Screen scraping, an approach to wrapping legacy applications, typically takes a thin-client approach. Screen scraping is discussed in chapter 11.

5.2.1.2 The Fat-Client Approach

As we see in Figure 5.5, when taking a fat-client approach client machines implement both the user interface and the business logic of an application. Servers typically only supply data to client machines with little or no processing done to it.

Client machines implement both the user interface and the business logic of an application.

The main advantage of this approach is that you've moved a lot of the processing off the server and onto client machines, taking advantage of the processing power of those machines. Unfortunately there are several disadvantages: first, you typically need better client machines resulting in higher hardware costs. Second, it is potentially harder to maintain (although see the following tip) as you need to update code on the client

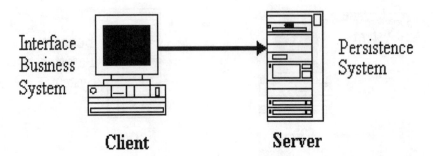

Figure 5.5.
Two-tier
client/server
taking a fat-client
approach.

machines for business updates. Third, there is most likely a lot more data going over the network as there is little processing being done to it by the server.

TIP

Make Your Application Smart Enough to Update Itself

Applications, or better yet, classes, should know their version number. When a user logs onto a server, the application should automatically ask the server what the latest version number of the code is, and if the application is out of date, then it should update itself automatically before starting. This is really easy to do and dramatically simplifies the release process for applications—critical for iterative development.

5.2.2 Three-Tier Client/Server

*Application
servers encapsu-
late access to
other servers on
the network, pro-
viding a single
point of contact
for clients.*

The *three-tier client/server* architecture, shown in Figure 5.6, addresses many of the flaws of the two-tier approach. It introduces the concept of an *application server*, which may or may not exist on its own physical machine, that acts as an interface to the other servers on the network. The basic idea is that now client machines only need to send requests to the application server, which in turn sends the appropriate requests to the other servers on the network, processing the responses and sending it back to the client.

Although at first this appears slow because of the added overhead of the application server, experience actually shows that application servers reduce the overall response time of a request. This happens because application servers are often directly connected to the other servers that they are front-ending, eliminating network overhead.

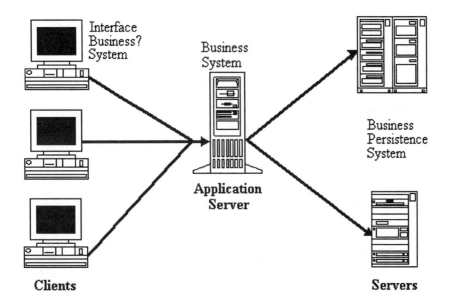

Interface
Business?
System

Business
System

Application
Server

Business
Persistence
System

Clients

Servers

Figure 5.6.
Three-tier
client/server.

Furthermore, because application servers process the responses of the other servers and only send back the information actually needed by the client machines, network traffic is reduced, thereby reducing the time to fulfill the request.

Application servers often improve the efficiency of client/server applications.

There are several advantages to the three-tier approach. Because the application server encapsulates access to the other servers on the network, client machines only have to connect to the one application server, simplifying their knowledge of the network. Furthermore, only the programmers responsible for developing the application server need to intimately understand the business rules, allowing application programmers developing client applications to have a more shallow understanding of the business. This also implies that application designers are free to put as much or as little business knowledge in client applications. The main disadvantage of this approach is that the application server now becomes your bottleneck.

Client/server architectures have been the mainstay of structured/procedural development for many years, although as we will see in the next section, OO and C/S are a very good fit, potentially much better than procedural and C/S ever were.

> **DEFINITIONS**
>
> *Three-tier client/server*—In this client/server architecture, client machines send requests to an application server, which then sends requests to other servers on the network to fulfill the original request.
>
> *Application server*—A component of a three-tier C/S architecture that encapsulates access to other servers on the network, supplying the business logic for combining the responses from those servers.

5.3   Distributed Classes

In a single-machine environment you have little choice as to where to place the classes that form your application—there's only one machine to put them on. Up until now we really haven't considered how to organize the design of our classes in a networked environment. Networked environments bring up several interesting questions for the designers of OO applications: How do you split up business logic and distribute it among the computers on your network? Which machine(s) should a class be implemented on? How can I take advantage of the numerous computers on the network to make my applications the most efficient?

Distributed classes is an architecture for organizing the logic of your application in which you put classes on specific computers on your network based on their specific behaviors. Because you have access to

> **TIP**
>
> *How to Achieve the Benefits of Distribution*
>
> The benefits of distribution—taking advantage of the availability of multiple processors, can be achieved only when the application is designed to do so.

> **DEFINITION**
>
> *Distributed classes*—An architecture in which the logic of your applications is organized by putting classes on computers on your network based on their specific behaviors.

multiple computers, doesn't it make sense to organize your classes on those computers in such a way as to take advantage of this available computing power?

5.3.1 *"Traditional" Client/Server Using Object Technology*

The "traditional" approaches to client/server applications can be implemented using object technology as well as with structured/procedural technology. Although your applications will still suffer from all of the difficulties (described in section 5.2 above) inherent in client/server applications, at least these problems will be reduced via the productivity enhancements provided by OO technology. Applying OO techniques to developing traditional client/server applications is probably the vast bulk of OO development efforts today, although OOCS and applets are coming on strong. We discuss these two techniques in the next section.

5.3.2 *Taking a Peer-to-Peer Approach — Object-Oriented Client/Server*

In the 1970s, only 40% of an IS department's budget was spent on maintenance. Now upwards of 90% is, motivating us to find ways to inexpensively develop software that is also inexpensive and easy to maintain. This is what object-orientation (OO) is all about. At the same time, we need to create applications that can access existing information stored in various databases on different hardware platforms. These applications must appear to be heterogeneous. This is what client/server is all about. Object-oriented client/server techniques attempt to meet the needs of developers for the 1990s and beyond.

OOCS assumes that you have access to a *peer-to-peer architecture*. Peer-to-peer architectures are based on the concept that multiple servers work together to support the needs of client machines, allowing any machine to send a message to any other machine. Although server design becomes more complex, peer-to-peer architectures increase the opportunity of reducing or eliminating bottlenecks.

The basic question that we need to answer is: "How do we organize the classes of our application so that they take best advantage of the resources available on the network." Although most C/S development experts will tell you to put the data on the server(s) and the interface on the clients, there is a little more to it than that. Although this advice appears sound, how do you design an application to take advantage of a peer-to-peer architecture? How do you minimize network traffic? What queries should the server(s) be able to respond to? OOCS techniques help you to answer these questions.

The fundamental concept in OOCS design is that you need to determine which business classes will appear on each computer. Of the classes that should appear on a server, you need to determine which server (in a peer-to-peer environment you have a choice, in a single-server environment you don't) they will appear on. To do this we will take an approach modified from the book *Designing Object-Oriented Software* (Wirfs-Brock, Wilkerson, & Wiener, 1990) to create OOCS applications. The modifications reflect insights gained both from experience developing these systems and from insights provided by our class-type architecture. Our basic approach will be to organize our class diagrams into a collection of subsystems, a subsystem being a potential server. Note that there may be subsystems (servers) within other subsystems (not all servers in a peer-to-peer network are directly accessible by client machines).

> **DEFINITION**
>
> *Peer-to-peer architecture*—An architecture based on the concept that any computer can potentially send messages to any other computer on the network.

The steps of OOCS design are as follows:

- identify subsystems

- simplify your overall design

- implement subsystems

5.3.2.1 Identify Subsystems

The first stage of developing an OOCS architecture for your application is to identify the various subsystems within it. There are four steps to this process:

1. Handle interface and persistence classes

2. Define class contracts

3. Simplify inheritance and aggregation hierarchies

4. Define subsystems

5.3.2.1.1 Handle Interface and Persistence Classes

The easiest part of identifying subsystems is to first deal with interface and persistence classes. Interface classes are generally implemented on client machines, unless the class is needed for technical support reasons, then it MAY be implemented on a server. Persistence classes are implemented wherever persistent business classes are implemented (otherwise how else would you make them persistent?).

Interface classes are implemented on the client, persistence classes are implemented wherever persistent business classes are.

5.3.2.1.2 Define Class Contracts

To decide where business classes should go, you first need to identify the *contracts* supplied by each class. A contract is any service/behavior of an object that other objects request of it. In other words, it is a method that directly responds to a message from other classes. The best way to think about it is that contracts define the external interface, or abstraction, of a class.

Let's look at an example. Consider the class diagram showing the account hierarchy in Figure 5.7, and the corresponding collaboration diagram of Figure 5.8. Because subclasses inherit the contracts of their superclasses, contracts for the class **Checking Account** include:

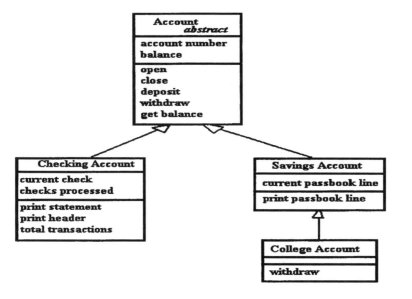

Figure 5.7.
The accounts hierarchy.

Figure 5.8.
Collaboration diagram showing the interaction between the teller workbench and accounts.

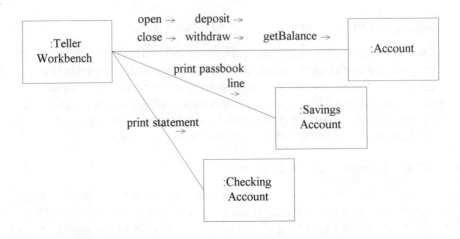

- Open

- Close

- Deposit

- Withdraw

- Get balance

- Print statement

DEFINITION

Contract—Any service/behavior of an object or server that other objects or servers request of it.

The methods illustrated in Figures 5.7 and 5.8 would not be considered contracts because they are methods that are invoked internally within an object: (a) print header and (b) total transactions.

5.3.2.1.3 Simplify Hierarchies

For the sake of identifying servers, inheritance and aggregation hierarchies can often be simplified. For inheritance hierarchies you can either choose to ignore any subclasses that do not add new contracts, or you can simply consider the entire hierarchy a single class that supports all of the contracts of that hierarchy. For aggregation hierarchies you can ignore any of the parts classes as long as they are not involved in relationships with other classes.

Let's consider some examples. For the account hierarchy in Figure 5.7 we could either ignore the class **College Account** because it

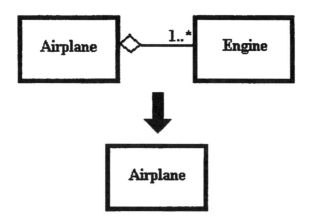

Figure 5.9.
Simplifying an aggregation hierarchy.

doesn't add any new contracts, or simply consider the entire account hierarchy as one class, **Account**. Collapsing the entire hierarchy is almost always the preferred approach as it greatly simplifies your task of identifying servers. Furthermore, experience shows that entire hierarchies inevitably end up on the same server anyway so we might as well consider them one class right from the beginning.

Now consider the aggregation hierarchies of Figures 5.9 and 5.10. We can collapse the airplane hierarchy of Figure 5.9 to appear as the single class airplane because engines don't have any sort of relationships with other classes. In Figure 5.10 we can't collapse the team aggregation because the class **Employee** has an object relationship with the class **Position**. Instances of **Employee** and **Position** collaborate with one another (if this wasn't the case then we wouldn't need to maintain the relationship between the two classes) and this is information that we need to consider when defining subsystems.

By collapsing aggregation and inheritance hierarchies you simplify your model, making it easier to analyze when you define subsystems.

Collapsing inheritance hierarchies is almost always preferable to simply ignoring subclasses that don't add new contracts.

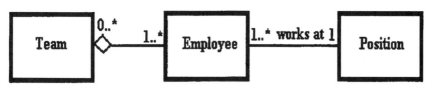

Figure 5.10.
An aggregation hierarchy you can't simplify.

5.3.2.1.4 Defining Subsystems

A *subsystem* is a set of classes that collaborate among themselves to support a cohesive set of contracts and as a result can be considered blackboxes. The basic idea is that classes, and even other subsystems, are able to send messages to subsystems to either request information or to request that an action be performed. On the outside subsystems appear simple, but on the inside they are often quite complex because they encapsulate the behavior of many classes. Hmmm... is it just me or do subsystems sound a lot like servers?

A class should be part of a subsystem only if it exists to fulfill the goals of that subsystem. To determine whether or not a class belongs in a subsystem you need to analyze the collaborations that it is involved with. We define a *server class* as one that receives messages but does not send them, a *client class* is one that sends messages but does not receive them, and a *client/server class* is one that both sends and receives messages.

The main goal when defining subsystems is that you want to split your design into several subsystems in such a way as to reduce the amount of information flowing between them. Any information passed between subsystems, either in the form of messages or the objects that are returned as the result of a message send, represents potential traffic on your network. You want to minimize network traffic so as to reduce the response time of your application. To minimize network traffic you want to design your subsystems in such a way so that most of the information flow occurs within the subsystems and not between them.

The main goal is to minimize network traffic so as to speed up your application.

The following are rules of thumb for defining subsystems:

1. **Server classes belong in a subsystem and will often form their own subsystems.** A server class will potentially form its own subsystem because it is the "last stop" for message flow within an application. Unfortunately server classes are very rare.

2. **Client classes do not belong in a subsystem.** Client classes only generate messages and don't receive them, whereas the purpose of a subsystem is to respond to messages. Therefore client classes have nothing to add to the functionality offered by a subsystem.

3. **When two classes collaborate frequently, it is an indication that they should be on the same subsystem.** If two classes interact a lot, especially when that interaction involves large objects, then by including them in the same subsystem you reduce the potential network traffic between them.

4. **You can have subsystems that are only accessed by one other subsystem.** Sometimes you'll find that one subsystem receives messages only from a particular subsystem. This is typically an indication that either the two subsystems should be merged or at least that the two machines on which the subsystems reside can be connected via a private link, avoiding the need to put the one machine on the network.

5. **C/S classes belong in a subsystem, but there may be a choice as to which subsystem they belong to.** This is where you need to look at the information flow going into and out of the class to figure out where it belongs. We'll consider an example below.

DEFINITIONS

Subsystem—A set of classes that collaborate among themselves to support a set of cohesive set of contracts.

Server class—A class that receives messages but does not send them.

Client class—A class that sends messages but does not receive them.

Client/server class—A class that both sends and receives messages.

5.3.2.1.5 An Example—The Bank Case Study

Let's look at the bank case study from *The Object Primer*. Figure 5.11 is a high-level overview of the bank's class diagram, showing the main classes of the application. The **Account Accessor** class hierarchy, as well as **Account Statement** and **Area Report** are all interface classes and everything else are business classes.

Figure 5.11.
The bank case
study.

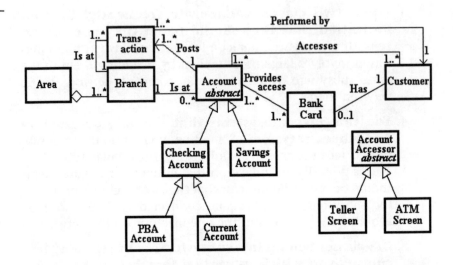

The first thing that we'll do draw a simplified collaboration diagram for the bank that shows the general message flow between classes and has the class hierarchies simplified. In Figure 5.12 we see that
the **Account Accessor** and **Account** inheritance hierarchies can be
compressed, whereas the **Area-Branch** aggregation hierarchy cannot
because **Branch** is associated with other classes. By compressing the
hierarchies our model becomes easier to analyze as there are fewer
classes to deal with.

*Compressing
class hierarchies
makes our model
easier to analyze.*

The next step is to determine which classes are client classes, which
are server classes, and which are client/server classes. In Figure 5.13 we
have labeled client classes with a "c," server classes with an "s," and left
client/server classes alone. Note that all of our interface classes are

Figure 5.12.
The bank case
study after
simplifying
hierarchies.

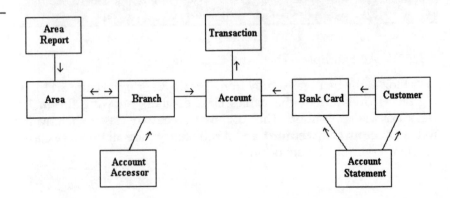

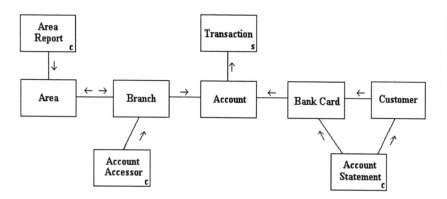

Figure 5.13.
Identifying pure client classes and pure server classes.

client classes, which is what you would expect because they typically don't receive messages from other classes (please refer to the class-type architecture in chapter 3 to verify this). Also note that we have a server class: **Transaction**.

Once we have identified each type of class we are now in a position to start defining subsystems. In Figure 5.14 we have identified four potential subsystems. I chose to make **Transaction** its own subsystem because of the large volume of transactions that get posted every day, perhaps millions, this volume pretty well requires a dedicated machine just for this (actually, we might choose to implement this server as several machines). The combination of **Area** and **Branch** could form their own subsystem because the two classes send messages to one another and because when they are put together they only receive messages from the one class **Area Report**. The combination of **Transaction** and **Account** could be a subsystem because together they would form a server, and because timely access to account information is mission-critical to a bank. **Customer** and **Bank Card** also form a potential subsystem.

Figure 5.14 isn't the only way that our application could be divided into subsystems. It might actually be better to combine subsystems 3 and 4 into one, putting **Account**, **Transaction**, **Customer**, and **Bank Card** onto one server. As with any aspect of design there are always alternatives.

5.3.2.2 Simplify Your Overall Design

Once you've identified potential servers you still need to simplify your design further before you can actually begin implementing

Figure 5.14.
Potential
subsystems.

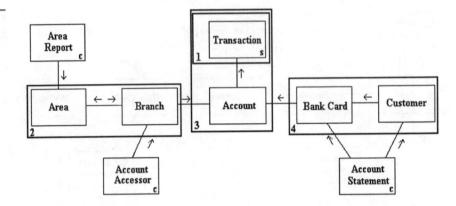

them. To do so you need to (a) define subsystem contracts and (b) simplify subsystem interfaces by collapsing subsystem contracts.

5.3.2.2.1 Define Subsystem Contracts

Subsystem contracts are the collection of class contracts that are accessed by classes outside of the subsystem (class contracts that are only used by classes within the subsystem are not included). For example, in Figure 5.13 the subsystem contracts for subsystem 2 (**Area-Branch**) are the ones of **Area** that are accessed only by **Area Report**. The contracts of **Branch** are the result of message sends from Area, and some of the contracts of **Area** may be the result only of messages from **Branch**, so none of these contracts would be included as subsystem contracts.

Rules of Thumb:

DEFINITION

Subsystem contracts—The collection of the class contracts of all of the classes that respond to messages sent from classes external to the subsystem.

- If all of the contracts of a server class are included in the contracts provided by the subsystem, you should consider making the server class its own subsystem that is external to the current subsystem.

- If none of the contracts of a server class are included in the subsystem contract (i.e., these contracts are only accessed by classes internal to the subsystem), then the server class should be defined as a subsystem internal to the present subsystem.

- The contracts of a subsystem should be cohesive; i.e., they should make sense being together. If they don't then you probably have multiple subsystems.

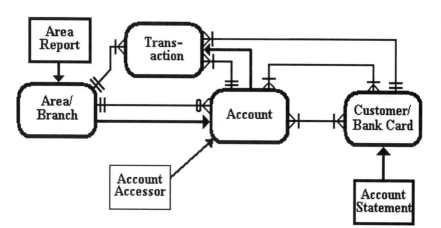

Figure 5.15.
The final OOCS design for our bank case study.

5.3.2.2.2 Simplify Subsystem Interfaces by Collapsing Subsystem Contracts

Depending on your initial design, it may be possible to collapse several contracts into one to reduce the number of different types of messages sent to a subsystem. By reducing the number of contracts for a subsystem we simplify its interface, making it easier to understand and hopefully use. For example, consider the contracts for the **Account-Transaction** subsystem of Figure 5.13 (subsystem #3). To reduce the number of contracts we could consider collapsing **Withdraw** and **Deposit** into a single **Change Balance** contract that takes as a parameter either a positive or negative amount.

5.3.2.3 Implement Subsystems

We've identified potential subsystems within our design and then we simplified them. So what? We've drawn some bigger bubbles around some smaller bubbles, that's it. To implement subsystems we need to define *router classes* that accept incoming messages sent to the server and then pass them on to the appropriate classes. A router class encapsulates the functionality provided by the server, providing an interface through which its clients can interact with it.

Once router classes have been implemented for each subsystem, each subsystem effectively becomes a potential server. In a single-server environment, all of the subsystems would be put on the same server. In a peer-to-peer environment, each subsystem could be placed on its own server. In Figure 5.15 we see the final design for our system, using the

> **DEFINITION**
>
> ***Router class***—A class that accepts incoming messages sent to a server and passes them on to the appropriate classes, providing an interface through which clients interact with the server.

Ambler class diagramming notation, with the servers shown as rounded rectangles.

5.3.3 Applets

A third way to implement distributed classes is via the use of applets. An applet is a small application, perhaps as little as one class, that is transmitted to a client machine from a server and then run on the client machine. In Figure 5.16 we see that applets typically implement interface logic that provides access to business functionality on the server. Applets may also include a limited form of business logic, often for basic data/object verification.

Figure 5.16.
Distributing classes via applets.

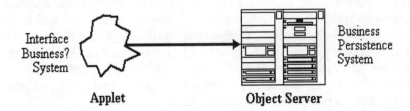

Interface
Business?
System

Applet

Business
Persistence
System

Object Server

The fundamental advantage of applets are that they are current—any applet that a user needs is downloaded from the server when it is needed. This allows developers to create and maintain applets iteratively, releasing new versions whenever they want to with the knowledge that the next time the user needs it that the user will automatically get it. The main disadvantage is that applets are geared toward simple applications made out of a few screens. Applications that require many screens are often too large to constantly download to users. Another disadvantage is that the bulk of the business logic is on the server, making it a bottleneck.

As we'll see in chapter 7 one of the main strengths of Java is its support for applet development. We will also see that it is likely that Java will evolve from being based on distributed classes into something resembling distributed objects. At least that's what I hope will happen.

5.4 Distributed Objects

Although distributed classes are a step in the right direction, they still have a way to go. One problem with distributed classes is that a specific class is only on the machine(s) that you have specifically put it on. For example, when you need a customer object you send a message to one of the machines that stores customers to have it transmitted to you across the network. You work with that customer and then transmit any changes back to the original machine. Is this the way it has to be? No! Why can't that customer object now reside on your machine until someone else needs it? If this customer is yours, perhaps because you are the sales representative assigned to that customer, then why should you have to transmit it back and forth across the network all the time? That doesn't make any sense.

Distributed objects consists of an architecture for organizing the logic of your applications in such a way as to allow objects to dynamically reside on the machines that are the most appropriate for the current situation. The fundamental idea is that distributed objects aren't limited to the machines where they were originally created, instead they are able to move freely about and go wherever they are needed. Distributed-object environments by their very nature have a peer-to-peer architecture, basically a scheme in which objects collaborate with each other across a network.

Distributed objects consists of an architecture in which objects dynamically reside on various machines on your network.

The enabling technology for distributed objects is the *object request broker* (ORB), a middleware technology that lets objects invoke methods on other objects that exist elsewhere on the network. ORBs basically manage the communication between disparate objects on the network. The messages sent between objects may be requests for information, requests to do something, or requests along the line of "come here I need you." In many ways an ORB is the OO equivalent of transaction processing (TP) monitors from the structured world.

ORBs are the enabling technology of distributed objects.

In Figure 5.17 we see an example of a distributed object environment where different kinds of applications—running on mainframes, personal computers, and even computers connected to your network remotely—send messages to various kinds of objects on your network. These objects may reside anywhere, even the machines sending the

Figure 5.17.
Distributed
objects.

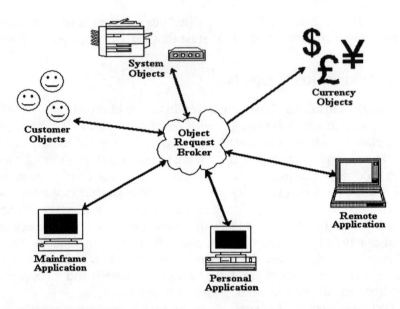

original messages. Not only that, but the objects on the network might also send each other messages—perhaps customer objects send the **name** message to currency objects so that the customer's currency of choice can be included on a statistics report that gets printed monthly. Although Figure 5.17 doesn't show it well, customer and currency objects can reside anywhere on the network and don't have to exist all on the same machine. Customer objects could exist on each and every machine connected to the ORB.

> *ORBs effectively encapsulate the implementation details of objects by providing a common and consistent manner for communication between objects.*

By providing a mechanism where objects can communicate with one another in a common and consistent manner, ORBs facilitate the integration of systems. The main point of ORBs is that they encapsulate the implementation details of objects—developers no longer need to be concerned about the location of an object, about the language it was written in, or about the hardware that it resides on to be able to write applications that interact with them. A systems integrator's dream.

DEFINITIONS

Distributed objects—An architecture in which objects dynamically reside on the machine that is most appropriate at the time. Objects move freely about the network and are not limited to where they may go.

Object request broker—A middleware technology that allows objects to send messages across the network to other objects.

In a distributed-object environment applications are basically implementing smart views of business objects, the clusters of interface classes that we will discuss in chapter 9. The interface classes should send messages to the ORB, which then passes them onto the appropriate objects.

5.4.1 Common Object Request Broker Architecture

CORBA, the *Common Object Request Broker Architecture*, is an approach to distributed objects recommended by the *Object Management Group* (OMG), a consortium of organizations that are working together to develop a set of standards for distributed-object computing. CORBA basically defines the services to be performed by an ORB, providing an *interface definition language* (IDL) that specifies a standard approach to defining the interface for objects. The CORBA IDL provides a mechanism for wrapping objects, discussed in chapter 11, which effectively hides the implementation details of an object.

CORBA is an OMG specification that defines the services to be performed by an ORB.

CORBA OBJECT SERVICES OVERVIEW

CORBA currently defines 16 services (Orfali, Harkey, & Edwards, 1995) that an ORB should perform. These services are as follows:

Change management service—This service provides the ability to track the various versions of your objects as they evolve over time. For example, an employee object may move from position to position within your organization, getting raises and promotions as they do so. While all of this is happening the employee is changing state: one day he or she is a programmer, and the next day he or she is a project leader. The change-management service tracks these changes in such a way that it is possible to restore the employee object back to previous states if required, perhaps for reporting purposes.

Collections service—This service provides the ability to work with multiple objects as if they were a single object, allowing queries (see below) to return collections of objects as well as single objects. For example, if a student object has taken several seminars over her time at a university, we are able to deal with those seminars as a single object instead of being required to work with each one separately. This would allow us to easily write the code needed to output a transcript (report card) because we'd be able to quickly loop through the collection of seminars telling them to output their information appropriately.

continued

CORBA OBJECT SERVICES OVERVIEW

continued

Concurrency control service—This service provides a lock manager to support object concurrency, allowing users to work with the same object simultaneously without writing over each other's work. For example, two users might want to work with the "Tom Paris" customer object at the same time—perhaps one is printing his name on a report, whereas the other is updating his address information. We will discuss concurrency issues in chapter 10.

Event service—This service allows object to dynamically register their interest, or non-interest, in specific events. For example, when a report object is printing itself out it will indicate to the ORB that it is interested in any printer errors that may occur so that it can redirect itself to another output device if there is a problem. Once printing is complete, the report object will tell the ORB that it is no longer interested in the status of the printer. The advantage of this is that the printer merely needs to inform the ORB that something's wrong so that the ORB can inform any interested object.

Externalization service—This service provides a standard approach to getting data into and out of an object via streaming. Objects often have to be communicated across a non-network link—perhaps the object needs to be sent via modem to a remote computer. Because we can only communicate data, we need a mechanism for converting objects to data and data to objects so that they can be transmitted between disparate computers/networks. This conversion process is called *object streaming*.

Licensing service—This service provides the ability to meter the use of objects to ensure fair compensation for their use, making it possible to "rent" software to people for specific periods of time or for specific amounts of usage. Perhaps you need to use a sophisticated drawing program for a presentation that you want to make but can't justify the expense of buying it outright. Because you need it only for this presentation, you decide to rent it at a fraction of the price of the entire package. The licensing service informs the maker of the software how much you used it so that you can be billed properly.

Life cycle service—This service defines the basic OOCRUD operations discussed in chapter 10 for creating, copying, moving, and deleting objects.

continued

CORBA OBJECT SERVICES OVERVIEW

continued

Persistence service—This service provides a single interface for storing objects persistently on a variety of storage mechanisms, including object databases, relational databases, and flat files.

Properties service—This service provides the operations that allow you to associate properties with any object that are above and beyond their current set of attributes. Consider our previous example where we rented a drawing application. Let's assume that instead of renting from the original developer of the software, we instead rented it from a software rental company that buys and then rents out software to its customers, just like video stores rent movies to their customers. This software rental store has two fee schedules: one based on a single user, and one based on an unlimited number of users accessing it. For this scheme to work, the software rental company uses the properties service to associate the rental plan that the user is paying for to the rented software (the developer of the drawing program never thought that his software would be rented in such a manner, so never built this ability into their product).

Query service—This service provides basic query functions for objects and is based on the ANSI SQL3 specifications and the OQL standards from the Object Database Management Group.

Naming service—This service allows objects to locate one another by name, regardless of where they are on the network. The naming service basically acts like the telephone white pages, associating the name of an object with their address on the network. This is what allows the ORB to send messages to the right object on the network. For example, a user working with a seminar registration screen might want to sign up Montgomery Scott to an advanced seminar, "DYL 200—Dylithium Accelerator Mechanics." The screen object would send the ORB the message, "Seminar 'DYL 201' addStudent 'Montgomery Scott'." The ORB would use the naming service to look up both the seminar object and the student object, sending them the appropriate messages. The point to be made is that the sign-up screen doesn't need to know where on the network the business objects are that it interacts with; the ORB encapsulates that knowledge.

continued

CORBA OBJECT SERVICES OVERVIEW

continued

Relationship service—This service provides a way to create dynamic associations between objects that know nothing of each other, as well as a mechanism for traversing those associations. You can use this service to maintain referential integrity between objects and to enforce aggregation relationships.

Security service—This service provides a way to secure servers from clients by managing access rights and by providing authentication of objects, as well as defining schemes for encryption and electronic signatures. Objects should only be willing to accept messages from objects that are allowed to send it messages in the first place; therefore a security mechanism needs to be available to define what each object in the system is allowed to do.

Time service—This service provides the ability to synchronize the clocks on all machines so that it looks like the entire network is operating on the same time. This is important because it is possible to work with the same object simultaneously on various machines, so we need to be able to identify the order in which any changes must be applied to the object. Without a common time clock this is impossible.

Trader service—This service provides an indication of what objects do, allowing other objects to discover what messages may be sent to them, as well as the parameters that they need to send. This is basically a matchmaking service similar in concept to the yellow pages—objects advertise what they can do, and other objects use the trader service to find the right object that provides the services that meet their needs.

Transaction service—This service provides two-phase commit coordination among recoverable objects using either flat or nested transactions, making it possible to write several objects simultaneously into their respective persistence mechanisms. The transaction service helps to maintain the integrity of objects so that they are consistent with each other. For example, when an order is made by a customer, the items on that order need to be shipped out. When we remove an item from inventory to put it on the order, we must ensure that both the **StockOnHand** attribute of the inventory item object and the appropriate **Order Item** object gets created at the same time—if the inventory item

continued

CORBA OBJECT SERVICES OVERVIEW

continued

object gets updated but the order item isn't created properly, then the inventory item won't accurately reflect the actual level of the stock (the item will still remain in stock because it won't get shipped out). We have a similar problem when the inventory item object doesn't get updated but the order item object does get created. The objects in your system must remain consistent with each other; this is facilitated by the transaction service.

CORBA defines the standards needed by companies developing ORBs so that objects can interact with one another in a consistent manner. CORBA has the advantage that it is supported by virtually all vendors in the computer industry. The main disadvantage is that each vendor extends CORBA in their own unique way with the result that not all implementations of CORBA are able to work together.

CORBA is supported by virtually all vendors in the computer industry, although each vendor has extended CORBA in their own manner.

DEFINITIONS

Object Management Group—A consortium of organizations that work together to create standards for the distributed object computing.

Common Object Request Broker Architecture—An OMG specification defining a distributed-object architecture. CORBA specifies how to develop OO applications that are able to connect and communicate with other CORBA-compliant (and potentially non OO) applications.

Interface definition language—A standard language for defining the interface of an object.

Object streaming—A process where an object is converted to data so that it can be stored or transmitted, eventually being converted back into an object afterward.

5.5 What We've Learned

In this chapter we discussed how the architecture for application development is becoming more distributed, evolving from centralized mainframes to client/server computing to distributed classes to distributed objects. We covered in depth how to design applications to take advantage of an object-oriented client/server (OOCS) architecture.

References

Fingar, P., Read, D., Stikeleather, J. (1996). *Next Generation Computing—Distributed Objects for Business*. New York: SIGS Books.

Orfali, R., Harkey, D., & Edwards, J. (1995). *The Essential Distributed Objects Survival Guide*. New York: Wiley.

Wirfs-Brock, R., Wilkerson, B., & Wiener, L. (1990). *Designing Object-Oriented Software*. Englewood Cliffs, NJ: Prentice Hall.

Part III

Object-Oriented Construction

Chapters

6 • *Measuring and Improving the Quality of Your Work—OO Metrics*
7 • *Choosing an OO Language—Comparing the Leading Languages*
8 • *Building Your Application—Effective OO Construction Techniques*
9 • *Making Your Applications Usable—OO User Interface Design*
10 • *Making Your Objects Persistent—OO and Databases*
11 • *Integrating Legacy Code—Wrapping*

> *Things that are measured get improved,*
>
> *so the trick must be to measure the right things.*

Chapter 6

Measuring and Improving the Quality of Your Work — Object-Oriented Metrics

What We'll Learn in This Chapter

What metrics are and why they're important for object-oriented (OO) development.

Which metrics work for OO and which ones don't.

What metrics to use for estimating projects, improving your development efforts, selecting the right tools, and improving your development process.

How to use metrics effectively on your OO development projects.

Project managers are constantly inundated with questions about the status of their project. How good is our design? Can we start coding now? How long will the project take? How big is the project? How much will it cost? How many people do we need? Questions that are difficult, if not impossible, to answer with any certainty without taking measurements of specific factors that address these issues. But what should you measure? A good question.

One of the reasons, very often the main reason, that firms move into object orientation is that they want to improve the quality of the applications that they develop. They want systems that are easier to maintain. They want systems that are easier to extend. They want to develop systems better, faster, and cheaper. The question is "How do you know that you've succeeded?" In this chapter we'll see that metrics are used to answer this question.

There are a lot of object-oriented (OO) development environments and techniques available to you. Although this sounds good, the problem is that it isn't always clear which ones are the best ones for you. How well is CRC modeling working in your organization? Is it helping to increase the quality of the systems that you build? What about use-case scenarios? Which language is the most effective one for your needs? Smalltalk? C++? Are you using the concept of inheritance correctly? How about polymorphism?

You have a lot of options available to you, and you want to make the best choices. Chances are that you're going to have to experiment a fair bit, trying several techniques and tools and then comparing and keeping the ones that are best for you. You might even decide to get daring and start tweaking the development techniques you've chosen. You need to find a way to compare and contrast the tools and techniques that you're using if you want to find and potentially improve the ones that are best for you. The bottom line is that you're going to have to start collecting metrics.

6.1   What Are Metrics and What Can They Do for/to Me?

Metrics provide insight into exactly what we do and how we do it.

A metric is a measurement, pure and simple. By taking measurements in a consistent manner we become aware of what it is that we do and how well we do it. This means that we can identify both what does and doesn't work well for us, which potentially allows us to intelligently estimate exactly how much time, effort, and resources will be required to complete a project.

> **DEFINITION**
>
> *Metric*—A measurement. In our case, a measurement of some factor involved in OO development.

Metrics are used for (although not always successfully):

1. **Estimating projects.** One of the most important uses of metrics is in the estimation of projects. Based on our previous experiences, we use metrics to estimate the time, effort, and cost of a project. This allows your organization to effectively manage its resources and set its development priorities.

2. **Improving your development efforts.** Metrics can be used to measure the quality of your development efforts. It can be used to pinpoint the weak areas of your design, providing you with the opportunity to fix any problems before they get out of hand.

3. **Selecting tools.** There are several metrics that can be used to compare the effectiveness of tools. Every tool has its strengths and its weaknesses, and you want to find the right collection of tools that are the best fit for your organization.

4. **Improving your development approach.** Many firms are using metrics to analyze and improve their overall approach to application development. It is one thing for me to say that CRC modeling works well (and it does), and it is another for you to have the cold hard numbers showing it to be true for your organization. Metrics provide those cold hard numbers.

Throughout this chapter I'm going to refer to the work of Mark Lorenz and Jeff Kidd (1994) a lot. They wrote an excellent book called *Object-Oriented Software Metrics* that describes OO metrics in detail and I highly suggest that you pick it up. What I've done in this chapter is to take several of the choice metrics that they discuss, as well as a few of my own, and put my own spin on them. I think that you'll find this chapter to be a really useful introduction to this exciting subject.

6.2   Estimating Projects

No matter what the project is, you always need to estimate how long it will take, how much money it will cost, and how many people need to be involved in it. This section provides a high-level overview of several metrics that you can use to base your estimates on.

The metrics that you can use as inputs to estimating OO projects are as follows:

- Number of key classes
- Person days per class
- Classes per developer
- Number of reused classes
- Function and feature points

TIP

You Have to Revisit Your Estimates Throughout the Project

Because things change—new people come onto the project, people leave the project, new tools become available, your schedule slips—you should occasionally go back and update your estimates. This helps to show your progress, or lack of progress, on the project, as well as provide an indication of the effort needed to complete the project. This is important so that upper management can decide to add more resources to the project, to leave the project alone, or to stop it before too much time and money have been lost.

6.2.1 Number of Key Classes

The number of key classes is a count of the classes that are deemed to be of central importance to the business (Lorenz & Kidd, 1994). If you've created a CRC model, this metric is very easy to calculate—it's the number of business and actor classes (as opposed to screen or report classes) that you've identified. If you haven't created a CRC model, then it's the count of all your business-layer classes (not interface, persistence, or system classes) in your model. This metric is useful because it can be combined with the number of person days per class metric (see below) to estimate the effort required for your project.

6.2.2 Person Days per Class

The person days per class metric (Lorenz & Kidd, 1994) is a simple multiplier used to estimate the effort required to develop a system. The basic idea is that based on past experience you know how many days it will take someone to develop an "average class" and then use this metric to estimate how long it will take to develop the entire project. The problem with this approach is that there are so many factors to take into account, see the soapbox below, that this is a lot harder than you'd think. For example, some of the factors that you need to take into account the type of class, the size of the class, the language that you are programming in, the skill of the programmer writing it, and the complexity of the class. There are published figures for some of these factors, but frankly they were all collected from different organizations using different methods from different projects written in different development environments at different times. To be honest with you I'm simply not confident that any of these figures are accurate enough to use on a project.

6.2.3 Classes per Developer

The classes per developer metric (Lorenz & Kidd, 1994) is an estimate of how much code a single developer can reasonably expect to "own." This metric can be used to estimate the number of people needed on a project, as you simply divide the number of key classes by the classes per developer.

SCOTT'S SOAPBOX

Estimating the Size of a Project is Really Tough

Project estimating is really tough to do, no matter how good your metrics are. There are several fundamental problems associated with estimating that can often be very difficult to factor in. First of all, different people have different skills. If you don't know what people are going to be on the project, or what skills they are bringing to the table, it is very difficult to estimate how much effort will be involved to complete the work. Second, tools improve rapidly. The productivity estimates for today's tool might not be applicable to tomorrow's updated release of that tool. Third, techniques improve. OO development techniques are still in their infancy and as a result we're learning as we're going. Fourth, as a result of the first three difficulties, we are often using apples as a basis to estimate how many oranges we're going to need—your new project will have a different team of people, use different tools, and use different techniques than the projects you are using as a basis for your estimate. Realistically, how good can your estimate be?

Lorenz and Kidd report that on short-term projects 20 classes is reasonable, whereas on a long-term project 40 classes is reasonable. The difference lies in the fact that on long-term projects, say over 12 months, developers have a greater opportunity to learn the classes that they work with, hence they can be responsible for more classes. My own experience, based on several C++ and Smalltalk projects, leads me to believe that more realistic figures would be 10 and 20 for C++ projects and 25 and 50 for Smalltalk projects. The reason is simple: Although the business functionality is the same, there is significantly less code to understand and maintain with Smalltalk than with C++. This for the most part is because Smalltalk is a higher level language than C++.

A significant point that Lorenz & Kidd point out is that as time goes on your mature classes need less effort to develop and maintain (they're mature), resulting in a steady increase in the number of classes each developer can look after.

6.2.4 Number of Reused Classes

This metric is a count of the classes in your repository that are ACTUALLY being reused on multiple projects. In other words, how many classes are being used in two or more applications? You might even want to collect two versions of this metric—the number of reused classes that were developed in house, and the number of reused classes you purchased in addition to your development environment. The first version of this metric gives you a measure of the quality of your own work (or if the number is low perhaps it's a measure of the politics in your organization) and the second version is a measure of how well you're taking advantage of the third-party object market.

It isn't reusable until it's actually been reused.

Don't be afraid if this number is low at first because it takes time to develop reusable classes. You can go into OO development with a lot of good intentions, believing that you'll be able to develop reusable classes right away. Although it would be really nice if you did, unfortunately it doesn't work like that. My experience has been that no matter how good a design job you do, the first cut of your classes at best will be about 80% of the way to being reusable. It isn't until your class has been reused, and typically reworked, by two other developers on two other projects that you can reasonably say that your class is truly reusable. Think of it like this: you can't possibly know all of the needs of all of the people that will reuse your work, so you really can't develop classes that are reusable right off the bat. That's just the way it is.

6.2.5 Function and Feature Points

Function and feature points are two similar approaches to estimating the size of an application. Function points were first introduced by A.J. Albrecht (1979) of IBM in the late 1970s so that it would be possible to compare projects developed in disparate environments. The basic idea is that you count five items: the inputs to the application, the outputs from it, inquiries by users, the data files that would be updated by the application, and the interfaces to other applications. Once you have these figures, you multiply by the following figures: 4, 5, 4, 10, and 7, respectively, add the results to get your function point estimate.

Function points are used to estimate the functionality provided by an application, regardless of the language it was developed in.

Function points worked reasonably well for simple management information system (MIS) applications, but unfortunately they often proved to be inadequate for estimating complex applications, the types of applications that object-oriented development is well suited for. In 1986 Capers Jones of Software Productivity Research (Jones, 1995) introduced the concept of feature points, a superset of function points, to correct this problem. Jones introduces a new measurement, algorithms, giving it a weighting of 3. Additionally, he reduces the data file weighting from 10 to 7. His studies have shown that feature points appear to work better for complex applications, whereas producing similar measurements as do function points for simpler applications.

Feature points are used to measure complex systems.

I suspect that feature points, or a modification of them, will prove to be very successful for comparing OO applications. Although a count of "significant" methods could be substituted for an algorithm count, I suspect that what would work best would be to substitute a count of the key classes for the algorithm count, and to substitute a new corresponding multiplier.

Although function and feature points are a useful approach to comparing applications, even for applications that are developed using different tools and techniques, they can be difficult and expensive to collect. Point counting is a skill that few people have and is a time-consuming process, even for people who are experienced at doing it. Function/feature points can also be used to measure the productivity of developers and of development tools, if only for the reason that they help to remove the differences between environments when you are estimating.

Function/feature points are difficult and expensive to collect.

TIPS

It Often Boils Down to Experience

The best estimates are made by the people who have done the work before, so if you can find someone experienced in what you're doing and ask him or her for their gut feeling, chances are pretty good that it'll be the best estimate you'll come up with.

Don't Forget the "Don't Forgets"

Don't forget to estimate for:

- Vacations and illnesses

- Both user and developer training

- Losing developers part-way through the project

- Testing

- Documentation

- How aggressive deadlines are

6.3 Improving Your Development Efforts

Metrics can be used to identify portions of your development efforts that need to be reworked.

The second most common use for metrics, although in my opinion probably the most important, is to help improve your development efforts. You can use metrics to identify problem areas in your application—perhaps your design can be improved, or perhaps your code needs some reworking—long before they show up as bugs detected by your users. By collecting metrics you are able to pinpoint portions of your development efforts that need to be looked at and potentially improved, increasing the quality of the systems that you develop.

In this section we'll talk about

- Analysis metrics

- Design metrics

- Code metrics

- Testing metrics

6.3.1 Analysis Metrics

The metrics that you can use to measure the quality of your analysis efforts are

- Percentage of key classes

- Number of use cases

- Function points

6.3.1.1 Percentage of Key Classes

Although the number of key classes (Lorenz & Kidd, 1994) metric is used to estimate the size of a project, it can also indicate whether or not you've completed your analysis. Of all the classes you've identified, either through CRC (class responsibility collaborator) or class diagramming, the percentage of key classes should typically be between 30 and 50%. If the percentage is low, say 10–15%, then that is a good sign that you still need to do some more analysis. Remember, you have to know what it is your users want before you can begin building it.

Key classes typically account for 30-50% of the classes in your system.

6.3.1.2 Number of Use Cases

The number of use cases that you've identified can also be used as an indicator of whether or not you've completed your analysis. My experience has been that small applications (a few months of development) usually have between five and ten use cases, medium-sized projects (less than a year of development) have between 20 and 30, and large projects typically have 40+. I don't have any hard data to back up this advice, so take it with a grain of salt.

This metric is basically the same as the number of scenario scripts metric proposed by Lorenz and Kidd (1994) although I use it differ-

---

MEANWHILE, BACK TO REALITY

You can really get yourself into trouble if you misjudge how many use cases are applicable to the project and then base your estimate on the use-cases. The moral of the story is to use more than one metric to estimate the size of the project—if the results are close, then you're probably OK; if they're wildly different, then you had better investigate further.

ently. Lorenz and Kidd suggested that this metric could be used to estimate the size of a project, although I simply don't see how you could estimate with any form of accuracy using this metric. Perhaps I'm wrong about this, but I don't think so.

6.3.1.3 Function Points

Screens with high function point counts should be revisited.

Although function points can be used for project estimating, they can also be used to identify screens or sections of your user interface that need to be rethought. Complex screens that provide a lot of function points can often be difficult to understand by your users. As a result, any screen with a high function point count should be given a second look to see if it needs to be simplified or broken up into several screens.

6.3.2 Design Metrics

In this section we will discuss a suite of metrics, some of which contract one another, which are commonly used to evaluate the quality of OO designs. Not only do these metrics measure important aspects of your design but they are also easy to automate, making them easy to collect.

Metrics that can be used as a basis to improve your design are as follows:

- Method count
- Number of instance attributes
- Inheritance tree depth
- Number of children
- Global usage
- Number of class attributes
- Number of ignored methods

6.3.2.1 Method Count

One metric that is very easy to collect yet often proves useful is the method count of a class (Chidamber & Kemerer, 1991). Classes with large numbers of methods are most likely to be application specific,

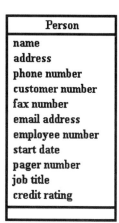 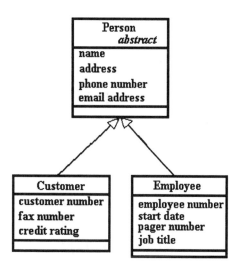

Figure 6.1.
Two approaches to modeling people.

whereas classes with fewer methods have a tendency to be more reusable. Although this isn't always true, I find it worthwhile to get a method count for all the classes in my application, and then take a look at the ones that appear to have an unusually high count as compared to the other ones. Considering these classes, I then ask myself whether or not they might be applicable to another project in the future. If so, then I rethink their design to make them more reusable, if possible.

Classes with unusually high numbers of methods are often application specific and therefore not reusable. Rethink their design.

6.3.2.2 Number of Instance Attributes

One indicator of whether or not you are using inheritance effectively is the number of instance attributes in a class (Lorenz & Kidd, 1994). Whenever you have a lot of instance attributes in a single class, say more than ten, there is a good chance that you have modeled more than one concept in that class. This is very common when you have what should be two classes that have a one-to-one relationship between them. In Figure 6.1 we see two versions of how to model people.

In Figure 6.1 the customer class on the left has a significant number of instance variables. Looking at the class we see that we are really modeling two different types of people, customers and employees. Rethinking our approach, we create a Person class hierarchy made up of three classes, Person, Customer, and Employee. If you remember, we presented an even better approach to this in the form of the Business Entity pattern in chapter 4.

Figure 6.2.
A sample class hierarchy with an inheritance depth of three.

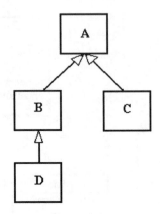

6.3.2.3 Inheritance Tree Depth

Deep inheritance hierarchies result in classes that are often difficult to understand.

Another metric that indicates potential difficulties with the way that you've used the concept of inheritance is the depth of your inheritance trees (Chidamber & Kemerer, 1991). The depth of an inheritance hierarchy is defined as the maximum number of classes from the root of their hierarchy to its lowest leaf class, including the root class. For example, in Figure 6.2 the depth of the inheritance hiearchy is three.

The basic problem is that deeper trees constitute greater design complexity. The lower down the tree a class is the more it inherits, and the more that it inherits the harder it is to understand. If it's harder to understand, then it's harder to maintain and enhance. The general feeling in the object community is that if the depth of an inheritance tree is greater than five then you need to revisit its design. You are often able to replace inheritance relationships with object relation-

---

DEFINITIONS

Root class—The top class in an inheritance hierarchy.

Leaf class—A class within an inheritance hierarchy that doesn't have other classes inheriting from it.

Inheritance tree depth—The maximum number of classes from the root of a class hierarchy to it's lowest node, including the root class.

Application-specific class—Any class that is used in a single application.

ships, as we saw in the Business Entity pattern and the Roles Played pattern in chapter 4. You might also want to consider combining classes. For example, in Figure 6.2 the only class that inherits from class B is class D. You might want to consider combining the two classes if you suspect that nothing else is going to need to inherit from B and if class D isn't application specific (application specific classes don't get reused by other applications).

6.3.2.4 Number of Children

A metric that is related to the inheritance tree depth, and which contradicts it, is the number of children of a class (Chidamber & Kemerer, 1991). Although we want to avoid the complexity that results from inheritance tree depth, it is generally better to have depth than breadth, because it promotes reusability through inheritance. One way that the number of children can be used to evaluate the quality of your use of inheritance is to look at where in the class hierarchy your classes are. You see, classes higher up usually have more subclasses than those lower down because they have less application-specific code (and hence are more reusable). Whenever you create classes that are specific to the application that you are working on you typically inherit from the existing class hierarchy at your disposal. This usually results in application-specific classes being lower down in the class hierarchy, classes that are often the only children of their superclass.

6.3.2.5 Global Usage

The global-usage metric (Lorenz & Kidd, 1994) is a count of how many global variables you are using in your application. You want to minimize the use of global variables because they increase the coupling within your application, making it harder to maintain and enhance. My rule of thumb is that if you've got any global variables at all then you're in trouble. Don't put them in your design and especially don't put them in your code. Furthermore, just because you're using a language that doesn't directly support global variables (although you could argue that a class itself is a global variable) it doesn't mean that you don't have any globals. You can use class variables, or singleton classes discussed in chapter 4, to simulate globals.

6.3.2.6 *Number of Class Attributes*

By counting the number of class attributes (Lorenz & Kidd, 1994) you get an indication of the quality of your design. Classes with more than three or four class attributes are often masking a coupling problem in your application. You see, class attributes can be used as global variables within an application, and the use of global variables increases coupling. The only valid use of a class variable is to share common information among the instances of that class. If you're using class variables in some sort of scheme to speed up the processing of your application then chances are good that you're abusing the concept. The CPU (central processing unit) cycles that you're saving had better be incredibly critical to your application to justify the increase in coupling.

6.3.2.7 *Number of Ignored Methods*

The final design metric is one of my own, and that's a count of ignored methods. Remember how we talked about pure inheritance in *The Object Primer* (Amber, 1995a), showing that it leads to greater reusability because it says that subclasses should inherit everything from their superclass? Well, this metric is all about finding the places where we haven't achieved this. Although there is nothing wrong with overriding a method to expand its functionality, there is a problem when you override to take away its functionality. In other words, you have effectively ignored it. Ignored methods within a class are an indication that it isn't inheriting all of the methods of its superclass, or in other words it violates the principle of pure inheritance. If at all possible you should aim for having no ignored methods in your classes. You won't always be able to achieve this, but you should try your best.

DEFINITIONS

Pure inheritance——A subclass inherits everything from its superclass.

Override——The redefinition of a method or attribute in a subclass.

Ignored method——An inherited method that is overridden with a method that has no functionality.

6.3.3 Construction Metrics

In addition to measuring the quality of your design, you also want to apply metrics to improve the quality of your code. Although one of the metrics presented in this section is specific to Smalltalk, the others are language neutral. As with the design metrics discussed previously, these metrics are also easy to automate. One thing that I would like you to keep in mind when you are reading this section is that the important thing is for coders to understand the thinking behind the metrics because that's what leads to good code. One problem with construction metrics is that coders with a hacker mentality usually don't like other people evaluating their work, so keep this in mind too.

Metrics that can be used as a basis to improve the quality of your code include the following:

- Method size

- Method response

- Comments per method

- Percentage of commented methods

- Strings of message sends

6.3.3.1 Method Size

If you want to write methods that are easy to maintain then they should be small, one should hope for less than 10 statements for Smalltalk code and 30 statements for C++ (Smalltalk is a higher level language than C++, resulting in few lines of code). I believe in something I call the 30-second rule—I should be able to look at any method and completely understand it in less than thirty seconds (Ambler, 1995b). This implies that methods must be both small and well commented (they should do one thing and one thing only). If methods are difficult to understand, then they are difficult to maintain and enhance, increasing your maintenance costs.

Large methods are difficult to maintain and enhance.

Furthermore, if a method is large it is a good indication that your code is actually function oriented as opposed to object oriented (Lorenz & Kidd, 1994). Objects get things done by collaborating with each other and not by doing everything themselves. This results in short methods, not long ones. Although you'll occasionally run into long methods, they're few and far between. If your methods are long it's an indication that there's a problem. In chapter 8 we will see several techniques for writing good methods.

6.3.3.2 Method Response

The more messages that get invoked by a method the harder it is to test.

We want to reduce the method response (Chidamber & Kemerer, 1991) of a method. Method response is a count of the total number of messages that are sent as a result of a method being invoked. The exact definition of method response is recursive, it is the count of all message sends within a method, plus the method response of each method invoked by those message sends. The reason why this is an important metric is that methods with high method-response values indicates that the method is difficult to test as you have to test all the code that gets invoked. Another potential problem is the potential for high coupling. Remember, the only way an object can send a message to another object is when it knows about that other object, implying that there is some coupling between the two objects. The higher the method response, the greater the chance of coupling.

We have a problem—the method-response metric contradicts the method-size metric. To get a low method response you need larger methods, and to get smaller methods you need to increase the method response. That's OK, as neither metric is accurate 100% of the time. Sometimes methods are large but there's nothing wrong with them, and sometimes they have a high method response and nothing's wrong with them.

6.3.3.3 Comments per Method

A very useful metric for estimating the quality of your code is the number of lines of comment per method (Lorenz & Kidd, 1994). My experience has been that good methods have more lines of comments than lines of code. Too few comments indicates that other programmers will have a difficult time trying to understand your code, and

---

DEFINITION

Method response— A count of the total number of messages that are sent as a result of a method being invoked.

too many comments indicates that you're wasting too much time documenting it. In section 8.3.2 we go into detail about how to document your code thoroughly and efficiently.

6.3.3.4 Percentage of Commented Methods

Related to comments per method is the percentage of methods with comments (Lorenz & Kidd, 1994). Although I instantly want to say that this figure should always be 100%, the reality is that it doesn't have to be. This is because you don't really need to document setters—methods that set the value of attributes. Once you ignore setters this metric should be 100%, however, and if it isn't then you've done a poor job.

6.3.3.5 Strings of Message Sends

A string of message sends is a Smalltalk coding convention in which a series of messages is sent to the same object, as we can see in Figure 6.3. Although this technique is often suggested as good style (Goldberg & Robson, 1989) I agree with Lorenz and Kidd (1994) that this is pure hogwash. The main problem is that by doing this you effectively ignore any error messages coming back, increasing the chance that your application crashes from run-time errors. For example, what would happen if **message2** didn't work properly? The code would crash, that's what would happen!

```
aMethod
        | anObject |
        anObject new; message1; message2; message3; message4.
        ^ anObject.
```

Figure 6.3.
A string of
message sends.

If there is a potential that a message send won't work, perhaps because of problems out of your control, you had better capture and deal with the error messages intelligently. Strings of message sends don't allow you to do this (at least without the addition of an exception handler added around the code) and as a result you should avoid their use if possible.

DEFINITION

String of message sends—A series of messages is sent to the same object.

SCOTT'S SOAPBOX

LOC Doesn't Mean Anything

Would you be impressed if someone told you that the code for his or her application, when printed out, made a stack 2 inches high? Would you accept this figure as a valid measurement of how much work they had done? Of course not—that wouldn't make any sense. Would you be impressed if someone told you that he or she wrote 30,000 lines of code (LOC) for an application? Would you accept it as a valid measurement of how much work was done? Although many people would, LOC is just as invalid a measurement of effort as is the height of the code printout stack. Here's why.

Given the number of lines of code, 30,000 in this case, the number of lines that can be printed on a page, say 60, and the thickness of a sheet of paper, say 1/250th of an inch, I can quickly calculate that a 30,000-line program, when printed out, results in a stack of paper 2 inches high. The measurements are the same. If you wouldn't accept the paper-stack-height metric as valid, why would you consider the LOC metric valid?

Furthermore, even if you do still accept LOC as a valid measurement, how are you going to use it? Is a 30,000-line C++ program better than a 20,000-line C++ program, or is it the other way around? Perhaps the second program is designed better, making it both easier to develop and maintain. Is a 30,000-line C++ program written in vendor-A C++ the same as a 30,000-line C++ program written in vendor-B C++? Is a 30,000-line C++ program better than a 5,000-line Smalltalk program? You just don't know.

At best, an estimate of the lines of code in a program might be able to tell you how much effort you'll need to spend coding. It doesn't tell you how much time you'll spend in analysis, design, or testing. I might spend months analyzing and designing a 30,000-line application that provides significant functionality. Or I might spend just a few days designing one that provides very little. The lines-of-code metric, whereas easy to collect, has virtually no meaning whatsoever except in that it might prove as an estimate as to how hard your system will be to maintain (although without an estimate of the quality of your code, LOC is still meaningless).

6.3.4 Testing Metrics

Most programmers don't like testing (which is one reason why you should have a quality assurance [QA] person overseeing the testing effort), however, the fundamental fact is that testing is a critical component of the development process and that it's worth our while to try to improve it whenever we can. The metrics presented in this section should help you to do just that.

Metrics that you can use to improve the quality of your testing efforts are: (a) problem reports per class, and (b) percentage of tested use-case scenarios.

6.3.4.1 Problem Reports per Class

Although counting the number of problems (bugs) in a class occurs after the fact, it is still a useful metric (Lorenz & Kidd, 1994) to collect. The 80/20 rule seems to apply with bugs—80% of your errors will be in 20% of your classes. By counting the number of problems per class, you can quickly determine which classes are the weak links of your application chain. Furthermore, if some of the classes you identified as buggy are key classes for your application, you know you're in serious trouble and need to deal with those ones right away.

Eighty percent of your bugs will be in 20% of your classes.

T I P

Have the Key Classes Developed by Your Best People

The success of your application often depends on the quality of your key classes—if your key classes are flaky, then your application is flaky. As a result, it makes sense to put your best people on these classes because they're the ones who are mostly likely to do the best job.

6.3.4.2 Percentage of Tested Use-Case Scenarios

The most important testing metric that you can take, one that is often calculated long before your official testing phase begins, is the percentage of tested use-case scenarios. You basically count the number of scenarios that you worked through with your users and divide it by the total number of scenarios that you identified. If you haven't tested 100%

Test all of your use cases before you begin coding.

of your scenarios, then you've got some more use-case scenario testing to perform. Remember, the least expensive time to test is during analysis which is also where you make the most mistakes (Ambler, 1995b).

6.4 Choosing the Right Tools

It's really hard to choose the right tools, especially when you're first getting into OO. Between not yet having the experience to know what's important in a tool, and having to wade through all the marketing hype, you need some help. Although we discussed many of the factors that you should look at when choosing tools, there are still a couple of metrics that are useful when trying to choose which language vendor is best for you.

Metrics that you can use as a basis for choosing the right language vendors are: (a) comments per method, and (b) percentage of commented methods.

> **TIP**
>
> *Establish Your Priorities First*
>
> To get the best tool for the job you first must understand what that job is so that you can establish the tool features that are critical to your specific project. In chapter 7 we'll discuss many of the factors that you want to consider when evaluating tools.

6.4.1 Comments per Method and Percentage of Commented Methods

Good development environments come with good source code. Bad development environments...

Just as the comments per method and the percentage of commented-methods metrics are useful for judging the quality of your own code, they are also useful for judging the code supplied in the development environments that you purchase. Look at the source code provided with the language you are using. How good are the comments? The poorer the quality of the comments the more difficult the language is to learn and to work with. Furthermore, coders will generally look to the provided source code for examples of how to do things. If the base source code included with the environment is poorly commented, chances are the code that gets developed using that environment will also suffer from the same types of problems.

6.5 Improving Your Development Approach

All of the metrics presented in section 6.3 that are used to improve your development efforts can also be used to improve your development approach. If the metrics you are collecting keep turning up the same sort of problem over and over again, it's a good indication that you need to step back and ask yourself what the source of the problem is and how you can avoid it in the future. The metrics can also be used to compare techniques—is the quality of your analysis better on projects for which you spent a lot of time CRC modeling versus projects for which you spent more time class diagramming? Or is there no difference at all? Use the metrics that you gather to identify the tools and techniques that work best for you, as well as the tools and techniques that don't work so well. Act on this information and improve your approach to system development.

Learn from both your successes and your mistakes.

6.6 Metrics Success Factors

There's more to metrics than just taking a few measurements and reporting them to upper management. If you want to put together a successful metrics program within your company, then I suggest you heed the following words of advice:

1. **Don't use metrics to judge people.** If you begin to use metrics to evaluate people, or to judge their work, your metrics program will fail. People aren't stupid. Once they realize that metrics are being used to judge them they'll begin to fudge the numbers, or even worse not collect them at all. I realize that it's incredibly tempting to use the metrics collected about a system to evaluate the skills and abilities of the people involved in building the system. I also realize that once you do you'll never be able to trust the measurements you receive again, dashing your hopes of an effective metrics program.

2. **Don't use single metrics by themselves.** There isn't a single metric that will give you an accurate picture of even a portion of your development efforts. You need to combine metrics, even metrics that contradict one another, if you want to gain a true understanding of what works well for you and what doesn't.

3. **Decide what you want to measure first.** Although you need to collect more than one metric, you don't need to collect them all. You should first decide on what you want to measure, then you should choose the metrics that are the most applicable.

4. **Automate collection of simple metrics.** As we mentioned earlier, there are a lot of metrics that can be collected automatically by your development tools. For some development environments you can purchase metrics tools from third-party vendors, and for other environments you'll have to build the tools themselves. If the collection of metrics becomes too onerous then your metrics program will fail.

5. **Simple metrics aren't enough.** Although automating the collection of simple metrics is a good start, chances are it isn't enough. Many of the metrics that we discussed in this chapter will need to be collected by hand.

6. **Make it easy to collect metrics.** If the collection process is perceived by developers as being too onerous then they either won't collect them or even worse will collect them the wrong way.

7. **Do some more reading.** What we've presented in this chapter is only a start. Furthermore, there is an active research community out there focused specifically on object-oriented metrics. Journals such as the *Communications of the ACM, IEEE Software*, and the *Journal of Object-Oriented Programming (JOOP)* occasionally publish papers on OO metrics. Keep your eye out for them.

8. **Apply the right metric to the right class-type layer.** Some metrics are more applicable than others to each individual class type (as presented in chapter 3). In Table 6.1 we

Table 6.1. CHOOSING THE RIGHT METRIC FOR EACH CLASS-TYPE LAYER

Metric	Interface	Business	Persistence	System
Classes/developer	Poor	Good	Average	Good
Comments/method	Good	Good	Good	Good
Feature points	Good	Poor	Poor	Poor
Function points	Average	Poor	Poor	Poor
Global usage	Good	Good	Good	Good
Inheritance tree depth	Poor	Good	Average	Good
Method count	Poor	Good	Average	Good
Method response	Poor	Good	Good	Good
Method size	Average	Good	Good	Good
Number of children	Poor	Good	Average	Good
Number of class attributes	Poor	Good	Poor	Poor
Number of ignored methods	Poor	Good	Average	Good
Number of instance attributes	Poor	Good	Poor	Average
Number of key classes	Poor	Good	Poor	Poor
Number of reused classes	Average	Good	Good	Good
Number of use cases	Good	Good	Poor	Poor
%/commented methods	Good	Good	Good	Good
Percentage of key classes	Poor	Good	Poor	Poor
Percentage of tested use cases	Poor	Good	Poor	Poor
Person days/class	Good	Good	Good	Good
Problem reports/class	Good	Good	Good	Good
Strings/message sends	Good	Good	Good	Good

%/ = percentage of

provide an indication (Good, Average, Poor) of how applicable each metric is for each class-type layer. When you read the table, please keep in mind the following considerations:

- Interface classes are typically small (the usually represent a single screen/window).

- Business classes range in size (although are usually larger) and are usually the most critical.

- Persistence classes are seldom modified once built.

- System classes are often numerous and complex.

6.7 What We've Learned

Metrics are an important but not yet fully understood aspect of object-oriented development. Metrics can be used as input into estimating projects, improving your development efforts and approach, and for selecting tools. In this chapter we discussed several important metrics that are applicable to object-oriented development efforts.

References

Albrecht A.J. (1979). "Measuring application development productivity." *Proceedings IBM Applications Development Symposium*, Guide International and Share, Inc., IBM Corporation.

Ambler, S.W. (1995a). *The Object Primer: The Application Developer's Guide to Object Orientation*. New York: SIGS Books.

Ambler, S.W. (1995b). "Avoiding brittle OO code" in *Software Development*, Miller Freeman Press, December.

Chidamber S.R., & Kemerer C.F. (1991). "Towards a suite of metrics for object-oriented design." *OOPSLA'91 Conference Proceedings*. Reading MA: Addison-Wesley, 197–211.

Goldberg, A., & Robson, D. (1989). *Smalltalk-80: The Language*. Reading MA: Addison-Wesley.

Jones, C. (1995, March). "What are function points?" http://204. 96.51.2/library/funcmet.htm [Internet]. Software Productivity Research.

Lorenz, M., & Kidd, J. (1994). *Object-Oriented Software Metrics*. Englewood Cliffs, NJ: Prentice-Hall.

> *You want to select the language(s) that are best for you*
> *in the long run, not what looks good in the*
> *short term or is today's current fad.*

Chapter 7

Choosing an Object-Oriented Language — Comparing the Leading Languages

What We'll Learn in This Chapter

What features to look for in an object-oriented (OO) language.

We'll compare and contrast the leading OO development languages:
C++, Smalltalk, Java, and ObjectCOBOL.

How to develop for the world of electronic commerce.

What other development tools you may need to
successfully build OO applications.

In this chapter we will discuss what features to look for in an OO language,
describing the main features of each of the leaders. We will also compare and
contrast the languages as well as discuss how to build electronic commerce
applications using OO development languages.

It wouldn't be right to have a book about OO development without covering the most common OO development languages. It needs to be pointed out, however, that this book isn't about OO programming, it's about OO development. Although I could easily write a book about each language covered in this chapter I'm not going to. The fact is that all I want to do is to give you a brief overview of what each language is like and what is typically used for, that's it. If you want more then I highly suggest that you pick up one or more of the books that I've listed in the references section at the end of this chapter.

7.1 What to Look For in an OO Language

Because no one language is ideal for all situations, you need to understand the strengths and weaknesses of each. Before you can judge which OO language is best suited for you, you need to understand the various features that OO languages should support. The following list delineates what one should look for in an OO language.

1. **Inheritance support.** You want to determine how the language supports inheritance, there being only three answers: it doesn't, it supports single inheritance, it supports multiple inheritance.

2. **Typing.** Typing is a mechanism that attempts to ensure that the objects being worked with are type consistent. The basic issue is this: if we know the type of an object then we know what behaviors it exhibits, otherwise we can only send it messages and hope for the best. Typing can be weak, strong, or untyped.

3. **Binding.** Binding is a mechanism that connects an object to its type/class. With static binding the type/class is bound at compile time, whereas with dynamic binding the type/class is bound at run time.

4. **Garbage collection.** Garbage collection is the term used to refer to the memory-management scheme used by an OO application, the basic issue being how and when do you get rid of objects in memory that are no longer being used? There are two types of garbage collection: automatic and manual. With automatic garbage collection the language automatical-

ly manages memory for you, reducing development, testing, and maintenance costs. With manual garbage collection the onus is on the programmer to manage memory himself or herself, increasing the cost of the application but giving coders complete control over memory management.

5. **Language level.** One question that you need to ask yourself is whether or not a language is "low level" or "high level." Low-level languages provide access to the underlying system, perhaps direct access to memory and operating system calls. The advantage of low-level languages is that you have complete control over your environment; the problem is that you typically have to write a lot of code to achieve this. High-level languages, on the other hand, abstract and encapsulate the functionality provided by the system, requiring far less coding but preventing programmers from accessing system-specific functionality. In short, low-level languages are very good for systems programming and high-level languages are more appropriate for application programming.

6. **Language purity.** There are two classifications of OO languages based on their origins: hybrid and pure. A hybrid OO language is one that supports structured/procedural programming constructs as well as object-oriented ones. Hybrid OO languages are typically extensions of existing procedural ones. Pure OO languages support only OO programming constructs, forcing programmers to do things the proper OO way.

7. **Enforcement of encapsulation.** A language enforces encapsulation when the only way to gain access to an attribute is via a method. By enforcing encapsulation a language increases the chances that programmers will do "the right thing" and reduce coupling between their classes. How a language enforces encapsulation, if it does so at all, is a pretty good indication as to how maintainable the code will be that is written in that language.

SCOTT'S SOAPBOX

When Is a Language Considered OO?

As far as I'm concerned, a language is considered OO when it meets all of the following criteria:

- It supports inheritance

- It supports polymorphism

- It enforces encapsulation

It should be simple to define the class **Employee** to be a subclass of **Person**, and if it takes more than one line of code to do so, then something's wrong. That's what I consider inheritance support. It should also be simple to treat instances of **Customer** and instances of **Employee** as if they were the same types of objects, and it should be easy for a **Customer** object to become an **Employee** object. That's what I consider polymorphism support. If a language doesn't support inheritance and polymorphism without extra coding, then it isn't even in the running to be considered object oriented.

The third issue deals with enforcement of encapsulation. Every modern language supports encapsulation, but not all of them enforce it. Encapsulation is one of the underlying principles of OO, and if your language allows you to easily go around encapsulation, then in my mind you are going around OO, and that isn't any good.

SCOTT'S SOAPBOX

Automatic Garbage Collection Is the Way to Go

Many people see manual garbage collection—the necessity of managing memory yourself—as a virtue. Frankly, I think that they're nuts. I've got better things to do than write code to create and destroy objects, and don't even get me going about wasting time looking for memory leaks (a memory leak is when you haven't properly managed the removal of an object from memory and as a result you have left part or all of the unwanted object in memory, effectively losing that memory space).

continued

SCOTT'S SOAPBOX

continued

With automatic garbage collection I know that my objects will be cleaned up when I'm done with them, without requiring me to write a single line of code. Furthermore, I know that the garbage collector has been written by one or more professionals who specialize in memory management—people who know far more than I do about garbage collection. Sure, I lose a little bit of control, but who cares? Unless I'm writing an embedded device driver for a piece of hardware, then I shouldn't have to worry about managing memory. Automatic garbage collection is the appropriate approach to managing memory 99.9% of the time.

By the way, most languages that support automatic garbage collection also allow you to define when you want it done, providing you with some control after all.

SCOTT'S SOAPBOX

The Pure Versus Hybrid Debate

A debate has been raging for years in the object community over which is better: pure or hybrid OO languages. I intend to wade into this debate with the opinion: Who cares? Yes, your code will more than likely be harder to maintain if you use a hybrid language. Yes, over the long-term pure languages lead to a better and faster understanding of the OO paradigm than the use of hybrid OO languages. However, the use of a hybrid OO language is often more palatable to experienced coders who balk at the idea of becoming a novice again after years of being an expert in their field. Hybrid languages aren't perfect, but they are here to stay—so let's get on with our lives and forget about it.

DEFINITIONS

Static typing—The class/type of an object is associated to it at compile time.

Dynamic binding—The class/type of an object is associated to it at run time.

Garbage collection—Memory management in an OO application.

Garbage collector—The object(s) responsible for garbage collection.

Memory leak—When you haven't properly managed the removal of an object from memory and have effectively lost some of the memory space that it takes up.

Pure OO language—An OO language that supports only OO programming constructs.

Hybrid OO language—An OO language that supports both structured/procedural and OO programming constructs.

7.2 The Leading OO Languages

There are currently four OO languages that I would consider to be the leaders: C++, Java, ObjectCOBOL, and Smalltalk. Some have been around for decades, whereas others have been around a couple of years. In this section we will discuss their various features, concentrating on when and why you should use each one.

7.2.1 C++

C++ is best suited for systems programming.

C++ is a hybrid OO language based on C that was originally designed at AT&T in the early 1980s (Ellis & Stroustrup, 1990). At the time of this writing, C++ is the most popular OO language on the market due in large part to the vast number of C shops that migrated to it in the late 1980s and early 1990s. C++ is used on various micro, mini, and mainframe platforms, and although it is a low-level language best suited for systems programming, it is also used for application development. C++ supports both static and dynamic (through pointers) binding, weak typing, and both single and multiple inheritance. C++ does not enforce encapsulation and it requires manual garbage collection. Figure 7.1 contains the code for a simple C++ method.

```
int* incrementCounter(char *aParameter)
{
        int iCounter;           // Define a counter

        this->set(&iCounter);   // Sets the initial counter value via
                                   an internal method

        iCounter++;             // Increments the counter

        return &iCounter;       // Returns the address of counter
}
```

Figure 7.1.
Example of C++
source code.

There is a lot to the C++ language, making it difficult to learn. Good C++ programmers have to understand pointers and memory management from C, often proving very difficult for novice OO developers. The main advantages of C++ are that it is a proven language and that it is supported by many vendors. The main disadvantages are its low-level nature and its complexity, making it both difficult to learn and to maintain.

7.2.2 Java

Java (Anuff, 1996) is a new OO language that officially popped onto the development scene in May of 1995. Java is used to develop applets, small programs that are transmitted across the Internet to users running a Java Virtual Machine (interpreter). With Java you add marketing bells and whistles to your World Wide Web (WWW) pages, and if you're very aggressive you'll use it to create applications that actively support electronic commerce by your organization. An example of Java source code is shown in Figure 7.2; notice its similarity to C++.

Java is best suited for Internet application programming.

Java is a high-level language based on C++ that only supports single inheritance, has automatic garbage collection, is weakly typed, is statically bound, and like C++ does not enforce encapsulation. At the time of this writing the main advantages of Java are that it is highly portable (although as more vendors get involved this could rapidly change) and that it is designed for the needs of Internet development. The main disadvantages are that it is an unproven, immature language and that it suffers from significant run-time performance problems.

Figure 7.2.
Example of Java
source code.

```
void PositiveOrNegative(int value)
{
        //  Indicate if the value is positive or negative
        if (value < 0)
        {
          System.out.println("Negative");
        }
        else
        {
          System.out.println("Positive");
        }
}
```

SCOTT'S SOAPBOX

The Future of Java

Java is currently in its first version so it is difficult to predict its future, although as we'll see in section 7.3, I think that it is clearly key to the future of electronic commerce. The Java Virtual Machine is currently being embedded in most common PC/workstation operating systems—virtually guaranteeing that it will be universally supported by the computer industry. The problem that I see is now that everyone has gotten onto the Java bandwagon, we will soon see numerous flavors of Java, one from each vendor, just as we see numerous flavors of other standard languages such as C++ and Smalltalk. How long Java source code will remain "portable" is questionable.

DEFINITIONS

Java Applet—Small programs written in Java that are transmitted to, and run on, a client workstation from a server.

Java Virtual Machine—The interpretive environment that runs Java apples.

7.2.3 ObjectCOBOL

ObjectCOBOL is a hybrid OO language that is an extension of COBOL (Arranga & Coyle, 1996). Its high-level nature makes it ideal for application development, although because of its newness it is still unproven. ObjectCOBOL supports both single and multiple inheritance, weak and strong typing, and dynamic binding. Depending on the vendor, encapsulation is either supported or enforced and garbage collection is either automatic or manual. Figure 7.3 provides an example of ObjectCOBOL code.

ObjectCOBOL is best-suited for application programming.

```
Method-Id. "Increment Counter".
* Increments the internal counter for this object
Procedure Division.
        Add 1 to Counter.
        * Output the value of the counter
        Invoke Self "Output Counter" Returning Counter.
        Exit Method.
End Method "Increment Counter".
```

Figure 7.3.
Example of ObjectCOBOL source code.

The main advantage of ObjectCOBOL is mindshare—this is the object-oriented language that Corporate America has been waiting for. The main disadvantages are that it is still immature and not proven, and that its hybrid nature will probably lead to non-OO (read poor) code.

SCOTT'S SOAPBOX

Is History Repeating Itself?

Many C shops in the late 1980s and early 1990s adopted C++ as their language of choice. Although some C shops went through the process of evaluating their options and went out and picked the best language for the type of programs they were writing, for the most part the vast majority said to themselves, "We know C, therefore we should move to C++." On the surface this sounds like a good decision, but the reality was that many C shops had a horrendous time moving to OO.

continued

SCOTT'S SOAPBOX

continued

The fundamental problem that C shops ran into was that when experienced C programmers try to learn C++, they are often unable to make the transition. The reason for this is simple: whenever you learn something new, you always run into problems that you can't immediately solve—this is simply part of the learning process. When experienced C programmers run into a problem learning C++ they unfortunately have the necessary skills to code around the problem, which is what people tend to do. The end result of this is that although the short-term problem gets solved by coding around it, the programmer never learns how to code it correctly. In other words, the programmers **never truly learn OO**.

The general consensus is that the vast majority of people who consider themselves C++ programmers are really only writing C programs that use a few objects—they aren't writing true OO C++ code. The interesting thing is that when you take the same programmers and put them in a Smalltalk environment, they pick up OO development easily. This is because Smalltalk is a pure OO language that doesn't allow programmers to code around problems; instead, it forces them to do things the proper OO way.

I'm afraid that the potential is there for the same problem to occur when COBOL shops decide to move into OO. Their tendency will be to say to themselves, "We're a COBOL shop; therefore ObjectCOBOL is the way to go." I'm afraid that just like C programmers had difficulties learning C++, we'll find that COBOL programmers will have problems learning ObjectCOBOL.

When you move programmers into an OO version of the development environment that they are familiar with, then the odds are very good that they won't learn the OO development concepts that you want them to. This means that your organization will not see many of the benefits of OO that it was hoping for. Although this strategy is very tempting from a short-term point of view, it more often than not hurts you badly in the long run. Let's learn from the mistakes of the past.

7.2.4 Smalltalk

Smalltalk (Goldberg & Robson, 1989) is a pure OO language that was originally developed at Xerox PARC in the 1970s and early 1980s. Smalltalk was first used for application development in the mid-1980s, but came into its own in the early 1990s. Smalltalk supports single inheritance, enforces encapsulation, supports dynamic binding, is untyped, and has automatic garbage collection. Smalltalk's high-level nature makes it ideal for OO applications programming. Figure 7.4 offers an example of Smalltalk code.

Smalltalk is best suited for OO application programming.

```
accountBalance
    " Answers back the balance of the account "
    (accountBalance isNil) ifTrue: [
      self accountBalance: 0.
    ].
    ^ accountBalance.
```

Figure 7.4.
Example of Smalltalk source code.

Smalltalk is being used in the financial industry, in the telecommunications industry, in the aerospace industry, in manufacturing, and in government. Its main advantages are that it is a simple language that is easy to learn and that it is proven and mature. The main disadvantages are that like C++ there are a lot of classes to learn and that its interpretive nature means that Smalltalk code typically runs between 5% and 10% slower than similar C++ code.

7.2.5 Comparing the Leading OO Languages

In Table 7.1 (following page) is found a chart that compares the features of the four leading OO languages.

7.3 Understanding Electronic Commerce on the Internet

Most companies are either starting to do business on the Internet or soon will be, and because this environment is significantly different than what organizations are used to I want to provide a few words of

Table 7.1. COMPARING THE LEADING OO LANGUAGES

Features	C++	Java	ObjectCOBOL	Smalltalk
Language type	Hybrid	Pure	Hybrid	Pure
Best suited for	Sys. Prog.[1]	Int. Applets[2]	App. Prog.[3]	App. Prog.
Market penetration	Very high	High	MBG[4]	High
Language level	Low	Medium	High	High
Learnability	Difficult	Medium	Medium	Medium
Inheritance support	S&Mult.[5]	Single	S&Mult.	Single
Encapsulation	Supported	Supported	Vendor-specific	Enforced
Typing	Weak&strong	Weak	Weak&strong	Untyped
Binding	Static&dynamic	Static	Dynamic	Dynamic
Garbage collection	Manual	Automatic	Vendor-specific	Automatic

[1]System Programming; [2]Internet Applets; [3]Application Programming;
[4]Medium but growing; [5]Single and multiple.

Understanding e-commerce will prove to be the key to success in the 21st century.

advice. From all appearances it looks as if Java is being used for both Internet and Intranet (networks that run internally within your organization) development. Because the electronic-commerce aspects of Internet development are so new to us I wish to concentrate on that use of Java here; although I realize that Intranet development is incredibly important it's not what I want to concentrate on. I truly believe that organizations that understand the issues surrounding electronic commerce (e-commerce) are the ones that are going to succeed in the 21st century, and the ones that don't will flounder at best, and will fail at worst.

In this section we will discuss the following issues:

- An electronic-commerce architecture
- Payment processing
- International issues

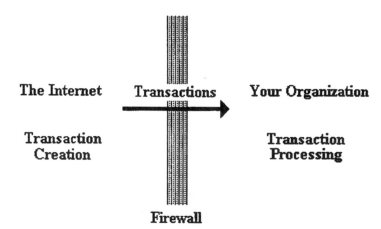

Figure 7.5.
A high-level architecture for electronic commerce.

The Internet   Transactions   **Your Organization**

Transaction   **Transaction**
Creation   **Processing**

Firewall

- Selling physical and virtual products on the web
- Taxes on electronic commerce
- Using Java and Smalltalk to support e-commerce

7.3.1 An Architecture for Supporting Electronic Commerce

In Figure 7.5 above we see a high-level overview of e-commerce on the Internet. The basic idea is that your potential customers go to your World Wide Web page, find a product or service that they wish to purchase from you, and then purchase it while they are at the web page. There are three components to this architecture: the Internet, a firewall, and your organization. The Internet is where you will interact electronically with your customers, your firewall will provide you with reasonable protection against people who wish you harm, and your organization's systems will process the business transactions generated on the WWW by your customers. Later in this chapter we will discuss a development approach that uses Java and high-level OO languages, such as Smalltalk or ObjectCOBOL, to support this architecture.

To understand why we need to change our systems infrastructure we must first put the requirements of electronic commerce into perspective. We're talking about the WORLD wide web, and that means international commerce. Doing business internationally means handling multiple languages, multiple currencies, multiple cultures, mul-

> **DEFINITIONS**
>
> *Electronic commerce*—Any form of commerce in which the buyer of a product or service uses a computer to interact with the computer system of the seller of that product or service.
>
> *Internet*—A collection of inter-connected computers that people can log onto to share information, to communicate, to be entertained, and to perform electronic commerce transactions.
>
> *Intranet*—A network internal to your organization that is built either partially or completely from Internet-based technology.
>
> *World Wide Web*—A component of the Internet that provides users with the ability to move from computer system to computer system by following predefined links among those systems.

tiple tax laws, and multiple shipping/customs rules. It's a whole new ball game, folks, and we need to step up to the plate right now.

7.3.2 Payment Processing on the Internet

You have to accept multiple currencies.

Without a doubt accepting multiple currencies is the easiest issue to deal with when doing business electronically. The American dollar isn't the only currency in the world, and it isn't unreasonable to expect that people will want to do business in German marks, English pounds, French francs, and even Canadian dollars (eh). The easiest solution to this issue is to quote prices on the net in your currency of choice, probably US dollars, and then convert to the other currency at the time of the sale.

In the short term credit-card transactions will prove to be the most popular payment type.

In addition to various types of currency you should also be able to accept multiple payment types. Credit-card transactions are fairly easy to process electronically and have the advantage that credit-card processors will do the currency exchange for you automatically. The big issue with credit cards is security, but by the time this book goes to print the major credit-card companies should have addressed this issue.

Credit cards, however, aren't the only game in town. Just as I can go down to the grocery store and use my bank debit card to buy food, I should also be able to use it to purchase products on the net.

Processing bank debit cards is a little harder than processing credit cards, but as the American financial industry consolidates itself over the next few years this will become less and less of a problem. *Bank debit cards will grow in importance over time.*

I also see wire transfers being a significant payment type for electronic commerce, especially for large orders between companies. I hope financial institutions will be able to get a mechanism in place to take advantage of the huge opportunity presented by the Internet. In addition to wire transfers I also see electronic purchase orders as a popular payment mechanism on the net. *Wire transfers may also prove popular.*

You should expect to see electronic/digital cash (e-cash) evolve over time, ultimately becoming the dominant payment type on the net. The main issue is one of acceptance, and I fear that it will take a generation or two for e-cash to truly catch on. Just as it was difficult centuries ago to convince people to start trading their cows and chickens for these new things called coins, it is just as difficult today to convince people to trade their hard-earned money for a collection of bits called e-cash. *E-cash will potentially dominate e-commerce in the long run.*

7.3.3 It's the WORLD Wide Web — International Issues

Language is another issue that is fairly easy to get our minds around—everyone doesn't read, write, and speak English. Although English is arguably the most popular language in the world, it isn't universal. German is quickly becoming the language of business in Europe, in large part because Germany is much more proactive in integrating Eastern European countries than are its trading partners. Spanish and Portuguese are the languages of business in South America, with Japanese and various dialects of Chinese used in most of Asia.

The point to be made is that if you truly want to do business on the web you're going to have to be able to support several languages. To do this you need a robust user interface that is easy to modify, a requirement that is well supported by the class-type architecture of chapter 3. Although this chapter didn't directly address supporting multiple languages, the interface class layer puts you into a position to support several languages in your user interface without forcing you to change your underlying business classes. *You'll need to support multiple languages.*

Another issue that needs to be considered when doing business on the web is culture. There are thousands of unique cultures around the world, each of which has its own ways of doing business and its own taboos. Did you know that in some Middle Eastern countries red is a forbidden color? Did you know that color is spelled "colour" in Canada

You need to understand the culture of the people you are trying to sell to.

and England? Make a small error in the design of your user interface and you risk offending millions of potential customers. The moral of the story is that if you want to be able to do business in these countries effectively you had better take the time to understand them and learn their unique nuances.

7.3.4 You Can Sell Both Physical and Virtual Products Internationally

You can sell more than just widgets.

Electronic commerce also opens up opportunities for selling virtual products—software, online newspapers and magazines, and electronic libraries to name a few. Unlike selling physical products such as widgets to customers you'll find that selling virtual products is a significantly different endeavor. How do you price a virtual product? How do you ensure that it isn't copied and resold unbeknownst to you (should you even care)? How do you predict how many copies you'll sell? Interesting issues that we simply don't have answers to yet.

You also need to address the issue of shipping and customs—what can you sell to Cubans? How about Russians? Japanese? Canadians? Brazilians? Americans? Depending on the nation that your customers live in you are able to sell and ship different products to them as defined by the trade agreements your country has with theirs. Forgetting the complexities of understanding the ever-changing trade agreements between nations, how do you even know what country a person is in? How do you know you aren't illegally selling a virtual product to someone? For example, what's stopping a Cuban from getting an Internet address through a Canadian provider and purchasing virtual products from an American company? You'd never know you committed a felony until the police came knocking on your door. Don't underestimate shipping and customs issues.

7.3.5 Don't Forget Taxes

As a Canadian I'm probably a little more aware of taxes than a lot of other people—without a doubt this is to my detriment. Taxes on electronic commerce are going to be a huge issue, one that probably won't be resolved quickly. If an American company sells a product to an Italian consumer via an electronic order made on a web server they operate in Germany, what taxes get applied: American, German, or Italian? What rates do we charge? Whom do we submit them to?

Taxes are collected at international, federal, state, and municipal levels. Tax rules are incredibly complex and constantly changing. In Canada we have a tax called the GST that is grossly convoluted in its calculation. When you buy donuts (the national delicacy, eh) the GST is applied when you buy five but isn't when you buy six, although if you buy seven then you're paying the GST again. It seems that donuts are considered a staple when purchased in multiples of half a dozen but are considered snacks otherwise and hence should be taxed. This is only one of hundreds of unusual rules associated with the GST. Can you imagine trying to keep track of tax rules from thousands of countries, states, and cities? The point to be made is that tax collection is going to be a huge issue for anyone wanting to do business on the web.

As more and more business is done on the Internet I suspect that we will see an online tax-calculation service that organizations can access for a fraction of a cent per transaction. Calculation and remittance of sales taxes on an international scale are far too complex for most organizations to handle, but will prove to be a lucrative business for anyone who wants to provide these services online.

We'll soon see online tax services on the Internet that encapsulate the complexities of tax calculation and remittance.

7.3.6 Using Smalltalk/ObjectCOBOL and Java to Develop Electronic Commerce Applications

It is clear that supporting electronic commerce, the issues of which are summarized in Table 7.2, will prove to be more difficult than many people think. I believe that to successfully do so your organization will need to develop a system architecture that is robust enough to deal with the constantly changing complexities of international electronic commerce. It isn't bad enough that you need to support multiple languages, multiple currencies, and multiple payment mechanisms; you also need to support tax laws and trade agreements that change daily. To put it bluntly, doing business on the web is a complex and constantly changing environment. Oh, and by the way, now that you're doing business internationally you now have six billion potential customers, so expect to receive a few more orders than usual once you're up and running on the web.

Realistically, Java will be used to create relatively simple applets that collect basic information from your customers, package the information into a transaction, and then send the transaction through your firewall to be processed by the applications within your organization. Although simple, Java applets are the key to doing business in the Internet.

Table 7.2. ELECTRONIC COMMERCE DEVELOPMENT CHECKLIST

Have you taken into consideration being able to:

- Process multiple currencies?
- Process multiple payment types?
  - Credit/debit cards
  - Wire transfers
  - Electronic/digital cash
  - Purchase orders
- Do business in several languages?
- Support various cultures and beliefs?
- Identify what you can and cannot sell to people?
- Support sale of both physical and virtual products?
- Collect and submit the appropriate taxes?
- Limit the information you reveal to your competition?
- Process orders made by six billion potential customers?
- Leverage existing legacy applications?

Applets will be simple for several reasons: first, Java is still immature as a language and still needs to grow before it can be used for complex applications. Second, the bandwidth on the Internet is limited and that effectively limits the size of the Java applets that you can reasonably transmit. Third, you want to limit the amount of information that you reveal to your competition on the Internet. Few organizations today hand their mission-critical applications over to their competition and it won't be any different with Java on the Internet (remember, anybody can go to your web page, even your competition). The short story is that you'll provide basic editing and validation logic in your applets, as well as whatever logic is needed to package the data into a packet to be transmitted through your firewall. Anything more and you're playing with fire.

If your Java applets don't encapsulate the complexities of doing business on the web that we discussed earlier, then where does all of that go? The answer is that it belongs on your side of the firewall. The basic idea is that your Java applets create and transmit standard transactions to your mission-critical applications and are processed there. You handle the complexity of electronic commerce within your internal applications where you can control and maintain it.

As shown in Figure 7.6, either Smalltalk or ObjectCOBOL is your best choice for creating the mission-critical applications that you need to

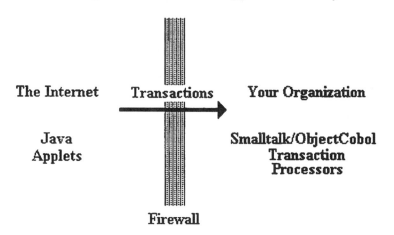

The Internet   **Transactions**   **Your Organization**

**Java
Applets**   **Smalltalk/ObjectCobol
Transaction
Processors**

Firewall

Figure 7.6.
Using Java and Smalltalk together to meet the needs of electronic commerce.

support the needs of electronic commerce. Because they are both high-level, object-oriented development environments they are able to support the complexities forced on you by the web.

Many organizations either are trying to modify their existing legacy applications or are trying to put an object-oriented wrapper around them so that newer programs can access them. Although some of these efforts will prove to be successful, I wouldn't put any money on them. Think of it like this: do your old applications truly support the needs of electronic commerce? Probably not. Just like you can't create a silk purse out of a sow's ear, you can't create a modern application out of the ancient legacy code of yesteryear. If you want to do business on the web you're going to have to rewrite your mission-critical applications using a combination of Java and Smalltalk/ObjectCOBOL, it's as simple as that.

7.4 Beyond Programming Languages — Other Development Tools

Programming languages aren't the only tools that are used during development, and there are several categories of tools that you want to choose from when putting together a development environment. These categories are as follows:

1. **OOCASE tools.** Object-oriented computer-aided system engineering (OOCASE) tools aid in the development effort by supporting various analysis-and-design modeling techniques. Sophisticated OOCASE tools will support both forward and reverse engineering. Forward engineering refers to the generation of code from a model or set of models and reverse engineering refers to the generation of models from source code. I'm a firm believer that CASE tools need to support both of these features in order to be an effective alternative for developers, because without these features your model quickly gets out of synch with your code.

2. **Off-the-shelf reusable code.** Reusable code can be purchased in one of several forms: class libraries, frameworks, or components. A class library is a collection of generic classes that serve various purposes, for example class libraries of GUI (graphical user interface) widgets are very common. Frameworks are

collections of classes that provide a robust set of functionality to which you can add new classes to specify features that are unique to your application. For example, you might purchase a human-resources (HR) framework that provides the basic HR functionality, or a manufacturing-process framework that provides basic manufacturing plant automation functions. Components are often touted as the poor man's objects because even though they encapsulate certain functionality they typically can't be inherited from. As with class libraries it is common to see component libraries for GUI widgets, the main difference being that class libraries are more extensible.

3. **OO repositories.** The main purpose of a repository is that it is a tool that is used to store and retrieve your development work. A repository is critical for team-developed systems, as it provides the mechanism for developers to share their work. In addition to storing source code (in the form of class libraries), your documentation and analysis/design models should also be stored in the repository. In short a repository is a centralized database in which you can check-in and check-out versions of your development work.

4. **OO testing tools.** This is any tool that aids in either the definition of OO test cases, the storage of OO test cases, or the running of OO test cases. Sophisticated OO testing tools should support a large percentage of the FLOOT (full life-cycle object-oriented testing) techniques presented in chapter 11.

DEFINITIONS

CASE—Computer-aided system engineering.

CASE tool—A tool that supports the creation of models and potentially both forward and reverse engineering.

Class library—A collection of classes, typically purchased off-the-shelf, which you can reuse and extend via inheritance.

continued

DEFINITIONS

continued

Component—Reusable code, typically purchased off-the-shelf, which you can reuse but not extend via inheritance.

Forward engineering—The generation of source code from a model by a CASE tool.

Framework—A collection of classes that together provide sophisticated, generic functionality, which can be extended via the addition of subclasses to meet your specific needs.

OOCASE tool—A CASE tool that supports OO development.

Repository—A centralized database in which you can check-in and check-out versions of your development work, including documentation, models, and source code.

Reverse engineering—The generation of a model from source code by a CASE tool.

Testing tool—Any tool that aids in either the definition of test cases, the storage of test cases, or the running of test cases.

7.5   *What We've Learned*

In this chapter we briefly reviewed the leading OO development languages, concentrating on their basic features as well as what they are best suited for. We also discussed many of the issues involved with developing electronic commerce applications. We finished the chapter with a discussion an overview of non-language OO development tools.

References

Anuff, E. (1996). *Java Sourcebook: A Complete Guide to Creating Java Applets for the Web*. New York: Wiley.

Arranga, E.C., & Coyle, F.P. (1996). *Object-Oriented COBOL*. New York: SIGS Publishing.

Ellis, M.A., & Stroustrup, B. (1990). *The Annotated C++ Reference Manual*. Reading, MA: Addison Wesley.

Goldberg, A., & Robson, D. (1989). *Smalltalk-80: The Language*. Reading, MA: Addison-Wesley.

Object-oriented construction is very similar to, yet at the same time
different from, procedural/structured development. Successful
OO programmers realize this, unsuccessful ones don't.

Chapter 8

Building Your Application — Effective Object-Oriented Construction Techniques

What We'll Learn in This Chapter

Why the right attitude is everything when coding object-oriented (OO) applications.

How to work with attributes effectively
to make your applications easier to maintain and enhance.

How to develop high-quality methods and classes.

What tools you can use to enhance the development process.

How to organize your development efforts around
the class-type architecture in an effective manner.

One of the most important lessons that you can learn about building applications is that there is more to it than coding. In this chapter we will discover a multitude of techniques that you can use to improve your application construction efforts. Everything covered in this chapter is applicable to any object-oriented (OO) language that you work in. This is important because it will help to *give you skills that you can apply when you are working in any OO development environment, and not just in the one that you have today. The best skills are the ones that you can transfer to your next project.*

Programming, or more accurately construction, is an important part of the development process. We'll discuss solutions for several common coding problems as well as how to organize your development efforts around the class-type architecture presented in chapter 3. The most important lesson that you can learn in this chapter is that good programmers realize that there is more to development than programming and that great programmers realize that there is more to development than development. Although mysterious, I hope that by the end of this chapter you'll agree that this statement is true.

8.1 Attitude Is Everything

The real secret to object-oriented construction isn't what language that you choose, or what testing tool, or what debugger, it's the way that you approach the development process. It's your attitude, not your tool set that makes you a good developer.

In this section we'll see that:

- There's more to development than just coding

- There's more to development than development

- You need to get the design right first

- You need to develop in small steps

- You need to work closely with your users

8.1.1 There's More to Development Than Just Coding

Good developers understand the entire development process.

The point to be made is that good developers understand that there's more to development than coding, there's analysis, design, testing, and implementation too. Until you understand the big picture and how you fit into it you will never reach your full potential as a devel-

---

SCOTT'S SOAPBOX

Iterative Development, Incremental Development, and Hacking

There are a lot of "cowboy programmers" out there who jump into coding without giving adequate thought to analysis and design. Although these people may write some very efficient code, it is often very difficult, if not impossible, to maintain by other people. What really irks me is when cowboy programmers justify their questionable practices by calling it "iterative development" or "incremental development." Pure hogwash.

Incremental development is all about releasing applications in parts. You typically implement the basic application functionality in the first release, and then over time you add more and more features to the application on a regular basis. When taking an incremental approach, it's common to see quarterly or even monthly releases of an application.

Although you don't need an OO development environment to do incremental development, it certainly helps. One of the main benefits of object orientation is high extensibility, a measure of how easy it is to modify or extend an application. By definition, you need an environment that provides great extensibility if you want to take an incremental approach to development over a long period of time. OO and incremental development go hand-in-hand.

Hacking is all about programming when you really don't know what you're coding. In order to justify this development approach, hackers will often claim that they are actually doing iterative development. Don't be fooled. How can you possibly justify coding when you don't know what it is you're building? Like I said previously, you ALWAYS have to start the development process with at least a little bit of analysis and design. The bottom line is that it's iterative development when you know what you're coding—it's hacking when you don't.

---

oper. I'm not saying that you need to be an expert at every part of the development process, but what I am saying is that you need to understand the fundamentals.

8.1.2 There's More to Development Than Just Development

The second important lesson that developers need to learn is that there's more to development than just development! There's also maintenance and support, and in fact an application will spend the

Good developers develop with maintenance in mind, not development.

vast majority of its lifetime in maintenance (post-development). The average computer program spends 80 to 90% of its lifetime being maintained and only a very small portion being developed.

There's something that I call the *development/maintenance trade-off*—decisions that speed up the development process often harm you during maintenance, whereas decisions that improve the maintainability of your system can often increase the time that it originally takes you to develop it. At least in the short term. You see, code that is more maintainable is much more likely to be reused than code that isn't. If it's hard to maintain it's also hard to reuse. The things that make your code maintainable—documentation, paragraphing, intelligent naming strategies, good design—many of the things that we talk about in this chapter all take time and money during the development process. Although they will pay for themselves many times over during maintenance, the short-term pain is often enough to motivate you to put them off for a later date, a date that more often than not never comes. Your real trade-off is this: do you invest a little bit of time and effort during development to greatly reduce your future maintenance efforts? I think that the answer is yes, how about you?

The development/maintenance trade-off boils down to an ounce of prevention being worth a pound of cure.

> **DEFINITION**
>
> *Development/maintenance trade-off*—Development techniques that speed up the development process often have a negative impact on your maintenance efforts, whereas techniques that lead to greater maintainability negatively impact your development efforts, at least in the short term.

8.1.3 You Need to Get the Design Right First

Would you feel comfortable walking over a bridge that was put together without a plan, just with the hard work of a group of construction workers who felt they knew what they were doing? Of course you wouldn't because you'd be afraid that it could fall down at any minute. Why should your users be comfortable with working with software built by a group of programmers who felt they knew what they were doing? How comfortable would you be when you're taking a flight somewhere if you were to find out that the air-traffic-control system was written without first putting together, and then following, a really solid design? Think about it.

Have you ever been in a situation where some code needs to be changed that your code relies on? Perhaps a new parameter needs to be passed to a method, or perhaps a class needs to be broken up into several classes. How much extra work did you have to do to make sure that your code works with the reconfigured version of the code that got changed? How happy were you? Did you ask yourself why somebody didn't stop and think about it first when he or she originally wrote the code so that this didn't need to happen? That they should have DESIGNED it first? Of course you did. If you take the time to figure out how you're going to write your code before you actually start coding, you'll probably spend less time doing it and potentially reduce the impact of future changes on your code simply by thinking about them up front.

The time invested in design pays off in spades during programming.

8.1.4 You Need to Develop in Small Steps

I've always found that developing in small steps, writing a few methods, testing them, and then writing a few more methods is often far more effective than writing a whole bunch of code all at once and then trying to fix it. It's much easier to test and fix ten lines of code than 100, in fact, I would safely say that you could program, test, and fix 100 lines of code in 10 10-line increments in less than half the time than you could write a single one-hundred line block of code that did the same work. The reason for this is simple. Whenever you're testing your code and you find a bug you almost always find that bug in the new code that you just wrote, assuming of course that the rest of the code was pretty solid to begin with. You can hunt down a bug a lot faster in a small section of code than in a big one. By developing in small incremental steps you reduce the average time that it takes to find a bug, which in turn reduces your overall development time.

Developing in small incremental steps is significantly faster than developing large portions of code at once.

There's a small caveat that I'd like to point out. Developing in small, incremental steps is faster only in interpreted environments like Smalltalk that allow you to see the effects of changes to your code instantly or on small applications that can be compiled quickly in environments like C++ that don't support interpreted development. When your applications takes several hours to compile you probably can't afford to write a few lines, compile it, then test it.

8.1.5 You Need to Work Closely with Your Users

If there's one common theme in this book series it's that good developers work closely with their users. Users know the business. Users are the reason why developers create systems, to support their work. Users pay the bills, including the salaries of developers. You simply can't develop a successful system if you don't understand the needs of your users, and the only way that you can understands their needs is if you work closely with them.

8.2 Working with Attributes Effectively

In this section we will discuss several techniques for dealing with attributes (variables) that will make your applications easier to develop, easier to maintain, and easier to enhance. The techniques that we will cover fall into one of two categories: (a) naming attributes, or (b) accessor methods.

8.2.1 Naming Attributes

The way that you name attributes is a critical factor in how easy it is to understand your code. I am a firm believer that your variables' names should be full English descriptions and that you should set a naming standard and always stick to it. Furthermore, if there is a commonly accepted naming convention for the environment that you are working in then that is the naming convention that you should follow.

TIP

Any Naming Convention is Better Than None
Pick a naming convention and stick to it. Your naming convention might not be perfect (I have yet to see a perfect one), but it is far preferable to not having one at all. Without setting a naming convention, you have absolutely no hope of writing consistent code. The greater the consistency of your code, the easier it is to understand and maintain.

8.2.1.1 English Descriptors

The most important part of setting an attribute-naming convention for your project, and for your organization as a whole, is that the convention should be based on using full English descriptors for attribute names. This means that variable names such as **x1** and **x2** aren't valid, although **accountNumber** and **customerCounter** are. A good attribute name indicates how the attribute is used or what it does.

An attribute name should describe what it does and/or how it is used.

Also notice how mixed case is used to form the names – whenever an attribute name is made up of several words the second, third, fourth, etc., words are capitalized. For example, we would have the attribute **customerFirstName** not **customerfirstname**. As you can see, it is easier to read and understand the full name of an attribute when you use mixed case.

If you are going to use short forms, which I advise against, then you must define a standard set of abbreviations. For example, how do you intend to abbreviate "number?" Do you use nbr, no, or num? Although this sounds like a small issue, consistency in the way that you name attributes is important so invest a little time setting standards for abbreviations if you intend to use them.

Avoid using abbreviations in attribute names.

> **TIP**
>
> *Relax Your Naming Convention for Loop Counters*
> The only time that I will ever break the convention of giving attributes and/or variables full English descriptors is for loop counters. It is quite common to see allowance for variable names such as **x**, **y**, or **z** to be used as loop counters because they are quite common and they are only being used as counters and not for anything "important." The decision is yours—you just have to come up with a strategy and stick to it.

8.2.1.2 Common Naming Conventions for the Different Languages

In Table 8.1 we see a summary of some of the standard-attribute naming conventions for the leading object-oriented languages. It's always preferable to choose an industry standard rather than to roll your own. The work of defining the standard is already done for you and chances are people from outside your team are also using, reducing your training costs if you bring them onto your project.

Table 8.1. STANDARD ATTRIBUTE NAMING CONVENTIONS

Language	Standard Naming Convention
C++	Hungarian notation — e.g., iCustomerNumber
Java	English words — e.g., customerNumber
ObjectCOBOL	English words —e.g., customerName
Smalltalk	English words — e.g., customerNumber

THE HUNGARIAN NOTATION

The Hungarian Notation for Naming Attributes

The "Hungarian Notation" (McConnell, 1993) is based on the principle that an attribute should be named using the following approach:

xEeeeeeeEeeee

where **x** indicates the base type of the attribute, and **EeeeeEeeeee** is the full English descriptor. The base type might be:

a for array	**p** for pointer	**i** for integer
li for long integer		**f** for float

The main advantage of the Hungarian Notation is that developers can quickly judge from the name of the variable its type and how it is used. The problem is that in dynamically typed languages, or in any language that supports polymorphism for that matter, it might not be possible to determine the type of an attribute when you code it.

If you intend to modify an existing standard to meet the specific needs of your project, perhaps you want to define a list of standard abbreviations, then make any change in such a way as to have it as an enhancement to the standards and not a rewrite of it. The fundamentals of the standards discussed above are very solid and have been proven over time, so my suggestion is that you should really think twice before making major modifications.

8.2.2 Accessor Methods

In addition to naming conventions, the maintainability of attributes is achieved by the appropriate use of *accessor methods*, methods that provide the functionality to either update an attribute or to access its value. Accessor methods come in two flavors: *setters* and *getters*. A setter modifies the value of a variable, whereas a getter obtains it for you.

Accessor methods are typically given the same names as the variables that they access. For example, the following Smalltalk and C++ examples in Figures 8.1 and 8.2, respectively, show the accessor methods for the account number attribute.

Accessor methods increase the maintainability of your classes by encapsulating attributes.

```
accountNumber
        ^ accountNumber.

accountNumber: aNewNumber
        accountNumber := aNewNumber.
```

Figure 8.1.
Examples of Smalltalk getter and setter methods, respectively.

```
accountNumber()
{
        return (accountNumber);
}

accountNumber( int aNewNumber)
{
        accountNumber = aNewNumber;
}
```

Figure 8.2.
Examples of C++ getter and setter methods, respectively.

Although accessor methods obviously add overhead, they help to hide the implementation details of your class. By having at most two control points from which a variable is accessed, one setter and one getter, you are able to increase the maintainability of your classes by minimizing the points at which changes need to be made.

Consider the implementation of bank account numbers. Currently account numbers are stored as one large number, but what would happen if the bank decided to store account numbers as two separate figures, a four-digit branch ID and a six-digit one that is unique within the branch. Without the use of accessors a change this simple usually has huge ramifications. Every piece of code accessing account numbers would need to be modified. With getters and setters, we only need to make a few minor changes as seen in Figure 8.3 (written in Smalltalk).

Figure 8.3.
Smalltalk accessors for accountNumber.

accountNumber
    " Answer the unique account number, which is the con catenation of the branch id with the internal branch account number "

    ^ (self branchID) * 1000000 + (self branchAccountNumber).

accountNumber: aNewNumber
    " Sets the branch ID and internal branch account number for this account "

    self branchID: (aNewNumber div: 1000000).
    self branchAccountNumber: (aNewNumber mod: 100000).

Notice that in Figure 8.3 we used other accessor methods in our accessor methods. Although the code was fairly straightforward, we didn't directly access any variables. Don't forget, the implementation of **branchID** and **branchAccountNumber** could easily change at some point in the future.

8.2.2.1 Getters for Constants

Unfortunately, there is one slight problem with our code in Figure 8.3—it doesn't work! Testing it, we find that the setter method

DEFINITIONS

Accessor method—A method that is used to either modify or retrieve a single attribute.

Getter method—An accessor method that retrieves the value of an attribute.

Setter method—An accessor method that modifies the value of an attribute.

accountNumber: doesn't update branch account numbers properly (it drops the left-most digit). That's because we used 100,000 instead of 1,000,000 to extract **branchAccountNumber**. Although we could directly update the constant there's a much better solution: always use accessor methods for constants.

Use accessor methods to get the value of constants.

accountNumberDivisor
    " Answers the divisor to extract branch ids from account numbers"
    ^ 1000000.

Figure 8.4.
Using accessor methods to get the value of constants.

accountNumber: aNewNumber
    | divisor |
    divisor := self accountNumberDivisor.
    self branchID: (aNewNumber div: divisor).
    self branchAccountNumber: (aNewNumber mod: divisor).

By using accessors for constants in Figure 8.4 we decrease the chance of bugs and at the same time increase the maintainability of our system. When the layout of an account number changes, and we know that it eventually will (users are like that), chances are that our code will be easier to change because we've both hidden and centralized the information needed to build/break up account numbers.

8.2.2.2 Getters for Classes

When you stop to think about it, classes are effectively the global variables of the object world. If you change the name of a class it can force you to update any method in your application that sends a message to it. Furthermore, even if you never change the name of a class you can still be forced to change your code, or to at least subclass methods, whenever you add subclasses.

Let's consider an example. In Figure 8.5 we see how a class diagram evolves over time. We introduce two new classes to support our organization's selling products and services to corporate customers. The basic idea is that residential customers have accounts, whereas corporate customers have corporate accounts. Before the change customer objects would send the **Open** message to the account class to open a new account and the **List** message to it to list all the accounts that the

Figure 8.5.
Adding new
subclasses.

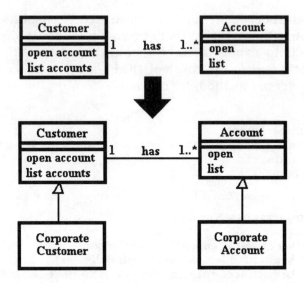

Figure 8.5.
Adding new
subclasses.

customer has. When the **CorporateCustomer** class directly inherits these methods then corporate customer objects would be opening normal accounts and listing the normal accounts they are associated with—this isn't what we want. So what do we do, copy the **open account** method and the **list accounts** method and change the appropriate lines of code to send messages to **CorporateAccount** instead of **Account**? There has to be a better way.

Use getters to provide the classes that you need access to.

The solution to this problem is to create an instance method in the **Customer** and **CorporateCustomer** classes that answers the corresponding account classes. In other words, we need a getter method that provides the class. Smalltalk examples for **Customer** appear in Figure 8.6.

With the code written like this the only method that needs to be changed in **CorporateAccount** is the accessor that provides the corresponding class from the **Account** hierarchy. Taking this approach **CorporateCustomer** can take advantage of the existing business logic inherited from **Customer** with very minimal changes to the code.

8.2.2.3 Getters for Booleans

The way that you write getters for booleans, attributes that have either the value true or false, can affect the robustness of your code.

Methods in Customer
    accountClass
        " Answers back the corresponding account class
          for customers "

        ^ Account.

    openAccount
        " Opens a new account for this customer "

        (self accountClass) openForCustomer: self.

    listOfAccounts
        " Answers back the list of accounts for this cus
          tomer "

        (self accountClass) listAccountsForCustomer: self.

Method in CorporateCustomer
    accountClass
        " Answers back the corresponding account class
          for corporate customers "

        ^ CorporateAccount.

Figure 8.6.
Using getters to
retrieve classes.

Consider the following Smalltalk accessor method in Figure 8.7:

    isPersistent
        " Indicates whether or not this object occurs in
          the database "
        ^ isPersistent.

Figure 8.7.
A getter method
for a boolean.

    This method works fine when the variable **isPersistent** has been initialized, but doesn't when it hasn't been. Chances are very good that the getter methods for booleans are being used in comparisons that assume the getter method returns either true or false. If **isPersistent** hasn't been initialized, then the getter for it answers **nil** and your comparison crashes. Not good. A better solution is presented in Figure 8.8.

Figure 8.8.
A bullet-proof
boolean getter.

isPersistent
    " **Indicates whether or not this object occurs in the database** "
    ^ **isPersistent == true.**

*You can bullet-
proof your
boolean getters
by comparing the
attribute they are
getting to the
value for true.*

By answering back the comparison of the variable **isPersistent** with true, we are guaranteed that the accessor method **isPersistent** always answers back a boolean, true when **isPersistent** is true and false when it is either false or uninitialized. A little extra typing results in bullet-proof code. Not that this approach for booleans is faster than lazy initialization, which is presented below in section 8.2.2.5 because we only do a single comparison (actually an equivalency comparison, which is really fast).

8.2.2.4 Naming Accessors

*Give accessors
the same names
as their corre-
sponding attrib-
utes.*

Common convention in the industry, as we saw in Figure 8.2, is to name accessors after the attributes that they access. For example, the Smalltalk accessors for the attribute **accountNumber** would be **accountNumber:** and **accountNumber**, and the corresponding C++ accessors for **iAccountNumber** would be **iAccountNumber(int iNewAccountNumber)** and **iAccountNumber()**.

The main advantage of this approach is that it is easy to remember and follow, the disadvantage is that when you change the name of the attribute you should also change the name of the corresponding accessors.

8.2.2.5 Lazy Initialization

The real problem is that all variables need to be initialized before they are accessed. There are two lines of thought to initialization: initialize all variables at the time the object is created (the traditional approach) or initialize at the time of first use. The first approach uses special methods that are invoked when the object is first created, called constructors in C++ or initialize methods in Smalltalk. Although this works, it often proves to be error prone. When adding a new variable you can easily forget to update the constructor/initialize method. An alternative approach is called *lazy initialization*, where attributes are initialized by their getter methods, as shown in Figure 8.9.

```
accountBalance
    " Answers back the balance of the account "
    (accountBalance isNil) ifTrue: [
        self accountBalance: 0.00.
    ].
    ^ accountBalance.
```

Figure 8.9.
Using lazy initial-
ization to guaran-
tee the value of
an account bal-
ance is always
set.

This version of **accountBalance** first checks to see if the variable **accountBalance** is uninitialized by sending it the **isNil** message, and if it is we set it to zero. We've added the overhead of checking if a variable is initialized, but we gain in maintainability because we know that variables are always initialized. This is a trade-off that is often worth making, especially for attributes that aren't regularly used and that require lots of memory.

*Lazy initializa-
tion is commonly
used for attri-
butes that aren't
regularly
accessed or that
are very large or
cumbersome to
initialize.*

DEFINITIONS

Constructor—A C++ member function (method) that allocates the memory needed for an instance of a class. Constructors are also used to set the initial value for attributes too.

Initialize method—A Smalltalk method that sets the initial values for attributes. In Smalltalk memory is allocated automatically when objects are instantiated.

Lazy initialization—An approach in which the initial value of attributes is set in their corresponding getter methods.

TIP

Use Lazy Initialization for Objects Currently in Your Database

It is quite common to use lazy initialization for attributes that are actually other objects stored in the database. For example, when you create a new inventory item you don't need to fetch whatever inventory item type from the database that you've set as a default. Instead, use lazy initialization to set this value the first time it is accessed so that you only have to read the inventory item type object from the database when and if you need it.

8.2.2.6 Documenting Accessors

Document your attributes in their corresponding getters.

A really effective approach to documenting an attribute is to put the documentation in the corresponding getter method for it. By setting this as a standard, programmers know where to go to either read or update the documentation for attributes, increasing the chance that the documentation will be kept up to date. My experience is that documentation that is internal to the code has a much greater chance of being maintained by developers than external documentation, so I always favor internal documentation approaches to external.

Whenever lazy initialization is used in a getter you should document why the default value is what it is. If the default value for an account balance is zero add a one-line comment in the code saying why that is. When you do this you take the mystery out of how attributes are used in your code, improving both its maintainability and extensibility.

8.2.2.7 The Advantages of Accessors

Accessors improve the maintainability of your classes in the following ways:

1. **Updating attributes.** You have single points of update for each attribute, making it easier to modify and to test.

2. **Obtaining the values of attributes.** You have complete control over how attributes are accessed and by whom.

3. **Obtaining the values of constants and the names of classes.** By encapsulating the value of constants and of class names in getter methods when those values/names change you only need to update the value in the getter and not every line of code where the constant/name is used.

4. **Bullet-proofing Booleans.** Getters for Booleans can be written in such a way that they always return a boolean.

5. **Initializing attributes.** The use of lazy initialization ensures that attributes are always initialized and that they are initialized only if they are needed.

6. **Reduction of the coupling between a subclass and its superclass(es).** When subclasses access inherited attributes

only through their corresponding accessor methods, it makes it possible to change the implementation of attributes in the superclass without affecting any of its subclasses, effectively reducing coupling between them.

7. **Encapsulating changes to attributes.** If your attributes change you can potentially modify your accessors to provide the same ability as before the change, making it easier for you to respond to the change.

8.3 Writing High-Quality Methods

Just as the way that you work with attributes impacts the quality of your code, the manner in which you write methods affects both the maintainability and extensibility of your code. In this section we will discuss naming conventions for methods, documentation conventions, and several tips and techniques for improving their quality.

8.3.1 Naming Methods

Like attributes, methods should be given full English descriptors that describe what they do. Furthermore, those names should be in the active voice. For example, the name **openAccount** is in the active voice, whereas **accountIsOpened** is in the passive voice. The difference is that in the first name we are indicating what is being done to something and in the second we indicate what was done to it. One really good approach is to start the name of a method with a strong, active verb—open, print, close, erase, activate, start, stop—to ensure that the method name is in the active voice.

Give methods full English names that start with strong, active verbs.

8.3.2 Documenting Methods

Every method should include some sort of header documentation at the top of the source code that documents all of the information that is critical to understanding it. This information includes, but is not limited to the following:

1. **What and why the method does what it does.** Other people who are going to use your code need to know what it does and why it does it. By documenting what it does you make

it easier for others to determine if they can reuse your code. Documenting why it does it you make it easier for other to put your code into context. You also make it easier to determine whether or not a new change should actually be made to a piece of code (perhaps the reason for the new change conflicts with the reason why the code was written in the first place).

2. **What a method must be passed as parameters.** You also need to indicate what parameters, if any, must be passed to the method, how they will be used, and what type of class they are an instance of. This information is needed so that other programmers know how to use your methods.

3. **What a method returns.** You need to document what, if anything, a method returns so that other programmers can use the return value/object appropriately.

4. **How a method changes the object.** If a method changes an object—for example the withdraw method of a bank account modifies the account balance—this needs to be indicated. This information is needed so that other programmers know exactly how a method invocation will affect the object.

5. **Include a history of any code changes.** Whenever a change is made to a method you need to document when the change was made, who made it, why it was made, who requested the change, who tested the change, and when it was tested and approved to be put into production. This history information is critical for the future maintenance programmers who are responsible for modifying and enhancing the code.

6. **Examples of how to invoke the method if appropriate.** One of the easiest ways to determine how a piece of code works it to look at an example, so consider including an example or two of how to invoke the method in its documentation.

7. **Document any assumptions that you've made.** All assumptions that you make when programming a method must be documented. This is important for two reasons: First, it provides a very good indication as to what your method does or doesn't handle. Second, it gives you an opportunity to CYA (cover your a**) in case your assumptions prove to be wrong or if a change in the business or technical environment negates your assumptions.

In addition to documentation at the beginning of a method, documentation is needed throughout the method to make it easier to understand and maintain.

8.3.2.1 Internal Code Documentation and Whitespace

Internal documentation and the use of whitespace is critical for writing maintainable methods. All control structures, such as loops and ifs, as well as any complex sections of code should be documented. Consider the following Smalltalk method in Figure 8.10:

```
withdraw: amount
| fileStream dateTime |
(self balance < amount) ifTrue: [
^ 'Not enough funds in account'.
].
self  balance: (self balance - amount).
dateTime := (Date today) + (Time now).
fileStream := File open: 'c:\L2000.TXT'.
fileStream notNil ifTrue: [
fileStream append: accountNumber.
fileStream append: dateTime.
fileStream append: 'W'.
fileStream append: amount.
fileStream append: Cr.
fileStream close.
].
```

Figure 8.10.
Smalltalk code that is difficult to maintain.

Although this code is fairly short, it isn't immediately obvious what it does or why it does it. Although we could read the code to try to understand it, this process is often time-consuming and error prone. A better version appears in Figure 8.11.

The addition of just a few comments makes this method much easier to understand. We've documented what parameters are passed to the method, what they are, and how they're to be used. We've also documented what the method returns. Throughout the main body of code we've also documented what each section of code does, as well as why we're doing it. Indicating why something is done is significantly more important than what is being done—you can always look at the code and figure out what it's doing, but you often can't figure out why. Therefore you should document any applicable business rules right in the code itself.

```
withdraw: amount
" Debit the provided amount from the account and post a trans
action.

Passed: A positive amount of money ( of class Float).

Answers: The receiver when the withdrawal is successful,
otherwise a string describing the problem encountered."

| fileStream dateTime |

" Don't allow the account to become overdrawn"
(self  balance < amount) ifTrue: [
^ 'Not enough funds in account'.
].

" Debit the account by the amount of the withdrawal  "
self  balance: (self balance - amount).

" Post a transaction so that we have a
  record of this transaction (for statements, ...)"
fileStream := File open: 'c:\L2000.TXT'.
fileStream notNil ifTrue: [
fileStream append: accountNumber.
dateTime := (Date today) + (Time now).
fileStream append: dateTime.
fileStream append: 'W'.        " Changed to uppercase 'W' on Jan
                                 7 1997 by request of Finance"
fileStream append: amount.
fileStream append: Cr.
].
```

*Whitespace
makes your code
easier to under-
stand and
maintain.*

Note how a few blank lines, called *whitespace*, help to make the code more readable. Whitespace makes code more maintainable by breaking it up into small, easy-to-digest sections. Insert whitespace in your code whenever you need to separate out a section of it. Also notice that in Figure 8.11 we put a line between the initial method comments and the definition of the temporary variables to separate out the code from the documentation.

DEFINITION

Whitespace—Blank lines in your code that are used to distinguish between sections.

TIPS

Tips for Creating Effective Documentation

The best way to document code is to write the comments before you write the code. This gives you an opportunity to think about how the code will work before you write it and will ensure that the documentation gets written. Alternatively, you should at least document your code as you write it. Because documentation makes your code easier to understand, you are able to take advantage of this fact while you are developing it. The way I look at it, if you're going to invest the time writing documentation, you should at least get something out of it.

If statements in your code must be executed in a defined order, then you should ensure that this fact gets documented. There's nothing worse than making a simple modification to a piece of code, only to find that it no longer works, then spending hours looking for the problem, only to find that you've gotten things out of order.

8.3.3 Paragraphing Your Code

Another way to improve this method is to paragraph it. Paragraphing refers to the way that code is indented on a page. Code should be indented within both the scope of a method and within the scope of a control structure. After paragraphing, the code in Figure 8.12 is easier to read, and hence easier to maintain.

```
withdraw: amount
      "  Withdraw.... "

      | fileStream dateTime |

      "  Don't allow the account to become overdrawn"
      (self  balance < amount) ifTrue: [
            ^ 'Not enough funds in account'.
      ].

      "  Debit the account by the amount of the withdrawal  "
      self  balance: (self balance - amount).
```

Figure 8.12.
Paragraphing your code makes it easier to understand and maintain.

continued

Figure 8.12.
(continued)

```
"  Post a transaction so that we have a
    record of this transaction (for statements, ...)"
fileStream := File open: 'c:\L2000.TXT'.
(fileStream notNil) ifTrue: [
        fileStream append: accountNumber.
        dateTime := (Date today) + (Time now).
        fileStream append: dateTime.
        fileStream append: 'W'.
        fileStream append: amount.
        fileStream append: Cr.
        fileStream close.
].
```

I have always found that using the tab key and not the space bar is the most effective way to paragraph code. There's less typing to do and your paragraphing will be more consistent (one tab vs. 2/3/4 spaces).

DEFINITION

Paragraphing—The indenting of your code to make it more readable.

TIP

People First, Technology Second

The primary goal of your development efforts should be that it is easy for other people to understand. If nobody else can figure it out, then it isn't any good. Use naming conventions. Document your code. Paragraph it.

8.3.4 Methods Should Always Do Something

Methods should always do something and not pass the buck as in the following Smalltalk code shown in Figure 8.13:

Figure 8.13.
A method that simply passes the buck.

```
display: selectedCustomer
        ^ CustomerDisplay display: selectedCustomer
```

Not only does this method do nothing, it adds to the "spagettiness" of your application. It complicates your program without adding any value. A better solution is to have the original object send a message directly to **CustomerDisplay**, effectively cutting out the middle-man. If you do find yourself in a situation where you need to do this, it does happen, then document why. For example, in Figure 8.13 it is very likely that the **display:** method is invoked when the user double-clicks on an item in a list, indicating they want to see the details of whatever they selected. An appropriate method might be "Display the customer selected from the list by the user."

8.3.5 Methods Should Do One Thing Only

Another issue pertinent to writing maintainable methods is that they should do one thing and one thing only. This is basically a cohesion issue in that methods that do one thing are much easier to understand than methods that do multiple things. For example, our **withdraw:** method does two things: It debits the amount from the account AND it posts a transaction. Even if we didn't need to post transactions in other methods, such as **deposit:**, we'd still be better off from a maintenance point of view by pulling the transaction posting code out of **withdraw:** and putting it into its own method, as we see in Figure 8.4. The act of reorganizing our code, or any of our development efforts, is called *refactoring*.

Methods should do one thing and one thing only.

```
withdraw: amount
        " Withdraw.... "

        | fileStream dateTime |

        " Don't allow the account to become overdrawn"
        (self balance < amount) ifTrue: [
                ^ 'Not enough funds in account'.
        ].

        " Debit the account by the amount of the withdrawal "
        self balance: (self  balance - amount).
```

Figure 8.14.
Refactoring our method so that it does one thing and one thing only.

continued

Figure 8.14.
(continued)

" Post a transaction so that we have a
record of this transaction (for statements, ...)"
" Changed to uppercase 'W' on Jan 7 1997 by request of
Finance"
self postTransaction: 'W' amount: amount.

postTransaction: aTransactionType amount: amount
" Post transactions to a flat-file so that we can maintain
a record of the activities on the bank's accounts. "

```
fileStream := File open: 'c:\L2000.TXT'.
(fileStream notNil) ifTrue: [
        fileStream append: accountNumber.
        dateTime := (Date today) + (Time now).
        fileStream append: dateTime.
        fileStream append: aTransactionType.
        fileStream append: amount.
        fileStream append: Cr.
        fileStream close.
].
```

TIP

Methods That Do One Thing Are Easier to Develop, Test, and Maintain

Methods that do one thing and one thing only are typically shorter and easier to write. Furthermore, they are easier to understand by other programmers and are easier to test because they do only one thing.

DEFINITION

Refactoring—The act of reorganizing OO development efforts. Refactoring will often comprise the renaming of methods, attributes, or classes; the redefinition of methods, attributes, or classes; or the complete rework of methods, attributes, or classes. Your analysis, design, or coding efforts can often be refactored.

8.3.6 Do One Thing per Line

Back in the day of punch cards it made sense to try to get as much functionality as possible on a single line of code, but considering it's been over fifteen years since I've even seen a punch card I think we can safely rethink this approach to writing code. Whenever you attempt to do more than one thing on a single line of code you make it harder to understand. Why do this? We want to make our code easier to understand so that it is easier to maintain and enhance. Just like a method should do one thing and one thing only you should only do one thing on a single line of code, assuming of course you aren't using punch cards.

Do only one thing on each line of code.

8.3.7 The 30-Second Rule

I've always believed that another programmer should be able to look at your method and be able to fully understand what it does, why it does it, and how it does it in less than 30 seconds. If he or she can't, your code is too difficult to maintain and should be improved. Thirty seconds—that's it.

8.3.8 Specify Order of Message Sends

A really easy way to improve the understandability of your code is to use parentheses, also called "round brackets," to specify the exact order of operations. Consider the two lines of Smalltalk source code in Figure 8.15. They both do the exact same thing, yet which one is easier to understand? The second one is because it specifies exactly what order messages will be sent in. I don't have to know the rules of the order of messages (this would be called the order of operations for procedural languages) in Smalltalk to be able to understand the second line of code. It gets the last name via an accessor, then it gets the first name, then it concatenates the two.

Code can be made more understandable by the usage of parentheses to specify the order of message sends.

```
fullName := self lastName concatWithComma: self firstName.

fullName := (self lastName) concatWithComma: (self firstName).
```

Figure 8.15.
Two versions of the same Smalltalk line of code.

Before you say that I broke the "one-thing-per-line rule," I would claim that each line of code only did one thing; put the person's name in lastname-firstname order. I don't count the use of a getter to get the value as an attribute as something that counts as a "thing," although concatenating the two names does.

8.3.9 Polymorphism the Right Way — Avoiding Case Statements

Finally, the misuse (or often lack of use) of polymorphism often leads to difficult to maintain code. Ninety-nine point nine percent (99.9%) of the time this issue manifests itself in the use of case statements[1] that are based on the class of an object. Consider the method in Figure 8.16 for withdrawing money from a bank account:

Figure 8.16.
Nested logicals and case statements based on the type of an object often indicate bad code.

```
withdraw: amount
      " Withdraw ....."

    I type I
    type := self class.           " Answers the class of the receiver "
    (type isKindOf: SavingsAccount) ifTrue: [
          " Some code....."
    ] ifFalse: [
          (type isKindOf: CheckingAccount) ifTrue: [
                " Some code "
          ] ifFalse: [
                " etc.... "
          ].
    ].
```

The problem here is that when we add a new type of account we have to modify this method, along with any others (such as **deposit:**) that also take this strategy. A potential maintenance nightmare. A better approach is to define a **withdraw:** method for each account class (assuming that withdrawing is different for each type of account), and simply send an account object the message **withdraw:** whenever we want to withdraw from it. Simple, elegant, and significantly easier to maintain.

---

[1] In C++ and Java, case statements are implemented via the switch command. In Smalltalk, you have to write the equivalent of cascaded ifs.

8.4 Creating Maintainable Classes

Although the maintainability of your classes is driven mostly by your analysis-and-design efforts there are a few issues that need to be addressed during construction. The first thing that you must do during construction is to allow your class diagram to drive the development of your classes. We saw in chapter 3 that class diagrams are used as input into the coding process, and all I'm saying here is that you need to recognize this during construction. Class diagrams reflect both your analysis-and-design efforts, the two things that you must do before you begin coding.

Analyze it, design it, then program it.

The second thing that you need to do is ensure that your classes are named appropriately. Once again you need to use English descriptors, such as **SavingsAccount** and **InventoryItem**. Class names are nouns 99.9% of the time.

Use full English descriptors for the names of classes.

The third arguement for creating maintainable classes is that if you follow the advice about attributes and methods in the previous sections your classes should be easy to maintain and to enhance already.

TIP

Try to Reuse Existing Classes

Avoid creating new classes whenever you can; instead try to reuse existing classes. Unless you're on the first OO project in your organization, chances are pretty good that some of the classes that you need have already been created for other projects. Look for them and use them on your project. Reuse is the key to success in the object world.

Finally, the *Law of Demeter* provides some very interesting suggestions for making your classes more maintainable.

8.4.1 The Law of Demeter

Demeter was an OO research project in the late 1980s and early 1990s, and out of that project came the Law of Demeter, which suggests restrictions of where objects can send messages in order to make them more maintainable. The Law of Demeter states that objects should only send messages to:

- Themselves

- Their direct or indirect superclasses

- Other objects returned directly from their own methods

- An object passed to them as a parameter to a method

- Their class

The important thing to understand is what an object shouldn't be sending messages to. Objects shouldn't send messages to objects that have been returned by invoking a method in an object other than themselves. This restriction helps to reduce coupling in a system by reducing the knowledge that objects have of each other. Let's consider an example.

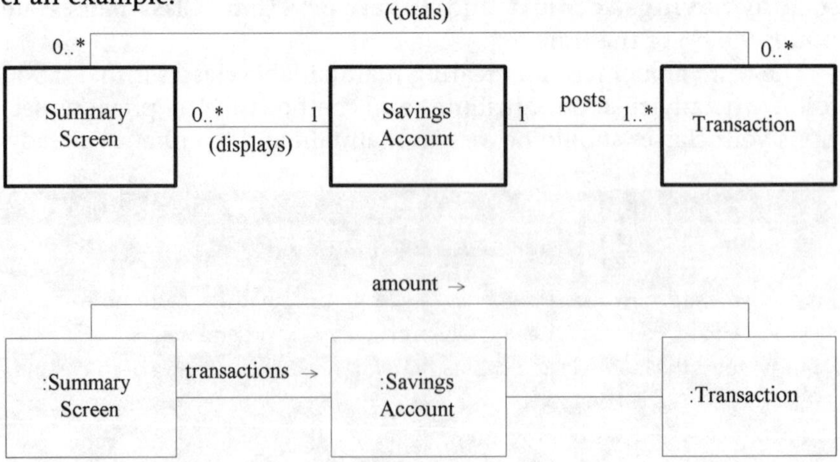

Figure 8.17.
Displaying account information.

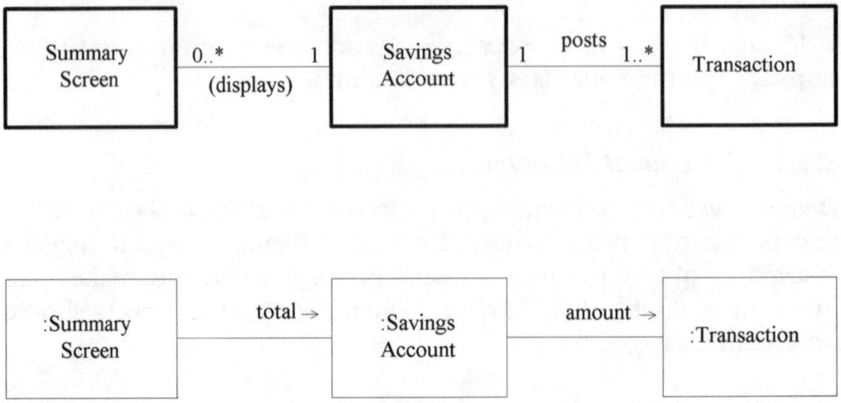

Figure 8.18.
Displaying account information.

In Figures 8.17 and 8.18 we see two approaches for building a summary screen that displays the total of a series of transactions posted to an account. In the first approach the screen object sends a message to an account object requesting the transactions for a given period of time. Once it has them, it then sends messages to each transaction requesting the amount. In the second example the summary screen sends a message to the savings account requesting the total transaction amount for a given period of time, the account then gets the amount of each transaction, adds them up, and passes the result back to the summary screen. Which approach is better?

According to the Law of Demeter, the second approach is better because the summary screen sends a message only to an object that is returned by one of its methods (the savings account would be returned by an accessor method within the screen object), and then this object does the necessary work. The advantage of this approach is that the coupling within the system is minimized. Summary screen objects only need to know that they have to send a single message to a savings account to get the job done, whereas in the first approach it has to know to send a message to an account to get the transactions, then it has to know to send a message to each transaction. Taking the first approach the class **Summary Screen** is coupled to both **Savings Account** and **Transaction**, whereas with the second approach it is only coupled to **Savings Account**.

The Law of Demeter reduces coupling between classes, increasing the maintainability of your application.

8.5   Programming Techniques and Approaches

In this section I would like to quickly share some solutions to common issues that I have used over the years and have found to be quite effective. We'll discuss how to implement instance relationships, how to implement error-handling strategies, and how to implement call-back methods.

8.5.1 Implementing Instance Relationships

Throughout this entire book we've ignored the issue of how to implement the instance relationships that our objects are involved in. We've said that instance relationships are maintained through a combination of attributes and methods, but we haven't said exactly how it's done. Until now.

Figure 8.19.
Implementing
instance relation-
ships.

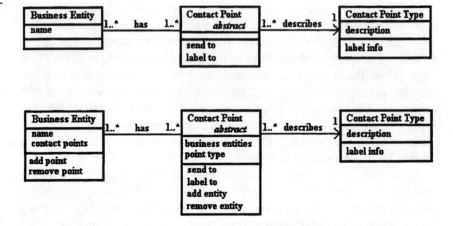

In Figure 8.19 we see two versions of a class diagram: one that takes our "standard" approach of not showing how to implement instance relationships, and a second one that does. Using this as an example, lets discuss how to implement the three types of instance relationships.

1. **Many-to-many relationships.** Many-to-many relationships require the largest amount of work to implement because each object involved in the relationship must maintain a collection of references to the other objects that it is related to. In Figure 8.19 we see that there is a many-to-many relationship between business entities and contact points. The class **Business Entity** has an attribute called **Contact Points**, which is a collection (perhaps implemented as an array or linked list) of instances of the class **Contact Point**. The methods **Add point** and **Remove point**, respectively, add a contact point into the collection or remove a contact point from the collection. In the class **Contact Point** we have the attribute **Business Entities** and **Add entity** and **Remove entity**, which serve the same sort of purpose.

2. **Many-to-one relationships.** Many-to-one relationships can be implemented much more easily. In Figure 8.19 there is a many-to-one relationship between **Contact Point** and **Contact Point Type**. The easy way to maintain this relationship is to have an instance of **Contact Point Type** as an attribute of **Contact Point**. In short, it should be enough that instances of **Contact Point** know what "type" they are. If it

isn't enough, for some reason you need to traverse the relationship between instances of **Contact Point Type** and **Contact Point**, perhaps you want to easily find out what contact points are of what type, then the **Contact Point Type** class would need to maintain a collection of **Contact Point** objects and have corresponding add and delete methods.

3. **One-to-one relationships.** One-to-one relationships are the easiest to maintain as you only need to have an instance attribute in either one or both classes, just as we did for the easy approach for maintaining many-to-one relationships.

As you might have guessed, aggregation relationships are handled the exact same way as instance relationships.

8.5.2 Error Handling

When serious errors (database errors, network errors, run-time code errors) occur during execution of an application what should happen? Should you ignore the problem? Should you display an error message and let the user deal with it? Should you try to deal with it proactively? I'm a firm believer (Ambler, 1997) that when an error occurs in an application then it is the application's responsibility to try to deal with that error as best it can. In Figure 8.20 we see an error-handling approach that does just that.

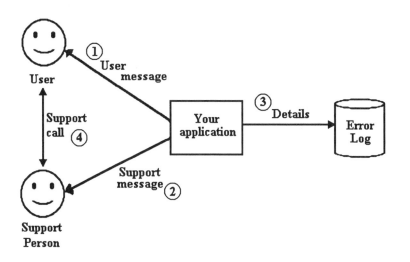

Figure 8.20.
Error-handling process overview.

1. **Display the error message.** An error message will be displayed on the user's screen in language that the user can understand. Messages like "Error NCC1701—Dylithium quantifier" aren't sufficient. However, something like "The dylithium quantifier in engineering is not responding and will be automatically recalibrated in the next 20 seconds. If this error persists please call support at x1234" is much more informative. Good error messages provide an indication of what is wrong, what needs to be done to address the problem, and whether or not the appropriate support person has been informed (if not, then the support phone number will be included in the message).

2. **Display the message on the support person's screen.** For all errors requiring a support person to deal with them an informative message should be immediately displayed on the appropriate person's screen. This message will include the name of the user, his or her extension, the application he or she is using, the screen he or she is on, and the description of the error message.

3. **Record the error into the log.** The details of an error should be recorded in an error log. This will allow you to hunt down and fix errors more effectively and perform statistical analysis of response times, and so on.

4. **The support person helps the user if need be.** If the support person needs more information to deal with the problem then he or she can quickly phone the user while that person is still dealing with the problem. (I've seen situations where a support person calls a user while they are still reading the message on the screen.) Alternatively, if the user needs more help then he or she can call support. The really neat thing about this approach is that the system informs both parties how to contact the other one by including the phone numbers in the messages.

You can easily support your users in a proactive and timely manner.

There are several advantages to this approach to handling errors. First, it is fairly simple to implement. Second, it allows you to support your users proactively and in a timely manner, as support people can get involved in solving a problem while it is occurring, without forc-

---

TIPS

Tips for Error Handling

You'll need to maintain configuration information about whom to send support messages to, or at least to what terminal they need to be sent.

You also want to ensure that the error transactions aren't lost so that you have an accurate record of what happened. The problem is that it can be really hard to write out to the error log when the database is down. This implies that you have to be prepared to write error transactions out to an alternative source—perhaps into a temporary file on your user's computer.

You'll want to eventually distinguish between types of errors, because the support person does not need to be informed of all of them. For example, if the database goes down when a hundred users are online, the support person only needs to have only one message box displayed on their system, not one hundred.

You may want to allow the support people to input a common message that would automatically be displayed when an error occurs. For example, if the database is down and the support people know that it will be available in a few minutes, they should be able to type this into the system so that this information is included in the error message displayed to the users.

---

ing people to seek out help. Third, by posting error messages you are in a position to analyze both what is wrong with your system and how well your support people deal with those problems.

8.5.3 Callback Methods and Message Dispatchers

Although it is very easy to say that objects work together by sending each other messages, it isn't always that easy to get the message to the right object. Consider the following scenario: an inventory-item object realizes that its stock levels are running low so it needs to reorder itself by sending a message to the appropriate supplier object. The supplier object in turn passes the order onto the real-world supplier via an EDI (electronic data interchange) transaction message. To ensure that everything works out properly, it needs to have a message sent back to it once the actual order has been placed (because orders can take several days to process, the inventory item object can't afford to sit around and wait for a return value). How do we implement this?

One way to solve this problem is to use what is called a *callback method*. The basic idea is that when the inventory item sends the order message to the supplier object it also includes a parameter indicating what message to send it once the order was made. The method that is invoked in response to this message is a callback method. In Figure 8.21 we see that inventory-item objects send the **order** message to supplier objects, one of the parameters of that message is the fact that the supplier object should send back the **reorder complete** message once the order has been made, even if it is days later. The advantage of this approach is that instances of **Supplier** don't need to know what message to send back to objects that send it messages, it only needs to be told what message to send back. This helps to reduce coupling between **Supplier** objects and the objects that send it messages.

Callback methods help to reduce the coupling between classes.

Figure 8.21.
An example of a callback method.

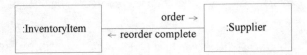

Now let's consider what happens at the supplier. Assuming the supplier also has an OO system, when the order comes in (via EDI) it needs to have that order routed to the right object to handle it. To implement this, we use a *message-dispatcher* object which passes the order message to the appropriate stock object. In Figure 8.22 we see how this would be modeled.

Figure 8.22.
A message-dispatcher object passes a message onto the appropriate object.

DEFINITIONS

Callback method—When object A communicates with object B, it may request that at some time in the future object B send it message C whenever a certain event happens (such as a process ending). The method that responds to message C is termed a callback method.

continued

> ### DEFINITIONS
>
> *continued*
>
> *Message dispatcher*—An object that exists solely to pass messages onto other objects. Objects will often register themselves with a message dispatcher to inform it of what events they are interested in being informed about.

8.6 Organizing Construction Around the Class-Type Architecture

Although we covered this material in chapter 3 it's definitely worth repeating again. In Figure 8.23 we see the four main layers of our class-type architecture: interface classes that make up the screens and reports of your application, business classes that model the business domain, persistence classes that provide access to permanent storage, and system classes that provide access to operating system features. Because each layer is different there are different skills required to develop classes in each layer.

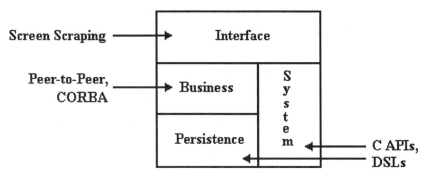

Figure 8.23.
The class-type architecture.

The development skills needed vary with each layer:

Interface classes—Analysis skills such as prototyping, use-case scenario development, and interface flow diagramming, are critical to the successful development of interface classes. User interface design skills are of the utmost importance when developing interface classes, skills that we cover in chapter 9.

Business classes—Analysis-and-design skills such as CRC (class responsibility collaborator) modeling, class diagramming, and process modeling, are the skills most needed to develop business classes. Programming skills are also important, but rank second when compared to analysis-and-design skills. We covered these skills in *The Object Primer* (Ambler, 1995) and in chapter 2.

Persistence classes—Design-and-programming skills are of the most importance here, as well as a thorough understanding of database concepts (which we cover in chapter 10).

System classes—Design-and-programming skills are important for developing system classes, and an understanding of wrapping is also important, a topic that we will cover in chapter 11.

The important lesson to learn here is that there is more to developing systems than programming. Although I truly believe that programming is one of the most exciting career fields to be in, I also believe that development is even more exciting. Take any opportunity that you get to expand your development horizons.

8.7 What We've Learned

Good programmers realize that there is more to development than programming. Great programmers realize that there is more to development than development.

In this chapter we detailed numerous techniques for improving the quality, maintainability, and extensibility of your code. We covered approaches to developing solutions to common problems, such as error handling and implementing relationships, and we described several categories of OO developments. We ended by reiterating the different development skill sets needed for each layer of our class-type architecture. The chart contains a summary of the tips and techniques that we learned in this chapter.

OO-DEVELOPMENT TIPS AND TECHNIQUES

General Guidelines:

- Good developers understand the entire development process
- Good developers develop with maintenance in mind, not development

continued

OO-DEVELOPMENT TIPS AND TECHNIQUES

General Guidelines (continued):

- Decisions that speed up the development process often harm you during maintenance
- Decisions that improve the maintainability of your system can often increase the time that it originally takes you to develop it
- The time invested in design pays off in spades during programming
- Your development efforts should be easy for other people to understand
- Analyze it, design it, then program it
- Support your users in a proactive and timely manner

Guidelines for Attributes:

- Pick a naming convention and stick to it
- An attribute name should describe what it does and/or how it is used
- Use mixed-case to distinguish words in an attribute name
- Avoid abbreviations, although if you must have them, then at least define a standard set of them
- Don't directly access attributes; instead, use accessor (getter and setter) methods
- Document your attributes in their corresponding getters

Guidelines for Methods:

- Give methods full English names that start with strong, active verbs
- Internal documentation in methods increases their maintainability; you should document:
  — what and why the method does what it does
  — what a method must be passed as parameters
  — what a method returns
  — how a method changes the object
  — a history of any code changes
  — examples of how to invoke the method, if appropriate
  — any assumptions that you've made

continued

OO-DEVELOPMENT TIPS AND TECHNIQUES

Guidelines for Methods (continued):

- The best way to document code is to write the comments before you write the code
- Whitespace makes your code easier to understand and maintain
- Paragraphing your code makes it easier to understand and maintain
- Use the tab key to paragraph code, not the space key
- Methods should do one thing and one thing only
- Methods that do one thing are easier to develop, test, and maintain
- Do only one thing on each line of code
- It should be possible to look at a method and understand it in less than 30 seconds
- Nested logicals and case statements based on the type of an object often indicate bad code

Guidelines for Accessors:

- Give accessors the same names as their corresponding attributes
- Use getter methods to get the value of constants
- Use getters to provide the classes that you need to access to
- Bullet-proof your boolean getters by comparing the attribute they are getting to the value for true
- Use lazy initialization for attributes that aren't regularly accessed or that are very large or cumbersome to initialize
- Use lazy initialization for attributes that are currently objects stored in your persistence mechanism

Guidelines for Classes:

- Use full English descriptors for the names of classes
- The Law of Demeter reduces coupling between classes
- According to the Law of Demeter, objects should only send messages to:

continued

OO-DEVELOPMENT TIPS AND TECHNIQUES

Guidelines for Classes (continued):

— themselves

— their direct or indirect superclasses

— other objects returned directly from their own methods

— an object passed to them as a parameter to a method

— their class

References

Ambler, S. (1995). *The Object Primer: The Application Developer's Guide to Object Orientation.* New York: SIGS Books.

Ambler, S. (Feb. 1997). *Handling Object-Oriented Errors: Software Development 5(2).* San Francisco: Miller Freeman.

McConnell, S. (1993). *Code Complete: A Practical Handbook of Software Construction.* Redmond, WA: Microsoft Press.

Suggested Readings

Meyer, B. (1988). *Object-Oriented Software Construction.* London: Prentice Hall International.

Page-Jones, M. (1995). *What Every Programmer Needs to Know About Object-Oriented Design.* New York: Dorset House.

Skublics, S., Klimas, E.J., & Thomas, D.A. (1996). *Smalltalk with Style.* Englewood Cliffs, NJ: Prentice-Hall.

Users work with real-world objects to perform their jobs. Shouldn't they work with objects in their computer systems too?

Chapter 9

Making Your Applications Usable — Object-Oriented User Interface Design

What We'll Learn in This Chapter

What are object-oriented user interfaces (OOUIs)?

How are OOUIs different from non-OOUIs and how are they the same?

How do you design effective OOUIs?

How do you prototype OOUIs?

Object-oriented applications should have object-oriented user interfaces. Although this statement sounds obvious, the fact of the matter is that very few systems built using OO technology actually have an OOUI. To create effective OOUIs we need to understand what they are. We also need to understand some of the fundamentals of user-interface design and the fundamentals of prototyping. Designing an object-oriented user interface isn't hard, but it is hard to design one that is easy to use.

For most people the user interface is the system.

Designing user interfaces that are easy to use and to understand is a skill, and designing *object-oriented user interfaces* is no different. For the vast majority of people the user interface is the system. Not the database. Not the program code.

You can reduce the overall cost of your application by investing the time to make its user interface easy to use.

Interface design is important for several reasons. First of all, the more intuitive the user interface the easier it is to use, and the easier it is to use the cheaper it is. The better the user interface the easier it is to train people to use it, reducing your training costs. The better your user interface the less help people will need to use it, reducing your support costs. The better your user interface the more your users will like to use it, increasing their satisfaction with the work that you have done.

Applications that are difficult to use won't be used.

The point to be made is that the user interface of an application will often make or break it. Although the functionality that an application provides to users is important, the way in which it provides that functionality is just as important. An application that is difficult to use won't be used. Period. It won't matter how technically superior your software is or what functionality it provides, if your users don't like it they simply won't use it. Don't underestimate the value of user interface design.

9.1 What Are Object-Oriented User Interfaces?

What are the features that make one interface object oriented (OO) but another one not OO? We need to understand the answer to this question before we can understand how to develop effective OOUIs. There are three important factors (Collins, 1995) that make a user interface object oriented:

1. Users perceive and act on interface objects

2. Users can classify interface objects based on how they behave

3. In the context of what users are trying to do, all the interface objects fit together into a coherent overall representation.

The first factor says that users should see the interface objects (objects displayed in the user interface of a system) that they are working with on the screen and they should be able to work with those objects. For example, a shipping application would allow us to work with the packages that we need to ship as well as the vehicles that we use to ship the products. Perhaps we should be able to *drag and drop* packages onto the vehicles to load them (dragging and dropping is a technique in which you use a pointing device, typically a mouse, to select an object on the screen and then move it on top of another screen object).

Users can work with objects on the screen in a manner similar to how they use the corresponding real-world objects.

The second factor implies that users should be able to identify similar objects by what they do and how they do it. Perhaps in our shipping example users see boat objects, truck objects, and airplane objects on the screen. They should be able to drag and drop packages onto any one of them so that the package can be scheduled on that vehicle appropriately. When the user double-clicks (with the mouse the user selects the same object twice in rapid succession) on any of the vehicle objects the appropriate detail screen should be displayed. Double-clicking on an airplane would display the arrival and departure datetimes, as well as the cities the airplane is arriving/departing in/from and a manifest showing the packages for each leg of the journey. Double-clicking on a truck would show the deliveries that it will make for that day. Or perhaps for both of these objects double-clicking on them would display an appropriate map showing each destination they will be making deliveries to and the route that each vehicle will take. Double-clicking on each destination would reveal the manifest of what is to be delivered there. The point to be made is that users should be able to work with all type of vehicles in a manner that is consistent to the way that they operate in the real world.

Users should be able to identify and classify objects by how the objects behave.

The third factor implies that the context in which an object is being used should define the behavior that it will exhibit. In our shipping application, when we double-click on a truck it's delivery route should be displayed. Assuming that our shipping company maintains their vehicles, what should happen when we double-click on the same truck in the garage part of our application? We don't want to see a delivery schedule, instead we probably would want to see a list of the work to be done on the truck, the status of the work, and an estimate of when the truck will be back on the road. In short, depending on the context of the situation an object will react differently.

Users expect objects to do the right thing depending on the context of the situation.

Is this enough? Well...I would add two more requirements of an object-oriented interface: Interface objects are inheritable and interface objects are polymorphic. Because inheritance is one of the fundamental concepts of OO it makes sense that it should be possible for one interface object to inherit from another. For example, it would be reasonable that the class **Truck** inherits from the class **Vehicle**. Furthermore, we should be able to replace interface objects with other interface objects. Perhaps one type of truck is used by your shipping warehouse on the East Coast but when we open up a second warehouse on the West Coast we decide to use another type of truck. We shouldn't have to change our application for the new warehouse, the only thing that we need to do is replace the Truck class, probably via inheritance, so that the trucks at the new warehouse do the right thing.

DEFINITIONS

Object-oriented user interface—A style of user interface in which users directly interact with objects using the computer, just as they work with them in the real world.

Interface object—An object displayed as part of the user interface for an application. This includes widgets such as buttons and list boxes, icons, screens, and reports.

Drag and drop—A technique in which a person uses a pointing device (typically a mouse) to select an object on the screen and then uses the mouse to move the object on top of another screen object.

9.1.1 An OO Bank Teller Application

To get a feel for what an OOUI might look like, let's consider the user interface for a teller application for our banking case study. In Figure 9.1 we see a straightforward design of a teller application that was programmed using Smalltalk. It has menus based on the main objects that tellers work with and even has the ABC company logo and slogan on the screen. It looks nice, but is it object oriented? No. Where are the objects? Sure we have menu items that eventually lead us to customers and accounts but I don't SEE any customers or accounts. We can do a lot better than this.

In Figure 9.2 we see an object-oriented version of our application. Notice how we now have icons representing the classes that bank tellers interact with, accounts and customers, as well as stacks of deposit slips, withdrawal slips, and transfer slips. All of the real-world objects that tellers normally use to do their job appear on their screen.

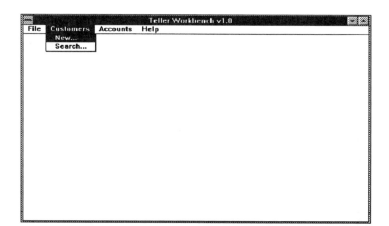

Figure 9.1.
A standard graphical-user-interface desktop for a bank teller application.

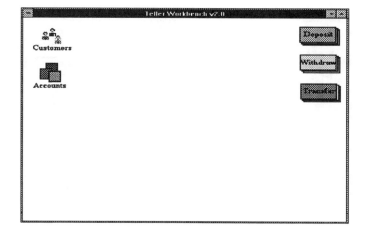

Figure 9.2.
An object-oriented version of the application.

Tellers interact with the objects on the screen in one of two ways—either they double-click on them or they peel objects off of them. By peeling a customer off the Customers icon users will be presented with a "Add-a-New-Customer Screen" or by double-clicking on the Customers icon users will be taken to the customer-search screen shown in Figure 9.3.

Users input their search criteria into the editing fields on the screen in Figure 9.3 and then press the search button to list their results in the field below. From that list they are able to select one or more customers and drag and drop them onto their workspace so that they can work with them. Alternatively, they could just double-click on the customer

Figure 9.3.
Double-clicking
on the customers
icon leads to a
search screen.

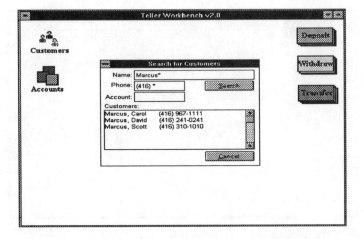

Figure 9.4.
Several customer
objects have been
dragged onto the
teller workspace.

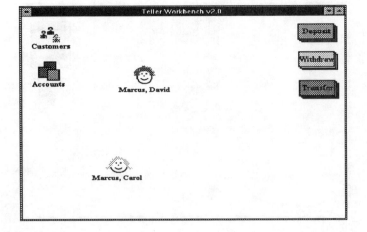

*Users should be
able to look at
an object on the
screen and
immediately
know what it is
and, if appropri-
ate, know its cur-
rent status.*

they want to work with directly from this list. In Figure 9.4 we see what
the screen looks like when we select several customers from the customer search screen, and in Figure 9.5 we see the customer-edit screen
that we reach whenever we double-click on a customer object.

Notice how in Figure 9.4 the names of the customers are displayed
for each customer icon so that we can distinguish between them. The
basic concept is that users should be able to look at an object on a
screen and know what it is, and potentially even know its current status. For account objects we might want to display their type (savings,
checking, ...), their account number, and their current balance. With

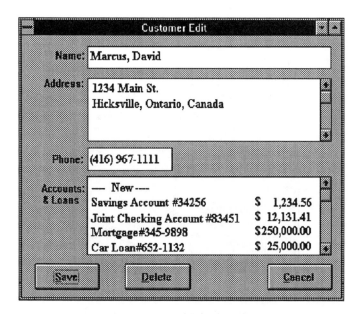

Figure 9.5.
Double-clicking
on an individual
customer leads to
an editing screen.

this information a bank teller could know immediately what can be
done with an account, perhaps there isn't enough money to allow the
customer to make the withdrawal from one account but in another
account there is.

Notice that on the customer-edit screen there is a list of accounts that
the customer has. Just as you can drag customer objects onto the workspace from a list of customers you should also be able to drag account
objects from a list of accounts onto the workspace. This exemplifies an
important characteristic of good user interfaces—they're consistent. We
discuss issues like consistency in greater detail in section 9.2.2.

*Consistency is
critical for devel-
oping a good
user interface.*

What should happen when we peel off an object from the stack of
deposit slips? We could display a deposit editing screen like the one
shown in Figure 9.6 that would allow us to input the deposit to be
made, but before we develop this screen we should first ask ourselves if
this is the best approach. We know what deposit slips look like in the
real world, so why don't we design our deposit-edit screen to look like
one? Figure 9.7 shows such a deposit slip edit screen.

Although tellers should be able to input the account number and the
customer number into the deposit slip edit screen if they like, there
should be an easier way. We have the account objects on the screen, as
well as the customer objects. Perhaps if we allow the teller to drag and

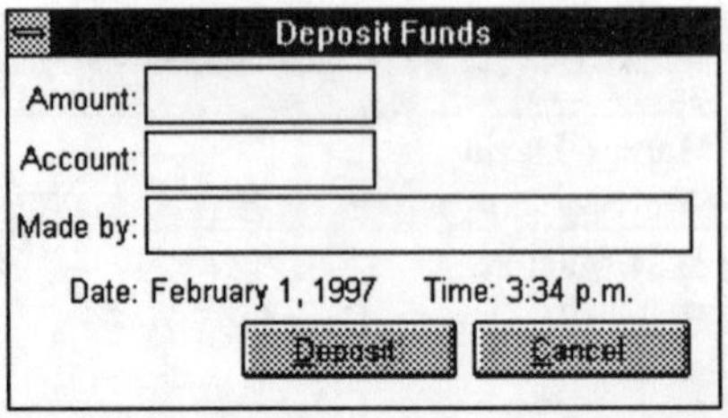

Figure 9.6.
A standard GUI
screen for
inputting
customer
deposits.

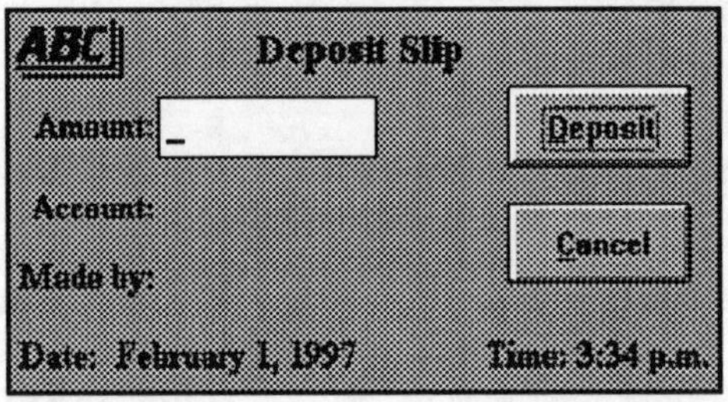

Figure 9.7.
An object-ori-
ented approach
for inputting
customer
deposits.

*Make it easy for
your users to
work with
objects.*

drop an account onto the deposit slip the proper account number would be automatically put onto the slip and if the deposit slip was dragged on top of an account object the same thing should happen. Deposit slips and customers would interact in the same manner. Furthermore, to maintain consistency within your application the same sort of things should happen for withdrawal and transfer slips as well.

9.1.2 Why OOUIs Are Different but the Same

The main difference between an object-oriented user interface and a standard graphical user interface is the fact that in a GUI the user works with windows and widgets to manipulate business objects, whereas with an OOUI users work with visual representations of those business objects.

*OOUIs are an
extension of
GUIs.*

In many respects OOUI is simply an improvement on GUI. OOUIs still use all of the components that make up GUIs—windows, menus, and widgets—but use them in such a way that users are able to work directly with business objects. In short, the distinction between an OOUI and a GUI is the way in which people use them.

> ### SCOTT'S SOAPBOX
>
> *Your User Interface Isn't Object-Oriented Just Because...*
>
> First, you don't have an OOUI just because it's a GUI. OOUIs might use many of the same components as GUIs, but never forget that it is the way in which your users interact with the interface that defines whether or not it is object-oriented. Second, you don't have an OOUI just because you used an OO development language. You can use languages like Smalltalk and ObjectCOBOL to develop both OO and non-OO interfaces. Third, you don't have an OO just because you used graphics or multimedia features in interesting ways. OOUIs are all about how people interact with business objects, not about how slick you've made the interface look.

9.2 Designing Effective User Interfaces

Before we can discuss how to build object-oriented user interfaces we must first understand how to design effective user interfaces. Because good interface designers understand the basics of *human factors*, the study of how humans interact with machines, we'll begin by covering some of its fundamentals. We'll then review a collection of tips and techniques that will help you to improve the user interfaces that you design.

9.2.1 Human Factors, the Study of People Using Machines

Human factors reveals many implications for how to design effective user interfaces. By understanding the basics of how people work with computers you will gain important insights for designing the interface of your applications. In this section we will discuss two fundamental issues in human factors—mental models and metaphors.

9.2.1.1 Mental Models

A *mental model* is an internal representation of a person's conceptualization and understanding of a system (Mayhew, 1992). In other words, it is the way that a person looks at the world. It is important to understand the mental models of your users so that you can develop user interfaces that users can comprehend and work with. Furthermore, you want to help users form accurate mental models of the way that an application works so that they can understand it and work with it effectively.

Consistency helps people to build accurate mental models.

Consistency in an application is critical for helping users to form an accurate mental model. For example, if a help screen is displayed every time the user presses the **F1** key then your users will very quickly build into their mental model that if they need more information all they need to do is press **F1**. On the other hand, if they have to do different things on different screens to get help information—perhaps **F1** works in some places, but **F2** in others, perhaps on some screens there's a Help button, whereas on others it's a Tips button, and perhaps on some screens help isn't available at all—then your users will have a very difficult time learning how to get the help information that they need. Perhaps the only thing that they will add to their mental model is that it's too much effort trying to find information

SCOTT'S SOAPBOX

User Interface Standards Are a Must

You want to ensure consistency among the applications developed in-house, preferably one that is recognized as an industry standard. For some reason people don't like interface standards—they think that standards somehow stifle their creativity. Pure hogwash. User-interface standards define how widgets such as menus, buttons, entry fields, and lists should look and feel. They also provide suggestions for how and when they should be used. In other words user-interface standards tell you how to work with the basic building blocks of user interfaces.

Consider the analogy of physical construction: the building you work in is made out of standard components, standard building blocks, such as 2x4s, plates of glass, concrete, and various pipes and wires: all standard materials that you can purchase at your local building-supply store. The building next to yours is also built from the same materials, as is the one beside it. Although all of these buildings are made from standard components they are all different, having different styles and architectures.

Just like architects can use standard components to design unique buildings, developers can use standard widgets to build unique applications. Don't waste your time being creative at the level of menu items and entry fields; instead invest it and be creative at the level of applications. Your users would rather have an application that is easy to use and meets their needs instead of a really neat button.

online, and therefore they should just phone the support desk whenever they need help. A very expensive and unfortunately very common problem in many organizations.

9.2.1.2 Metaphors

Another way to do this is to use a familiar metaphor in the design of your application's user interface. A *metaphor* is a set of concepts, terms, and objects that the user is familiar with that are used in the design of a user interface to make it easier to understand and use. For example, in Figure 9.8 we see a very common metaphor used by many of today's popular operating systems called the "desktop metaphor." The basic idea is that because computers are now replacing many of the tools formerly used by business people—file folders to store paper information, phone books to look up phone numbers, schedulers to keep track of appointments, and waste paper baskets to throw out unwanted objects—then your computer system should look like the tools that it is replacing. This will make you system easier to understand and to learn by anyone who is already familiar with the real-world tools that it is replacing.

Let's do another example. In Figure 9.9 we see a "card catalog" metaphor for searching for books in a library. Physical card catalogs are quickly being replaced by computer systems that are easier to maintain and that provide greater search functionality. The problem is that library patrons aren't willing to take a training course on how to use the system; instead, they need something they can walk up to and use immediately. Because they already know how to use a card catalog it makes a perfect metaphor for the computer system that is replacing it. The basic idea is that users would first open one of the drawers to search by author, title, or subject. Doing this an open drawer would be dis-

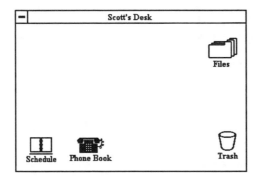

Figure 9.8.
A desktop metaphor.

Figure 9.9.
A library catalog
metaphor.

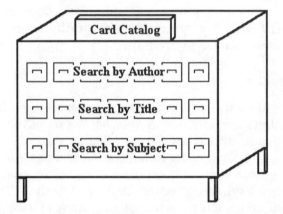

played, perhaps with tabs for each letter of the alphabet displayed. The user would then select a tab and be shown another series of tabs of the authors, titles, ... beginning with that letter. They would then select the appropriate tab again and be shown the books that match their selection. Very similar to a card catalog in the real world.

Choosing effective metaphors can be difficult. One problem that you face is that you probably can't pick a metaphor that everyone recognizes. In our library example people who have been to a library before will immediately recognize a card catalog (Figure 9.9). But what about people who have never seen a card catalog? Furthermore, a related problem that you also run into is the difficulty that people might not recognize the metaphor that you are using in the future. Business people of today might recognize a schedule book, but as they are replaced by electronic organizers, the validity of the schedule book being part of the desktop metaphor will slowly erode.

*It is quite diffi-
cult to choose
an effective
metaphor that
will stand the
test of time.*

DEFINITIONS

Human factors—The study of how people interact with machines.

Mental model—An internal representation of a person's conceptualization and understanding of a system.

Metaphor—A set of concepts, terms, and objects that the user is familiar with that are used in the design of a user interface to make it easier to understand and use.

9.2.2 Enough User Interface Design Tips to Sink a Ship, and Then Some

In this section we will cover a series of user interface design tips that will help you to improve the object-oriented interfaces that you create.

1. **Consistency, Consistency, Consistency.** The most important thing that you can possibly do is make sure that your user interface works consistently. If you can double-click on items in one list and have something happen then you should be able to double-click on items in any other list and have the same sort of thing happen. Put your buttons in consistent places on all of your windows, use the same wording in labels and messages, and use a consistent color scheme throughout. Consistency in your user interface allows your users to build an accurate mental model of the way that it works, and accurate mental models lead to lower training and support costs.

2. **Set standards and stick to them.** The only way that you'll be able to ensure consistency within your application is to set design standards and then stick to them. The best approach is to adopt an industry standard and then fill any missing guidelines that are specific to your needs. Industry standards, such as the ones set by IBM (1993) and Microsoft (1995), will often define 95–99% of what you need. By adopting industry standards you not only take advantage of the work of others you also increase the chance that your application will look and feel like other applications that your users purchase or have built.

   Set organization-wide standards and stick to them.

3. **Explain the rules.** Your users need to know how to work with the application that you built for them. When an application works consistently it means you only have to explain the rules once. This is a lot easier than explaining in detail exactly how to use each and every feature in an application step by step.

4. **Support both novices and experts.** Although our library-catalog metaphor might be appropriate for casual users of the system, library patrons, it probably isn't all that effective for expert users, librarians. Librarians are highly trained people

who are able to use complex search systems to find information in the library, therefore you should consider building a set of search screens just for them.

5. **Navigation between screens is important.** If it is difficult to get from one screen to another then your users will quickly become frustrated and give up. When the flow between screens matches the flow of the work that the user is trying to accomplish, then your application will make sense to your users. Because different users work in different ways, your system will need to be flexible enough to support their various approaches.

6. **Navigation within a screen is important.** In Western societies people read left to right and top to bottom. Because people are used to this should you design screens that are also organized left to right and top to bottom. You want to organize navigation between widgets on your screen in a manner that users will find familiar to them.

7. **Word your messages and labels appropriately**. The text that you display on your screens is a primary source of information for your users. If your text is worded poorly then your interface will be perceived poorly by your users. Using full English words and sentences, as opposed to abbreviations and codes makes your text easier to understand. Your messages should be worded positively, imply that the user is in control, and provide insight into how to use the application properly. For example, which message do you find more appealing "You have input the wrong information" or "An account number should be 8 digits in length." Furthermore, your messages should be worded consistently and displayed in a consistent place on the screen. Although the messages "The person's first name must be input" and "An account number should be input" are separately worded well, together they are inconsistent. In light of the first message, a better wording of the second message would be "The account number must be input" to make the two messages consistent.

8. **Understand your widgets.** You should use the right widget for the right task, helping to increase the consistency in

your application and probably making it easier to build the application in the first place. The only way that you can learn how to use widgets properly is to read and understand the user-interface standards and guidelines that your organization has adopted.

9. **Look at other applications with a grain of salt.** Unless you know that another application has been verified to follow the user-interface standards and guidelines of your organization, you mustn't assume that the application is doing things right. Although it is always a good idea to look at the work of others to get ideas, until you know how to distinguish between good user-interface design and bad user-interface design you have to be careful. Too many developers make the mistake of imitating the user interface of another application that was poorly designed.

Don't assume that the user interfaces of other applications are designed well.

10. **Use color appropriately.** Color should be used sparingly in your applications, and if you do use it you must also use a secondary indicator. The problem is that some of your users may be color blind and if you are using color to highlight something on a screen then you need to do something else to make it stand out if you want these people to notice it. You also want to use colors in your application consistently so that you have a common look and feel throughout your application.

11. **Follow the contrast rule.** If you are going to use color in your application you need to ensure that your screens are still readable. The best way to do this is to follow the contrast rule: use dark text on light backgrounds and light text on dark backgrounds. It's very easy to read blue text on a white background but very difficult to read blue text on a red background. The problem is there isn't enough contrast between blue and red to make it easy to read, whereas there is a lot of contrast between blue and white.

12. **Use fonts appropriately.** Old English fonts might look good on the covers of Shakespeare's plays, but they are really hard to read on a screen. Use fonts that are easy to read, such as serif fonts like Times Roman. Furthermore, use your fonts consistently and sparingly. A screen using two or three fonts effec-

tively looks a lot better than a screen that uses five or six. Never forget that you are using a different font every time you change the size, style (bold, italics, underlining, ...), typeface, or color.

13. **Gray things out, don't remove them.** You often find that it isn't applicable to give your users access to all the functionality of an application at certain times. You need to select an object before you can delete it, so to reinforce your mental model the application should do something with the delete button and/or menu item. Should the button be removed or grayed out? Gray it out, never remove it. By graying things out when they shouldn't be used people can start building an accurate mental model as to how your application works. If you simply remove a widget or menu item instead of graying it out, then it is much more difficult for your users to build an accurate mental model because they only know what is currently available to them, and not what isn't available. The old adage that "out of sight is out of mind" is directly applicable here. If it's out of mind, then it's out of your mental model.

14. **Use non-destructive default buttons.** It is quite common to define a default button on every screen, the button that gets invoked if the user presses the Return/Enter key. The problem is that sometimes people will accidentally hit the Enter/Return key when they don't mean to, consequently invoking the default button. Your default button shouldn't be something that is potentially destructive, such as delete or save (perhaps your user really didn't want to save the object at that moment).

15. **Alignment of fields.** When a screen has more than one editing field you want to organize the fields in a way that is both visually appealing and efficient. As shown in Figure 9.10, I have always found that the best way to do so is to left-justify edit fields, or in other words make the left-hand side of each edit field line up in a straight line, one over the other. The corresponding labels should be right justified and placed immediately beside the field. This is a clean and efficient way to organize the fields on a screen.

16. **Justify data appropriately.** For columns of data it is common practice to right justify integers, decimal align floating point numbers, and left justify strings.

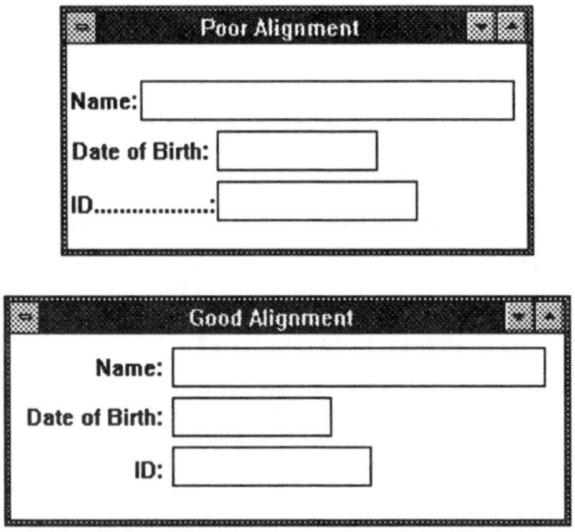

Figure 9.10.
Alignment of
fields is critical.

17. **Don't create busy screens.** Crowded screens are difficult to understand and hence are difficult to use. Experimental results (Mayhew, 1992) show that the overall density of the screen should not exceed 40%, whereas local density within groupings shouldn't exceed 62%.

18. **Group things on the screen effectively.** Items that are logically connected should be grouped together on the screen to communicate that they are connected, whereas items that have nothing to do with each other should be separated. You can use whitespace between collections of items to group them and/or you can put boxes around them to accomplish the same thing.

19. **Open windows in the center of the action.** When your user double-clicks on an object to display its edit/detail screen then his or her attention is on that spot. Therefore it makes sense to open the window in that spot, not somewhere else.

20. **Pop-up menus shouldn't be the only source of functionality.** Your users can't learn how to use your application if you hide major functionality from them. One of the most frustrating practices of developers is to misuse pop-up, also called context-sensitive, menus. Typically there is a way to use the mouse on your computer to display a hidden pop-up menu that provides access to functionality that is specific to the area of the screen that you are currently working in.

9.3 Developing Effective Object-Oriented User Interfaces

In this section we are going to discuss several factors that are important to the successful development of object-oriented user interfaces. We'll begin by arguing that the concept of an application might no longer be valid in the object world and that objects are what we are really developing now. We'll then follow with a discussion of what you need to do to design interface objects successfully, and then we'll cover how to prototype OOUIs.

9.3.1 Applications Are No More, Just Objects

In the structured world an application is a program, or collection of programs, that provides a coherent set of functionality for its users. In the object world we don't have programs, we have objects. An application, if you want to call it that, is defined as a collection of classes that work together to provide a coherent set of functionality for its users.

Whenever a single class changes it potentially impacts several "applications."

The question that I pose to you is: do we really need applications any more? To answer this question, consider the class **Customer**. Because many applications work with customer objects the **Customer** class needs to be included in each of these applications. The problem with this approach is that when we make a change to **Customer** we need to release new versions of any application that includes this class. This seems to be a lot of unnecessary work, especially when the changes are small. Wouldn't it be easier to just release the **Customer** class instead of all the "applications" that include it?

New functionality should be released in small clusters of business objects and their corresponding interface classes, avoiding the need to release entire applications when only a few classes have changed.

What we really need is an environment into which we can add new versions of classes, or even new classes, in such a way as to not require us to release a new application. When we consider our class-type architecture from chapter 3 we quickly realize that whenever we change a business class such as **Customer** we will probably need to change its corresponding interface classes as well. For example, in Figure 9.11 we see that there are three interface classes associated with the business class **Truck**. The point to be made is that the changes to **Truck** are localized to itself and to its interface classes, so that when we do make modifications to the class **Truck** all we really want to release are these classes and not every class that makes up the applications that include **Truck**.

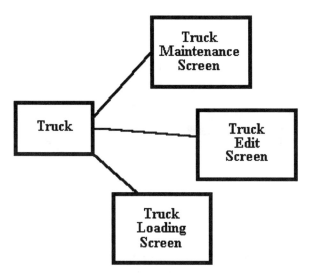

Figure 9.11.
The business class
Truck and its
corresponding
interface classes.

If we are going to be able to release clusters of business classes and their corresponding interface classes, then we need environments that can accept and integrate them into the existing "application." One approach is to have an OO desktop environment that has the ability to accept new clusters, integrate them into the existing functionality, and then allow the user to work with them. In Figure 9.12 we see the basic architecture of such an environment, a Desktop object that contains clusters of business objects and interface objects, which together provide the functionality that we formerly would have considered to be an application.

There are several advantages to this approach. First, we are now able to release only the classes that change and not be forced to release entire applications, allowing us to deliver new functionality to our users quicker. Second, it is now easier to deliver configured environments that include only the classes that users need to do their work. Although there are always similarities between the responsibilities of users, it is also quite common to find that people have their own unique set of needs and as a result need their own unique application. The desktop approach allows us to deliver on this need by providing access to only the classes that each specific user needs. For example, if one user needs to work with customer and account objects, then they will be released the customer and account clusters. If another user works only with customers, then they will only be released the customer cluster.

The desktop approach allows us to release functionality quicker and to configure functionality to the specific needs of our users.

Figure 9.12.
"Applications"
are really just
collections of
interacting
business objects
and their
corresponding
interface objects.

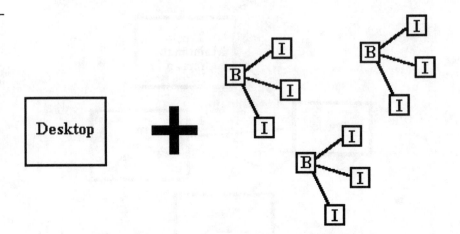

In a lot of ways the concept of Java applets discussed in chapter 8 is a simplified form of what I'm talking about here. I fully expect that Java will evolve into this sort of an approach and, I hope, something even better. It is difficult to do this with other OO languages, although I have managed it with one version of Smalltalk applications quite successfully. The secret to doing it in Smalltalk is that you need to be able to release your application packager/compiler along with your application's image so that you can repackage any new classes or versions of classes that you are sent. With C++ applications you should be able to release dynamic-link libraries (DLLs), library (LIB) files, or your environment's equivalents to do the same thing.

It's still an application-centric world, but we can look forward to that ending someday soon.

Although the desktop concept is easier said than done, as OO development environments evolve over the next few years we'll start to see a move away from application thinking to desktop thinking. Until then I'm afraid that we are still in an application-centric world, so I'll continue to use the word "application" throughout this book to remain consistent with the environments that we are all currently working in.

9.3.2 You're Working with Objects Too, Not Just Windows

The desktop provides users access to the objects that they need to do their job.

In an object-oriented "application" you need to define a desktop, also known as a application or home screen, from which the user works. In Figure 9.2 we saw the design of an object-oriented desktop for our bank teller application. On the desktop the objects that the user works with are displayed, both the objects that they are currently working with as well as other objects that they might need later. For example, we had accounts, customers, and transaction slips.

When designing an OOUI it is important that the objects that users work with on the screen actually look, feel, and behave just like they do in the real world. Bank tellers work with customers, accounts, and deposit slips in the real world, therefore these are the kinds of objects that they should work with on the computer screen. Shippers work with trucks, planes, and boats to schedule shipments, therefore that's what they should work with on the computer screen. All of these interface objects.should provide the (pertinent) functionality of their real-world counterparts.

Interface objects should look, feel, and behave just like the real-world objects that they represent.

TIP

Get Someone Who Can Draw

You want to use pictures, icons, and visual designs that look like the real-world things that they represent. Truck objects should look like trucks. Deposit-slip objects should look like deposit slips. This means that if you want to develop a truly object-oriented user interface you'll need to have access to people with the artistic talent to draw the pictures that you need. Perhaps you have these skills, but I certainly don't.

9.3.3 Modeling Object-Oriented User Interfaces

A really good question that OO professionals have debated for years is—should interface classes be shown on your class diagrams? In my first book, *The Object Primer* (Ambler, 1995), I showed interface classes in several of my class diagrams. The reason why I did this was because I wanted to explain several OO concepts that are best described by using interface classes and because I wanted to show that there is more to OO than just working with business classes. I don't typically show interface classes on class diagrams, however, because there are other diagrams that are better suited for interface classes, namely interface-flow diagrams which we discussed in chapter 2. Interface-flow diagrams show the relationship between interface objects, and when combined with documented prototypes for each interface object provide an excellent model of the user interface for your system.

The combination of interface-flow diagrams and prototypes is very useful for modeling interface classes.

Figure 9.13.
The iterative steps
of prototyping.

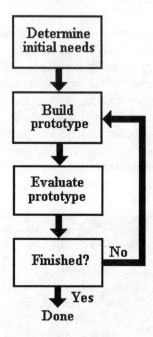

9.3.4 Prototyping Object-Oriented User Interfaces

Prototyping is an iterative analysis technique in which users are actively involved in the mocking-up of screens and reports. The purpose of a prototype is to show people the possible design(s) for the user interface of an application. As we see in Figure 9.13, there are four steps to the prototyping process:

1. **Determine the needs of your users.** The requirements of your users drive the development of your prototype as they define the business objects that your system must support. You can gather these requirements in interviews, in CRC (class responsibility collaborator) modeling sessions, in use-case modeling sessions, and in class diagramming sessions. Refer to chapter 2 for an overview of the various object-oriented analysis-and-design techniques that can be used to gather requirements.

2. **Build the prototype.** Using a prototyping tool or high-level language you develop the screens and reports needed by your users. The best advice during this stage of the process is

to not invest a lot of time in making the code "good" because chances are high that you may just scrap your coding efforts anyway after evaluating the prototype.

3. **Evaluate the prototype.** After a version of the prototype is built it needs to be evaluated. The main goal is that you need to verify that the prototype meets the needs of your users. I've always found that you need to address three basic issues during evaluation: what's good about the prototype, what's bad about the prototype, and what's missing from the prototype. After evaluating the prototype you'll find that you'll need to scrap parts, modify parts, and even add brand-new parts.

4. **Determine if you're finished yet.** You want to stop the prototyping process when you find the evaluation process is no longer generating any new requirements, or is generating a small number of not-so-important requirements.

DEFINITION

Prototyping—An iterative analysis technique in which users are actively involved in the mocking up of the user interface for an application.

TIP

Your Prototype Must Be Doable

Never prototype something that you can't build. If you know that your application will be implemented with a text interface, perhaps on a mainframe, don't build a prototype with a graphical user interface. If you can't build it, or at least won't be able to build it, then don't show it to your users. It isn't fair to build up their expectations, nor is it easy to explain later on why they won't be getting what you showed them.

9.3.4.1 Documenting Prototypes

Prototypes need to be documented so that the developers who are going to build the actual application being prototyped know what is needed. One approach is that every high-level interface object, typically screens and reports, be described exactly as it is to be used. The

Figure 9.14.
An object-
oriented
approach for
inputting
customer
deposits.

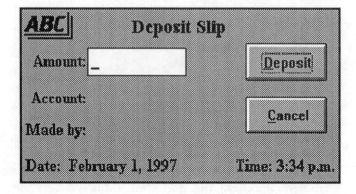

means you need a sentence or two describing its purpose, an indication of other interface objects that it interacts with, and a sentence or
two describing each component of the interface object.

Let's consider an example. In Figure 9.14 we have our deposit slip
interface object, and in Table 9.1 we have an example of how to document it.

T I P

Document Interface Objects Only Once They're Stable

During the prototyping process it will quickly become obvious which interface
objects (screens, reports, etc.) you've "got" and which ones you don't. Once
you understand an interface object and are reasonably assured that it won't
change much, if at all, then you document it. If the interface object is likely to
undergo more changes, then you shouldn't invest any time documenting it
because much of the stuff that you are documenting might be discarded, the
documentation included.

9.3.4.2 Prototyping Tips and Techniques

We've covered the fundamentals of the prototyping process, so now
let's discuss several tips and techniques that you can use to create
truly world-class OO prototypes.

1. **Look for real-world objects.** OOUIs allow users to work
   with the real-world objects they are used to. Therefore you

---

Table 9.1. DOCUMENTATION FOR THE DEPOSIT SLIP INTERFACE OBJECT

DEPOSIT SLIP

Purpose: Allows tellers to deposit funds into customer accounts.

Interacts With:

Customers—Customers can be dropped onto deposit slips and deposit slips can be dropped onto customers.

Accounts—Accounts can be dropped onto deposit slips and deposit slips can be dropped onto accounts.

Components:

Amount field—The amount of the deposit, to be filled in manually by the teller. Allows only positive numbers with up to two digits after the decimal point, displayed in the currency format of the country the application is being run in.

Account field—The account into which the deposit is being made. The teller will either drag and drop an account onto the deposit slip or drag and drop the slip onto the account.

Made by field—The customer making the account. The teller either will drag and drop a customer onto the deposit slip or will drag and drop the slip onto the customer.

Date field—Auto-filled by the application to the current date.

Time field—Auto-filled by the application to the current time.

Deposit button—Makes the deposit, posting the appropriate transaction, and updates the balance in the account. Before making the deposit it checks to see that a customer and an account have been indicated, as well as ensures that a positive, non-zero amount is being deposited. The deposit slip is "shrunk" into an icon and placed on the teller application desktop along with any other transactions made for this customer.

Cancel button—Closes the deposit slip without making the actual deposit. The deposit slip is not added to the desktop as an icon.

---

should start by looking for these kinds of objects and identify how people interact with them.

2. **Work with the real users.** The best people to get involved in prototyping are the ones who will actually use the application when it's done. These are the people who have the most to gain from a successful implementation, and these are the ones who know their own needs best.

3. **Set a schedule and stick to it.** By putting a schedule in place for when you will get together with your users to evaluate the prototype, you set their expectations and you force yourself to actually get the work done. A win–win situation.

4. **Use a prototyping tool.** Invest the money in a prototyping tool that allows you to put screens together quickly. Because you probably won't want to keep the prototype code that you write, code that's written quickly is rarely worth keeping, you shouldn't be too concerned if your prototyping tool generates a different type of code than what you intend to develop in.

5. **Get the users to work with the prototype.** Just like you want to take a car for a test drive before you buy it your users should be able to take an application for a test drive before it is developed. Furthermore, by working with the prototype hands-on they will quickly be able to determine whether or not the system will meet their needs. A good approach is to ask them to work through some use-case scenarios using the prototype as if it is the real system.

6. **Understand the underlying business.** You need to understand the underlying business before you can develop a prototype that will support it. Perform interviews with key users, read internal documentation of how the business runs, and read documentation about how some of your competitors operate. The more you know about the business the more likely it is that you'll be able to build a prototype that supports it.

7. **There are different levels of prototype.** I like to successively develop three different types of prototypes of a system: A hand-drawn prototype that shows its basic/rough functionality, an electronic prototype that shows the screens but not the data that will be displayed on them, and then finally the

screens with data. By starting out simple in the beginning I avoid investing a lot of time in work that will most likely be thrown away. By successively increasing the complexity of the prototype as it gets closer to the final solution, my users get a better and better idea of how the application will actually work, providing the opportunity to provide greater and greater insight into improving it.

8. **Don't spend a lot of time making the code good.** At the beginning of the prototyping process you will throw away a lot of your work as you learn more about the business. Therefore it doesn't make sense to invest a lot of effort in code that you probably aren't going to keep anyway.

9.4   What We've Learned

In this chapter we discovered what it means for a user interface to be truly object-oriented: you users work directly with objects on the screen exactly as they would in the real world. We also discussed how to build successful object-oriented user interfaces (OOUIs), and a summary of the numerous design tips and techniques that we covered is summarized in the chart below.

USER INTERFACE DESIGN TIPS AND TECHNIQUES

Mental models and metaphors

- Understand the mental models of your users.

- Be consistent in your applications as this reinforces the development of accurate mental models.

- Use a familiar metaphor to help users build accurate mental models.

- Pick a metaphor that will stand the test of time.

General guidelines

- Be consistent in a user interface, it's critical.

- Set user interface standards and stick to them.

continued

USER INTERFACE DESIGN TIPS AND TECHNIQUES

continued

- Choose industry standards so as to increase the chance that your applications will look and feel like other applications developed external to your organization.

- Explain the rules of how your application works to your users. If it's consistent, then the rules should be simple and few in number.

- Support both novices and experts.

- Word text consistently, positively, and in full English.

- Look at other applications with a grain of salt because not everyone understands good user interface design.

- Display the objects that your users need to do their jobs on the desktop.

- Think in terms of clusters of business objects and their corresponding interface objects, not in terms of applications.

- Interface objects should look, feel, and behave exactly like the real-world objects that they represent.

Screen design

- Navigation between screens and on screens are both important.

- Understand your widgets so that you know how to apply them properly.

- Use color sparingly and always have a secondary indicator.

- Follow the contrast rule—put dark text on light backgrounds and light text on dark backgrounds.

- Use fonts sparingly and consistently.

- When items are unavailable gray them out; don't remove them if you want your users to form accurate mental models.

- Use non-destructive default buttons.

continued

USER INTERFACE DESIGN TIPS AND TECHNIQUES

continued

- Left justify edit fields and right justify their labels.

- Right justify integers, decimal-align floating point numbers, and left justify strings.

- Don't create busy/crowded screens.

- Use group boxes and whitespace to group logically related items on the screen.

- Open windows in the center of the action.

- Pop-up menus shouldn't be the only source of functionality.

Prototyping

- The requirements of your users drive the development of your prototype.

- During evaluation ask: What's good about the prototype, what's bad about the prototype, and what's missing from the prototype?

- Stop the prototyping process when you find the evaluation process is generating few or no new requirements.

- Look for real-world objects and identify how users work with them.

- Work with the people who will use the application when it's done.

- Set a prototyping schedule and stick to it.

- Use a prototyping tool.

- Get the users to work with the prototype, to take it for a test drive.

- Understand the underlying business.

- Don't invest a lot of time in something that you'll probably throw away.

- Document interface objects once they have stabilized.

continued

**USER INTERFACE DESIGN TIPS
AND TECHNIQUES**

continued

- For each interface object that makes up a prototype, document
    - Its purpose and usage
    - An indication of the other interface objects it interacts with
    - The purpose and usage of each of its components

References

Ambler, S. (1995). *The Object Primer: The Application Developer's Guide to Object Orientation.* New York: SIGS Books.

Collins, D. (1995.) *Designing Object-Oriented User Interfaces.* Redwood, CA: Benjamin/Cummings.

IBM (1993). *Systems Application Architecture: Common User Access Guide to User Interface Design.* IBM Corporation.

Mayhew, D.J. (1992). *Principles and Guidelines in Software User Interface Design.* Englewood Cliffs, NJ: Prentice Hall.

Microsoft (1995). *The Windows Interface Guidelines for Software Design.* Redmond, WA: Microsoft Press.

Suggested Readings

Laurel, B., Ed. (1990). *The Art of Human–Computer Interface Design.* Reading, MA: Addison-Wesley.

Weinschenk, S., & Yeo, S.C. (1995). *Guidelines for Enterprise-Wide GUI Design.* New York: Wiley.

> *Persistence is a virtue.*

Chapter 10

Making Your Objects Persistent — Object-Orientation and Databases

What We'll Learn in This Chapter

Why your persistence strategy is important for successful application development.

What terminology is commonly used with respect to persistence.

How to map objects to flat files.

How to map objects to relational databases, concentrating on several critical topics: the impedance mismatch; mapping objects to tables; implementing object relationships; inheritance mapping strategies; and mapping success factors.

How to use object-oriented databases and object/relational databases as your persistence mechanism.

Persistence deals with the issue of how one ensures that the objects that he or she works with last, or persist, between invocations of object-oriented applications. In other words, persistence addresses one's strategy for saving objects to permanent storage. There are four common mechanisms used to store objects:

flat files, relational databases, object-oriented databases, and object/relational
databases. Although you may have heard that mapping objects into a relational
database is a nightmare, and it can be if you make a mistake, we'll see in this
chapter that using relational databases to store your objects
is a very viable approach to persistence.

The vast majority of business objects must be persistent, or in other words they need to be saved to permanent storage so that you can work with them in the future. Fortunately or unfortunately depending on your point of view, we have several mechanisms that we can use to make our objects persistent: flat files, relational databases, object-oriented databases, and object/relational databases. We will cover each of these mechanisms in detail, discussing the issues for how to use them to make your objects persistent.

10.1 Getting Started — Some Common Terminology

Before we can discuss the issues involved with making objects persistent, we must first ensure that we have a common base of terminology.

COMMON PERSISTENCE TERMINOLOGY

Persistence—The issue of how to store objects to permanent storage. Objects need to be persistent if they are to be available to you and/or to others the next time your application is run.

Persistence mechanism—The permanent storage facility used to make objects persistent. Examples include relational databases, object databases, flat files, and object/relational databases.

Persistence layer—The collection of classes that provide business objects the ability to be persistent. The persistence layer effectively wraps your persistence mechanism.

Object identifiers (OIDs)—A unique identifier assigned to objects—typically a large integer number. OIDs are the object-oriented equivalent of keys in the relational world.

continued

COMMON PERSISTENCE TERMINOLOGY

continued

Database proxies—An object that represents a business object stored in a database. To every other object in the system the database proxy appears to be the object that it represents. When other objects send the proxy a message, it immediately fetches the object from the database and replaces itself with the fetched object, passing the message onto it. See the Proxy pattern in chapter 4 for more details.

CRUD—Acronym for create, retrieve, update, delete. The basic functionality that a persistence mechanism must support.

OOCRUD—Object-oriented CRUD

Reading into memory—When you obtain an object from the persistence mechanism but don't intend to update it

Retrieving into memory—When you obtain an object from the persistence mechanism and will potentially update it

Transaction—A transaction is a single unit of work performed in a persistence mechanism. A transaction may be one or more updates to a persistence mechanism, one or more reads, one or more deletes, or any combination thereof

Concurrency—The issues involved with allowing multiple people simultaneous access to your persistence mechanism

Lock—An indication that a table, record, class, object, ... is reserved so that work can be accomplished on the item being locked. A lock is established, the work is done, and the lock is removed

Read lock—A type of lock indicating that a table, record, class, object, ... is currently being read by someone else. Other people may also obtain read locks on the item, but no one may obtain a write lock until all read locks are cleared

Write lock—A type of lock indicating that a table, record, class, object, ... is currently being written to by someone else. No one may obtain either a read or a write lock until this lock is cleared

Pessimistic locking—An approach to concurrency in which an item is locked for the entire time that it is in memory. For example, when a customer object is edited a lock is placed on the object in the persistence mechanism, the ob-

continued

COMMON PERSISTENCE TERMINOLOGY

continued

ject is brought into memory and edited, and then eventually the object is written back to the persistence mechanism and the object is unlocked. This approach guarantees that an item won't be updated in the persistence mechanism while the item is in memory, but at the same time it disallows others to work with it while someone else does.

Optimistic locking—An approach to concurrency in which an item is locked only for the time that it is accessed in the persistence mechanism. For example, if a customer object is edited, a lock is placed on it in the persistence mechanism for the time that it takes to read it in memory, and then it is immediately removed. The object is edited and then when it needs to be saved it is locked again, written out, then unlocked. This approach allows many people to work with an object simultaneously, but also presents the opportunity for people to overwrite the work of others (we'll discuss this later).

SQL—Structured Query Language, a standard mechanism used to CRUD records in a relational database

SQL3—The latest version of SQL that includes extensions that support object-oriented concepts

SQL statement—A piece of SQL code

Key—One or more columns in a relational data table that when combined, form a unique identifier for each record in the table

Associative table—A table in a relational database that is used to maintain a relationship between two or more other tables. Associative tables are typically used to resolve many-to-many relationships

ODMG—Object Database Management Group, a consortium of most of the ODBMS vendors who together set standards for object databases

OQL—Object Query Language, a standard proposed by the ODMG for the selection of objects. This is basically SQL with object-oriented extensions that provide the ability to work with classes and objects instead of tables and records

Object adapter—A mechanism that both converts objects to records that can be written to a persistence mechanism and converts records back into objects

continued

> ### COMMON PERSISTENCE TERMINOLOGY
>
> *continued*
>
> again. Object adapters can also be used to convert between objects and flat-file records
>
> ***Data dictionary***—A repository of information about the layout of a database, the layout of a flat file, the layout of a class, and any mappings among the three.

10.2 Saving Your Objects into Flat Files

A common approach to making objects persistent is to save them into a *flat file*. A flat file is a single file that is used to store information—a text file, a word-processing file, or an image file. For our purposes, we'll use flat files to store objects that can be read/written sequentially one object at a time. For example, when a user exits from an application we might want to write out all of the objects in the system to a text file, allowing us to read them the next time we work with the application.

Flat files are a valid option for making objects persistent.

Although you might be quick to dismiss flat files when you are building an MIS (management information system) application, you should think again. It is quite common to use flat files to store configuration objects, to write transaction objects out to a log file, to generate files so that you can share objects with other systems, or simply to generate an e-mail message that you send to someone as part of a workflow application. The point to be made is that flat files are a valid alternative for use as your persistence mechanism.

10.2.1 An Approach to Mapping Objects to Flat Files

What we're going to concentrate on is a strategy for writing and reading a series of objects into a flat file. The strategy that we will discuss can be used for transaction logs, for configuration files, and for creating summary files of objects so that they can be shared with other,

> ### DEFINITIONS
>
> ***Flat file***—A single data file in which information is stored.
>
> ***MIS***—Management information system.

typically non-OO applications. It is my experience that this strategy covers about 90% of what you'll use flat files for. The other 10% typically requires custom coding, such as saving a spreadsheet to a file or sending an e-mail. My experience is that if you can do the generic stuff you can also do the custom stuff.

The first thing that you need to do is come up with a layout for the flat file. The typical strategy is to have one object per line in the file with the attributes of the object starting and ending at a specific position, or column, in the file. For example, a customer object could be stored in a flat file by having the person's name in the columns 1 to 40, his or her date of birth in columns 41 to 48, and the customer's phone number in columns 49 through 59.

You start by determining a layout for your flat file.

Once you've created your file layout you need to decide how you're going to implement reading and writing your objects to it. If your only requirement is to write a single class of objects to a single file then you had might as well just write the specific code for that class and that file. If, however, you need to create several files you'll want to use a data dictionary.

In Figure 10.1 we see an approach that uses a data dictionary to provide the mapping information needed to read and write objects into flat files. On a per-attribute basis the information stored in the data dictionary would include:

Data dictionaries can be used to provide the information for mapping objects into flat files.

- the name of the attribute

- the name of the class that it is part of

- the file name that it maps into (if you need to support more than one file)

- the start position/column in the file

- the end position/column in the file

- the type of the attribute (string, number, date, float, ...)

- any necessary formatting information

Based on the information contained in the data dictionary, it should be simple to create a **Flat File Map** class that can read and write objects into flat files. A class diagram to do this is presented in Figure 10.2. The class **Flat File Map** provides the basic file I/O functionality, whereas **Mapped Attribute** encapsulates the information stored in the data dictionary.

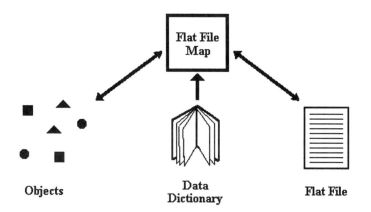

Figure 10.1.
A data dictionary
is used to define
the mapping
between objects
and the flat file.

Objects   Data
Dictionary   Flat File

The biggest design decision will be how **Flat File Map** reads and writes objects: does it read/write sequentially or can it perform random access in the file and treat it like a database? Sequential access is straightforward and can typically be handled by the **FileStream** classes that should come included with your development language. Random access implies that you need some sort of strategy for determining where in the file the object should be read from/written to. Random access also implies that you should be able to easily delete from the file as well (with sequential access you simply don't write the object out again if you want to delete it).

Random access into a flat file requires a lot more work than sequential access.

The short story is that although flat files are often used to store objects, it is much more common to use relational databases to make objects persistent for most MIS applications.

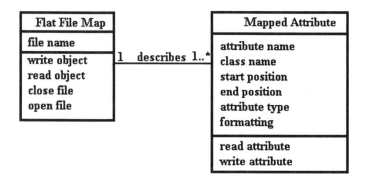

Figure 10.2.
A class diagram
showing the
design for
mapping objects
to flat files.

10.3 The Current Reality — Relational Technology and OO Applications

Although we'll see that object-oriented database management systems (OODBMSs) are designed specifically for OO applications, you can still store objects (well, at least the attributes of an object) in a relational database. Please note that there is more to storing objects in a relational database than just saving the values of their attributes. You must also store enough information to maintain the relationships that each object is involved with, including both object relationships and aggregation relationships. To further complicate the issue, the OO feature of inheritance throws in a few interesting complications that must be addressed. Who said life was easy?

REASONS FOR USING RELATIONAL DATABASES

Reasons for Using Relational Databases to Store Objects

All of these reasons may not be valid for you, or perhaps all of them are. Anyway, below is a list of the common reasons for using relational technology with OO:

- You have a large investment in relational technology

- Your legacy data is an asset that your organization doesn't want to risk

- There isn't an OO database available <u>yet</u> that meets the needs of your application

- Your application is very transaction-intensive

- Relational databases are a proven technology that you can trust

- Most OO applications can be supported by relational technology and yours is one of them

- People understand relational databases, so it's one less thing for them to learn when moving to OO

- Non-OO applications may need to access your data

The fact is that relational databases are what's being used by the vast majority of OO developers to store objects. The reason is simple—relational databases are a mature technology that works. OO databases, on the other hand, are technically sexy but unfortunately they often lack the features required to support mission-critical applications. Although this won't be true forever, the current reality is that many OO developers are forced to use relational databases to store objects.

Many OO developers use relational databases to store their objects.

In this section we will discuss issues such as the following:

- Normalization, of both relational databases and object-oriented designs

- How to overcome the object/relational impedance mismatch

- How to map objects into a relational database

- How to build a persistence layer that uses relational databases as the persistence mechanism

- The myths of mapping objects to relational databases.

DANGER, WILL ROBINSON, DANGER!

I need to warn you that in this section we'll be looking at both class diagrams and data models. The bad news is that the notation for class diagrams is very similar to the notation for data models, so watch out!

10.3.1 Normalization

Just like a class diagram shows the design of an OO system, a data model shows the design of a relational database. In this section we will discuss both data normalization and class normalization, techniques that improve the design of data models and class diagrams, respectively.

DEFINITION

Data model—A diagram used to communicate the design of a (typically relational) database. Data models are often referred to as entity-relationship (ER) diagrams.

Figure 10.3.
The data entity
Student.

Student
<u>Student number</u>
Name
Address
Phone number
! Seminar ID
! Seminar location
! Seminar start date
! Seminar end date
! Seminar time
! Professor ID
! Professor name
! Course name
! Course number

10.3.1.1 Data Normalization

Data normalization is a process by which you organize the data within a relational database in such a way as to reduce and even eliminate data redundancy. Although there are five levels of data normalization (1NF through 5NF), the first three are the ones that are most commonly used and hence will be what we concentrate on here. The first three levels of normalization are as follows:

1. First normal form (1NF)

2. Second normal form (2NF)

3. Third normal form (3NF)

10.3.1.1.1 First Normal Form (1NF)

To put data entities into 1NF you remove repeating groups of data.

A data entity is in *first normal form (1NF)* when it contains no repeating groups of data. A database is in 1NF when all of its data entities are in 1NF. For example, in Figure 10.3 we see that there are several repeating fields (indicated by an exclamation point) in the data entity **Student**. These fields are used to record the fact that students take several seminars. Although the first version of student could work, perhaps we would have 20 sets of the repeating fields, in which case it

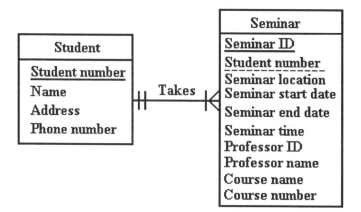

Figure 10.4.
The data entity
Student in 1NF.

wouldn't work very well. What happens when a student takes more than 20 seminars? Do you create a second student record for them? What about the students who only take one or two seminars? Do we really want to waste all that storage space in the database for the 18 sets of empty seminar fields? I don't think so.

Figure 10.4 shows how to put **Student** into 1NF by removing the repeating group and creating a new student called **Seminar**. The advantage of this approach is that we have a seminar record for each seminar that a student takes, no more, no less. This saves space in the database if a student only takes one or two courses while at the same time providing the flexibility to allow students to take as many seminars as they'd like. To maintain the relationship between **Seminar** and **Student** we introduce the *foreign key* **Student number**, which is indicated by a dashed underline. A foreign key is an attribute(s) of a data entity that makes up a primary key of another entity.

10.3.1.1.2 Second Normal Form (2NF)

A data entity is in *second normal form (2NF)* when it is in 1NF and when every non-key attribute, any attribute that is not part of the primary key, is fully dependent on the primary key. A database is in 2NF when all of its data entities are in 2NF. For example, consider the data entity **Seminar** in Figure 10.4—**Course name** isn't dependent on the complete key of **Seminar**. To identify the name of a course we should only have to know the course number and not the **Seminar ID** as well (if a course is taught 5 times in one term there is one seminar record for

To put data entities into 2NF you make sure that all non-key attributes depend on the complete key.

Figure 10.5.
The data entity
Seminar in 2NF.

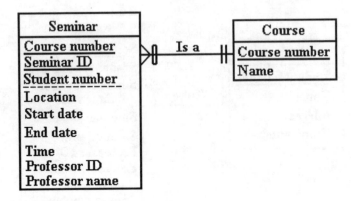

each, with seminar ids 1, 2, ...). Because we don't want to store the
name of a course in five places (what would happen if we change the
name of the course?), we introduce in Figure 10.5 the new data entity
Course, which maintains the name of a course and is keyed on the
attribute **Course number**.

10.3.1.1.3 Third Normal Form (3NF)

*To put data enti-
ties into 3NF you
ensure that all
attributes direct-
ly depend on the
key.*

A data entity is in *third normal form (3NF)* when it is in 2NF and when
all of its attributes are directly dependent on the primary key. A database is in 3NF when all of its data entities are in 3NF. For example, consider **Seminar** in Figure 10.5—the attribute **Professor name** isn't
directly dependent on the combination of **Course number** and
Seminar ID, instead it is directly dependent on **Professor ID**. To
resolve this issue we create a new data entity called **Professor**, shown
in Figure 10.6, which maintains the name of professors. The advantage

Figure 10.6.
The data entity
Seminar in 3NF.

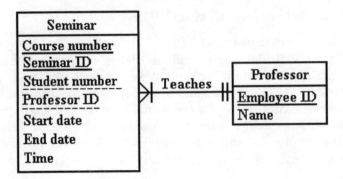

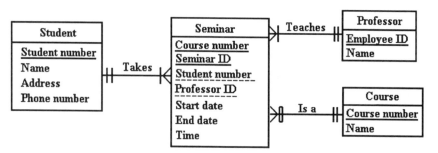

Figure 10.7.
The complete data model in third normal form.

of this is that the name of a professor is stored in one place only, when the name changes we only need to change it in one place.

10.3.1.1.4 Normalization in a Nutshell

Figure 10.7 summarizes the resulting data model after normalizing **Student**. Notice how key information, like the name of a course, is stored only once. This means that we only have one record to update if the name changes, and that the name will be changed consistently throughout the database.

TIP

How to Remember the Rules of 3NF

To remember the first three rules of data normalization you only need to remember the following saying: a database is in third normal form when every attribute depends on the key, the whole key, and nothing but the key, so help me Codd.

10.3.1.2 Class Normalization

In many ways data normalization deals with both the coupling between data entities and the cohesion of data entities. Because data normalization addresses two issues that are important to us in object-oriented design, it seems reasonable that we should attempt to take advantage of them when creating class diagrams. The problem is that data normalization only deals with the issue of normalizing data, it doesn't address the normalization of functionality as well. *Class normalization* is

DEFINITIONS

Data normalization—A process in which data in a relational database is organized in such a way as to reduce and even eliminate data redundancy.

Non-key attribute—Any attribute of a relational table that is not part of the primary key.

Foreign key—An attribute(s) of a data entity that makes up the primary key of another data entity. Foreign keys are used to maintain relationships between data entities.

First normal form (1NF)—A data entity is in 1NF when it contains no repeating groups of data. A database is in 1NF when all of its data entities are in 1NF.

Second normal form (2NF)—A data entity is in 2NF when it is in first normal form (1NF) and when all of its non-key attributes are fully dependent on its primary key. A database is in 2NF when all of its entities are in 2NF.

Third normal form (3NF)—A data entity is in 3NF when it is in second normal form (2NF) and when all of its attributes are directly dependent on the primary key. A database is in 3NF when all of its data entities are in 3NF.

a process by which you organize the behavior within a class diagram in such a way as to increase the cohesion of classes while minimizing the coupling between them.

In this book I'd like to propose the following steps of class normalization:

1. First object normal form (1ONF)

2. Second object normal form (2ONF)

3. Third object normal form (3ONF)

10.3.1.2.1 First Object Normal Form (1ONF)

A class is in *first object normal form (1ONF)* when specific behavior required by an attribute that is actually a collection of similar attributes is encapsulated within its own class. A class diagram is in 1ONF when

```
          Student
    _____
    student number
    name
    address
    phone number
    seminars
    _____
    add seminar
    drop seminar
    print schedule
    change professor
    change course name
    seminar length
```

Figure 10.8.
The class Student.

all of its classes are in 1ONF. For example, consider the class **Student** in Figure 10.8, which implements the behavior for adding and dropping students to/from seminars. The attribute **seminars** is a collection of seminar information, perhaps implemented as an array of arrays, that is used to track what seminars a student is assigned to. The method **add seminar** signs the student up to another seminar, whereas **drop seminar** removes them from one. **print schedule** produces a list of all the seminars the student is signed up to so that the student can have a printed schedule. **Change professor** and **change course name** make the appropriate changes to data within **seminars**. Because this is obviously clunky to code let's try to improve our design.

In Figure 10.9 we see how **Seminar** was created to encapsulate the behavior required by instances of **Student**. **Seminar** has both the data and the functionality required to keep track of when and where a sem-

To put a class into 1ONF you need to encapsulate behavior for directly manipulating data contained in a collection.

Class normalization helps to increase the cohesion within a class diagram.

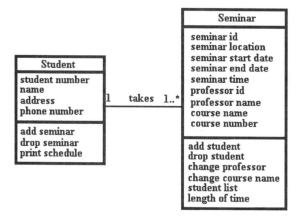

Figure 10.9.
The class Student in 1ONF.

inar is taught, as well as who teaches it and what course it is. It also implements the functionality needed to add students to the seminar and drop students from the seminar. By encapsulating this behavior in **Seminar** we have increased the cohesion within our design—**Student** now does student kinds of things and **Seminar** does seminar types of things, whereas before **Student** did both student and seminar things.

Notice how we've introduced the method **student list** to **Seminar**, which prints out the list of students taking a seminar so that the professor teaching the seminar can keep track of who should be attending it. The point to be made is that because **Seminar** now encapsulates the behavior needed to maintain seminars it is now a lot easier to introduce this kind of functionality. Previously, when **Student** implemented seminar behavior, it would have been very difficult to do something like this.

Class normaliza-tion increases the flexibility within a class diagram.

When you compare Figure 10.4, where we put the data entity Student into first normal form, and Figure 10.9, where we put the class Student into first object normal form, it becomes clear that 1ONF is simply an OO version of 1NF. With 1NF you remove repeating groups of data from a data entity, with 1ONF you remove repeating groups of behavior from a class. Conceptually this is very similar.

1ONF is simply the object-orient-ed equivalent of 1NF.

10.3.1.2.2 Second Object Normal Form (2ONF)

To put a class into 2ONF you need to encapsu-late the behavior that is needed by more than one instance into its own class.

A class is in *second object normal form (2ONF)* when it is in first object normal form (1ONF) and when "shared" behavior that is needed by more than one instance of the class is encapsulated within its own class(es). A class diagram is in 2ONF when all of its classes are in 2ONF. For example, consider the class **Seminar** in Figure 10.9, which implements the behavior of maintaining both information about the course that is being taught in the seminar and about the professor

---

TIP

You Need to Consider Both Data and Functionality

Notice that when we put the CLASS Student into 1ONF in Figure 10.9, we nor-malized both the data attributes and the methods, unlike when we put the DATA ENTITY Student into 1NF in Figure 10.4, where we only normalized the data. The point to be made is that because objects have both data and func-tionality, we need to consider both aspects during class normalization.

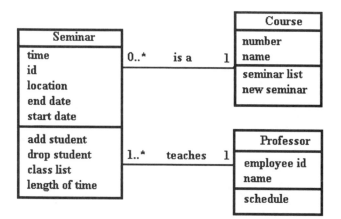

Figure 10.10.
The class Seminar
in 2ONF.

teaching that course. Although this approach would work, it unfortunately doesn't work very well. When the name of a course changes you'd have to change the course name for every seminar of that course. That's a lot of work.

In Figure 10.10 we see a better solution for implementing **Seminar**. We have introduced two new classes, **Course** and **Professor**, which encapsulate the appropriate behavior needed to implement course objects and professor objects. As before, notice how it has been easy to introduce new functionality to our application. **Course** now has methods to list the seminars that it is being taught in (needed for scheduling purposes) and to create new seminars because popular courses often need to have additional seminars added at the last moment to meet student demand. The class **Professor** now has the ability to print out a teaching schedule so that the real-world person has the information needed to manage his or her time.

Second object normal form in a lot of ways is the object-oriented equivalent of second normal form and third normal form. Where 2NF and 3NF are concerned with reducing the data redundancy within a database, 2ONF is concerned with reducing the behavioral redundancy (i.e., increase the cohesion) within an OO application.

2ONF is the OO equivalent of 2NF and 3NF combined.

10.3.1.2.3 Third Object Normal Form (3ONF)

A class is in *third object normal form (3ONF)* when it is in second object normal form and when it encapsulates only one set of cohesive behaviors. A class diagram is in 3ONF when all of its classes are in 3ONF. For example, consider the class **Student** in Figure 10.10, which encapsu-

Figure 10.11.
The class Student
in 3ONF.

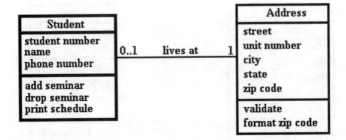

> **TIP**
>
> *Look at Subsets of Behavior*
>
> The real trick for putting things into 2ONF is to look at subsets of behavior within a class and ask yourself if this should be its own class. For example, in Figure 10.9 we had some behavior specific to professors—the attributes Professor name and Professor ID and the method Change professor. This is a pretty good indication that you need to consider creating a class to implement these behaviors.

lates the behavior for both students and addresses. By removing the address behavior from **Student** and encapsulating it in **Address**, as we see in Figure 10.11, we make the two classes much more cohesive—**Student** implements what it is to be a student and **Address** implements what it is to be an address. Furthermore, it makes our system more flexible as there is a very good chance that students aren't the only things that have addresses.

The problem is that we aren't done—**Address** still needs to be normalized. In Figure 10.11 we see that there is behavior within address that is associated only with zip codes, formatting, and validation to be specific. For example, based on the zip code it should be possible to determine whether or not the city and state are valid. This realization leads to the class diagram presented in Figure 10.12, which splits **Address** into four distinct classes: **Address**, **Zip Code**, **City**, and **State**. The advantage of this approach is twofold—first of all, the zip-code functionality is implemented in one place, increasing the cohesiveness of our model. Second, by making zip codes, cities, and states their own separate classes we can now easily group addresses based on various criteria for reporting purposes, increasing the flexibility of our

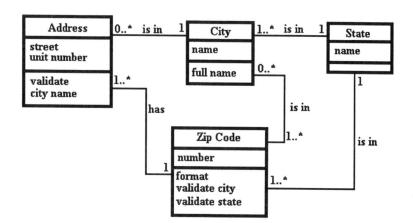

Figure 10.12.
The class Address
in 3ONF.

application. The main drawback is that to build a single address we have to build it from four distinct objects, increasing the code that we have to write. It's the same old trade-off that we've lived with for years: flexibility versus amount of code.

Let's consider one more example and put the **Seminar** class of Figure 10.10 into 3ONF. We see that **Seminar** implements "date-range" behavior—it has a start date and an end date, and it calculates the difference between the two dates. Because this sort of behavior forms a cohesive whole and because it is more than likely needed in other places, it makes sense to form the class **Effective Date** of Figure 10.13 to encapsulate it.

10.3.1.2.4 Class Normalization in a Nutshell

Figure 10.14 shows the resulting class diagram for Student in 3ONF. Notice how each class is highly cohesive, encapsulating a single set of related behavior. Also notice how each class is easy to understand quickly, making it easier to maintain and to enhance.

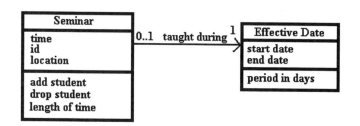

Figure 10.13.
The class Seminar
in 3ONF.

Figure 10.14.
The complete
class diagram in
3ONF.

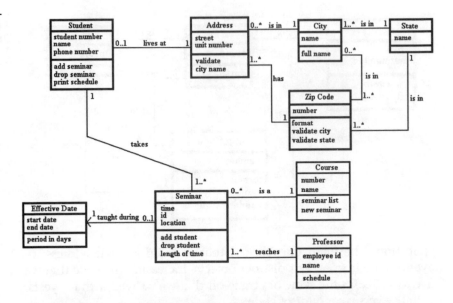

> ### DEFINITIONS
>
> *continued*
>
> encapsulated within its own class. A class diagram is in 1ONF when all of its classes are in 1ONF.
>
> **Second object normal form (2ONF)**—A class is in 2ONF when it is in first object normal form (1ONF) and when "shared" behavior that is needed by more than one instance of the class is encapsulated within its own class(es). A class diagram is in 2ONF when all of its classes are in 2ONF.
>
> **Third object normal form (3ONF)**—A class is in 3ONF when it is in second object normal form (2ONF) and when it encapsulates only one set of cohesive behaviors. A class diagram is in 3ONF when all of its classes are in 3ONF.

10.3.2 Overcoming the Object/Relational Impedance Mismatch

We need to deal with the impedance difference between the relational approach and the object paradigm. The *object/relational impedance mismatch* refers to the fact that relational theory is based on relationships between tuples, making it easy to do ad hoc queries against a database, whereas the object paradigm is based on a network of interacting objects that for the most part would prefer to be traversed as opposed to queried. To traverse objects within a database we must be able to follow the relationships between them, and to follow the relationships between two objects we must first be able to save these relationships in the database.

Object orientation and relational theory are based on different premises, increasing the difficulty of mapping objects to relational.

   In this section we will first discuss an approach to uniquely identify objects and then we describe how to implement the relationships between objects—inheritance, instance relationships, and aggregation relationships—so that we may minimize the impedance mismatch between object and relational technology.

> ### DEFINITION
>
> *Object/relational impedance mismatch*—The difference resulting from the fact that relational theory is based on relationships between tuples that are queried, whereas the object paradigm is based on relationships between objects that are traversed.

10.3.2.1 Implementing Object Identifiers (OIDs)

OIDs are typically implemented as large integer numbers.

We need to assign unique identifiers to our objects so that we can distinguish between them. A very good way to accomplish this is to assign each object an attribute called an object identifier (OID). OIDs are typically implemented as very large integers that are used as the key values in relational database tables. The main advantage of OIDs is that your keys are as simple as possible—a single numeric field.

OIDs allow us to simplify our key strategy within a relational database. Although OIDs don't completely solve our navigation issue between objects (fundamentally relational databases simply aren't set up this way), they do make it easier. You still need to perform table joins to read in an aggregate of objects, such as an invoice and all of its line items, but at least it's doable.

OIDs make it easier to automate maintenance of relationships.

Another advantage is that the use of OIDs also puts you into a position in which it is fairly easy to automate the maintenance of relationships between objects. When all of your tables are keyed on the same type of column, in this case OIDs, it becomes very easy to write generic code to take advantage of this fact. You merely need to record information about relationships in your data dictionary and then modify your class **PersistentObject** to act on this information. A little bit of programming, but it provides significant bang for your buck. We'll discuss the issues involved with doing this in section 10.3.3 that follows.

OIDs should have no business meaning.

A very critical issue that needs to be pointed out is that OIDs should have absolutely no business meaning whatsoever. Nada. Zip. Zilch. Zero. Any column with a business meaning can potentially change, and if there's one thing that we learned over the years in the relational world it's that it's a fatal mistake to give your keys meaning. If your users decide to change the business meaning, perhaps they want to add some digits or make the number alphanumeric, you need to make changes to your database in every single spot where you use that information. Anything that is used as a primary key in one table is virtually guaranteed to be used in other tables as a foreign key. What should be a simple change, adding a digit to your customer number, can be a huge maintenance nightmare. Yuck!

To give you an example, consider telephone numbers. Because phone numbers are unique many companies use them as keys for their customers. Although this sounds like a good idea, you're actually asking for trouble. I live near Toronto, Canada and because of the increased use of cellular phones, modems, and fax machines the local phone company was recently forced to divide the phone numbers of the 416 area code between 416 and 905. What's less work, changing the phone numbers in a few tables that had them as non-key columns or changing lots of tables that used them as either primary or foreign keys, not to mention the changes needed to your indexes? Moral of the story: OIDs should have no business meaning.

10.3.2.1.1 Strategies for Assigning OIDs to Objects

One key issue that you need to consider is how you intend to assign OIDs to your objects. There are three basic approaches to this:

1. **Use the SQL MAX() function.** The basic idea behind this approach is that you process an SQL statement that takes the maximum of all the OIDs currently used a data table, add one to it, assign the OID to the object you intend to insert into the database, and then write it out. This approach works well for relational databases that have optimized the MAX() function for numeric key fields but very poorly for those that haven't. The biggest problem with this approach is that you need to maintain a write lock on the table for a brief instance of time so that you can take the MAX and write out the new object. If you don't put the write lock on the table you run the risk of having two users trying to insert two objects into the table at the same time with the same OID.

2. **Maintain a separate OID value table.** With this approach you keep an extra table in the database that maintains the last assigned OID value for each class in your application. To get a new OID value you go to this table, get a write lock on the appropriate record, add one to the OID value stored there, update the record, and then assign that OID to the object that you want to add into the database. The advantage is that it doesn't force you to write lock the entire table that you are inserting a new object into, but the disadvantage is that the "last assigned OID" table can become a bottleneck in your system.

3. **Do a MAX() but write real quick.** To avoid the table-locking issue of the first approach you can take the MAX() to determine the largest OID, then immediately write the record to the table with the new OID value in it. If you do have two

Figure 10.15.
A simple class
diagram for our
bank.

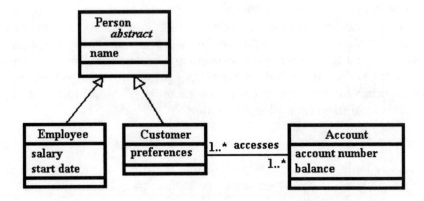

people attempting this simultaneously what will happen is one will insert the new record and the other one's insert will fail (because there's already a record in the database with that key value). Then what should happen is the transaction that failed should go through this process again, perhaps repeating several times before giving up. The advantage of this approach is that it is simple and fast, the disadvantage is that when there are a lot of people trying to create new objects in the database their efforts can collide with each other.

10.3.2.1.2 How Unique Should Your OIDs Be?

Another key issue with OIDs is that you need to decide how unique they will actually be. Will they be unique only within the scope of a single class? Within the scope of a class hierarchy? Or within the scope of your entire business model? To address this issue let's consider the class diagram presented in Figure 10.15.

If we make our OIDs unique within the scope of a class we could very well assign the same value of OID to an employee, to a customer, and to an account. For example, Kira Nurees the employee could have OID value 1701, Jadzea Dax the customer could have OID 1701, and an account object could also be assigned OID 1701. Although this sounds like it works, what happens when Jadzea is hired on at the bank? We can't just create a new employee object for her and give it the OID 1701 because Kira already has OID 1701. The only solution is to reassign Jadzea a new OID that is unique for both customers and employees, update her customer record and any associative tables that include her OID and then create the new employee record. Yuck!

If we make OIDs unique within the scope of a class hierarchy then this problem goes away—there will never be a customer who has the same OID as an employee, and vice versa. We do have a problem if an account becomes a person, or a person becomes an account, but frankly this isn't going to happen. Objects typically change type within the scope of their class hierarchy, so this approach should work for us 99.99% of the time.

To support poly-morphism nicely OIDs should be assigned at least within the scope of a class hierar-chy.

If we make OIDs unique within the scope of the entire business model then we don't have to worry at all if objects change type on us. The problem we do run into is that it is difficult to assign OIDs effectively—we basically need one point of control for assigning OIDs. Although you can alleviate this problem by assigning blocks of OIDs to each class hierarchy, perhaps accounts get OIDs 1 to 999,999 and persons get OIDs from 1,000,000 to 1,999,999 the fact still remains that you need to manage these blocks somehow. Yuck again!

Making OIDs unique across all objects is really tough to do.

10.3.2.2 Implementing Inheritance in a Relational Database

By using OIDs to uniquely identify our objects in the database we greatly simplify our strategy for database keys (table columns that uniquely identify records), making it easier to implement inheritance, aggregation, and instance relationships. First let's consider inheritance, the relationship that throws in the most interesting twists when saving objects into a relational DB. The problem basically boils down to: "How do you organize the inherited attributes within the database?" The way in which you answer this question can have a major impact on your system design.

Let's first look at an example that we will use in comparing various approaches to implementing inheritance in a relational database. In Figure 10.16 we see two versions of a class diagram for the **Person** hierachy: the original version of the hierarchy with the class **Person**, **Employee**, and **Customer** and the second version with the addition of the class **Executive**. This simple maintenance change will help us to understand the differences between the various approaches that we will discuss.

In the class diagram of Figure 10.16 we will assume that it is possible that a person can be both an employee and a customer at any given point in time, or perhaps either just a customer or just an employee. The main difference between executives and employees is that executives get an annual bonus and employees don't.

Figure 10.16.
A class diagram showing two versions of the Person class hierarchy.

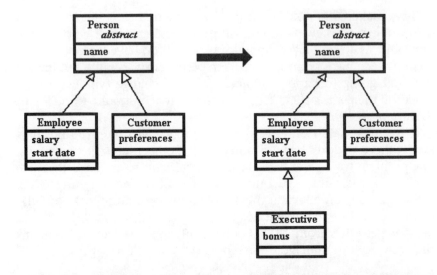

TIP

Important Factors to Consider When Implementing Inheritance in a Relational DB

Ease of implementation—This is always a critical factor.

Ease of data access—If your users are going to access the database that you create for end-user reporting, then you need to provide a database that is easy for them to understand and easy for them to get data out of. The more normalized a database is, the harder it will be for users to retreive the data because they will need to access more tables to get it.

Coupling—The less normalized a database is, the greater the coupling within it, making it harder to maintain and enhance.

Speed of data access—Speed of data access is often critical because the more normalized your data is, the more tables that need to be read from/written to, which means speed of access goes down.

Ease of assigning OIDs—Your strategy for assigning OIDs is also important if you intend to store the data for a single object in more than one table. The basic issue is: how do you ensure that the same value for the OID is used in each table that the object is stored in?

continued

> **IMPORTANT FACTORS**
>
> *continued*
>
> **Polymorphism**—If you have objects that will change their type and/or that will take on simultaneous roles, then you need to consider this in your design. For example, if the person Tom Paris can be both a customer and an employee of your organization at the same time, how are you going to support this? What happens when Tom is a customer, but then gets hired on as an employee? Very important considerations.

There are three fundamental solutions to implementing inheritance in a relational database:

1. Use one table for an entire class hierarchy

2. Use one table per concrete class

3. Use one table per class.

10.3.2.2.1 Use One Table for an Entire Class Hierarchy

One approach to implementing inheritance relationships in a relational database is to map an entire class hierarchy into one table, where all the attributes of all the classes in the hierarchy are stored in it. In Figures 10.17 and 10.18 we see the two versions of the data model for our **Person** hierarchy. Notice how we've used the generally accepted practice of underling the attribute being used for the key field, **OID**. Also notice that when we added the **Executive** class, all we needed to do was add the **Bonus** attribute to the table to support it. Nice and easy.

The advantages of this approach are that it is simple—polymorphism is supported when a person either changes roles or has multiple roles (i.e., the person is both a customer and an employee) and it is

Person
<u>OID</u>
Type
Name
Preferences
Salary
Start Date

Figure 10.17.
A data model using one table for the original Person hierarchy.

Figure 10.18.
A data model
using one table
for the new
Person hierarchy.

Person
OID
Type
Name
Preferences
Salary
Start Date
Bonus

This approach is simple, supporting polymorphism reasonably well, and making OID assignment and ad hoc reporting easier.

This approach increases coupling within your application, wastes space in your database, and requires the addition of an attribute indicating the type of the object.

easy to assign OIDs to objects because all of the objects are stored in one table. Ad hoc reporting is also very easy with this approach because all of the data you need about a person is found in one table.

The disadvantages are that every time a new attribute is added anywhere in the class hierarchy a new attribute needs to be added to the table. This increases the coupling within the class hierarchy—if a mistake is made when adding a single attribute it could affect all the classes within the hierarchy and not just the subclasses of whatever class got the new attribute. It also wastes a lot of space in the database, for example customer objects don't have **Salary**, **Bonus**, or **Start Date** attributes so all that storage space is being wasted for every customer object—if we have thousands or even millions of customers that's a serious issue. Finally, we need to add an artificial attribute called **Type** that indicates the type of person the object is so that when we retrieve the object we know what it is. Note that this technique only works if person objects can only have a single role at a time.

10.3.2.2.2 Use One Table per Concrete Class

Another approach is to use one table for each concrete class in your application, in which each table includes both the attributes and the inherited attributes of the class that it represents. In Figures 10.19 and 10.20 we see how we have separate tables for **Employee**, **Customer**, and **Executive**. Notice how when we created the table **Executive** we

Figure 10.19.
A data model
using one table
per concrete class
for the original
Person hierarchy.

Employee
OID
Name
Salary
Start Date

Customer
OID
Name
Preferences

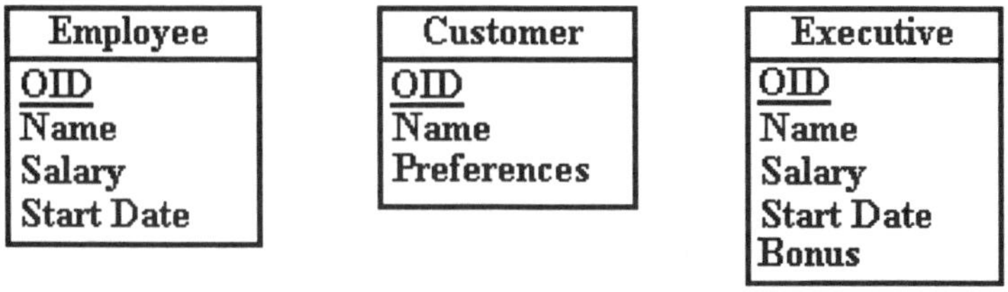

Employee	Customer	Executive
OID	OID	OID
Name	Name	Name
Salary	Preferences	Salary
Start Date		Start Date
		Bonus

Figure 10.20.
A data model using one table per concrete class for the new Person hierarchy.

repeated all of the attributes of **Employee** and added **Bonus**. Also notice how none of the attributes of **Customer** appear in either **Employee** or **Executive**.

This approach supports ad hoc reporting very well.

The main advantage of this approach is that it is still fairly easy to do ad hoc reporting as all the data you need about a single class is stored in only one table. It is still easy to assign OIDs to objects as long as polymorphism, the ability of objects to change their type, isn't an issue.

There are several disadvantages, however. First, when we modify a class we need to modify its table and the table of any of its subclasses. For example, if we were to add height and weight to the person class we would need to add it in all three of our tables, a lot of work. Second, whenever an object changes its role, perhaps we hire one of our customers, we need to copy the data into the appropriate table and assign it a new OID, once again a lot of work. Third, it is difficult to support multiple roles and still maintain data integrity. For example, if someone is both a customer and an employee then there will be records stored in each of the **Customer** and **Employee** tables, respectively. If the person changes his or her name then both of the records need to be updated appropriately. You're just asking for data to get out of synch taking this approach.

This approach makes it more difficult to modify existing classes and more difficult to support polymorphism.

10.3.2.2.3 Use One Table per Class

The third approach is to use one table per class, regardless of whether or not the class is concrete. Taking this approach we create one table per class, the attributes of which are the OID and the attributes that are specific to that class. In Figures 10.21 and 10.22 we see that the data model for our database is almost identical to our class diagram. To store an employee object in these models you would have a record for it in the **Person** table to store its name and a record in the **Employee** table to store its start date and salary. The two records would have the same value for their OID so that we can put the employee object together again.

Figure 10.21.
A data model
using one table
per class for the
original Person
hierarchy.

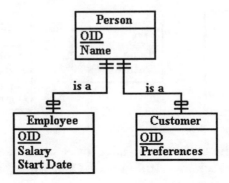

The main advantage of this approach is that it conforms to object-oriented concepts the best. It supports polymorphism very well because you merely have records in the appropriate tables for each role that an object might have. It is also very easy to modify superclasses and add new subclasses as you merely need to modify/add one table.

This approach is the closest to the OO paradigm.

There are several disadvantages to this approach. First of all, you end up with many tables in the database, one for every class. Second, it takes longer to read and write data using this technique because you need to access multiple tables. This problem can be alleviated if you organize your database intelligently by putting each table within a class hierarchy on different physical disk-drive platters (this assumes that the disk-drive heads all operate independently). Third, ad hoc reporting on your

Figure 10.22.
A data model
using one table
per class for the
new Person
hierarchy.

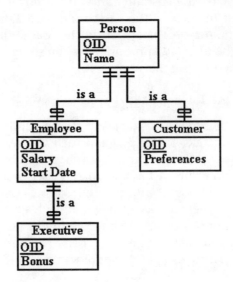

database is difficult if you don't add views on your data tables to make it easier. For example, a view could be created that makes the combination of the **Employee** and **Person** table appear as one, making it easy for users to get at employee information. Except for the problem of having a lot of data tables, all of the problems that we've discussed in this paragraph can be addressed with a little bit of extra code in your persistence layer, which we will discuss later in this chapter.

This approach requires a sophisticated approach in your persistence layer.

TIP

Use a Data Warehouse for Ad Hoc Reporting

Ease of ad hoc reporting against your database might not be as big an issue as we think. Most organizations now have *data warehouses*—large databases used for reporting purposes. Instead of performing queries against your production database, which negatively affects its performance, users report against copies of the original data that is stored in your data warehouse. The advantage of this approach is that you can have multiple copies of the same data in the data warehouse: one copy for each way that the data is to be used. This allows you to tune the data warehouse for high performance, while at the same time allowing you to design your production database so it contains your live data in the manner that best supports the needs of your non-reporting applications.

DEFINITION

Data warehouse—A large database, almost always relational, that is used to store data for reporting purposes.

10.3.2.2.4 Comparing the Three Approaches

In Table 10.1 we see a quick summary of the trade-offs associated with each of the three approaches to implementing inheritance in a relational database. For the third approach, two of the categories contain two answers, one if a bare bones approach is taken and another if the more sophisticated approach that we discussed in the previous section is taken.

As we've seen, the bad news is that it takes a little bit of effort to implement inheritance effectively in a relational database. The good news is that once you've mastered implementing inheritance rela-

Table 10.1. COMPARISON OF THE THREE APPROACHES TO MAPPING INHERITANCE INTO A RELATIONAL DATABASE

Factors to Consider	One Table per Hierarchy	One Table per Concrete Class	One Table per Class
Ease of implementation	Simple	Medium	Difficult
Ease of data access	Simple	Simple	Medium/Simple
Ease of assigning OIDs	Simple	Medium	Medium
Coupling	Very high	High	Low
Speed of data access	Fast	Fast	Medium/Fast
Support for polymorphism	Medium	Low	High

tionships, you'll find that instance and aggregations relationships are fairly straightforward.

10.3.2.3 Implementing Instance Relationships and Aggregation Relationships

In chapter 8 we covered how to implement instance and aggregation relationships in detail from a programming perspective; now let's look at it from a database perspective. To do this we must understand the difference between the two types of relationships, how to implement relationships generally, and how to implement many-to-many relationships specifically.

10.3.2.3.1 The Difference Between Instance Relationships and Aggregation

From a database perspective the only difference between instance relationships and aggregation relationships is how tightly the objects are bound to each other. With aggregation, anything that you do to the whole in the database you almost always need to do to the parts, whereas with instance relationships that isn't the case. Let's consider an example to make this clearer.

Figure 10.23.
The difference between instance and aggregation relationships.

In Figure 10.23 we see three classes, two of which have an instance relationship between them and two with an aggregation relationship. Let's first consider retrieving the objects from the database. When we retrieve an airport object do we need to automatically retrieve all the airplane objects that it is associated with? Of course not—airports are still useful objects even when we don't have the airplanes that are parked there in memory. Now consider airplanes. When we retrieve an airplane do we need to retrieve the airport as well. No, airplanes are useful objects without the airport that the regularly park at. When we retrieve the airplane from the database do we need to retrieve the wings as well? You bet—airplanes have a lot of problem flying when their wings aren't there. When we retrieve a wing from the database you probably want to retrieve the airplane as well. From a retrieval point of view, aggregation and instance relationships are different in the fact that with aggregation you usually want to read in the part when you read in the whole, whereas with an instance relationship it isn't always as obvious what you need to do. Granted this is usually specific to the business domain, but this rule of thumb seems to hold up in most circumstances.

With aggregation when you retrieve the whole you usually have to retrieve the part as well.

Now let's consider deletion. When you delete an airport do you need to delete all the airplanes parked at it? Probably not. When you delete an airplane do you need to delete the airport. No. What about the wings? Unless your business domain allows you to put the old wings on another airplane you probably need to delete them along with the plane. Depending on your business rules, when you delete the wings you might want to delete the airplane as well.

With aggregation when you delete the whole you usually want to delete the part as well.

Finally, let's consider writing the objects to the database. Once again what you do to the airport says nothing about what to do with the airplane, and vice versa. To maintain consistence within the database you'll probably want to write both the airplane and its wings at the same time. A good rule of thumb with an aggregation relationship is that whatever you do to the whole you almost always end up doing to the part. At least from a database point of view.

Figure 10.24.
Implementing
relationships in a
relational
database.

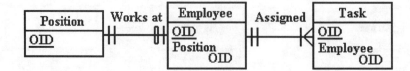

10.3.2.3.2 Implementing Relationships in Relational Databases

Relationships in relational databases are maintained through the use of *foreign keys*. A foreign key is a data attribute(s) that appears in one table but that is also used as the key of another table. Foreign keys allow you to relate a record in one table with a record in another. To implement one-to-one and one-to-many relationships, you merely have to include the key of one table in the other table. Let's look at an example.

In Figure 10.24 we see three classes, their keys (OIDs of course), and the foreign keys used to implement the relationships between them. First, we have a one-to-one relationship between **Position** and **Employee**. To implement this relationship we added the attribute **Position OID**, which is the key of **Position**, although we could just as easily have added a foreign key called **Employee OID** in **Position** instead. Second, we implement the many-to-one relationship (also referred to as a one-to-many relationship) between **Employee** and **Task** using the same sort of approach, the only difference being that we had to put the foreign key in **Task** because it was on the many side of the relationship. We can't put a foreign key in **Employee** because an employee can be assigned many different tasks. Some are assigned to only one task, some are assigned to several, and some might even be assigned to hundreds. There's simply no good way to implement a foreign key in **Employee** to relate it to **Task** in a relational database without either wasting space or requiring copies of employee records whenever an employee is assigned lots of tasks.

One-to-one and one-to-many relationships are implemented by adding a foreign key into one or both of the tables involved in the relationship.

DEFINITION

Foreign key—A non-key attribute(s) in one relational table that is the key of another. Foreign keys are used to maintain relationships between tables.

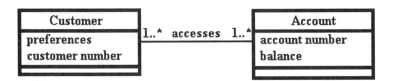

Figure 10.25.
Two classes with a many-to-many relationship between them.

10.3.2.3.3 Implementing Many-to-Many Relationships

We've seen that implementing one-to-one and one-to-many relationships is fairly straightforward, but what about many-to-many relationships? Can't we just have a foreign key in one or both of the tables and be done with it? No. In Figure 10.25 we see that there is a many-to-many relationship between customers and accounts. A single foreign key in either table doesn't cut it here because each record is associated with one or more of the other one. Wait a minute, why don't we just have attributes in each table that we'll use as foreign keys to the other one? We could have five fields in **Customer** that we'll use for account OIDs and five attributes in **Account** for customer OIDs. What do we do for customers with more than five accounts? Limit them to just five and risk losing their business? Add one or more dummy records just to store the additional accounts? Add more account OID fields? What happens when a customer goes past that limit, do we just add more? It should be clear that we need to take another approach than just adding foreign keys to existing tables to support many-to-many relationships.

Adding foreign keys to one or both of the tables won't work for many-to-many relationships.

To implement many-to-many relationships we need to introduce the concept of an associative table, a table whose sole purpose is to maintain the relationship between two or more tables in a relational database. In Figure 10.26 we see how to use an associative table to implement a many-to-many relationship. In relational databases the attributes contained in an associative table are traditionally the combination of the keys in the tables involved in the relationship. It has

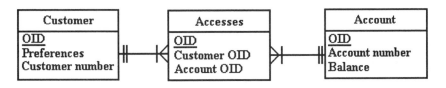

Figure 10.26.
Implementing a many-to-many relationship in a relational database.

been my experience, however, that it is easier to implement associative tables if you treat them as just another type of table—you assign them their own key field, in our case **OID**, and then add the necessary foreign keys to maintain the relationship. The advantage of this is that all tables are treated the same by your persistence layer, simplifying its implementation.

10.3.3 An Approach for Mapping Objects to Relational Databases

We've covered many of the issues involved in mapping objects to relational databases and with this knowledge we are now in a position where we can discuss how to build a persistence layer for relational databases. To do this, we must first see how to wrap access to the database itself, and then we need to encapsulate the wrapper so that business objects don't need to have any knowledge of how the database wrapper is built.

10.3.3.1 Wrapping Access to a Relational Database

The first step in building a relational persistence layer is to create classes that provide access to your relational database. You basically use the wrapping techniques that will be described in chapter 11, which create classes that make calls to a C-API or to a dynamic shared library (DSL) that is provided by either the database vendor or a third-party vendor.

Figure 10.27.
Wrapping the functionality of a relational database.

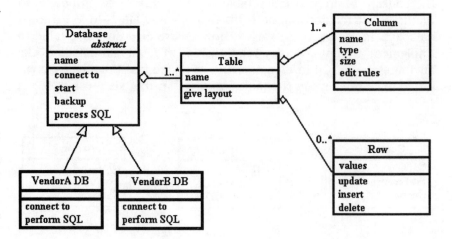

You might also choose to wrap a standard access mechanism such as Microsoft's ODBC (Open Database Connectivity), which can be used to access the databases of several vendors. Figure 10.27 illustrates a class diagram that shows how to access a relational database.

Although our class diagram only shows a very simple approach to wrapping a database, it does show the most critical features that we need. The class **Database** is the key as it provides the mechanism through which SQL statements can be processed against a relational database. The **ProcessSQL** method takes as a parameter a valid SQL statement and returns one of two things: a collection of rows representing the result of processing the statement, or an error message object indicating a problem (perhaps the SQL statement was invalid or the database connection is down).

The **Table** and **Column** classes are needed so that we know exactly how the database is designed. Databases are collections of one or more tables and tables contain one or more columns (also called fields or attributes). Without this basic knowledge we would be unable to map our business classes and their attributes to tables.

SCOTT'S SOAPBOX

Don't Hardcode SQL Statements in Your OO Code

Although it is possible to write several SQL statements for each one of your persistent business classes—statements to read, insert, update, and delete instances of the class—this strategy proves to be an onerous burden during both development and maintenance. Think of it like this: when your system potentially has several hundred or even several thousand business classes, the last thing that you want to have to do is maintain four times that many SQL statements to make your objects persistent. Take the time to create a generic persistence layer. By following the advice presented in this book, you'll find that mapping objects to relational databases is a lot easier than you originally thought.

Although this model gives you everything you need to both read and write data to/from the database, it isn't enough. You still need to encapsulate it so that business objects don't know how they are stored.

DEFINITIONS

Open database connectivity (ODBC)—A Microsoft standard for accessing relational databases. Effectively a standard for defining a database access wrapper that allows database vendors to provide a common interface to their product.

Dynamic shared library (DSL)—A library of function/procedure calls that exists outside of an application that is linked in at run time. Also known as a dynamic link library.

10.3.3.2 Encapsulating the Database Wrapper — Persistent Object

To reduce coupling in our applications, business objects shouldn't have to know how they are stored. To achieve this goal we need to introduce a new class, called **Persistent Object**, that encapsulates the classes that wraps access to your persistence mechanism, in this case a relational database. In Figure 10.28 we see a class diagram that shows the basics of how to develop a persistence layer for relational databases.

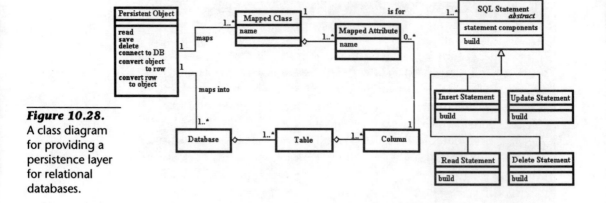

Figure 10.28.
A class diagram for providing a persistence layer for relational databases.

Persistent Object encapsulates the classes that wrap your database.

The class **Persistent Object** provides access to the basic OOCRUD (create, read, update, and delete) functionality needed to make objects persistent. Not only does it encapsulate the classes that wrap database access, it also encapsulates the process of converting objects into table rows, and table rows into objects. **Persistent Object** connects to databases and passes them SQL statements that return row objects that represent the objects requested by your application.

The classes **Mapped Class** and **Mapped Attributes** are created from information provided by your data dictionary (discussed below in the next section). There is one instance of **Mapped Class** for each business class in your system that needs to be persistent, and one instance of **Mapped Attribute** for each of its attributes and for any OIDs associated with the table(s) that the business class maps to.

Mapped Class uses instances of **Mapped Attributes** to create the SQL statements needed by **Persistent Object** to CRUD business objects. Because large portions of the SQL statements for inserting, deleting, updating, and selecting objects to/from the database are similar, we create instances of subclasses of **SQL Statement** for each **Mapped Class** object, speeding up the SQL statement creation process. Note that these are dynamic SQL statements that we are creating due to the fact that they are being created on the fly and are not being bound to the database (which would make them static SQL statements). For example, the SQL statement to retrieve customer objects from the database are identical except for the value of the OID, so why bother creating the entire statement every time when you only need to change the value of the OID? You can do the same thing for insert, delete, and update statements too.

Before you start sending me e-mail, yes, *dynamic SQL* does run slower than *static SQL*. A dynamic SQL statement is one that is generated by the application at run time, whereas a static SQL statement that is defined and bound to the database at compile time. There are always trade-offs in system development, and this is it when you're mapping objects. The efficiency loss with dynamic SQL, however, won't be an issue forever. Relational database (RDB) vendors are beginning to realize that more people are turning to dynamic SQL to read and write objects to their databases, and as a result their ability to process dynamic SQL efficiently is fast becoming the deciding factor for potential buyers. This is a big motivation for vendors to get their act together regarding dynamic SQL.

Dynamic SQL is slower than static SQL, but this issue is quickly being addressed.

This collection of classes provides the basis for implementing a persistence layer for relational databases. The only thing that we need now is the information to create the right instances of these objects so that our business classes are mapped to the right tables. We need a data dictionary to do this.

10.3.3.3 The Design for a Data Dictionary

The data dictionary provides the information needed to map objects into your database.

The **Persistent Object** class only becomes useful when you combine it with a data dictionary, which is the second step in reducing the effort of mapping objects to a RDB. You can implement your data dictionary as either a flat file or a table in your database. Figure 10.29 shows that the data dictionary is read when your application first starts so that the mapping information (objects) needed by your persistence layer can be instantiated.

Figure 10.29.
A data dictionary provides the information needed to map objects into a database.

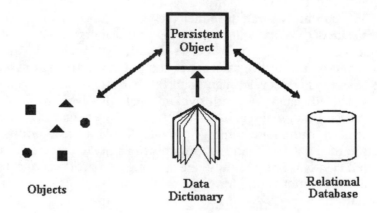

Objects   Data Dictionary   Relational Database

Persistent Object uses the information read in from the data dictionary to create dynamic SQL statements to read, write, and delete objects to/from the database. When your class diagram changes, and over time it always does, you'll only need to make the corresponding changes in your database and in the data dictionary. As you can see, the combination of the **Persistent Object** class and the data dictionary greatly reduces the maintenance effort required to map your objects into an RDB.

Before we move on, I just want to say a few more words about data dictionaries. First, it is fairly straightforward to include information about relationships between objects in your data dictionary, providing **Persistent Object** with the ability to maintain the relationships automatically. We'll talk about this more below. Second, for large systems it's worth your while to spend a day or two creating a small application to maintain your data dictionary. Third, instead of building all of this stuff you might just want to go out and buy it. Whenever possible you should buy, not build.

THE INFORMATION STORED IN YOUR DATA DICTIONARY

At a minimum, each row of your data dictionary should include the following fields:

- The name of the class being mapped
- The name of the attribute being mapped
- The name of the column that the attribute is being mapped to
- The name of the table that contains the column

You should also consider including:

- The name of the database the table is in (if your application accesses several databases)
- An indication if a column is being used as a key (in case you haven't standardized on OID as the key field)
- An indication if a column is being used as a foreign key (in case you intend to automate the maintenance of relationships) and for what table it is a foreign key

---

10.3.3.4 Taking a More Robust Approach

Up until this point there has been the implied assumption that you are starting fresh and can define your database to meet the needs of your OO application. In fact, we'll see later in this chapter that one of the secrets to success when mapping objects to relational databases is

You are often forced to work with a legacy relational database.

to let your class diagram drive your data model as this allows you to create the cleanest mapping possible. The bad news is that you are rarely in a position to start fresh but instead you have a legacy relational database whose design doesn't take the needs of mapping objects into consideration. It doesn't use OIDs, instead it uses fields with business meaning for keys instead. It doesn't take inheritance into account, and chances are it isn't even normalized.

There are two basic approaches to dealing with this situation. The first approach is to start fresh with a new database design and to convert the old data to the new design. Although at first look this sounds attractive, it rarely proves to be a viable alternative. Either there are too many legacy applications that would need to be changed to work with the new data, the cost of the conversion is simply too high, the conversion itself is too difficult, or all of the above.

The second approach is to extend your persistence layer to handle non-OID key fields and to map your objects to less than ideal database designs. This means that you'll have more code in your persistence layer and it will probably run a little slower trying to compensate for the design of the legacy database. Although this isn't ideal, it may be something that you can live with as you slowly replace existing legacy systems and databases with new and improved object-oriented versions of them.

10.3.4 The Seven Commandments for Mapping Objects to Relational Databases

I like to say that there are seven commandments to successfully mapping objects to relational databases. These commandments are:

1. **Thou shalt wrap access to thy database first.** Create the classes (Database, Table, Column, and Row) that provide basic access to your database first. Build your persistence layer one step at a time.

2. **Thou shalt encapsulate thy database wrapper second.** Once you have the classes built that wrap your database you need to encapsulate them with the class **Persistent Object** so that your business classes have no knowledge of how they are stored.

3. **Thy class diagram shall drive thy data model.** You are mapping objects to a relational database not a relational data-

base to tables. By creating your class diagram and then using it to define the tables that you need to store your persistent objects, you reduce the complexity of the mapping process by creating a clean database design.

4. **Thou shalt use only OIDs for keys.** OIDs are easy to understand, easy to implement, and they work. What more do you want?

5. **Thy OIDs shall have no business meaning.** Any attribute that has business meaning has the potential to be changed, and changing key fields always leads to tremendous amounts of work.

6. **Thou shalt use a data dictionary.** Data dictionaries that provide the information needed to define how to map objects to tables are critical if you want to have a persistence approach that is easy to maintain. When the business domain changes, and it always does, you shouldn't have to change any code in your persistence layer. Your business classes will change, and your database may need to change to reflect this, but from a persistence point of view the only other change should be in your data dictionary in order to reflect any new mappings.

7. **Thou shalt not map to a legacy database.** The design of legacy databases rarely reflects the needs of your object-oriented applications and as a result are often difficult, if not impossible, to map to effectively. If you can start fresh and let your class diagram drive the design of your database.

SCOTT'S SOAPBOX

So What's with the Attitude Problem?

In this soapbox I want to expose why we keep hearing that mapping doesn't work. First, let's go for an easy kill—employees of object database companies. I shouldn't have to point out that OODB people have a stake in shooting down relational databases. Don't get me wrong: I really like OODB, but I am a realist—I'll listen to what OODB people have to say when they're talking about object databases, but when they're talking about relational databases, I listen with a grain of salt.

continued

10.3.5 Looking into My Crystal Ball — OO and RDB in the Future

Considering the investment in legacy data that exists today and the reluctance of organizations to move away from it, I suspect that organizations will be mapping objects to relational databases for years to come. I also believe that relational databases will evolve in time, to become more like the object-relational databases that we'll discuss in section 10.5. Evolution, not revolution, will be the name of the game for the vast majority of organizations. Whether or not this will be the best strategy, only time will tell.

10.4 Persistence on the Leading Edge — Object-Oriented Databases

An *object-oriented database management system (OODBMS)* is used to store both the attributes and methods of objects. This is different than traditional databases that only store data. Remember, one of the key premises of object orientation is that data and functionality are now together in the form of an object. Therefore, you must be able to store both methods and attributes in an OODBMS. Don't worry, there isn't any code redundancy—there is only one copy of the methods stored for a class, not one copy of the methods for each instance of the class

At the time of this writing, object-oriented databases are just about to come into their own. In the late 1980s and early 1990s they were definitely in their infancy, but now they are easily into adolesence with adulthood around the corner. As a result it's worth our while to discuss the potential features that you may want in an object-oriented database.

> **DEFINITION**
>
> *Object-oriented database management system (OODBMS)*—A persistence mechanism that stores objects, including both their attributes and their methods.

10.4.1 *What to Look For in an OODBMS*

The object-oriented database system manifesto (Banchilhon, Delobel, & Kanellakis, 1992) defines the "13 golden rules" that define what it is to be an OODBMS. These 13 rules are:

1. **Thou shalt support complex objects.** It should be possible to build complex objects from simple ones, such as integers, strings, and booleans. Furthermore, it should be possible to work with those complex objects in the form of collections such as sets (collections of objects in which there is at most one copy of any object), tuples (the attributes of a single object), and lists/arrays (ordered collections of objects).

2. **Thou shalt support object identity.** Objects should have identity independent of their values. In other words, they should have a unique identifier that has no business meaning (see the requirements for OIDs in section 10.3.2).

3. **Thou shalt encapsulate thy objects.** An object database should provide the ability to store both the data of an object as well as its functionality. Furthermore, it should be possible to hide the implementation of the data and functionality, providing only an interface through which you interact with objects stored in the object database.

4. **Thou shalt support types or classes.** An object database must support some mechanism for coherently organizing objects, and this should be done either via the use of types or classes. Sets of types/classes effectively replace the notion of database schemas (table layouts) from relational databases.

5. **Thy classes or types shall inherit from their ancestors.** Just like an object-oriented language must support inheritance, an object-oriented database must also support it.

6. **Thou shalt not bind prematurely.** Because an object can change type (through polymorphism) and because it is possible that different classes/types in the database may implement the same behavior differently, we cannot bind the object to a class/type until run time. In other words, because we don't know the type of an object until we interact with it we can't identify its exact implementation until that time.

7. **Thou shalt be computationally complete.** It should be possible to write any kind of method imaginable using methods that will run in the database. You should take this rule with a little grain of salt. Our class-type architecture says that the persistence layer shouldn't be allowed to send messages to the user interface, so we really don't want computational completeness in the strict sense of the term.

8. **Thou shalt be extensible.** It should be possible to add new classes/types to the database.

9. **Thou shalt remember thy data.** It should be possible to CRUD (create, read, update, and delete) objects with an object database.

10. **Thou shalt manage large databases.** Object databases shouldn't be trivial and should be able to easily handle gigabytes, if not terabytes of objects.

11. **Thou shalt accept concurrent users.** It should be possible to have multiple users accessing an object database simultaneously.

12. **Thou shalt recover from hardware and software failures.** Object databases should support the full range of backup and recovery features expected of mission-critical databases.

13. **Thou shalt have a simple way of querying data.** It should be possible to get at the objects that exist in an object database in a simple and easy manner.

The 13 golden rules are very thorough, but the following list includes a few important features that I think are missing:

1. **Multiple inheritance support.** It's worth pointing out that if you are using a language that supports multiple inheritance, such as C++, then your object database should also support it.

2. **Distribution.** The ability to distribute an object database across multiple computers is quickly becoming a fundamental need for most organizations (Bukhres & Elmagarmid, 1996; Andleigh & Gretzinger, 1992). We discussed how to design applications for distributed architectures in chapter 5.

3. **Versioning.** Versioning of objects is a common need for many applications. Because objects change state over time and because there is often a need to look at different pictures in time, it should be possible to easily maintain previous versions of an object to support this need. Versioning is also important when it is possible that users may be working with, and potentially updating, one of multiple copies of the same object.

4. **Security**. It should be possible to restrict access to the object database at either the database, class, or object levels.

WHAT VERSIONING IN AN OBJECT DATABASE REALLY MEANS

Versioning in a relational database means that various snapshots, or copies, of a piece of data are stored over time. For the most part, versioning refers to keeping track of the history of the data, allowing you to restore its state as of any given time. Although this form of versioning works great for relational databases, it is inadequate for object databases.

The problem is that objects are made up of both data and functionality, so versioning just the data isn't good enough. You also need to version the function-

continued

WHAT VERSIONING IN AN OBJECT DATABASE
REALLY MEANS

continued

ality—that is, the methods—of an object too. For example, consider the class **FederalTax**. The rules for taxation are constantly changing—at least once a year. Keeping track of just the taxation rates year to year won't do; we also need to keep track of the methods that apply those rates. For an OODBMS to truly support versioning, it must be able to version both the attributes and the methods of objects.

DEFINITIONS

Object-oriented database system manifesto—The "13 golden rules" that define what it is to be an OODBMS.

Active persistent object—An object that exists in an object database that can be sent messages both from within and from without the object database.

10.4.2 Debunking the Myths of Object Databases

There are several myths in the object industry concerning object databases that I would like to address:

1. **Object databases aren't ready for prime time.** This myth completely ignores the fact that many mission-critical applications—trading applications on Wall Street, inventory control systems at large manufacturers, and prospecting databases of large oil companies—all use object databases.

2. **Object databases aren't good for transaction processing.** There are a lot of applications using object databases that are up and running today that process hundreds of thousands of transactions daily, including some of those mentioned above.

3. **Object databases don't scale.** This might have been true several years ago, but frankly there are lots of applications out there with very large databases.

4. **You can't query an object database.** In other words, you can put objects into an object database, but you can't get them out. I shouldn't even have to comment on this.

WHAT AN OBJECT DATABASE IS IN A NUTSHELL

Let's take a crack at a definition that we could give to upper management as to what an object database is:

An object database stores active persistent objects—objects that exist in the database that are able to receive messages from objects either inside or external to the database. In other words, objects can run on the server. It is possible to CRUD (create, read, update, and delete) objects in the database as well as share them simultaneously with other users based on their security access rights.

10.5 Taking a Hybrid Approach — Object/Relational Databases

An object/relational database is a persistence mechanism that encompasses many of the features of both relational databases and object-oriented database management systems by allowing you to store both data and objects. They offer the features of relational databases—the ability to work with tables made up of columns and rows—and with objects that encapsulate both data and functionality. As with an OODBMS, you are able to traverse objects easily in the database, supporting the complex relationships between objects that are often needed for many OO applications. The best of both worlds? Perhaps.

One way to look at object/relational databases is that they implement:

- the inheritance mapping features that we discussed in section 10.3

- methods in tables

- easy traversal between objects

- extensions to SQL that allow you to work with objects as well as data

The main advantage of object/relational databases is that they are an incremental improvement over what you already know—relational databases. The main disadvantage of this hybrid approach is that because you are able to work with both data records and with objects

---

DEFINITION

Object/relational database—A persistence mechanism that encompasses the features of both relational databases and OODBMSs by allowing you to store both data and objects.

SCOTT'S SOAPBOX

The Persistence Mechanism Market Will Go to...

At the time of this writing (December 1996), there are a couple of companies offering object/relational databases that have very impressive features. Although these products are all pretty solid, I highly suspect that the object/relational market will go to the mainstream relational database vendors as they add object-oriented extensions to their products. Although you can argue both sides of the "write from scratch" versus extending existing relational databases argument, the fact is that the vast majority of database customers would prefer to upgrade their existing databases rather than purchase a new one from another vendor.

Because today's mainstream relational database vendors will add object-oriented extensions to the products over the next few years, and because relational databases vastly overshadow both the OODBMS and object/relational markets, an object/relational database is probably in your future. This database will most likely be an upgrade of your existing relational database, if only for the simple reason that it's politically easier to sell the idea of a database upgrade to upper management than it is to sell the idea of a database conversion.

And what of OODBMSs? OODBMSs, although a very promising technology, will probably only be a "small" (several hundred million dollar) niche in the persistence-mechanism market. Great technology, but not good enough to replace the huge install-base of relational databases. (In 1996 the relational market was an estimated $6 billion.) Still, several hundred million dollars is nothing to sneeze at.

it is often tempting not to use the object-oriented extensions because they are foreign to your existing experience; instead you stick with what you know, what you consider safe.

10.6 What We've Learned

In this chapter we compared and contrasted the various technologies that can be used for persistence mechanisms: flat files, relational databases, object databases, and object/relational databases. We saw that all four technologies are valid alternatives for making objects persistent. We concentrated on mapping objects to relational technology since that is the current reality for the majority of developers and because a simple mistake when mapping can severely affect your application. We also discovered that both object-database technology and object/relational database technology have very promising futures.

References

Andleigh, P.K., & Gretzinger, M.R. (1992). *Distributed Object-Oriented Data-Systems Design*. Englewood Cliffs, NJ: Prentice Hall.

Banchilhon, F., Delobel, C., & Kanellakis, P., Eds. (1992). *Building an Object-Oriented Database System: The Story of O2*. San Mateo, CA: Morgan Kaufmann.

Bukhres, O.A., & Elmagarmid, A.K., Eds. (1996). *Object-Oriented Multidatabase Systems: A Solution for Advanced Applications*. Englewood Cliffs, NJ: Prentice Hall.

Suggested Reading

Kemper, A., & Moerkotte, G. (1994). *Object-Oriented Database Management: Applications in Engineering and Computer Science*. Englewood Cliffs, NJ: Prentice Hall.

Chapter 11

Integrating Legacy Code — Wrapping

What We'll Learn in This Chapter

Why we need to wrap.

What the approaches to wrapping are.

When, and when not, to use the following wrapping technologies: C APIs, dynamic shared libraries, screen scraping, peer-to-peer, and the Common Object Request Broker Architecture (CORBA).

The trade-offs of wrapping.

Information technology shops of today have a huge investment in information technology; unfortunately, the vast majority of it isn't object oriented (OO). In the 1980's it is estimated that over $1 trillion was invested in information technology in the United States alone. Needless to say organizations are motivated to retain as much of this investment as possible. Wrapping is a technique in which you make non-OO technology appear to be OO by putting a layer of OO code around it, which is often a critical part of any significant OO project.

343

A *wrapper* is a collection of one or more classes that encapsulates access to technology that isn't object-oriented to make it appear as if it is. A *wrapper class* is any class that is part of a wrapper. Wrapping, as shown in Figure 11.1, is used to provide OO applications access to hardware, operating system features, procedure libraries, function libraries, and even legacy applications. Wrapping allows you to retain your investment in older, non-OO technology by allowing you to reuse it in the new OO applications that you develop.

Figure 11.1.
Wrappers make non-OO technology appear to be OO.

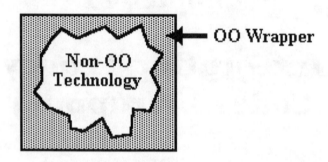

As we see in Figure 11.2, once non-OO technology is wrapped it can send and receive messages just like any other object or class in your application. In many ways wrapping is really the act of abstracting the "real" features, or the high-level features that you want from the thing that you are wrapping. From the point of view of the other objects in the system the wrapper appears just like any other object.

Wrapping is the act of abstracting the features that you want.

11.1 Why Wrap?

There are several reasons why we would want to wrap something. First, we often need to make specific calls to either the operating sys-

Figure 11.2.
Wrapped technology can send and receive messages just like other objects.

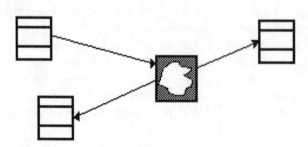

DEFINITIONS

Wrapper—A collection of one or more classes that encapsulates access to non-OO technology to make it appear as if it is OO.

Wrapper class—Any class that is part of a wrapper.

---

tem or to a piece of hardware. Perhaps your application needs to be able to automatically send e-mail to people, perhaps it needs to be able to send information to a printer, or perhaps it needs to connect to equipment that exists somewhere else on the network. By encapsulating system specific calls in an OO wrapper we hide their complexity, making it easier for other developers to access the same functionality as well as providing a single point of maintenance for what is being wrapped.

Wrappers are used to encapsulate system-specific calls to an operating system or to hardware.

Let's consider an example. In Figure 11.3 we see a class diagram for a simple wrapper of a printer. There are three classes—**Printer**, **Printer Document**, and **Printer Text**—that make up the wrapper. The basic idea is that you build a document from a series of **Printer Text** objects and then tell it to print itself. Instances of **Printer Text** can be marked as bold, underlined, and so on just like in a typical word processor. When the document is printed text object asks the printer for the specific codes that it needs to bold, underline, and so on itself. This way a document can be printed on any type of printer. Granted, there are many more robust ways to wrap access to a printer but if all you want to do is print out simple reports then this will do it.

A second reason for wrapping is the wish to reuse non-OO legacy code, perhaps in the form of function libraries or even legacy applications. Organizations simply can't afford to rewrite all of their exist-

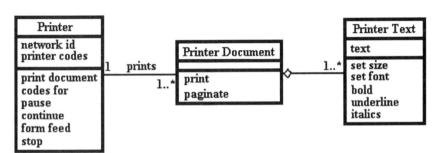

Figure 11.3.
A simple printer wrapper.

Wrappers are used to encapsulate legacy code.

Wrappers are used to extend the life of your investments in older technology.

Wrappers are used to integrate legacy applications and at the same time provide them with a modern user interface.

ing code, or at least can't rewrite it fast enough to meet the demands of the market that they are in. It is often quicker and less expensive to wrap this legacy code than it is to rewrite it.

By wrapping legacy code you can extend the life of your investments in prior technology. Furthermore, because it can often be easier to wrap than to rewrite, wrapping can often buy you enough time to rewrite and enhance the code that you wrap.

Third, wrapping can be used to both integrate existing systems into a cohesive whole as well as put a new face on your old workhorse applications. As we see in Figure 11.4, many organizations are using OO wrappers to build modern user interfaces to access functionality provided by older, often mainframe applications. In a few short weeks or months developers can put together a new object-oriented user interface (OOUI), which encapsulates access to one or more legacy applications. In short, users are quickly given "new," easy-to-use applications to help them do their work.

11.2 Approaches to Wrapping

Let's discuss several approaches to wrapping that you have available to you:

- Don't wrap at all
- Wrapping only hardware and operating system calls
- Scaffolding legacy applications

Figure 11.4.
Wrappers are used to integrate and provide new user interfaces for legacy applications.

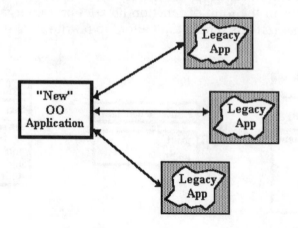

11.2.1 Leaving Things Well Enough Alone

One approach to wrapping is to not do it at all. Many people feel that you should just start fresh with objects and take a pure approach, not looking to the past at all. Although this sounds attractive, realistically you can rarely do this. Most organizations have too much invested in their legacy applications, hardware, and operating systems to simply throw it all away. Furthermore, you still find that you have to write your own wrappers for accessing hardware and specialized operating-system calls. Although OO development is swiftly becoming the norm, few hardware and operating-systems vendors provide OO wrappers for their products, even for the most common OO development environments.

Just because you can wrap doesn't mean that you have to.

11.2.2 Wrapping Only Hardware and Operating System Calls

Many organizations choose to wrap only the things that they absolutely have to, namely, hardware drivers and operating system calls. Wrapping output devices such as printers and plotters is very common, as well as input devices like scanners and light pens. Wrapping calls to the operating system, especially for network access, is also a very common need. As we discussed previously very few vendors provide wrappers that access their products, in fact you're often lucky enough to get a non-OO driver that works well for you. Although I expect to see the third-party-wrapper market to grow substantially in the next few years, at the present moment we still have to create our own wrappers for these things.

We still need to wrap hardware drivers and calls to the operating system.

11.2.3 Scaffolding Legacy Applications

As we saw in Figure 11.4, it is quite common to integrate access to legacy applications using OO wrappers, a process called *scaffolding*. Scaffolding allows developers to quickly put a new interface on top of a legacy application, allowing them to make it look as if they ported the application to a new hardware platform. Mainframe applications are often scaffolded by OO applications running on desktop computers/workstations.

Scaffolding can be done in one of two ways: You can wrap access to legacy applications and then never touch them again, or you can itera-

You often have to enhance the legacy applications that you have scaffolded. Where do you make the changes, in the legacy code or in your OO code?

tively replace and improve them. Sometimes you find yourself with a legacy application that is doing the job that you need it to do, although it is just hard to use. In these situations you can simply scaffold the application and leave it alone. More common, however, is that you find that you need to enhance portions of the legacy applications that you have scaffolded. In these situations you need to make a really hard decision. Do you make the changes to the legacy code or do you rewrite it using OO technology? Some of the deciding factors will include how long it will take you to make the changes on each platform, how much it will cost, when you need to get the changes made, and how hard it will be to maintain the changes that you need to make.

I have always found that the most important factor is whether or not you are able to split off the portions of the code that need to be changed and to rewrite them taking an OO approach. The main issue here is one of coupling. If the legacy system is highly coupled and difficult to modify, then it will be difficult if not impossible to split it up. Unfortunately, the primary reason why you are moving to OO technology is often the fact that your legacy code is highly coupled and difficult to maintain, negating your ability to iteratively rewrite your legacy applications.

DEFINITION

Scaffolding—A technique in which one or more legacy application is accessed through an OO wrapper to provide users with a modern user interface usually on a new hardware platform.

11.3 Wrapping Technologies

We've discussed several approaches that you can take to wrap, now let's talk about the various technologies that you can use. Because there are two distinct type of wrappers this section is split into two corresponding topics: (a) wrapping hardware and operating-system calls, or (b) wrapping legacy applications.

11.3.1 Wrapping Hardware and Operating-System Calls

Wrapping access to hardware and to the operating system is a very common technical requirement for most applications, something that is done during the development of system classes and persistence classes (see chapter 3 for a more detailed discussion of our class-type architecture). There are two basic technologies that are used for this type of wrapping: (a) C-APIs, and (b) dynamic shared libraries.

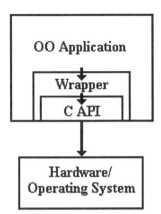

Figure 11.5.
Wrapping C-APIs.

11.3.1.1 C-APIs

The most common form of wrapping is to take a *C-API* (application-programming interface) and to put a layer of OO code on top of it to make it appear as if it is one or more objects to the rest of the system. C-APIs are commonly shipped with most hardware components and operating systems, allowing programmers to access them from their program code.

The basic idea, which is shown in Figure 11.5, is that you're effectively creating an OO layer between your application and whatever the C-API accesses. Your application interacts with the wrapper classes that you create, and the wrapper classes convert whatever messages they receive and turn them into the appropriate calls to the C-API. The wrapper classes also do whatever memory management needs to be done to facilitate the passing of data to and from the C-API (because C-APIs are procedural and not object oriented you pass data to them, not objects).

When wrapping a C-API you start by identifying the functionality, perhaps all of it, that you need to use. Following common OO conventions you then design one or more wrapper classes to encapsulate the functionality that you want from the C-API. You then have to write and test the wrapper code, and this is where the fun comes in.

The first problem is one of memory management. Because C expects programmers to manage memory C-APIs expect the same thing of you. You have to be able to both pass parameters to and accept return values from the C-API, implying that your wrapper classes need to be able convert objects to and from the expected C data types. This in turn

When wrapping a C-API you create a layer between your OO application and the C-API.

You need to determine what you want to wrap, design the wrapper class(es), and then code and test the wrapper.

You need to con-vert back and forth between objects and C data types.

Debugging becomes difficult because you're not sure where the problems really are.

implies that you have to do whatever is necessary to do the conversion, the main component of which is understanding and managing how the data is stored in memory.

The second problem is that you typically don't have the source code for the C-API, so you're never quite sure if a bug that you discover is really your fault or a problem with the C-API. Although the vendor of the C-API should have found all the bugs in it.

A major feature of wrapping C-APIs is that the C-API effectively becomes part of your OO application, as we saw in Figure 11.5. The C-API is linked in at compile time, or packaging time if you're a Smalltalk shop. Although wrapping C-APIs is a viable technique of any OO development environment, it is best suited for C++ applications because converting between C++ objects and C data types is straightforward.

DEFINITION

Application programming interface (API)—A set of function/procedure calls that access a component that is external to your system.

11.3.1.2 Dynamic Shared Libraries (DSLs)

Wrapping DSLs reduces the size of your exe-cutable/image.

It is common for developers to cre-ate a DSL from a C-API and then to wrap the DSL.

Another technology for wrapping hardware and operating system calls is *dynamic shared libraries* (DSLs), also called *dynamic link libraries* (DLLs). As we see in Figure 11.6, DSLs are very similar in concept to C-APIs, the main difference being that they are linked in at run time instead of compile time, reducing the size of your executable/image.

It is very common for developers to first wrap a C-API using C to produce a DSL and then wrap the DSL. This may be done for one of several reasons: Your OO language might be able to access DSLs but not C-APIs, you might need to share the DSL between several applications written in various languages, or you're already using DSLs for other things and don't want to have a mixed wrapping strategy.

DEFINITION

Dynamic shared library (DSL)—A library of function/procedure calls that exists outside of an application that is linked in at run time. Also known as a dynamic link library.

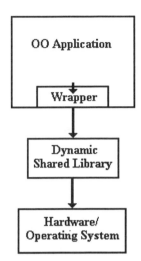

Figure 11.6.
Wrapping
dynamic shared
libraries.

11.3.2 Wrapping Legacy Applications

A *legacy application* is any application that is currently being maintained within your organization. Wrapping access to legacy applications is a common practice in many organizations. By wrapping legacy applications you can both extend their lifetime and give yourself a head start on developing the OO applications that replaces them. There are three main approaches to wrapping legacy applications:

- Screen scraping

- Peer to peer

- CORBA

11.3.2.1 Screen Scraping

With *screen scraping* an OO application "logs on" to a legacy

DEFINITION

*Legacy applica-
tion*—Any applica-
tion or system that is
difficult, if not
impossible, to main-
tain and enhance.

application and simulates the keystrokes that a user would make to access the functionality of the legacy application. From the point of view of the legacy application, it's just as if a user is using the application. Screen scraping effectively takes the "thin" 2-tier client/server approach that we saw in chapter 5, in which the client is the OO application and the server is the legacy application.

As we see in Figure 11.7 the basic idea is that a log-on session is set up between an OO application and the legacy application and then the

Figure 11.7.
Wrapping a
legacy application
via screen
scraping.

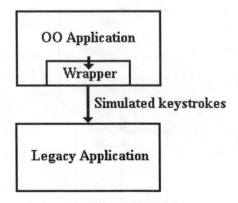

**With screen
scraping, an OO
application "logs
on" and simu-
lates the key-
strokes that a
user would nor-
mally make.**

wrapper sends keystrokes to the legacy application. The keystrokes
might be function keys to go to another screen, a combination of
arrow keys and the Enter key to select a menu item, tab keystrokes to
go between fields on an edit screen, or combinations of letters and
numbers to provide input to the edit fields.

The main advantages of screen scraping is that it is quick and requires
no knowledge of the underlying application, you only have to know
how to use it. The main disadvantage is that your OO application becomes highly coupled to the interface of the legacy application. A simple change in the interface such as the repositioning of fields or menu
items requires changes in the wrapper code in the OO application. Furthermore, screen scraping can result in very poor performance, especially when you need to traverse several screens before getting to the screen
that supplies the actual functionality that you want or when that functionality is provided by several screens working in conjunction.

> **TIP**
>
> *Assign Every Screen in Your Legacy Application a Unique Identifier*
>
> For screen scraping to work, the wrapper needs to be reasonably assured that
> it has gone to the right screen before it starts simulating keystrokes. For exam-
> ple, if you are wrapping the functionality to edit customer information, you
> first need to go to the customer-edit screen, verify that it got there, and then
> start sending the edit the customer data. Although it is easy for humans to
> determine that they are on the customer-edit screen, it is very difficult for your
> application if it doesn't have a unique screen identifer.
>
> *continued*

> **TIP**
>
> *continued*
>
> One approach for solving this problem is to put a unique number in a specific spot on each screen in the legacy application. This way, whenever your wrapper simulates the keystrokes to go to a new screen, it can easily look at the screen identifier to verify that it got to the right place. This is important whenever the legacy application performs inconsistently, a typical feature of mainframe applications because the number of users varies during the day (the more users, the slower it is). In situations such as this, your wrapper will simulate the keystrokes needed to change screens and then continuously poll the legacy application looking for the proper screen ID.
>
> If your users don't want to have a unique identifier showing on each screen of their legacy applications, you can put them on the screen in "invisible text." It is common for most development environments to have a text attribute that makes it invisible to users but visible to other software, specifically screen scrapers. This allows you to have the identifier that you need without having to clutter up the screens of your legacy application.

11.3.2.2 Peer to Peer

A second approach to wrapping legacy applications is to take a peer-to-peer approach in which your wrapper resides both in the OO application and around the legacy application, the two components communicating with one another via transaction calls. The basic idea, which we see in Figure 11.8, is to first write wrapper code that directly accesses the functionality provided by the legacy application by calling its internal subroutines. You then write wrapper code in your OO application that communicates with the legacy wrapper code by sending it transactions. It is quite common to see the transaction flow going in both directions, usually because a component of the legacy application has been replaced either partially or fully by the OO application.

DEFINITION

Screen scraping— A wrapping technique where the wrapper simulates the keystrokes that a user would normally make to drive the functionality of a legacy application.

The main advantage of peer-to-peer wrapping is that it is very fast because the legacy wrapper accesses the actual code that performs the business functionality. The disadvantage is that wrapper code exists for both the OO application and the legacy application, effec-

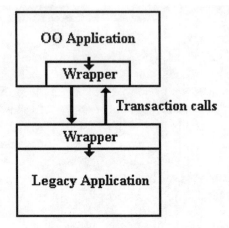

Figure 11.8.
Wrapping a
legacy application
via a peer-to-peer
approach.

tively coupling the wrapper code to the internals of the legacy application. It also requires that you have programmers for both development environments.

11.3.2.3 Common Object Request Broker Architecture (CORBA)

As we discussed in chapter 5, CORBA is a set of standards proposed by the Object Management Group (OMG) for supporting distributed object applications. Part of CORBA is the definition for an interface definition language (IDL) that provides a standard approach for defining the interface of an object. As we see in Figure 11.9 you use the CORBA IDL to wrap legacy applications (Mowbray & Zahavi, 1995), effectively making them look like objects to other CORBA-compliant applications. Your OO application is also wrapped by the CORBA IDL, perhaps this is even a built-in feature of your development environment, allowing it to send messages to and receive messages from the legacy application.

The main advantage of this approach is that it provides all objects in your system with a consistent interface, including both your OO code and your legacy-application code. The main disadvantage is that full-blown implementations of CORBA currently add significant overhead to your applications. Regardless of the overhead, CORBA has the support of the vast majority of the players in the computer industry as it provides a standard mechanism through which their products can interact. As a result, CORBA is most likely in your future.

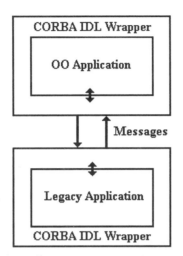

Figure 11.9.
Wrapping a
legacy application
via CORBA.

DEFINITIONS

Object Management Group (OMG)—A consortium of organizations that
work together to create standards for distributed-object computing.

Common Object Request Broker Architecture (CORBA)—An OMG specification defining a distributed-object architecture. CORBA specifies how to
develop OO applications that are able to connect and communicate with other
CORBA-compliant (and potentially non-OO) applications.

Interface Definition Language (IDL)—A standard language for defining the
interface of an object.

11.3.3 Comparing Wrapping Technologies — When to Use Each One

Using our class-type architecture from chapter 3 to guide us, let's
quickly review when you should use each wrapping technique. In
Figure 11.10 we see that screen scraping is typically used when you
want to create OO applications that are made up mostly of interface
classes. These interface classes front-end access to one or more legacy
applications that typically reside on a mainframe and are usually simple because they only need to contain the code to simulate the keystrokes expected by the legacy applications.

*You take differ-
ent wrapping
approaches for
different class
types.*

Figure 11.10.
When to use
each wrapping
technology.

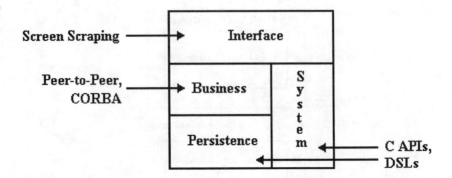

The peer-to-peer and CORBA approaches are used when you wish to create business classes that wrap the business functionality contained by a legacy application. Both approaches allow you to directly access the functionality provided by legacy applications. C-APIs and DSLs are typically used to access the low-level functionality provided by hardware and operating systems and as a result are the favorite approaches taken by developers of system and persistence classes.

Each wrapping technology requires a different set of development skills.

Table 11.1 provides a summary of the skills needed by developers for each wrapping technology. Although there are some common fea-

---

Table 11.1. The Skills Needed for Each Wrapping Technology

C-APIs	Intimate knowledge of C pointers and memory memory management. Intimate knowledge of con verting between objects and C data types
Dynamic shared libraries	Intimate knowledge of converting between objects and the data types required by the DSL
Screen scraping	Knowledge of how to use the legacy application being wrapped
Peer to peer	Intimate knowledge of the internals of the legacy application being wrapped. Programming skills for both the OO and legacy development environments
CORBA	Intimate knowledge of the internals of the legacy application being wrapped. An understanding of how the CORBA IDL works

tures among them, each technology requires a different skill set, implying that it is probably difficult to find a single developer who is good at all types of wrapping.

11.4 The Advantages and Disadvantages of Wrapping

There are several advantages and disadvantages to wrapping. On the advantage side you have the following:

1. **You can reuse existing investments in previous technologies.** You can wrap legacy code and hardware to make it available to your new, OO applications. This allows you to extend the life of technologies that your organization has invested in, making your OO development efforts more cost effective.

2. **You can quickly put a new face on old workhorse applications.** Yesterday's hard-to-use mainframe application can become today's slick, easy-to-use object-oriented application simply by wrapping it.

3. **You can buy yourself the time you need to rewrite legacy code.** Wrapping legacy code may not be ideal but it may save you a significant amount of development, especially when you are rewriting and extending an existing application.

4. **You can still use legacy code when you've lost the ability to maintain it.** Sometimes you've lost the key developer who knew the code inside out and backwards and/or sometimes you've even lost the code itself. Regardless of your situation, you can still wrap it and continue to use it in your OO applications.

On the disadvantage side you have the following:

1. **You have to maintain multiple sets of code.** You now have several sets of code to maintain: the legacy application code, the wrapper code, and the new OO application code. The more code the harder it is to maintain, particularly when the code was developed in several languages.

2. **It's no longer clear where to add new functionality.** It's very easy to say that all new functionality will go into your OO application, but it's often a different story when you find that large sections of your legacy application would need to be rewritten before you can add it. Sometimes its faster, at least from a calendar's point of view, to add new functionality to a legacy application than it is to add it to an OO application.

3. **Changes in the legacy application will affect your OO code.** Whenever the legacy application is modified the changes will need to be reflected in your wrapper code, and probably in your OO code itself.

4. **Few businesses or technologies are so stable as to permit wrapping.** It's really easy to say that you're going to wrap legacy code, but the reality is that both the business and technological environments change so quickly that you often can't get enough benefit out of the wrapped code to make it worth your while. One of the reasons why you moved to OO in the first place is because you needed a development environment that allows you to write code that's easy to maintain and enhance. The legacy code that you wrap typically doesn't meet these needs.

11.5 What We've Learned

In this chapter we discussed wrapping, a technique in which you write OO code that makes non-OO technology appear to be OO. Wrapping allows the OO applications that we develop to access hardware and non-OO code, even code that exists in the form of legacy applications.

There are three main approaches to wrapping: not wrapping at all; wrapping hardware and code libraries; and scaffolding legacy applications. We also saw that there are several technologies that can be employed in wrapping: C-APIs; dynamic shared libraries; screen scraping; peer-to-peer communication; and CORBA. Each of these technologies can be used for development of one or more of the four class types discussed in chapter 3.

References

Mowbray, T.J., & Zahavi, R. (1995). *The Essential CORBA: Systems Integration Using Distributed Objects*. New York: Wiley.

Suggested Reading

Berson, A. (1990). *APPC: Introduction to LU6.2*. New York: McGraw-Hill.

Otte, R., Patrick, P., & Roy, M. (1996). *Understanding CORBA: The Common Request Broker Architecture*. Englewood Cliffs, NJ: Prentice-Hall.

Part IV

Object-Oriented Testing

Chapters

12 • *Making Sure Your Applications Work—Full Life-Cycle Object-Oriented Testing (FLOOT)*

Chapter 12

Making Sure Your Applications Work — Full Life-Cycle Object-Oriented Testing (FLOOT)

What We'll Learn in This Chapter

Why we need to test our applications.

Which traditional testing concepts still work for object-oriented (OO) development and which don't.

How to test during all phases of the development life cycle: analysis, design, construction.

How to implement test cases within program code.

How to perform function, regression, stress, and user-acceptance testing.

Testing an object-oriented (OO) application is both very similar and very different as compared to testing a procedural application. The good news, if you can call it that, is that you still need to formulate test cases, you still need to document them, you still need to run and verify them, you still need both black-and-white box tests, you still need regression testing, and you still need stress test-

ing. The bad news, however, is that the new development concepts provided by the OO paradigm require new approaches to testing. In this chapter we will discover several key concepts required for testing object-oriented applications.

I'm a strong believer in something called *full life-cycle object-oriented testing* (FLOOT), which involves testing your object-oriented applications throughout the entire system development life cycle (SDLC). We'll see that there are many reasons why you want to test throughout the entire SDLC, not the least of which is if you leave testing to the end of a project it typically doesn't get done properly. In this chapter we will discuss a number of testing techniques that together form a FLOOT process (there has to be a music joke in here somewhere).

Before we begin, let's first define some common testing terms that will use throughout this chapter. The central document in testing is called the *master test plan*, which prescribes the testing approach for your application. You need to create a master test plan for every release of your application. A *test-procedure script* is the description of the steps that must be carried out to perform all or part of the master test plan. An *object-oriented test case*, referred to simply as a *test case*, is a collection of objects that are put into states that are appropriate to what is being

---

DEFINITIONS

Full life-cycle object-oriented testing (FLOOT)—A testing methodology for object-oriented development that comprises testing techniques that taken together provide methods to verify that your application works correctly at each stage of development.

Object-oriented test case—A collection of objects that are in states that are appropriate to what is being tested, message sends to those objects, and the expected results of those message sends that together verify that a specific feature within your application works properly.

Test log—A chronological tracking of your testing activities.

Test plan—A document that prescribes the approach to be taken during the testing process.

Test-procedure scripts—The description of the steps that must be carried out to perform all or part of a test plan.

tested, message sends to those objects, and the expected results of those message sends. Test cases are used to verify that a specific feature within your application works as you expected. A *test log* is a chronological recording of your testing activities.

12.1 Why FLOOT?

Why do we need to test throughout the entire development life cycle? We've always left testing to the end, isn't that the way it works? How can we test unless all the code is written, or at least a portion of the code? Valid questions. Here are some valid points that address these questions:

1. **The cost of fixing errors increases the later they are detected in the development life cycle.** The cost of fixing an error, as shown in Figure 12.1, snowballs the longer that it takes to detect it (McConnell, 1993). If you make an analysis error, a missed or misunderstood user requirement, and find it during the analysis process it is very inexpensive to fix. You merely change a portion of your analysis document. A change of this scope is on the order of $1 (you do a little bit of retyping/remodeling). If you don't find it until the design stage it is more expensive to fix. Not only do you have to change your analysis, you also have to reevaluate and potentially modify the sections of your design based on the faulty analysis. This change is on the order of $10 (you do a little more retyping/remodeling). If you don't find the problem until programming you'll need to update your analysis, design, and potentially even scrap portions of your code, all because of a missed or misunderstood user requirement. This error is on the order of $100, because of all the wasted development time based on the faulty requirement. Furthermore, if you find the error during testing, where we typically start looking for errors, the error is on the order of $1,000 to fix (you need to update your documentation, scrap/rewrite large portions of code, and so on). Finally, if the error gets past you into production, you're looking at a repair cost on the order of $10,000 plus to fix (you need to send out update disks, fix the database, restore old data, rewrite/reprint manuals, and so on). It is clear that we want to find and fix errors as early on in the development process as possible.

The earlier in the life cycle that we test our application the less expensive it is to fix any errors that we find.

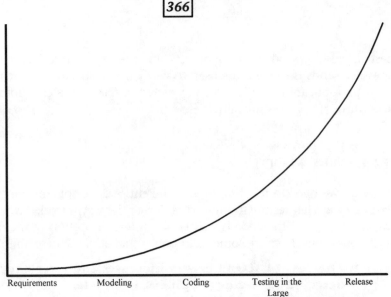

Figure 12.1.
The rising cost of
fixing errors.

2. **Developers don't like to test their systems.** Most developers are programmers at heart, not testers. They want to write code, not test it. To put it bluntly, many programmers simply aren't interested in testing, they'd rather be coding.

We must integrate testing into the entire development process.

3. **When left to the end of the life cycle, testing is often left out.** Projects are almost always late, and project managers are often desperate to get the project back on schedule. As a result, they start looking for places to cut corners, and because testing and documentation are often the only things that need to be worked on, they are often cut back or discarded completely. We can't afford to leave testing to the end of the development process anymore, instead we must integrate it into the entire development process.

To be successful we must involve our users early in the testing process.

4. **We test systems the way we think they're supposed to work, not in the way they actually get used.** Users have a tendency to use systems in completely different ways from those originally intended. The problem with this is that we didn't think they'd try some of the things that they do, and as a result they put the system through situations that it simply can't handle. The end result is that users must be involved as much as possible in the testing process.

One of the most important lessons that you can learn about object-oriented testing is that although many of the techniques are similar to those of structured testing, there are some very significant differences that you need to be aware of. When you consider the fact that the OO and structured/procedural paradigms share some common design principles, and that OO has taken them further and added several new ones, it is only reasonable to expect that we'd have to change our approach to testing OO applications. In this chapter we will cover several new OO testing techniques as well as several tried-and-true structured testing methods that are still applicable in the OO world.

Table 12.1 (following page) contains a list of the steps of the full life-cycle object-oriented testing (FLOOT) process, steps which we will cover in greater detail in this chapter.

12.2 Testing Your Previous Efforts — Regression Testing

The first thing that you need to do is ensure that the functionality your application previously supported still works. *Regression testing* is the act of ensuring that changes to an application haven't been adversely affected. We've all had experiences where we made a small change to a program, we then successfully tested the change that we made thinking that everything was fine, and then we put the program into production only to see it fail because our small change affected another part of the program that we had completely forgotten about. Regression testing is all about avoiding problems like this.

DEFINITION

Regression testing—The act of ensuring that previously tested functionality still works as expected after changes have been made to an application.

The reason why we're talking about regression testing first is because it's the very first thing that you should be thinking about when you begin testing your application. Users really get ticked off when functionality in an application that they are used to having no longer works. They get a lot more ticked off if new functionality doesn't work properly. How angry would you get if you took your car into a garage

---

TABLE 12.1 THE STEPS OF FULL LIFE-CYCLE OBJECT-ORIENTED TESTING (FLOOT)

Testing your previous efforts
- Regression testing

Testing your analysis
- Use-case analysis testing
- User-requirement reviews

Testing your design
- Technical-design reviews
- Requirements verification matrices

Testing your program code
- Code reviews
- Traditional testing techniques
    - Black-box testing
    - White-box testing
    - Boundary-value testing
    - Coverage testing
    - Path testing
- Method testing
- Class testing
- Inheritance-regression testing
- Class-integration testing
- Implementing test cases (in order of preference)
    - Built-in test cases
    - Separate testing hierarchies
    - Testing scripts (the traditional approach)
    - Test subclasses

Testing the entire application
- System testing
    - Function testing
    - Stress testing
    - Installation testing
    - Operations testing
- User acceptance testing
- Alpha and beta testing

---

to have a new stereo system installed just to discover afterward that the new stereo works but that the windshield wipers don't? Pretty mad. How angry do you think your users would get when a new release of an application no longer allows them to fax information to other people because the new e-mail feature that you just added has affected it somehow? Pretty mad.

Users expect that all of the functionality they had in a previous version of a system will either still exist or will be enhanced by new releases.

The quick answer as to how to do regression testing is to run all of your previous test cases against the new version of your application. Although this sounds like a good idea, it often proves not to be realistic. First, you may have changed part of, or even all of, the design of your application. This will mean that you need to modify some of the previous test cases as a result. Second, if the changes you have made truly affect only a component of the system, then potentially you only need to run the test cases that affect this single component. Although this approach is a little risky because your changes may have had a greater impact than you suspect, it does help to reduce both the time and cost of regression testing. In section 12.4.5 we'll see that requirement-verification matrices can be used to help you identify what components of your application need to be retested when you make a change.

Changes in the design may result in changes to your old testing procedures.

Regression testing is vitally important because of the tendency of developers to test only the new functionality that they added to a system and to assume that the old functionality that they didn't touch still works. You didn't touch the piece of code so you don't have to test it, right? Absolutely wrong! You have to put as much effort into testing the code that you didn't change as the code that you did change to ensure that you still support all of your application's previous functionality. You probably won't like it, but that's the way that it is.

Many developers assume that code they didn't change still works. You simply can't count on this, so please don't fall into this trap.

It is important to recognize that incremental development, a favorite approach in the object world, makes regression testing critical. Whenever you release an application you have to ensure that its previous functionality still works, and because you release applications more often when taking the incremental approach it means that regression testing becomes that much more important.

Incremental development dramatically increases the importance of regression testing.

12.3 Testing Your Analysis

In *The Object Primer* (Ambler, 1995) we saw that the most significant mistakes are those that are made during analysis. If you miss or misunderstand a user requirement, you automatically ensure that the system will not completely meet the needs of your users. Either it is missing a feature or a feature is implemented wrong. Analysis errors such as this often result in project failure, or at least in serious cost overruns to fix the problem.

There are three techniques that you may employ to test your analysis:

- use-case scenario testing

- prototype walkthroughs

- user-requirements reviews.

12.3.1 Use-Case Scenario Testing

Use-case scenario testing (Ambler, 1995) is a testing process in which users are actively involved with ensuring that user requirements are accurate. The basic idea is that a group of users, with the aid of a facilitator, step through a series of defined use cases to verify that the analysis model, typically a CRC (class responsibility collaborator) or class diagram, accurately reflects their requirements. Use-case scenario testing was previously discussed in greater detail in chapter 1.

The main point that needs to be made is that you need to verify that your model accurately reflects the problem domain. If it doesn't, then your project is in serious jeopardy. I would prefer to find this out early on in the project when I'm still in a position to do something about it rather than later when I probably can't. Wouldn't you?

12.3.2 Prototype Walkthroughs

During analysis it is quite common to create a *prototype*, a mock-up of the user interface, for your application. Prototyping, discussed in chapter 2, is an iterative process in which you work closely with your users to design the user interface for the application that you are developing. Although you will eventually create an interface design that your users like (one hopes), the question of whether or not the interface actually works still remains. This is why you need to do a *prototype walkthrough*.

A prototype walkthrough is an analysis-testing process in which your users work through a collection of use cases to verify that the design of a prototype meets their needs. The basic idea is that they pretend that the prototype is the real application and they try to use it to solve real business problems. Granted, they'll need to use their imaginations to fill in the functionality that the application is missing (such as reading and writing objects from/to permanent storage) but for the most part this is a fairly straightforward process. Your users simply sit down at the computer and begin to work through the use cases. Although they do this, it's your job to sit there and observe them, looking for places where the system is difficult to use or is just plain missing some features. In a lot of ways prototype walkthroughs are a lot like user acceptance tests, discussed in detail in section 12.3.2, the only difference being that you're working with the prototype instead of the real system.

Prototype walkthroughs quickly verify that your prototype meets the needs of your users.

12.3.3 User-Requirement Reviews

After you have gathered user requirements you need to document and present them to your users to both verify that they are accurate and to prioritize them. A user-requirement review is a formal process in which a facilitator puts together a group of users with the authority to confirm and prioritize the user requirements gather by a development team. This process could take from several hours to several days depending on the size of the project.

It is important to document, review, and prioritize user requirements so as to verify that what you are building will meet the needs

---

DEFINITIONS

Analysis error—When a user requirement is missed or misunderstood.

Prototype—A mock-up of the user interface of your application.

Prototype walkthrough—A process in which your users work through a collection of use cases using the prototype of the application as if it was the real thing. The main goal is to test whether or not the design of the prototype meets their needs.

Use-case scenario testing—A testing process in which users work through use cases with the aid of a facilitator to verify that the user requirements are accurate.

User-requirement review—A testing process in which a facilitated group of users verify and prioritize the user requirements gathered by a development team.

User-requirement reviews are used to verify that your application will meet the needs of your users and to define the scope of your project.

of your users and to define the scope of your project. Part of the pri-oritization process should be to provide an indication as to which release of the application a specific feature will appear in. User-requirement reviews are run in a manner similar to technical-design reviews, discussed in the next section, with the exception that busi-ness experts instead of technical experts review the work of the devel-opment team. User-requirement reviews are often used in addition to use-case analysis testing and prototype walkthroughs.

12.4   Testing Your Design

Just like you need to verify that your analysis is right; you also need to verify that your design is correct too. Remember, the sooner in the development life-cycle you discover errors, the less expensive they are to fix. There are two techniques for testing your design that we will discuss in this section: (a) technical-design reviews, and (b) require-ment-verification matrices.

12.4.1 Technical-Design Reviews

It isn't enough to test just your analysis efforts, you also need to test your design. *Technical-design reviews*, also called design walkthroughs, are a testing technique in which your design efforts are examined crit-ically by a group of your peers. The basic idea is that a group of quali-fied people, both technical staff and sometimes users, get together in a room and evaluate the design of the application that you are current-ly developing. The purpose of this evaluation is to determine if the design not only fulfills the demands of the user community, but is also of sufficient quality to be easy to develop, maintain, and enhance. When they are done properly, technical-design reviews can have a big payoff because they often identify deficiencies when they are still rea-sonably inexpensive to address.

In this section we will address the following issues:

1. What should be reviewed

2. How to perform a review

3. How to plan a review

4. Technical-review checklists

5. Tips and techniques for successful reviews

6. The advantages of technical reviews.

DEFINITION

Technical-design review—A testing technique in which the design of your application is examined critically by a group of your peers. This process is often referred to as a walkthrough.

12.4.1.1 What Should Be Reviewed?

The first question that you want to address is what you wish to review. Although technical reviews are often performed to evaluate documentation and program code as well as your design efforts, in this section we will concentrate on the issues involved in technical-design reviews. Technical-design reviews often address (Ince, 1994) issues such as how well the design will support the required functionality, as well as system properties such as response time, reliability, interfaces to other systems, target computers, operating systems, file/database/memory requirements and limitations, as well as the extensibility and maintainability of the design. You want to put your design through its paces to determine whether or not you've done a good job.

Some of the issues that I believe should also be addressed by a technical review include the following: Do you have it right? Have you documented your design/code properly (we discussed code documentation in chapter 8)? Will other people be able to understand your work (i.e., can you hand it off)? Does it conform to both your organizational standards and to industry standards? Is the project still on schedule? All of these questions are important and should not be taken lightly. Make sure they are covered in your technical reviews.

12.4.1.2 The Technical-Review Process

There are five basic steps to doing a formal technical review, be it a design review, a document review, or a program-code review. The steps of a technical review are as follows:

1. **The development team indicates that they are ready for review.** The development team must inform the technical-review manager when they are ready to have their work verified as well as what they intend to have reviewed, such as their application design, their documentation, or their program code.

2. **The review manager performs a cursory review.** The first thing that the review manager must do is determine if the development team has produced work that is actually ready to be reviewed. The manager will probably discuss the development team's work with the team leader and do a quick rundown of what they've produced. The main goal at this stage is to ensure that the work to be reviewed is good enough to warrant getting a review team together. You don't want to waste their time.

3. **The review manager plans and organizes the review.** Once the review manager has determined that work to be reviewed is ready, he or she must schedule a review room, any equipment needed for the review, invite the proper people (see section 12.4.1.3 below), and send out any materials that are needed ahead of time for the review.

4. **The review takes place.** Technical reviews can take anywhere from several hours to several days depending on the size of what is being reviewed. The entire development team should attend, or at least the people responsible for what is being reviewed, to answer questions and to explain/clarify their work. There will also be from three to five reviewers, as well as the review manager, all of whom are responsible for doing the review.

5. **The review results are acted on.** Depending on how formal the review, a document may be produced (informal reviews typically provide only verbal feedback) describing both the strengths and weaknesses of the work being reviewed. This document should provide both a description of any weakness, why it is a weakness, and possibly provide an indication of what needs to be addressed to fix the weakness. This document will be given to the development team so that they can act on it, and will be kept by the review manager to

be used at any follow-up reviews in which the work is looked at again to verify that the weaknesses were addressed.

12.4.1.3 Planning a Technical Review

As indicated in the previous section, technical reviews must be planned if they are to be successful. The plan is typically created by the review manager and should result in a *technical-review-plan document* that addresses the following issues:

1. **What is the goal of the review?** The review-plan document should describe what is to be reviewed, why it is important to your organization, and what the end goal of the review is. Typical goals include verifying that the user requirements will be met by an application, that the documentation for the system is sufficient, or that the models and diagrams conform to your organizations standards. The technical reviewers need a clear indication of what the goal is for the review if they are to come properly prepared.

2. **Who is to attend?** The review plan must include a list of who will attend the review as well as why they are to attend. The attendees will include the developers directly involved in the development of the work being reviewed; technical experts such as designers, database administrators, programmers, and project managers who have the skills and experience appropriate to review the work; key user representatives, if appropriate to what is being reviewed, who have a stake in the project; and possibly outside experts from other organizations who are experienced technical reviewers. These people are a must whenever you are reviewing a mission-critical system, as they can provide an unbiased opinion from a completely different viewpoint other than that of your fellow co-workers. There should also be a scribe to record the findings of the review process.

   Outside experts can provide unbiased opinions from new viewpoints.

3. **What information is required by the reviewers before the review?** The review plan will provide an indication of what is to be reviewed, including any documentation, review checklists, organizational standards, diagrams, models, or program code. This information should be includ-

ed as attachments to the review plan itself. The basic goal is to provide the reviewers with all the documentation that they need to prepare themselves ahead of time.

4. **What records/documentation will be produced?** The review plan should end with a description of the expected results of the review, providing an indication to everyone involved as to what they are expected to hand off to the development team. This helps to set appropriate expectations and helps to ensure that the development team benefits from the review itself. Why hold the review if you aren't going to use its results to improve the work under review?

DEFINITION

Technical-review plan—A document that describes the goal of a technical review, who is to attend and why, the information that the reviewers require before the review, and the records and documentation that will be produced by the review.

12.4.1.4 Technical-Review Checklists

In addition to the technical-review-plan document described in section 12.4.3, the technical review manager should send out all relevant design documents such as class diagrams and sequence diagrams to the review participants. Furthermore, checklists of review topics should be included in this package. These checklists help to ensure that you cover everything that needs to be covered and allow reviewers to prepare themselves.

When you are preparing your checklist you should let the goals of the technical review drive its development. For example, if one of the goals was to review the class diagram for the application, some of the items that should appear on the checklist are as follows:

- Was the company standard, the Ambler notation, used for the class diagram?

- Are the class symbols the same size?

- Has a requirement-verification matrix (see section 12.4.5 below) been created for the class diagram?

- Are the classes documented according to company standards?

- Are the methods documented?

- Are the attributes documented?

- Are the relationships documented?

- Is the correct cardinality and optionality documented for each relationship?

- When aggregation is being used, would an instance relationship be more appropriate? Vice versa?

- Is pure inheritance being used? If not, has it been properly justified?

- Are the classes partitioned cleanly (i.e., do they make sense)?

TIP

Look to the Problems of the Past to Create Checklists

A really good source of checklists are descriptions of technical problems that you have experienced in the past—they might not reveal all potential problems, but at least you can ensure that you won't make the same mistakes twice.

12.4.1.5 Tips for Performing Successful Technical Reviews

In my experience technical reviews are often one of the best ways to judge the quality of the application that you are building. Although there will always be things that need to be improved, you will find that you will often gain significant insights from the people reviewing your work, assuming of course the review process was successful. The following issues provide insight into how to organize and participate in a successful technical review.

1. **You're judging the design, not the people.** Never forget that you are reviewing the work of the development team, not the team members themselves. Whenever a technical review degenerates into personal attacks on people it almost always fails. Although this is easier said than done, you need to keep the review on a technical level and not on a personal one.

2. **Get the right people on the review.** When you are reviewing an object-oriented project, the technical people acting as reviewers must have an understanding of the object-oriented development process. I've seen OO projects thrown off track when they "failed" based on criticisms made by "expert" reviewers who didn't know a thing about OO. Never forget that OO development is different from structured development. What used to be a development truism in the past can often be irrelevant or just plain wrong for OO development. Unfortunately, people who haven't made the leap to OO may not realize this, or if they have they may not yet know what still works and what doesn't work. You can't review an OO project if you don't understand the OO development process to begin with.

3. **Get a skilled review manager.** Planning and facilitating technical reviews can be an arduous and complex task that requires the skills of a highly trained professional. Not only do they need to understand the review process, they also need the people skills to facilitate the reviews and the technical skills to understand what is being reviewed.

4. **Obtain consensus, not majority vote.** The goal of a technical review is to provide good, sound advice on how to improve what is being reviewed. The best way to do that is to come to a consensus within the group and not by letting a majority vote rule. The majority isn't always right and you have to invest the time needed to get everyone to agree to the correct approach. It isn't easy, but it's worth it.

12.4.1.6 *The Advantages of Technical Reviews*

There are several important advantages to technical reviews that are best described in the list (Hetzel, 1988) below:

- Reviews provide the best mechanism for reliably evaluating progress

- Reviews bring individual capabilities to light

- Reviews discover batches and classes of errors at once

- Reviews give early feedback and prevent more serious problems from arising

- Reviews train and educate the participant and have a significant positive impact on staff competence.

Technical reviews are an excellent way of ensuring that the design of your application will meet the needs of your users, be easy to extend and maintain, and will help to make the development of your application easier.

TIP

Get the Design Right First

Although I'm beginning to sound like a broken record, it's really worth your while to get your design right. The better your design, the less there is to code and the less there is to test. This reduces both the time it takes to develope the application and the cost to do so. The time invested in technical-design reviews can really pay off.

12.4.2 Requirement-Verification Matrices

Requirement-verification matrices (Ince, 1994) are used to relate user requirements to the portion(s) of your application that implement those requirements. For OO applications the names of classes are listed across the top of the matrix, the use cases for your application are listed along the left-hand axis of the matrix, and in the squares are listed the main method(s) in each class that are involved in fulfilling each use-case. The advantage of requirement-verification matrices is that they provide a mechanism to trace your design efforts back to your use-case definitions that actually describe the user requirements for your application. This enables you to both verify that your design meets the needs of your users and to determine what classes might be affected by a maintenance change for regression-testing purposes (section 12.2).

Let's consider an example. Table 12.2 presents a portion of a requirement-verification matrix for our bank case study. In this example we've described each user case briefly. Typically what happens is you simply put the unique number used to identify each use-case in the requirement column in order to save space in the matrix.

DEFINITION

Requirement-verification matrix—A document that is used to relate use cases to the portions of your application that implement those requirements. For OO applications, the names of classes are listed across the top of the matrix, the use cases are listed along the left-hand axis of the matrix, and in the squares are listed the main method(s) involved in fulfilling each use-case.

Table 12.2. **A Small Portion of a Requirement-Verification Matrix for the Bank Case Study**

Requirement	Savings Account	Customer	Transaction
Deposit money into an account	Deposit		Post
Withdraw money from an ATM	Withdraw	Supply PIN for verification	Post
Print bank statement	Print statement	Supply name and address	Supply transaction info

---

TIP

Use a Spreadsheet to Create Requirement-Verification Matrices

Because requirement-verification matrices can grow to be quite large for complex applications, I have found that it is a good idea to use a spreadsheet.

12.5 Testing Your Program Code

Testing object-oriented programming code in many ways is similar to testing structured/procedural code, although in many ways it is also different. In this section we will discuss many "traditional" testing concepts and even newer OO testing concepts. Don't worry—many of the new testing techniques that we'll discuss are actually extensions of structured testing techniques that have been modified to meet the needs of OO developers.

In this section we will cover the following code-testing techniques:

- code reviews
- traditional testing techniques
  - black box
  - white/clear box
  - boundary values
  - coverage testing
  - path testing
- object-oriented testing techniques
  - method testing
  - class testing
  - inheritance-regression testing
  - class-integration testing

The main goal of all of these testing techniques is to help us formulate a collection of test cases to put our program code through its paces. Before we formally test our program code, however, we should first perform a code review to help find deficiencies that testing often cannot detect.

TIP

Stabilize the Code Before Testing It

Don't start code testing until the portion of code that you intend to test is stable. Although we discussed in chapter 8 that the best way to program is to develop a little bit of code, test it, then develop another little bit and so on, I really don't spend a lot of time testing it at this point. You want to be fairly confident that your code works before you go on, but you shouldn't start your "real" testing until you're confident that the code is pretty well finished. The reason for this is simple. Whenever you make a change to your code, you have to test that change, so it doesn't make sense to test until the code is stable enough that there will be few, if any, changes made to it before it is put into production.

12.5.1 Code Reviews

Inspect your code first, then test it.

Technical reviews, discussed above in section 12.4, are used to determine the quality of your code as well as the quality of your design. Code reviews often reveal problems that normal testing techniques don't; in particular, poor coding practices that make your application difficult to extend and maintain. I am a firm believer that code reviews should be done before formal testing because once code has been formally tested and approved developers are rarely motivated to then have their code inspected. Their attitude is that the code works, so why bother looking at it again? The end result is that you should first review your code, act on the recommendations from that review, then test it.

Everything that we discussed about planning, running, and following-up technical-design reviews in section 12.4 applies to technical code reviews, the only difference being the issues that you address in the review. Code reviews should concentrate on quality issues such as:

- Naming conventions for your classes, methods, and attributes

- Code documentation standards and conventions
  - Have you documented what a method does?
  - Have you documented what parameters must be passed?
  - Have you documented what values are returned by a method?

TIPS

Tips for Using Coding Standards as Input to Technical Reviews

1. Document your coding standards. If you do intend to do code reviews, then you need to put together a document describing the coding standards and conventions that you expect programmers to adhere to. This document should be distributed before the project begins so that programmers know on what basis their code will be reviewed. In short, you have to define the rules of the game before you begin playing it.

2. Use the coding standards from this book. The coding practices that we discussed in chapter 8 can be used as a basis for your organization's coding standards.

— Have you documented both what and why a piece of code does what it does?

- Writing small methods that do one thing and one thing well

- Can the code be simplified?

Once your program code has been reviewed and approved, you must still verify that it works by formally testing it. In the following sections we will discuss both traditional and object-oriented techniques for testing your program code.

12.5.2 Traditional Testing Methods

I've told you that many traditional testing techniques are still applicable to object-oriented testing, whereas others aren't. Well, now it's time to put my money where my mouth is and discuss what traditional testing techniques are still viable in the world of OO development. In this section we will discuss black-box testing, white/clear box testing, boundary-value testing, coverage testing, and path testing.

TIP

Your Newest Code Is Probably Where the Errors Are

Although you're coding, you'll also be doing testing, at least a rough form of it. During this process any new errors that you find are almost always the result of the code that you just put in, so look there first.

12.5.2.1 Black-Box Testing

Black-box testing is a technique in which you create test cases based only on the expected functionality of a method, class, or application, without any knowledge of its internal workings. One way to define black-box testing, as shown in Figure 12.2, is that given defined input "A," we should get the expected results "B." The goal of black-box testing is to make sure the system can do what it should be able to do, but not how it does it. For example, a black-box test for a word processor would be to verify that it is able to read a file in from disk and then write it back exactly as it was originally. It's a black-box test because

Figure 12.2.
Black-box testing.

*Black-box test
cases are often
created from
analyzing use
cases.*

we can run it without having any knowledge of how the word processor reads and writes files.

The creation of black-box tests is often driven by the user requirements, typically documented by use cases, for the application. The basic idea is that we look at the user requirement and ask ourselves what needs to be done to show that the user requirement is met. For our bank case study one of our user requirements would be to support deposit, withdrawal, and get balance access to accounts via the use of automated teller machines (ATMs). This requirement would generate black-box tests such as: withdraw funds from a savings account using an ATM, deposit funds into an account at an ATM, and transfer funds between accounts using an ATM.

The advantage of black-box tests is that they allow you to prove that your application fulfills the user requirements defined for it. Unfortunately, black-box testing doesn't allow you to show that extra, often technical, features not defined by your users also work. For this you need to create white/clear-box test cases.

> **DEFINITION**
>
> *Black-box tests—*
> Test cases that verify
> that given input A
> the component/system being tested
> gives you expected
> results B.

12.5.2.2 White/Clear Box Testing

White-box testing, also called *clear-box testing*, is based on the concept that your program code can drive the development of test cases. The basic idea is that you look at your code and then create test cases that exercise it. In Figure 12.3 we see that with white-box testing we are

Figure 12.3.
White-box
testing.

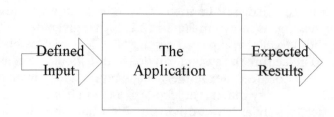

able to see the internal workings of an application, and that with this knowledge we create test cases that will run specific sections of code.

For example, assume that we have access to the source code that reads in files for a word processor. When we look at it we see that there is an IF statement (in Smalltalk that would be an **ifTrue:ifFalse:** message) that determines whether or not the file being read in is a word-processing file or a simple text file, and then reads it in appropriately. This indicates that we need to run at least three tests on this source code: one to read in a word-processor file, one to read in a text file, and one to read in a file that is neither a word-processor file nor a text file. By looking at the code we were able to determine new test cases to exercise the different logic paths within it.

The main advantage of white-box testing is that it allows you to create tests that will exercise specific lines of code that may not have been tested by simple black box-test cases. Unfortunately, it does not allow you to confirm that all the user requirements have been met, since it only enables you to test the specific code that you have written.

> **DEFINITION**
>
> *White-box tests*— Test cases that verify that specific lines of code work as defined. This is also referred to as clear-box testing.

12.5.2.3 Boundary-Value Testing

Boundary-value testing is based on the fact that you need to test your code to ensure that it can handle unusual and extreme situations. For example, boundary-value test cases for withdrawing funds from a bank account would include test cases such as attempting to withdraw $0.00, $0.01, –$0.01, a very large amount of money, and perhaps even a large negative amount of money. Furthermore, if there is a daily limit of $500 for withdrawals from automated teller machines you would want to create tests that verify that you could withdraw $500 on a single transaction, but not $500.01, and run the same tests for a collection of transactions that add up to the same amount.

The basic idea is that you want to look for limits defined either by your business rules or by common sense, and create test cases that test attribute values in and around those values. The main advantage of boundary-value testing is that it allows you to confirm that your program code is able to handle unusual or extreme cases.

> **DEFINITION**
>
> *Boundary-value tests*—Test cases that test unusual or extreme situations that your code should be able to handle.

Limits defined by your business rules and/or by your own common sense should be tested for to verify that your code does the right thing when it experiences them.

> ## TIP
>
> ### With Someone Else's Code Concentrate on Typical Situations
>
> If you are testing someone else's code, then spend more effort testing for typical situations than for boundary-value cases, especially if you already know that the developer has already tested the code. My experience has always been that programmers are really good at boundary-value testing. Boundary-value testing is typically pounded into computer science students in college, with the result that anyone who took programming courses in school is typically very good at it.

12.5.2.4 Coverage and Path Testing

Coverage testing ensures that all lines of code were tested. Path testing ensures that all logic paths were tested.

Coverage testing is a technique in which you create a series of test cases designed to test all the code paths in your code. In a lot of ways, coverage testing is simply a collection of white-box test cases that together exercise every line of code in your application at least once. *Path testing* is a superset of coverage testing that ensures that not only have all lines of code been tested, but all paths of *logic* have been tested as well. The main difference occurs when you have a method with more than one set of case statements or nested IF statements (two techniques that we saw in chapter 8 to be bad coding styles): to determine the number of test cases with coverage testing you would count the maximum number of paths between the sets of case/nested IF statements, and with path testing you would multiply the number of logic paths.

Let's consider an example. In Figure 12.4 we see a code-logic diagram for a method. In this method we see that we have two sets of case statements: the combination of **b**, **c**, **d**, and **e**, and the combination of **f**, **g**, and **h**. When each case statement is considered alone it has the following logic paths: **bcf**, **bdf**, and **bef**; **fgi**, and **fhi**, respectively. To coverage test this code you would need only three test cases that would cover the following paths through the code: **abcfgi**, **abdfhi**, **abefhi** (or **abefgi**—it doesn't matter). Although coverage testing would ensure that all code is tested, it doesn't ensure that all combinations of the code would be tested. Path testing, on the other hand, would use six test cases to test all logic paths present in the code. These logic paths would be: **abcfgi**, **abdfgi**, **adefgi**, **abcfhi**, **abdfhi**, and **adefhi**.

The main advantage of coverage testing is that it helps to ensure that all lines of code in your application have been tested, although it does-

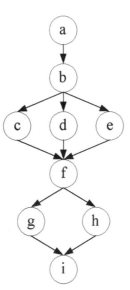

Figure 12.4.
The flow of code
in an example
method.

SCOTT'S SOAPBOX

Coverage and Path Testing Aren't as Important Anymore

Although I am a strong believer in both coverage and path testing, I'm a little leery about their use for object-oriented applications. Without a doubt there is value in exercising all of your code at least once. My experience, however, is that this often lulls programmers into a false sense of security that their code actually works. Sure, every line of code was run successfully, but does that mean the code actually works? Absolutely NOT in an OO environment.

For the most part, the problem has to do with polymorphism—the ability of objects to change their type. You might test some code that works fine when a specific object is customer, but later that same object might become an employee and your code crashes. The ability of objects to change type means that the ground is constantly shifting beneath you; the end result being that just because you have coverage tested and/or path tested successfully, it doesn't mean that your code is guaranteed to run perfectly in production. All that it means is that your source was exercised thoroughly.

Coverage and path testing are both good techniques in theory, but in object-oriented practice they often fall short of their ideal. Use these techniques; just don't completely rely on them.

> **DEFINITIONS**
>
> **Coverage testing**—The act of ensuring that all lines of code were exercised at least once.
>
> **Path testing**—The act of ensuring that all logic paths within your code were exercised at least once. This is a superset of coverage testing.

n't ensure that all of the combinations of the code have been tested. Path testing on the other hand does test all combinations of the code, but requires significantly more effort to formulate and run the test cases.

12.5.2.5 The Need for a New Testing Paradigm

Test data sets no longer make sense, instead we need test object sets.

I'd like to finish this section with a discussion of how we need to change our view of how to test applications. First of all, the concept of test data sets, a collection of data representing test cases that exercises a program, needs to be thrown out the window. Unlike structured applications that are built from a series of programs that work with data, object-oriented applications are built from interacting objects. We don't use data to exercise our programs anymore, we use objects. Therefore, instead of test data sets we need to create test object sets.

A new development paradigm implies that we need a new testing paradigm too.

Related to this is the need to rethink the concept of a test case. Instead of defining a test case as some data and some code to run against the data, we now have object-oriented test cases that are a collection of objects that have been put into a specified state and a series of messages sent to those objects to exercise them. In section 12.5.5 we'll discuss several strategies for implementing OO test cases.

12.5.3 New Testing Techniques for OO Program Code

Object-oriented code testing is a combination of old and new testing techniques.

There are three main categories of object-oriented testing techniques: method testing, class testing, and class-integration testing. Although we will explore each of these categories in greater detail, I want to first point out that the traditional testing techniques described in the previous section (black-box, white-box, boundary-value, coverage, and path testing) are all applicable approaches to help you define test cases for method, class, and class-integration testing. Object-oriented code testing is a collection of new and old techniques. The trick is to know which ones to use and which ones not to.

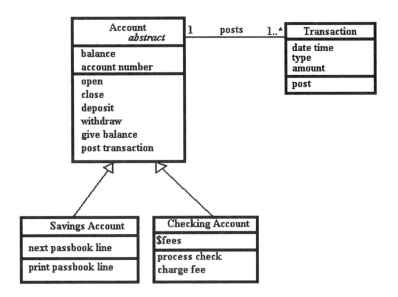

Figure 12.5.
A class diagram depicting a portion of our bank information system.

12.5.3.1 Method Testing

Method testing is the act of ensuring that your methods, called member functions in C++, perform as defined. The closest comparison to method testing in the structured world is the unit testing of functions and procedures. Although some people argue that class testing, discussed below, is really the object-oriented version of unit testing, my experience has been that the creation of test cases for specific methods often proves useful and should not be ignored. Hence the need for method testing. Figure 12.5 depicts a class diagram that we will define test cases for.

The first thing that you do is create test cases for the accessors, the methods that get and set the values of the attributes of an object. Accessors are simple, self-contained units that typically interact with only one attribute, the one that they get or set. In Figure 12.6 we see

---

DEFINITIONS

Unit testing—The act of testing small components of a system to ensure that they work. In the object world this is both method and class testing.

Method testing—The act of ensuring that a method (member function) performs as defined.

the Smalltalk code for the two accessors of the instance attribute **currentBalance** of the class **Account**. The first method is the *getter*, and the second method is the *setter*. The test cases for setters, accessor methods that set attribute values, are straightforward—you set the attribute, then compare its value to what you set it at.

Create specific test cases for accessor methods.

The test cases for getters, accessor methods that get the value of an attribute, are slightly more complex. You need to check that the default value for the attribute is set appropriately and that the getter works during normal execution of the system. The getter method in Figure 12.6 uses *lazy initialization*, a technique in which the getter initializes the attribute the first time it is accessed. If you don't use lazy initialization, then you must initialize the attribute at the time the object is first instantiated. Regardless of the approach you take to initialization, you must still test to see if the attribute is initialized properly. Modeling note: accessors typically aren't shown on class diagrams (as in Figure 12.5) because they are assumed to exist.

Figure 12.6.
Smalltalk source code for some of accessor methods of Account.

```
currentBalance
        " Get the current balance of this account  "
        (currentBalance isNil) ifTrue: [
                " The account must have just been opened, set the
                balance to zero "
                self currentBalance: 0.0.
        ].
        ^ currentBalance.


currentBalance: newBalance
        " Set the current balance for this account "
        currentBalance := newBalance.
```

To test the accessors shown in Figure 12.6 you need at least two test cases: one to test the getter to verify that it initializes the attribute properly, and one to test the setter which would include testing the getter (so you can compare the value of the attribute before and after). Note that you might decide to roll both of those test cases into one.

Once you're convinced that your accessors work then you should start addressing other method testing issues:

- Ensuring methods return the proper values

- Basic checking of the parameters being passed to the methods

- Ensuring the method does what the documentation says it does.

Let's look at an example. In Figure 12.7 we see the source code for withdrawing funds from an account. When creating test cases for this method, the first thing to do is create test cases around the parameter, **anAmount**, being passed to the method. Try boundary cases—passing it negative numbers, zero, positive numbers, very large numbers, the exact amount in the account, more than what is in the account, and less than what is in the account. These test cases will run through all lines of code and will allow you to check all possible return values. You should also try passing it unreasonable information—a string, an undefined value, and a date (I'm a strong believer in testing for things that shouldn't work). These test cases, in combination with the previous ones, should adequately test the parameters passed to the method. Finally, you should also look at the documentation for this method and create black-box test cases based on the business rules defined there.

```
withdraw: anAmount
        " Withdraw anAmount from this account "
        (self currentBalance >= anAmount) ifTrue: [
                " Post a withdrawal transaction "
                self postTransaction: #withdrawal amount:
                anAmount.
                " Debit the account "
                self currentBalance: (self currentBalance -
                anAmount).
        ] ifFalse: [
                " Don't allow the withdrawal if there isn't enough
                in the account "
                ^ 'Not enough funds in account.' asMessage.
        ].
```

Figure 12.7.
Smalltalk source code for the withdraw method of Account.

As you can see, the code in Figure 12.7 would fail several of the tests that are proposed above. Although the method fails the tests, what should we do about it? Should we add better parameter checking in the method, along with its associated overhead, or should we simply document what parameter values are acceptable and hope that the developers who use the method do what they're told? Both approaches are valid, you just need to decide which one you'll take and stick to it.

TIP

Tips for Better Method Testing

Over the years I have learned several important lessons about method testing that I'd like to share with you:

1. Dynamically typed languages like Smalltalk increase the difficulty of testing methods in isolation. Because you never know the type of an object, at least without unnecessarily increasing your application's overhead by checking an object's type, you need to be careful about what you pass as parameters to a method.

2. Method testing isn't enough. We still need class testing and class-integration testing.

12.5.3.2 Class Testing

Class testing is both unit testing and traditional integration testing at the same time. It is unit testing because you are testing the class and its instances as single units in isolation, but at the same time it is integration testing because you need to verify that the methods and attributes of the class work together. Class testing is an important component of the OO code-testing process.

For now assume that the other classes in the system work.

The one assumption that you need to make during class testing is that all other classes in the system work. Although this may sound like an unreasonable assumption, it is basically what separates class testing from class-integration testing, a subject discussed later. The main purpose of class testing is to test classes in isolation, which is difficult to do if you don't assume everything else works.

> **DEFINITION**
>
> *Class testing*—The act of ensuring that a class and its instances (objects) perform as defined.

12.5.3.2.1 Using State Diagrams to Drive Class Testing

The first thing to do when class testing is to look at the state diagram, if there is one, for the class you are testing. The interesting thing about this approach is that if a class is simple enough so that you didn't need to draw a state diagram for it, then chances are fairly good that your method tests are sufficient. Complex classes, however, require that you take a more thorough approach to design; hence the state diagram and a more thorough approach to testing. Therefore it makes sense to allow your state diagram to help drive the development of test cases.

State diagrams can drive the development of test cases.

  The state diagram in Figure 12.8 shows many interesting aspects of the class **Account**. We see the various states that an account may be in at any given time and the transitions between those states. Right away it becomes obvious that we need to create test cases that will put an account object into each of these states and then verify that the transitions out of that state actually work. For example, we would want to verify that when the account is active that we can query it, deposit into it, and withdraw money from it. Furthermore, we also want to verify that the transitions that shouldn't work for certain

Test for both valid and invalid transitions for leaving a state.

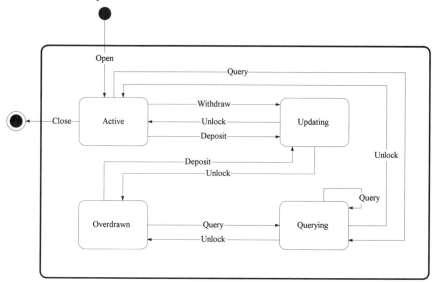

Figure 12.8.
A state diagram for Account.

states don't. For example, we see that we can't withdraw from a savings account when it is overdrawn so therefore we should create a test case to check this to verify that you can't in fact do the withdrawal.

To test the state diagram thoroughly we need to try every transition for each unique state and see if the class does what we expect. Note that whenever a transition can take you to more than one of several states, you'll need to test for each one. In Figure 12.8 we see that when that the **unlock** transition leads to either the **Active** or the **Overdrawn** state depending on the value of the account balance (if the balance is less than zero then the account is overdrawn). Therefore we'll need two test cases to test for this.

TIP

You Can Combine Test Cases

It's at about this point in the chapter that I think you'll become despondent as to how many test cases you'll have to create to properly verify your code. Don't worry, you can often combine several test cases into one. In other words, you can kill two potential error birds with one test-case stone if you want to. All you need to do is ask yourself what two or three test cases seem to fit together, and then write the code to test them all at the same time. It's as simple as that.

12.5.3.2.2 Inheritance-Regression Testing

Without a doubt the most important part of class testing is *inheritance-regression testing*—the running of the class and method test cases for all of the superclasses of the class being tested. For example, in Figure 12.5 we see that **CheckingAccount** inherits from **Account**. When we test **CheckingAccount**, we need to run all of the test cases for **Account** against it as well as any new test cases that we might identify.

You have to run the test cases of the super class on the subclass.

The motivation behind inheritance-regression testing is simple. It is incredibly naive to expect that errors haven't been introduced by a new subclass. New methods are added and existing methods are often redefined by subclasses, and these methods access and often change the value of the attributes defined in the superclass. It is very possible that a subclass may change the value of the attributes in a way that was never intended in the superclass, or at least was never expected. Personally, I would want to run the old test cases against my new subclass just to make sure everything still works.

```
withdraw: anAmount
        " Withdraw anAmount from this account "
        | returnValue |
        returnValue := super withdraw: anAmount.
        (returnValue isMessage) ifFalse: [
                " Charge a fee for withdrawing "
                self chargeFee: #processWithdrawal.
        ].
        ^ returnValue.
```

Figure 12.9.
Smalltalk source code for the **withdraw** method of CheckingAccount.

For example, in Figure 12.5 we see that the method **withdraw** is overridden (redefined) by **CheckingAccount**, the code for which is presented in Figure 12.9. The main difference is that we charge a fee for withdrawing from a checking account that we don't charge for savings accounts. Although this code will probably test out OK, there might be a potential problem that we overlooked—transferring money between accounts may not work properly anymore. Our bank insists that you must have sufficient funds in the account that you are transferring money from to complete the transaction. That means you need to check the balance, compare it with the amount to be transferred, and then perform the transfer if you have enough money. Simple enough. What happens when I have exactly $50 in an account and want to transfer $50 to another account? I should be able to do this from a savings account but not from a checking account because I wouldn't have enough money to cover the withdrawal fee. By running the **Account** test cases against **CheckingAccount** we will discover whether or not we're taking the fee into account when we transfer money between accounts.

I can't stress enough that inheritance-regression testing is critical to the success of your project. Just because it works in the superclass doesn't mean it'll work in your subclass. It's as simple as that.

DEFINITION

Inheritance-regression testing—The act of running the test cases of all the superclasses, both direct and indirect, on a given subclass.

> **TIP**
>
> ### Testing for Potential Inheritance Errors Is Critical
>
> The most important lessons I've learned over the years about class testing is that state diagrams often provide unique insights into testing, and that inheritance-regression testing is an absolute must. If you've done a clean job of inheritance, you have only added new functionality and not taken any away, then your test suite of the superclass should run without a hitch against the subclass and you'll have the peace of mind of knowing that your subclass works. If on the other hand your use of inheritance isn't so pure, then chances are pretty good that you've introduced errors into the system that you'll want to root out and fix. Inheritance-regression testing does this very well.

12.5.3.3 Class-Integration Testing

Look at the relationships between classes for insights into new test cases.

Class-integration testing addresses the issue of whether or not the classes in your system work together properly. Because we know that the only way classes, or to be more accurate the instances of classes, can work together is via sending each other messages, and that there must be some sort of relationship between those objects before they can send the message, then it is clear that the relationships between classes can be used to drive the development of integration test cases. In other words, our strategy should be to look at the association, aggregation, and inheritance relationships that appear on our class diagram to help us to formulate class-integration test cases.

DEFINITION

Class-integration testing—The act of ensuring that the classes, and their instances, that form an application perform as defined.

As we did previously, let's go for the easy test cases. For class-integration testing that means we should first create test cases to verify that the relationships between objects are being maintained properly. For example, in Figure 12.5 we see that there is an instance relationship, or association, between **Savings-Account** and **Transaction**. This relationship will be maintained in one of two ways: either a transaction "knows" what account it is posted against or the account maintains a list of all transactions that it posts, or perhaps a combination of the two. Anyway, we need to test that when a new transaction gets posted the right thing happens and that when a transaction gets deleted then the right thing happens as well. Furthermore, because it is possible for relationships to change between objects, if I sell you my house then the house object now has an "owned-by" relationship with you instead of me, we would want to test that the relationship is updated properly. In short we need to create test cases to verify we can both insert new objects into a relationship and remove existing objects from a relationship

We also need to test all messages being sent from one object to another. That's hard because the dynamic nature of objects makes it difficult to test them. You could send a message to an object when it is in one state and everything works fine, but send the same message to the same object when it is in another state and the system might crash. Yikes! Furthermore, the polymorphic nature of some OO languages allow objects to change type. One minute a person object might be an employee object, and the next minute it might be a customer object. Customer objects react to different messages than employee objects or may react differently to the same message. Because objects can change both state and type on the fly, it makes testing incredibly difficult.

To protect myself from these problems I believe in checking the return value of all messages to verify that they worked properly. (OK, I didn't do this with the **chargeFee:** message in Figure 12.9, but do as I say, not as I do). Although this takes a little extra coding, I can sleep at night knowing reasonably well that my applications work. (Actually I can sleep at night because I'm not being beeped to come in and fix my applications to be exact.) The testing implication of all this is that you need to generate test cases that will result in all important return values for a message being worked through. Although this sounds like a lot of work, the good news is that you have probably already created these test cases while you were method and class testing.

Let's consider an example. In Figure 12.10 we see part of the code for posting transactions. Notice how the return value from posting a transaction is checked to see if an error message was returned. We should run tests for situations in which the transaction is posted properly and for when it isn't (perhaps we'd need to take down the transaction server to force an error to come back). The point to be made is that we want to ensure that our **postTransaction:amount:** method works properly when the two classes, **Account** and **Transaction** are integrated.

In the long run, class-integration testing is affected the most by the quality of your code. The better the encapsulation within your system and the looser the coupling between classes then the easier it is to test. Bad coding practices result in your having to spend more time testing, and then fixing, your application.

Figure 12.10.
Smalltalk source
code for posting
transactions in
Account.

```
postTransaction: aTransactionType amount: anAmount
    " Post a transaction to record a change in this account "
    | aTransaction  returnValue |

    " Create the transaction "
    aTransaction := Transaction new.
    aTransaction account: self.
    aTransaction type: aTransactionType.
    aTransaction amount: anAmount.

    " Write the transaction to the transaction log "
    returnValue := aTransaction post.
    (returnValue isMessage) ifTrue: [
            " The transaction wasn't posted, do whatever's
            appropriate..... "
    ].
```

TIP

The Better the Design, the Less Code to Test

It is really worth your while to take the time to get your design right. Good designs often lead to significantly less code, and significantly less code means significantly less code testing.

12.5.4 Language-Specific Testing Issues

I can't stress enough the importance of testing for memory leaks in any language, especially C++, where you are required to manage memory yourself. It doesn't matter how trivial the leak is, even if it is only a couple of bytes per instance, eventually you'll run out of memory space.

12.5.5 Implementing Program Code Test Cases

An important decision in object-oriented testing is how you are going to implement your test cases. There are four common approaches to implementing OO test cases: build them right into your classes, create a separate testing hierarchy, create test subclasses, or create a test script. Each approach has its strengths and weaknesses, which are discussed below.

1. **Building test cases right into your classes.** The basic idea is that every class you create has several standard methods where you put your testing code: one or more class methods devoted to testing the functionality of the class itself, and one or more instance methods devoted to testing the objects of the class. You'll typically have a class method called **testClass** that tests all of the class methods and then creates one or more instances of the class, put each of them into a certain state, and then send the instances one or more **testObjectFor...** messages. The **testObjectFor...** methods puts the object through a series of related test cases. For example, the class **Account** may have methods called **testObjectForSimpleTransactions** and **testObjectForComplexTransactions**. The advantage of this approach is that it is easy for subclasses to inherit the test cases of their superclasses, an important consideration for inheritance-regression testing and for test-case reuse. It also increases the chance that developers will keep the test cases up to date because the testing code is right there in their face. The main drawbacks are that this approach increases the footprint of your released application, unless of course you strip out the testing methods, and that it requires you to perform testing in a uniform manner for all of your classes (which I think is an advantage).

2. **Creating a separate testing hierarchy.** Another common technique to implement test cases is to create a separate testing hierarchy that corresponds on a one-to-one basis with the classes that you want to test. The advantages of this approach are that you can still inherit test cases and that your testing code is separate from your "real" code. One disadvantage is that you now have two sets of code to maintain, increasing the chance that your developers won't keep the test code up to date. Another disadvantage is that encapsulation can hinder this approach; for example, how would you test private C++ member functions (methods)? Remember, private member functions are only accessible internally to the class itself, and not externally to testing classes. One way around this is to use either friend classes or mixin classes, both of which unfortu-

nately break the encapsulation of a class and may be used to justify or reinforce questionable coding practices within the rest of your application. C++ friends are rarely friendly from a maintenance point of view, so avoid them if you can.

3. **Creating a test script.** The traditional way to test is to create a series of testing scripts that would create a collection of objects, send them messages, and then compare the results of the tests to what was expected. The main advantage of this is that it is simple and straightforward, whereas the main disadvantage is that it is difficult to inherit test cases, which increases the complexity of your testing efforts.

4. **Creating testing subclasses.** You can also create testing classes that include only the code needed to directly test a "real" class from which it directly inherits. The basic strategy is to create one testing subclass for every class to be tested. This is similar in concept to a separate testing hierarchy: it's just that the testing subclass sends a series of messages to itself instead of to an instance of the object under test. The main advantage of this approach is that it works well for languages that support multiple inheritance because your testing subclass would inherit from both the class it tests and from the testing subclass(es) of that class's parent class(es), allowing it to inherit test cases. The main disadvantage is that by having separate testing classes you once again risk the chance of them getting out of synch with the classes that they supposedly test. This approach is also clumsy for single-inheritance languages like Smalltalk. If you want to inherit test cases then your class hierarchy will have testing subclasses intermixed with your "real" classes, forcing your "real" classes to inherit from testing classes. Yuck!

My experience has been that built-in test cases are your best bet. They're the easiest to maintain, they can be inherited, and they can be implemented in a manner that is easy to understand. As long as you follow a consistent naming strategy they are also easy to strip out of your code if you need to minimize the footprint, the total amount of storage and memory needed to run the application, of your final production release.

12.5.6 A Process for Successfully Testing Your Code

Although we have discussed many techniques for testing your OO program code, what we haven't talked about is how to go about actually doing the testing. Until now. The following is a list of several issues that need to be addressed when testing your code.

1. **Create a test plan first.** The most effective way to ensure that program code will be tested properly is to create a test plan before you begin coding. Program test plans can be basically thought of as a collection of documented code test cases. For each test case you need to describe it, indicate what method or class it relates to if applicable, any setup needs that must be met before the test can be run, and the expected results of the test.

2. **Review your test plan before you begin coding.** Before you begin coding you should do a technical walkthrough of the test plan. This will help to ensure that the plan is adequate and may even help you to discover deficiencies in your design.

3. **Review your test plan after you've coded.** After the code has been written you need to review your test plan again to ensure that it is still applicable. You often find that you have either left out planned functionality, have taken a different approach than you originally expected, or added new functionality when you realized that you needed it. The end result is that you need to revisit your test plan and update it to reflect these changes.

4. **Get someone else to test your code if possible.** The worst person to get to test your own code is yourself. You are often too close to the code that you wrote to test it adequately, so the best way to ensure that your code is tested properly is to get someone else to do it. At least that's what should happen in an ideal world. In reality, unfortunately, it often proves too time-consuming and costly to have someone test your code for you so you end up having to test it yourself. Luckily, if you've created a test plan you can often negate the disadvantages of testing your own code.

5. **Remember that it's a combination of old and new.** The trick to testing OO program code is to know how and when to use each technique, as well as what structured testing techniques you have to avoid. Don't forget that it's a whole new ball game.

12.5.7 The Strengths of Each Program Code Testing Technique

Table 12.3 summarizes how each program code testing technique is used to generate test cases. The important point to be made is that to properly test your code you need to use all of the testing techniques that we have discussed in this section.

Table 12.3. Comparing Code Testing Techniques

Testing Technique	Allows You to Verify That
Black-box testing	Your code meets the user requirements
Boundary-value testing	Your code handles extreme and unusual situations
Class-integration testing	Your classes work together
Class testing	A class works exclusive of other classes
Code reviews	Your code meets specified quality standards
Coverage testing	All lines of code have been tested
Inheritance-regression testing	A subclass has not adversely affected code inherited from other classes
Method testing	A method works exclusive of other methods and classes
Path testing	All logic paths within your code have been tested
White-box testing	Specific lines of code have been tested

12.6 Testing Your Application As a Whole

Although testing your analysis, your design, and your program code are all very important, they aren't enough. You also have to ensure that the complete application works. All of the components of the application work as they have been defined and the application must meet the needs of its users. To do this, there are several different approaches that we can employ:

- system testing
  - — function testing
  - — stress testing
  - — installation testing
  - — operations testing
- user-acceptance testing
- alpha and beta testing

12.6.1 System Testing

System testing is a testing process in which you aim to determine the system's capabilities and then fix any known problems so that the development team can assure themselves that the application is ready for user-acceptance testing (see section 12.6.2). System testing cannot be performed until after code testing is complete. You can't successfully test your application as a whole until you are reasonably confident that your code works. Development teams that try to do so quickly find that their application blows up in their faces. The following are the most common components of system testing: function testing, stress testing, installation testing, and operations testing.

System testing is performed after code testing to verify that your application is ready for user-acceptance testing.

> **DEFINITION**
>
> *System testing*—A testing process in which you find and fix any known problems to prepare your application for user- acceptance testing.

TIP

Tips for System Testing

1. **You can't test your application as a whole until all of the components have been tested.** If the separate pieces aren't working, there would be no way that they're going to magically work together. You can't begin system testing until your code has been successfully tested and fixed, otherwise your system test will quickly crash and you'll spend a lot more time and effort than you would have finding and fixing the problems.

2. **Testing your application's capabilities is more important than testing its components.** If the components don't work together to support the functionality of your users, then who cares if all of the separate components work perfectly? Your main goal in application development is to deliver an application that meets the needs of your users and that works.

12.6.1.1 Function Testing

Function testing is a system-testing process in which development staff verify that their application meets the needs of their users. The main idea is that they run through the main functionality that the system should exhibit to assure themselves that their application is ready for user-acceptance testing (UAT). It is during UAT that the users will confirm for themselves that the system meets their needs. In many ways the only difference between function testing and user-acceptance testing is who does it: testers and users, respectively.

Use cases can be used as input into creating function test plans.

Because system functionality was captured during analysis by use cases, use cases can be used to drive the development of your function test plan because they lay out the exact logic of how the system operates. You'll find that changes in the design of your application will force you to revisit your use cases to verify that they are still applicable. Once that's done you'll find that your use cases are often perfect input to defining the steps for testing each major function in your system.

DEFINITION

Function testing—A part of systems testing in which development staff confirm that their application meets the user requirements specified during analysis.

In addition to verifying that your system supports the functionality that your users require, you must also confirm that it can do so under harsh and unusual conditions. That's what stress testing is all about.

12.6.1.2 Stress Testing

Stress testing is a system-testing process in which you determine how well your application performs under high numbers of users, high numbers of transactions (testing of high numbers of transactions is also called *volume testing*), high numbers of data transmissions, high numbers of printed reports, and so on. The goal is to find the stress points of your application under which it no longer operates so that you can gain insights into how it will perform in unusual and/or stressful situations.

Stress testing proves that applications can still function during unusual situations.

Although stress testing must be performed during the system-testing process, it is also commonly done at the start of a project to verify whether or not a technical alternative works or simply to test the validity of your software. For example, many database administrators will set up a sample database and "pound it" with high numbers of transactions, access requests, and concurrent users to determine its strengths and weaknesses. At the end of a project the real database will be stress tested again to verify that it will meet the needs of peak demand periods.

Stress testing for the most part is a very technical process that should be performed by developers experienced in both the application and the aspect of it that they intend to stress. Stress testing will often take anywhere from several days to several months, depending for the most part on the complexity of what is being stressed and the number of environments that it must be stressed in. For example, one form of stress testing involves using the application on what is considered the minimal computer/network hardware/software configuration(s) to verify that it can be run in the environments that you say it can run in.

A *stress-test plan* should be created that defines exactly how you intend to go about "pounding" your application. How do you intend to stress the database? The network connection? The printer from which you will be printing reports? How many users logons do you wish to test your application under? All of these questions and more should be addressed in your stress test plan.

12.6.1.3 Installation Testing

Installation testing is a form of system testing in which the focus is on whether or not your application can be installed successfully. There are several important issues to be considered here:

- Can you successfully install the application into an environment that it hasn't been installed into before?

- Can you successfully install the application into an environment that it has been installed into before?

- Does configuration information get defined correctly?

- Does previous configuration information get taken into account?

- Are there replacements for existing user documentation?

- Is there a distribution plan for these documents?

- Is there a training plan for the application?

- Are any other applications affected by the installation of this one?

- Is there enough disk space/memory available on the machines of users for the application and does the application detect this?

12.6.1.4 Operations Testing

Operations testing is a type of system testing that verifies that the needs of operations personnel who have to support and keep the application up and running are met. Examples of the issues that must be addressed by operations testing includes the following:

- Is there operations documentation?

- Does it meet the documentation standards required by your operations department?

- Are there technical manuals available for every component (database, operating system, language, and so on) of the system?

- Is there an error-handling facility (see section 8.5.2) in place?

- Is someone available on call to answer questions if something goes wrong?

Without operations testing how can you be assured that your application will be supported properly once it is installed?

DEFINITION

Operations testing—The act of ensuring that the needs of operations personnel who have to support the application are met.

12.6.2 User-Acceptance Testing

After your system testing proves successful, your users must perform *user-acceptance testing*, a process in which they determine whether or not your application truly meets their needs. This means that you have to let your users work with the software that you produced. Because the only person who truly knows your own needs is you, the people involved in the user-acceptance test should be the actual users of the system—not their managers and not the Vice Presidents of the division that they work for, but the people who will work day in and day out with the application. Although you may have to give them some training to gain the testing skills that they will need, these are the only people who are qualified to do USER-acceptance testing.

Get the real users involved in user-acceptance testing.

Although problems reported by your users usually indicate real problems with your application, they sometimes reveal areas in which they need training.

The UAT process should take only a few days to a week at most. UAT is similar in concept to function testing, the main difference being that users do the testing and not developers. Your first step is to get your users working with the system so that they get a feel for what it is all about. Pay careful attention to their initial reactions. Initial reactions will reveal either deficiencies in your system or they will reveal areas in which your user community may need training. For example, many users when presented with a graphical user interface (GUI) for the first time may have difficulties working with it. You may have put together a perfectly good application, but because they didn't have an understanding of how GUIs work they may not have liked it.

Once the initial UAT period is over you want to get your users working through some of your simpler use cases and get them using the system to perform everyday tasks. You then have them slowly build up to more complex or esoteric functions in the application, giving them time to learn how to use the application on their job.

Users should drive the creation of the user-acceptance test plan.

A user-acceptance test plan defines exactly how your users intend to go about testing the application. Without such a test plan, you'll find that the user acceptance test process quickly becomes chaotic and does not produce the results that you want—verification of whether or not your application meets the needs of your users. Both users and development staff should be involved with the definition of the user-acceptance test plan, users providing the business knowledge and developers providing the testing expertise. Although your function test plan can be used as input in the development of your user-acceptance test plan, the important thing is to let your users drive the process of creating it so that you can be assured that the test plan accurately reflects their needs.

For software products that are sold by companies to other organizations, there is a process that is related to user-acceptance testing called alpha/beta-testing in which your users are actively involved in verifying that the application works, the main difference being that there really isn't a testing plan.

DEFINITION

User-acceptance testing (UAT)—The act of having users verify that an application meets their needs as they see them.

12.6.3 Alpha, Beta, and Pilot Testing

One of the major problems with testing is that you can only test for the things that you know about. As we have discussed before, unless you do the job of your users day in and day out you can never know it as well as they do. The implication of this is that you'll never be able to come up with as many real-life testing scenarios as they can. Furthermore, because your users typically outnumber you (so don't tick them off, or else!), and as they say, two heads are better than one, they can usually come up with better live tests than you can. Therefore it makes sense to get your users to test for you.

Two common approaches to this are *alpha testing* and *beta testing* (this is referred to as *pilot testing* for applications being developed for use by internal users). Alpha testing is a process in which you send out software that isn't quite ready for prime time to your users to let them work with it and report back to you the problems that they encounter. Although it is typically buggy and may not meet all of their needs, they get a heads-up on what you are doing a lot earlier than if they waited for you to release the software. Beta testing is basically the same process except that the software has a lot of the bugs that were found during alpha testing (beta testing follows alpha testing) ironed out of it.

DEFINITIONS

Alpha testing—A testing period in which pre release versions of software products that are often very buggy are released to users who need access to the product before it is to be officially released. In return these users are willing to report back to the software developers any problems they uncover. Alpha testing is typically followed by a period of beta testing.

Beta testing—Similar to alpha testing except that the software product is usually less buggy. This approach is typically used by software development companies who want to ensure that they meet as many of their client needs as possible.

Pilot testing—A testing process equivalent to beta testing that is used by organizations to test applications that they have developed for their own internal use.

Alpha and beta testing are an important part of the testing process for professional software development houses whose products need to run on many diverse computing environments. These companies typically can't afford to, or simply don't have the time to, set up test environments for every possible combination of hardware and operating systems that their software will be running on.

TIP

Be Proactive with Beta Testers

Companies that are the most successful with beta testing are those that are proactive with their beta testers. Provide beta testers with a mechanism to report problems to you easily. Call them on a regular basis to find out what they're thinking. When they report bugs, respond to them quickly, thanking them for the input and telling them specifically what's being done. Treat your beta testers well and they'll treat you well, and that's exactly what you want.

12.7   Software Quality Assurance and ISO 9000

Software quality assurance (SQA) is a set of processes and techniques that an organization uses to verify, test, and assure the excellence of the software that they develop. ISO (International Standards Organization) 9003 is the component of the ISO 9000 collection of quality standards that deals specifically with how organizations should manage their software quality-assurance programs. In a lot of ways ISO 9003 is seen as a subset of the ISO 9001 standard, as it defines how organizations should manage their entire quality-assurance programs, and not just software quality assurance.

A simplistic view of ISO 9000 is that it is a definition of how your organization produces the products and services that it sells to its customers, as well as the definition of how the customers can complain about what they have received. In a nutshell, ISO 9000 defines quality standards for the PROCESS by which your company operates. I believe that there is a lot of value in the ISO 9000 standards, and ISO 9003 in particular, for software developers. If you are serious about improving the software-testing process in your organization I highly suggest you look into both of them.

> ### SCOTT'S SOAPBOX
> #### ISO 9000 Says Nothing About the Quality of a Product
> Although ISO 9000 guarantees a quality process, it doesn't guarantee a quality product. To explain my point, a company that makes parachutes out of lead (instead of light-weight parachute silk) could gain their ISO 9000 certification as long as they define how they build the parachutes and how their customers can complain if they are unhappy about them. ISO 9000 certification only guarantees a quality process, not a quality product.

It is important for organizations to have an SQA program in place, as they can truly aid in improving the quality and excellence of internally developed software. SQA departments are typically responsible for aiding in, and often being responsible for, the testing process within a software development project. I've seen organizations in which SQA staff act as consultants on projects, helping staff to put together test plans, technical reviews, and even aiding in the testing itself. I've also seen organizations where the SQA department is directly responsible for testing software, not allowing deficient software to go into production until it meets the standards that they have set. In addition, I've unfortunately seen organizations in which the SQA department is all but ignored, with nobody taking advantage of their advice of their own free will and at the same time nobody being forced to either. Regardless of how the SQA department is being managed in your organization, I highly suggest that if you have access to one that you start working with them closely to help you with testing your OO applications. Although you may need to help them get up to speed on

Your SQA department can provide experts to help you with the testing process.

> ### DEFINITIONS
> **Software quality assurance (SQA)**—The process and techniques by which the development of software is verified, tested, and ensured to be of sufficient levels of excellence for your organization.
>
> **ISO 9001**—A standard defined by the International Standards Organization (ISO) that defines how organizations should manage their quality-assurance programs.
>
> **ISO 9003**—The standards defining how organizations should manage their software-quality assurance programs.

object-oriented development so they can understand your testing needs, there's always value in taking advice from experts. Go have a talk with them.

SQA departments are often the driving force behind bringing ISO 9003, and sometimes even the entire ISO 9000 quality standard, into your organization. Often the reverse is the case. In many organizations you'll see that SQA departments have been created as the direct result of bringing ISO 9000 in. SQA and ISO 9003 go hand in hand.

12.8 Testing Tips and Techniques

Before we wrap up this chapter I'd like to leave you with a few tips that I have discovered over the years to be really helpful when testing object-oriented applications.

1. **Successful tests find errors.** The main goal of testing is to find problems in your application so that you are able to fix them. If your tests don't find any problems, then the chances are infinitely more likely that you need to improve your testing techniques rather than that your application is perfect.

2. **Learn from your mistakes.** We can never find all of the errors in our applications and some of them will get past us and into production. Because I believe in making the best of a bad situation I always try to determine how the error got past me so that I can improve my testing strategy on the next application that I work on. The least you can do is add the problem to your technical-review checklists.

3. **Test throughout the life cycle.** By testing throughout the entire life cycle you both reduce the cost of fixing the errors that you find and you also increase the quality of your applications. When you leave testing to the end you increase the risk that testing won't be done properly, or perhaps won't even be done at all.

4. **Get training in testing.** The material that was covered by this chapter is just the tip of the testing iceberg. The only way to ensure that your developers will have the necessary skills to properly test systems is to invest in object-oriented-testing training courses for them.

5. **A new development paradigm implies a new testing paradigm.** Object-oriented development is significantly different than structured/procedural development. Many of the techniques that we used in the past to test structured applications are either no longer applicable or need to be reworked to meet the new needs of OO development.

6. **The better your design/code, the easier it is to test.** The simpler your design is, and the simpler your code is, the easier it is to test. The time and effort that you invest up front to creating a good design and writing good code will pay off in spades when you test it. Like my grandfather says, "do it right and do it once."

7. **Create a Software Quality Assurance department.** Software quality-assurance departments aid in creation of testing procedures, guidelines, and plans. They also aid in the technical review process. SQA people are experts at ensuring that your applications meet the standards of quality expected by your user community, and can be an excellent resource during the testing process by providing advice and expertise. If you have an SQA department in your organization take advantage of the fact and get them involved as early as possible in your projects.

8. **Create a master test plan.** At the beginning of a project it is highly suggested that you create a *master test plan* (Hetzel, 1988) that fully describes your testing procedures. This document will be updated and revised throughout the project with the addition of the other test plans that we discussed throughout this chapter. The main advantage of this is that the master test plan provides you with a common repository for all of your testing efforts.

9. **Test to the importance of the system.** I would hope that you would put significantly more effort into testing an air-traffic control system than you would a "hello world" program. You need to invest enough time and effort in testing so that you are comfortable that if there is a problem with the application, its consequences would be acceptable to yourself AND to your users.

10. **Consider paying for every error found.** A really successful way to motivate your testers is to consider paying for every
error that they find. I've seen schemes in which a pot of money
was allocated to the testing process. For every problem the tester
found he or she got so much of the pot and whatever was left at
the end of testing was split among the development team. I've
also seen user-acceptance tests where every original problem
found by a user resulted in them being given a bottle of wine
(Ontario wine of course, among the best you can buy, eh?).

DEFINITION

Master test plan—A document, typically created at the beginning of the project but that is updated throughout, which describes your testing strategies.
Other test plans are included as components of the master test plan.

12.9   Full Life-Cycle Object-Oriented Testing Overview

We've discussed a wide range of testing techniques, and now we really need to put them into perspective. Figure 12.11 shows the relationships among the testing techniques described in this chapter. The
first thing that needs to be pointed out is the fact that regression testing needs to be considered at all stages of testing. The second point is
that we need to distinguish between *testing in the small* and *testing in
the large*. Testing in the small is a term we use to refer to testing com-
OO testing is one ponents of our system—the application prototype, portions of the
of the steps of design, some methods, or some classes. For the most part, analysis
OO development, testing, design reviews, and code-testing techniques are all approach-
hence it can be es to testing in the small. Testing in the large refers to testing tech-
performed either niques that are used to test the entire system, or at least very large
serially or itera- components of it, at once. System testing and user-acceptance testing
tively. are considered to be testing-in-the-large techniques.

Although I have drawn the FLOOT process in a linear manner, the
fact is that testing in the small for the most part can be an iterative
process. After you've done some analysis you can test it; after you've
done some design you can walk through it; after you've written some
code you can test it. As we saw in the Pinball System Development
Life Cycle (SDLC) in section 1.3, testing is in fact one of several of the

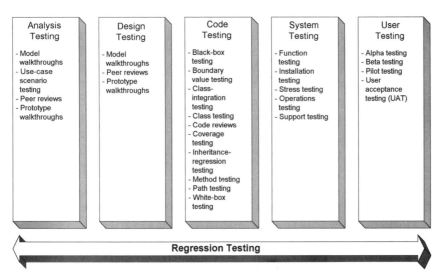

Figure 12.11. Overview of the FLOOT process.

Analysis Testing	Design Testing	Code Testing	System Testing	User Testing
- Model walkthroughs - Use-case scenario testing - Peer reviews - Prototype walkthroughs	- Model walkthroughs - Peer reviews - Prototype walkthroughs	- Black-box testing - Boundary value testing - Class-integration testing - Class testing - Code reviews - Coverage testing - Inheritance-regression testing - Method testing - Path testing - White-box testing	- Function testing - Installation testing - Stress testing - Operations testing - Support testing	- Alpha testing - Beta testing - Pilot testing - User acceptance testing (UAT)

Regression Testing

iterative steps of OO development. Testing in the large, however, becomes serial. You have to do it just before you release your application to your users. Testing in the large is often the largest step of your implementation effort, so looking at it like that you could easily say that implementation is one of the iterative steps of OO development, it's just that this step is done in a serial manner.

DEFINITIONS

Testing in the small—Any testing technique that concentrates on testing components of, or portions of, a system.

Testing in the large—Any testing technique that concentrates on testing the entire system as a whole, or at least very large components of it.

12.10 What We've Learned

In this chapter we saw that full life-cycle object-oriented testing encompasses a collection of techniques for verifying your analysis, design, and program code. Furthermore, we discussed techniques for ensuring that your application as a whole works properly. If there is one message that

I want to leave you with, it's that testing object-oriented applications is similar yet different from structured testing of the past. Although many of the fundamentals are the same, we've seen that concepts such as inheritance and encapsulation require changes in the approach that you take to testing applications. Although some developers look on testing as a necessary evil that should at best be tolerated, I look at testing as an opportunity to show to the world that my applications work just as I said they would. Which view do you think is better?

By the way, except for now, did you notice how I didn't use the word "bug" anywhere in this chapter? If that's not impressive, I don't know what is!

References

Ambler, S.W. (1995). *The Object Primer: The Application Developer's Guide to Object Orientation*. New York: SIGS Books.

Hetzel, B. (1988). *The Complete Guide to Software Testing, 2nd Edition*. New York: Wiley-QED.

Ince, D. (1994). *ISO 9001 and Software Quality Assurance*. London: McGraw-Hill.

McConnell, S. (1993). *Code Complete*. Redmond, WA: Microsoft Press.

Suggested Reading

Goglia, P.A. (1993). *Testing Client/Server Applications*. Boston, MA: QED Publishing Group.

Part V

Conclusion

Chapters

13 • Where to Go from Here—Personal Success Strategies

Chapter 13

Where to Go from Here — Personal Success Strategies

What We'll Learn in This Chapter

How to overcome the object-oriented (OO) learning curve.

What we've learned in this book.

By reading this book you've made a really good start at overcoming the OO learning curve, but that's all you've done, made a really good start. There's still a lot of work ahead of you. More reading, courses, mentoring, and lots of development work. There is a light at the end of the OO tunnel, and this chapter tells you how to get there.

As we saw in this book, there's a lot to object-oriented development. On the one hand, the object-oriented learning process can be long and difficult. Furthermore, there is no guarantee for success. On the other hand, you've gotten a really good start at it by reading this book. Now it's time to move on, however, down the never-ending road of continuous learning.

13.1 Advice for Overcoming the OO Learning Curve

1. **Pick up some other books.** Throughout this book I referred to some really good books. Although each of them takes a different approach to OO development, you'll find that there are several similarities between them. You should seriously consider reading at least one or two of them.

2. **Subscribe to some magazines and/or journals.** There are several object-oriented analysis-and-design magazines and journals, as well as numerous OO programming magazines. They provide leading-edge advice regarding OO development techniques. It's really worth your while to start reading some of them.

3. **Read, read, read.** I can't stress this strongly enough—you have to do a lot of reading. Object orientation is relatively new, and significant work is being done on it all the time. You need to keep up with the latest-and-greatest techniques, and the only way you can do this is by reading.

4. **Take some OO courses.** There are a lot of great object-oriented development courses out there, so sign up for a few of them. There is a lot of value in classroom training, and I highly recommend it. Take at least one OO analysis-and-design course, an "Introduction to XXX Programming" course, and an "Advanced XXX Programming" course, where XXX is your language of choice. OO can be hard to pick up on your own, and talking to an expert can really help.

5. **Bring in a mentor.** OO mentors are people who aid in the skills-transfer process. They are usually consultants or architects internal to your organization. The key is that they are

OO experts and have the communications skills to convey their expertise to others. OO mentors can help to significantly reduce the OO learning curve, and at the same time increase the chance of success for your project. OO mentoring is covered in detail in the third volume in this series.

6. **Sign onto the Internet.** There are several interesting newsgroups (a newsgroup is an electronic public forum where people can submit their ideas regarding a certain topic) that discuss object-oriented development issues on the Internet. Even if you don't participate in the discussions, there is always some valuable advice being given daily. The following list includes some of the newsgroups that you may wish to consider joining:

> **comp.databases.object**
> **comp.lang.c++**
> **comp.lang.smalltalk**
> **comp.object**
> **comp.software-eng**

7. **Drop by my web site, WWW.AmbySoft.Com** I've set up a web site dedicated to OO development issues, which include my online writings, links to paper publications that I write for, and links to other great OO development sites. It's worth bookmarking in your browser.

8. **Go to object-oriented conferences.** The newest OO tools and techniques can always be found at conferences such as OOPSLA (Object-Oriented Programming, Systems, Languages and Applications) and Object Expo. These conferences are advertised months in advance on the Internet and in magazines/journals.

9. **Don't forget that OO requires a mindset change.** It takes a long time to get up to speed in object orientation. You have to completely change the way that you think about systems, and that doesn't come easy, so don't get frustrated. You can do it if you want to.

10. **Don't forget that OO is more than just programming.** It isn't enough to use a programming language like C++ or

Smalltalk. You have to obtain OO analysis-and-design skills if you want to become a successful OO developer. It isn't what you want to hear, but many developers are destined to fail miserably because they refuse to accept this fact.

13.2   What We Learned in This Book

In *Building Object Applications* we explored several topics that are critical to your understanding if you wish to become an effective object-oriented developer. These topics can be broken down into the following categories:

Object-Oriented Architecture

- class-type architecture
- client/server architecture
- distributed classes
- distributed objects

Object-Oriented Patterns

- design patterns
- analysis patterns

Object-Oriented Analysis

- modeling techniques
- analysis metrics
- prototyping

Object-Oriented Design

- modeling techniques
- design metrics

Object-Oriented Design (continued)

- designing good classes
- object-oriented user-interface (OOUI) design
- designing distributed applications

Object-Oriented Construction

- the leading languages
- developing for the Internet
- working with attributes effectively
- writing effective methods
- creating maintainable classes
- programming techniques
- wrapping

Object-Oriented Persistence

- mapping objects to flat files
- mapping objects to relational databases
- object/relational databases
- object databases

Object-Oriented Testing

- full life-cycle object-oriented testing (FLOOT)
- analysis testing
- design testing
- code testing
- system testing
- user acceptance testing

Object-Oriented Testing (continued)

- regression testing
- quality assurance
- ISO 9000

13.3 Parting Words

If there is one message that I want to leave you with, one message that will truly prove beneficial to you in your career, it would have to be this:

> *Good developers know that there is more to development than programming.*

> *Great developers know that there is more to development than development.*

—Scott Ambler, April 1997

Appendices

Appendices

A • *Notation Summary*
B • *Visual Glossary*

Appendix A

Notation Summary

A.1 The Ambler Class Diagramming Notation, v2.0

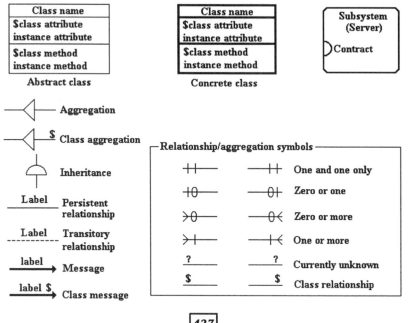

Figure A.1.
The Ambler class-diagram notation v2.0.

A.2 The Unified Modeling Language Class Diagramming Notation v1.0 (Simplified)

Figure A.2.
A simplified UML class-diagram notation.

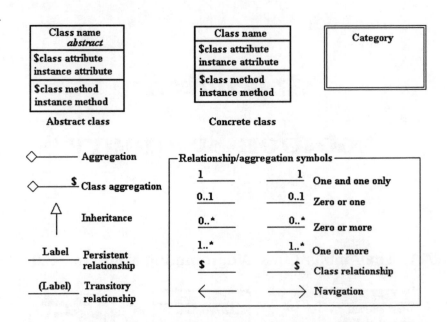

Important: The Relationship/aggregation symbols for class relationship are only proposed.

Appendix B

Visual Glossary

1NF — See First normal form.

1ONF — See First object normal form.

2NF — See Second normal form.

2ONF — See Second object normal form.

2-tier client/server — Clients and servers communicate with one another in a direct and highly coupled manner.

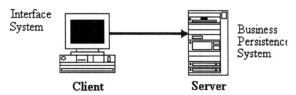

2-tier client/server architecture.

3NF — See Third normal form.

3ONF — See Third object normal form.

3-tier client/server — In this client/server architecture client machines send requests to an application server, which then sends requests to other servers on the network to fulfill the original request.

3-tier client/serv-
er architecture.

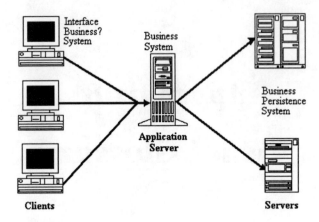

Abstract class — A class that does not have objects instantiated from it, but will provide functionality inherited by its subclasses.

Left: Abstract-
class notation
(Ambler). **Right:**
Abstract-class
notation (UML).

Abstraction — The definition of the interface of a class (what it knows and does).

Accessor method — A method that is used to either modify or retrieve a single attribute.

Active persistent object — An object that exists in an object database that can be sent messages both from within and from without the object database.

Actor — A person, organization, or external system that interacts with the application that we are currently developing.

Aggregation — Represents "is-part-of" relationships.

Left: Aggregation notation (Ambler). **Right:** Aggregation notation (UML).

Ambler			UML	
⊣⊦	⊣⊦	One and one only	1	1
⊣0	0⊦	Zero or one	0..1	0..1
≻0	0≺	Zero or more	0..*	0..*
≻⊦	⊣≺	One or more	1..*	1..*
?	?	Currently unknown		
$	$	Class relationship	$	$
		Navigation	←	→

Symbol combinations for aggregate and instance relationships **Left:** Ambler. **Right:** UML.

Alpha testing — A testing period in which pre-release versions of software products that are often very buggy are released to users who need access to the product before it is to be officially released. In return these users are willing to report back to the software developers any problems they uncover. Alpha testing is typically followed by a period of beta testing.

Analysis error — When a user requirement is missed or misunderstood.

Analysis pattern — An OO pattern that describes a solution to a business/analysis problem.

API — See Application-programming interface.

Application-programming interface (API) — A set of function/procedure calls that access a component that is external to your system.

Application server — A component of a 3-tier C/S architecture that encapsulates access to other servers on the network, supplying the business logic for combining the responses from those servers.

Application-specific class — Any class that is used in a single application.

Association — Another term for instance relationship.

Associative table — A table in a relational database that is used to maintain a relationship between two or more other tables. Associative tables are typically used to resolve many-to-many relationships.

Attribute — Something that an object or class knows. An attribute is basically a single piece of data or information. Attributes can be simple, like a string or integer, or can be a complex object, like an address or customer.

BDE — See Business-domain expert.

Beta testing — Similar to alpha testing except that the software product is usually less buggy. This approach is typically used by software development companies who want to ensure that they meet as many of their client needs as possible.

Black-box tests — Test cases that verify that given input A the component/system being tested gives you expected results B.

Boundary-value tests — Test cases that test unusual or extreme situations that your code should be able to handle.

Business classes — Business classes model the business domain. Business classes are usually found during the analysis process.

Business-domain expert (BDE) — Someone with intimate knowledge of all or a portion of the problem domain that you are modeling.

Callback methods — When object A communicates with object B, it may request that at some time in the future object B sends message M whenever a certain event happens (such as a process ending). The method that responds to message M is named a callback method.

Cardinality — Indicates how many objects are involved in a relationship.

Cardinality symbols (Ambler).

One   +   Many —<

CASE — Computer-aided system engineering.

CASE tool — A tool that supports the creation of models and potentially both forward and reverse engineering.

Category — See subsystem.

Class — A category of similar objects. A class is effectively a blueprint from which objects are created.

Class attribute — Information that is applicable to an entire class of objects.

Class diagram — Class diagrams show the classes of the system, their intrarelationships, and the collaborations between those classes.

Class hierarchy — A set of classes that are related through inheritance.

Class-integration testing — The act of ensuring that the classes, and their instances, that form an application perform as defined.

Class library — A collection of classes, typically purchased off-the-shelf, which you can reuse and extend via inheritance.

Class message — A message that is sent to a class, instead of to the instance of a class.

label $

Class-message
notation
(Ambler).

Class method — A method that operates on a class.

Class normalization — A process in which you organize the behavior within a class diagram in such a way as to increase the cohesion of classes while minimizing the coupling between them.

Class testing — The act of ensuring that a class and its instances (objects) perform as defined.

Class-type architecture — The classes of an application are organized into well-encapsulated layers according to their general properties.

The interaction between classes is often restricted based on the layer they belong to.

Client — A client is a single-user PC or workstation that provides presentation services and appropriate computing, connectivity, and interfaces relevant to the business need. A client is also commonly referred to as a "front-end."

Client class — A class that sends messages but does not receive them.

Client/server class — A class that both sends a receives messages.

Client/server (C/S) computing — An environment that satisfies the business need by appropriately allocating the application processing between the client and the server processes.

Cohesion — A measure of how much a method or class makes sense.

Collaboration — Classes work together (collaborate) to get things done.

Common Object Request Broker Architecture (CORBA) — An OMG specification defining a distributed-object architecture. CORBA specifies how to develop OO applications that are able to connect and communicate with other CORBA-compliant (and potentially non-OO) applications.

Component — Reusable code, typically purchased off-the-shelf, which you can reuse but not extend via inheritance.

Concrete class — A class that has objects instantiated (created) from it.

Left: Concrete-class notation (Ambler). **Right:** Concrete-class notation (UML).

Class Name
$class attributes instance attributes
$class methods instance methods

Class Name
$class attributes instance attributes
$class methods instance methods

Constructor — A Java or C++ member function (method) that allocates the memory needed for an instance of a class. Constructors are also used to set the initial value for attributes.

Contract — Any service/behavior of an object or server that other objects or servers request of it.

CORBA — See Common Object Request Broker Architecture.

Coupling — A measure of how connected two classes are.

Coverage testing — The act of ensuring that all lines of code were exercised at least once.

CRC (Class Responsibility Collaborator) card — A standard index card divided into three sections showing the name of the class, the responsibilities of the class, and the collaborators of the class.

Class Name	
Responsibilities	Collaborators

CRC card notation.

CRC model — A collection of CRC cards that describe the classes that make up a system or a component of a system.

CRC modeling — The act of creating a CRC model.

CRUD — Acronym for create, retrieve, update, delete. The basic functionality that a persistence mechanism must support.

Database proxies — An object that represents a business object stored in a database. To every other object in the system the database proxy appears to be the object that it represents. When other objects send the proxy a message it immediately fetches the object from the database and replaces itself with the fetched object, passing the message onto it. See the Proxy pattern in chapter 4 for more details.

Data dictionary — A repository of information about the layout of a database, the layout of a flat file, the layout of a class, and any mappings among the three.

Data entity — A person, place, thing, event, or concept. Data entities are drawn on data models and are similar to classes with the exception that they have data attributes, but do not have functionality (methods).

Data-entity nota-
tion.

Data flow — In a process model a data flow represents the movement of information, either physical or electronic, from one source to another.

Data-flow nota-
tion.

Data model — A diagram used to communicate the design of a (typically relational) database. Data models are often referred to as entity-relationship (ER) diagrams.

Data normalization — A process in which data in a relational database is organized in such a way as to reduce and even eliminate data redundancy.

Data store — In a process model it is a place where information is stored, such as a database or filing cabinet.

Gane & Sarson
data-store nota-
tion.

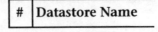

Data warehouse — A large database, almost always relational, that is used to store data for reporting purposes.

Design pattern — An OO pattern that describes a solution to a design problem.

Development/maintenance trade-off — Development techniques that speed up the development process often have a negative impact on your maintenance efforts, whereas techniques that lead to greater maintainability negatively impact your development efforts, at least in the short term.

DFD — See Data-flow diagram.

Distributed classes — An architecture in which logic of your applications is organized by putting classes on computers on your network based on their specific behaviors.

Distributed objects — An architecture in which objects dynamically reside on the machine that is most appropriate at the time. Objects move freely about the network and are not limited to where they may go.

do/ — A keyword used on a state diagram to document actions taken by an object while in a state.

Drag and drop — A technique in which a person uses a pointing device (typically a mouse) to select an object on the screen and then uses the mouse to move the object on top of another screen object.

DSL — See Dynamic shared library.

Dynamic model — See State diagram.

Dynamic shared library (DSL) —A library of function/procedure calls that exists outside of an application that is linked in at run time. Also known as a dynamic-link library.

Dynamic SQL — An SQL statement that is generated by an application at run time and then processed against the database. This is more flexible but much slower than static SQL.

Dynamic typing — The class/type of an object is associated to it at run time.

Electronic commerce — Any form of commerce in which the buyer of a product or service uses a computer to interact with the computer system of the seller of that product or service.

Encapsulation — The hiding of the implementation of what a class/object knows or does, without telling anyone how it's done.

Extensibility — A measure of how easy it is to add new features to a system. The easier it is to add new features, the more extensible we say the system is.

External entity — In a process model it is the source or destination of data that is external to the system being modeled. In a class diagram we would call this an actor class.

External-entity
notation.

Entity
Name

Fat-client approach — A 2-tier C/S architecture in which client machines implement both the user interface and the business logic of an application. Servers typically only supply data to client machines with little or no processing done to it.

Final state — A state (in a state diagram) from which no transitions lead out of. Objects will have zero or more final states.

First normal form (1NF) — A data entity is in 1NF when it contains no repeating groups of data. A database is in 1NF when all of its data entities are in 1NF.

First object normal form (1ONF) — A class is in 1ONF when specific behavior required by an attribute that is actually a collection of similar attributes is encapsulated within its own class. A class diagram is in 1ONF when all of its classes are in 1ONF.

Flat file — A single data file in which information is stored.

FLOOT — See Full life-cycle object-oriented testing.

Foreign key — An attribute(s) of a data entity that make up the primary key of another data entity. Foreign keys are used to maintain relationships between data entities.

Forward engineering — The generation of source code from a model by a CASE tool.

Framework — A collection of classes that together provide sophisticated, generic functionality, which can be extended via the addition of subclasses to meet your specific needs.

Full life-cycle object-oriented testing (FLOOT) — A testing methodology for object-oriented development that comprises testing techniques that taken together provide methods to verify that your application works correctly at each stage of development.

Function testing — A part of systems testing in which development staff confirm that their application meets the user requirements specified during analysis.

Garbage collection — Memory management in an OO application.

Garbage collector — The object(s) responsible for garbage collection.

Getter method — An accessor method that retrieves the value of an attribute.

Human factors — The study of how people interact with machines.

Hybrid OO language — An OO language that supports both structured/procedural and OO programming constructs.

IDL — See Interface-definition language.

Ignored method — An inherited method that is overridden with a method that has no functionality.

Information hiding — The restriction of access to attributes.

Inheritance — A concept that allows us to take advantage of similarities between classes by representing "is-a" and "is-like" relationships. (Inheritance notation is on the following page.)

Left: Inheritance notation (Ambler). **Right:** Inheritance notation (UML).

Inheritance-regression testing — The act of running the test cases of all the superclasses, both direct and indirect, on a given subclass.

Inheritance-tree depth — The maximum number of classes from the root of a class hierarchy to its lowest node, including the root class.

Initial state — The state in which an object is in when it is first created. All objects have an initial state.

Initialize method — A Smalltalk method that sets the initial values for attributes. In Smalltalk memory is allocated automatically when objects are instantiated.

Installation testing — The act of ensuring that your application can be installed successfully.

Instance — Another word for object. We say that an object is an instance of a class.

Instance attribute — Information that is specific to a single object.

Instance method — A method that operates on an individual object.

Instance relationship — Relationships, or associations, exist between objects. For example, customers BUY products.

Instantiate — To create an instance. When we create an object we say that we instantiate it from a class.

Interface — The set of messages an object or class will respond to.

Interface classes — Interface classes provide the ability for users to interact with the system. Interface classes typically define a graphical user interface (GUI) for an application, although other interface styles such as voice command or handwritten input are also implemented via interface classes.

Interface-definition language (IDL) — A standard language for defining the interface of an object.

Interface-flow diagram — A diagram that models the interface objects of your system and the relationships between them. Also referred to as storyboards.

Interface object — An object displayed as part of the user interface for an application. This includes widgets such as buttons and list boxes, icons, screens, and reports.

Internet — A collection of interconnected computers that people can log onto to share information, to communicate, to be entertained, and to perform electronic-commerce transactions.

Intranet — A network internal to your organization that is built either partially or completely from Internet-based technology.

ISO 9001 — A standard defined by the International Standards Organization (ISO) that defines how organizations should manage their quality-assurance programs.

ISO 9003 — The standards defining how organizations should manage their software quality-assurance programs.

Java applet — Small programs written in Java that are transmitted to, and run on, a client workstation from a server.

Java Virtual Machine (Java VM) — The interpretive environment that runs Java applets.

Key — One or more columns in a relational data table that when combined form a unique identifier for each record in the table.

Layer — A (class-type) layer encapsulates the broad functionality of a collection of classes that exhibit similar behaviors. Layers help us to identify, define, and potentially restrict how classes interact with one another.

Lazy initialization — An approach in which the initial value of attributes are set in their corresponding getter methods.

Leaf class — A class within an inheritance hierarchy that doesn't have other classes inheriting from it.

Legacy application — Any application or system that is difficult, if not impossible, to maintain and enhance.

Lock — An indication that a table, record, class, object, and so on is reserved so that work can be accomplished on the item being locked. A lock is established, the work is done, and the lock is removed.

Maintainability — A measure of how easy it is to add, remove, or modify existing features of a system. The easier a system is to change the more maintainable that system is.

Master test plan — A document, typically created at the beginning of the project but that is updated throughout, that describes your testing strategies. Other test plans are included as components of the master test plan.

Member function — The C++ term for method.

Memory leak — When you haven't properly managed the removal of an object from memory and have effectively lost some of the memory space that it takes up.

Mental model — An internal representation of a person's conceptualization and understanding of a system.

Message — A message is either a request for information or a request to do something.

Message notation
(Ambler & UML).

label ➤

Message dispatcher — An object that exists solely to pass messages onto other objects. Objects will often register themselves with a message dispatcher to inform it of the events that they are interested in being informed about.

Message-invocation box — The long, thin vertical boxes that appear on sequence diagrams that represent a method invocation in an object.

Message-invocation box notation.

Messaging — In order to collaborate, classes send messages to each other.

Metaphor — A set of concepts, terms, and objects that the user is familiar with that are used in the design of a user interface to make it easier to understand and use.

Method — Something that an object or class does. A method is similar to a function or procedure in structured programming.

Method response — A count of the total number of messages that are sent as a result of a method being invoked.

Method testing — The act of ensuring that a method (member function) performs as defined.

Methodology — In the context of systems development, it is the collection of techniques and approaches that you take when creating systems.

Metric — A measurement. In our case, a measurement of some factor involved in OO development.

Middleware — The technology that allows clients and servers to communicate with one another. This includes the network itself, its operating system, and anything needed to connect computers to the network.

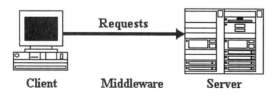

Middleware.

MIS — Management Information System.

Multiple inheritance — When a class directly inherits from more than one class, we say that we have multiple inheritance. Note that not all OO languages support multiple inheritance.

Multiple inheritance. **Left:** Ambler. **Right:** UML.

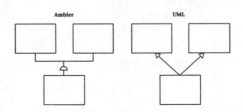

Non-key attribute — A non key attribute is any attribute of a relational table that is not part of the primary key.

Notation — The set of symbols that are used to document the analysis/design of a system.

Object — Any person, place, thing, event, screen, report, or concept that is applicable to the design of the system. Objects have both data and functionality that define its behavior.

Object adapter — A mechanism that both converts objects to records that can be written to a persistence mechanism and converts records back into objects again. Object adapters can also be used to convert between objects and flat file records.

Object Database Management Group (ODMG) — A consortium of most of the ODBMS vendors who together set standards for object databases.

Object identifier — An attribute that uniquely identifies an object. The object-oriented equivalent of a key.

Object Management Group (OMG) — A consortium of organizations that work together to create standards for the distributed object computing.

Object-oriented database management system (OODBMS) — A persistence mechanism that stores objects, including both their attributes and their methods.

Object-oriented database system manifesto — The "13 golden rules" that define what it is to be an OODBMS.

Object-oriented test case — A collection of objects that are in states that are appropriate to what is being tested, message sends to those objects, and the expected results of those message sends that together verify that a specific feature within your application works properly.

Object-oriented user interface (OOUI) — A style of user interface in which users directly interact with objects using the computer just as they work with them in the real world.

Object query language (OQL) — A standard proposed by the ODMG for the selection of objects. Basically SQL with object-oriented extensions that provide the ability to work with classes and objects instead of tables and records.

Object/relational database — A persistence mechanism that encompasses the features of both relational databases and OODBMSs by allowing you to store both data and objects.

Object/relational impedance mismatch — The difference resulting from the fact that relational theory is based on relationships between tuples that are queried, whereas the object paradigm is based on relationships between objects that are traversed.

Object request broker (ORB) — A middleware technology that allows objects to send messages across the network to other objects.

Object streaming — A process in which an object is converted to data so that it can be stored or transmitted, eventually being converted back into an object afterward.

ODBC — See Open database connectivity.

ODMG — See Object Database Management Group.

OID — See Object identifier.

OOCASE tool — A CASE tool that supports OO development.

OOCRUD — The object-oriented create, retrieve, update, and delete functionality performed by persistence classes.

OOD — Object-oriented design.

OODBMS — See Object-oriented database management system.

OO pattern — A model of several classes that work together to solve a common problem in your application's business or technical domain.

OOUI — See Object-oriented user interface.

Open database connectivity (ODBC) — A Microsoft standard for accessing relational databases. Effectively a standard for defining a database access wrapper that allows database vendors to provide a common interface to their product.

Operations testing — The act of ensuring that the needs of operations personnel who have to support the application are met.

Optimistic locking — An approach to concurrency in which an item is locked only for the time that it is accessed in the persistence mechanism. This strategy allows many people to work with an object simultaneously, but also presents the opportunity for people to overwrite the work of others (we'll discuss this later).

Optionality — Indicates whether or not it is mandatory that other objects are involved in a relationship.

Optionality symbols (Ambler).

May —○—

Must —+—

OQL — See Object query language.

Overload — The redefinition of a method with the exception that a different set, or different type, of parameter(s) is passed to it.

Override — A term used to indicate that we redefine attributes and/or methods in subclasses to provide slightly or completely different behavior.

Paragraphing — The indenting of your code to make it more readable.

Path testing — The act of ensuring that all logic paths within your code were exercised at least once. This is a superset of coverage testing.

Peer-to-peer architecture — An architecture based on the concept that any computer can potentially send messages to any other computer on the network.

Peer-to-peer wrapping — A legacy-application wrapping technique in which wrapper code in an OO application communicates with wrapper code on the machine running the legacy application that directly accesses its functionality.

Persistence — The issue of how to store objects to permanent storage. Objects need to be persistent if they are to be available to you and/or to others the next time your application is run.

Persistence classes — Persistence classes provide the ability to permanently store objects. By encapsulating the storage and retrieval of objects via persistence classes you are able to use various storage technologies interchangeably without affecting your applications.

Persistence layer — The collection of classes that provide business objects the ability to be persistent. The persistence layer effectively wraps your persistence mechanism.

Persistence mechanism — The permanent-storage facility used to store objects, such as a relational database, a flat file, or an object database.

Persistent memory — Main memory plus all available storage space on the network.

Persistent object — An object that is saved to permanent storage making it retrievable for future use.

Pessimistic locking — An approach to concurrency in which an item is locked for the entire time that it is in memory. This strategy guarantees that an item won't be updated in the persistence mechanism while the item is in memory, but at the same time disallows others to work with it while someone else does.

Pilot testing — A testing process that is equivalent to beta testing that is used by organizations to test applications that they have developed for their own internal use.

Polymorphic — Two classes are polymorphic when they exhibit the same public interface.

Polymorphism — Polymorphism says that an object can take any of several forms, and that other objects can interact with the object without having to know what specific form it takes.

Portability — A measure of how easy it is to move an application to another environment. Application environments may vary by the configuration of both their software and hardware. The easier it is to move an application to another environment the more portable we say that application is.

pre/ — A keyword used on a state diagram to document state preconditions.

Process — In a process model a process takes some data as input, does something to it, and then outputs it.

Process model — A diagram that shows the movement of data within a system. Similar in concept to a DFD but not as rigid and documentation heavy.

Gane & Sarson process notation.

Prototype — A mock-up of the user interface of your application.

Prototype walkthrough — A process in which your users work through a collection of use-cases using the prototype of the application as if it was the real thing. The main goal is to test whether or not the design of the prototype meets their needs.

Pure inheritance — A subclass inherits everything from its superclass.

Pure OO language — An OO language that supports only OO programming constructs.

Reading into memory — When you obtain an object from the persistence mechanism but don't intend to update it.

Read lock — A type of lock indicating that a table, record, class, object, and so on is currently being read by someone else. Other people may also obtain read locks on the item, but no one may obtain a write lock until all read locks are cleared.

Recursive transition — A transition is considered recursive when it leads into the same state that it originated.

Refactoring — The act of reorganizing OO development efforts. Refactoring will often comprise the renaming of methods, attributes, or classes; the redefinition of methods, attributes, or classes; or the complete rework or methods, attributes, or classes. Your analysis, design, or coding efforts can often be refactored.

Regression testing — The act of ensuring that previously tested functionality still works as expected after changes have been made to an application.

Repository — A centralized database in which you can check-in and check-out versions of your development work, including documentation, models, and source code.

Requirement-verification matrix — A document that is used to relate use cases to the portions of your application that implement those requirements. For OO applications, the names of classes are listed across the top of the matrix, the use cases are listed along the left-hand axis of the matrix, and in the squares are listed the main method(s) involved in fulfilling each use case. (The requirement verification matrix format is shown on the following page.)

Requirement-veri-
fication matrix
format.

Requirement	Class1	Class2
Req1		
Req2		
Req3		

Responsibility — A responsibility is anything that a class/object knows or does.

Retrieving into memory — When you obtain an object from the persistence mechanism and will potentially update it.

Reverse engineering — The generation of a model from source code by a CASE tool.

Root — The topmost class in a class hierarchy. Also called a root class.

Router class — A class that accepts incoming messages sent to a server and passes them onto the appropriate classes, providing an interface through which clients interact with the server.

Scaffolding — A technique in which one or more legacy applications are accessed through an OO wrapper to provide users with a modern user interface usually on a new hardware platform.

Screen scraping – A wrapping technique in which the wrapper simulates the keystrokes that a user would normally make to drive the functionality of a legacy application.

Second normal form (2NF) — A data entity is in 2NF when it is in first normal form (1NF) and when all of its non key attributes are fully dependent on its primary key. A database is in 2NF when all of its entities are in 2NF.

Second object normal form (2ONF) — A class is in 2ONF when it is in first object normal form (1ONF) and when "shared" behavior that is needed by more than one instance of the class is encapsulated within its own class(es). A class diagram is in 2ONF when all of its classes are in 2ONF.

Sequence diagram — A diagram that shows the types of objects involved in a use-case scenario, including the messages they send to one another and the values that they return.

Server — A server is one or more multiuser processors with shared memory that provides computing connectivity, database services, and interfaces relevant to the business need. A server is also commonly referred to as a "back-end."

Server class — A class that receives messages but does not send them.

Setter method — An accessor method that modifies the value of an attribute.

Single inheritance — When a class directly inherits from only one class, we say that we have single inheritance.

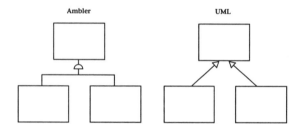

Single-inheritance notation.
Left: Ambler.
Right: UML.

Software quality assurance (SQA) — The process and techniques by which the development of software is verified, tested, and ensured to be of sufficient levels of excellence for your organization.

SQA — See Software quality assurance.

SQL — See Structured query language.

SQL3 — The latest version of SQL that includes extensions that support object-oriented concepts.

SQL statement — A piece of SQL code.

State — A state represents a stage in the behavior pattern of an object. A state can also be said to represent a condition of an object to which a defined set of policies, regulations, and physical laws apply. On state diagrams a state is shown as a horizontal, rounded rectangle.

State notation.

State diagram — A model that describes the states that an object may be in, as well as the transitions between states.

State precondition — A condition that must be met before a state can be entered.

State-transition model — See state diagram.

Static binding — The class/type of an object is associated to it at compile time.

Static SQL — An SQL statement that is defined and bound to the database at compile time. This is much less flexible but faster than dynamic SQL.

Stress testing — The act of ensuring that the system performs as expected under high volumes of transactions, high numbers of users, and so on.

Stress-test plan — The test plan that describes how you intend to go about stress testing your application.

String of message sends — A series of messages is sent to the same object.

Structured query language — A standard language used to access and modify data stored in relational databases.

Subclass — If class "B" inherits from class "A," then we say that "B" is a subclass of "A."

Substate — A specific state that is part of a more generalized superstate.

Subsystem — A set of classes that collaborate among themselves to support a set of cohesive set of contracts. Called a category in UML.

Subsystem contracts — The collection of the class contracts of all of the classes that respond to messages sent from classes external to the subsystem.

Subsystem (Server)	Category Name	Subsystem nota-tion (Ambler).
) Contract		

Superclass — If class "B" inherits from class "A," then we say that "A" is a superclass of "B."

Superstate — A general state that is decomposed into several substates.

System classes — System classes provide operating-system-specific functionality for your applications, or they wrap functionality provided by other tool/application vendors. System classes isolate you from the operating system (OS), making your application portable between environments by wrapping OS specific features.

System testing — A testing process in which you find and fix any known problems to prepare your application for user-acceptance testing.

Technical-design review — A testing technique in which the design of your application is examined critically by a group of your peers. This process is often referred to as a walkthrough.

Technical-review plan — A document that describes the goal of a technical review, who is to attend and why, the information that the reviewers require before the review, and the records and documentation that will be produced by the review.

Test log — A chronological tracking of your testing activities.

Test plan — A document that prescribes the approach to be taken during the testing process.

Test-procedure scripts — The description of the steps that must be carried out to perform all or part of a test plan.

Testing in the small — Any testing technique that concentrates on testing components of, or portions of, a system.

Testing in the large — Any testing technique that concentrates on testing the entire system as a whole, or at least very large components of it.

Testing tool — Any tool that aids in either the definition of test cases, the storage of test cases, or the running of test cases.

Thin-client approach — A 2-tier C/S architecture in which client machines implement only the user interface of an application.

Third normal form (3NF) — A data entity is in 3NF when it is in second normal form (2NF) and when all of its attributes are directly dependent on the primary key. A database is in 3NF when all of its data entities are in 3NF.

Third object normal form (3ONF) — A class is in 3ONF when it is in second object normal form (2ONF) and when it encapsulates only one set of cohesive behaviors. A class diagram is in 3ONF when all of its classes are in 3ONF.

Transaction — A transaction is a single unit of work performed in a persistence mechanism. A transaction may be one or more updates to a persistence mechanism, one or more reads, one or more deletes, or any combination thereof.

Transient object — See transitory object.

Transition — A transition is a progression from one state to another. A transition will be triggered by an event (either internal or external to the object). A transition is shown on a state diagram as an arrow leading from one state to another.

Transition nota-
tion.

label ➤

Transitory object — An object that is not persistent.

UAT — See User acceptance test.

Unified Modeling Language (UML) — The industry standard OO modeling notation proposed by Grady Booch, James Rumbaugh, and Ivar Jacobson. At the time of this writing, the UML is being considered by the OMG to make it the OMG standard.

Unit testing — The act of testing small components of a system to ensure that they work. In the object world this is both method and class testing.

Use case — A description of a real-world scenario that a system may or may not be able to handle.

Use-case diagram — A diagram that shows the use cases and actors for the application that we are developing.

Use-case scenario testing — The process of having a group of BDEs act out use-case scenarios to ensure that their CRC model handles the use-cases correctly.

User-acceptance testing (UAT) — The act of having users verify that an application meets their needs as they see them.

User-requirement review — A testing process in which a facilitated group of users verify and prioritize the user requirements gathered by a development team.

Volume testing — A subset of stress testing that deals specifically with determining how many transactions or database accesses that an application can handle during a defined period of time.

White-box tests — Test cases that verify that specific lines of code work as defined. This is also referred to as clear box testing.

Whitespace — Blank lines in your code that are used to distinguish between sections.

World Wide Web (WWW) — A component of the Internet that provides users with the ability to move from computer system to computer system by following predefined links between those systems.

Wrapping — Wrapping is the act of encapsulating non-OO functionality within a class making it look and feel like any other object within the system.

Wrapper — A collection of one or more classes that encapsulates access to non-OO technology to make it appear as if it is OO.

Wrapper class — Any class that is part of a wrapper.

Write lock — A type of lock indicating that a table, record, class, object, and so on is currently being written to by someone else. No one may obtain either a read or a write lock until this lock is cleared.

Index

A

abstract class
  definition, 9
abstraction
  definition, 6
  example, 6
accessor methods, 229
  advantages, 236
  definition, 230
  lazy initialization, 234
  naming convention, 234
  on models, 390
  testing, 389
  tips, 258
acting out scenarios, 23
actor classes
  and external entities, 71
actors
  definition, 58
aggregation
  applicability, 32
  class, 39
  defining, 32
  definition, 11
  deleting objects, 323

example, 11
implementing, 322
retrieving objects, 323
simplifying hierarchies, 152
vs. instance relationships, 322
writing objects, 323
alpha testing, 409
  definition, 409
Ambler notation
  best of breed, 55
  moving to UML, 34
  summary, 41
analysis
  metrics, 179
  testing, 369
analysis-and-design
  diagramming, 80
analysis classes, 88
analysis errors, 370
  definition, 21, 371
analysis patterns
  business entity, 128
  contact point, 128
  definition, 118
  Item-Item description, 126

analysis patterns (*continued*)
Place, 131
Shipping/Billing, 130
analysis testing, 369
and interface-flow diagrams, 76
prototype walkthroughs, 370
use case scenario testing, 370
API. *See* Application programming interface
applets, 160, 203
advantages, 160
and electronic commerce, 214
definition, 204
application programming interface
C-APIs, 349
definition, 350
application servers, 146
definition, 148
application testing, 403
applications
no more, 278
vs. desktops, 279
architecture
class type, 87
distributed classes, 148
distributed objects, 161
for electronic commerce, 209
object-oriented C/S, 149
peer-to-peer, 149
three-tier C/S, 146
two-tier C/S, 144
associations. *See* Relationships
associative tables, 325
definition, 294
attitude, 222
attributes
and states, 64
class, 33
definition, 6
effective, 226
finding, 31
instance, 33
metrics, 181, 184
naming conventions, 226
non-key, 304
tips, 257

B

bank case study, 42
BDEs. *See* Business domain experts
behavioral redundancy, 307
beta testing, 409
definition, 409
binding, 198
black-box testing, 383
definition, 384
booleans
getters, 232
boundary-value testing
definition, 385
boundary values
and states, 66
brainstorming, 14
pointers, 17
built-in test cases, 399
business classes, 88
and applets, 160
and CORBA, 356
and peer-to-peer wrapping, 356
and persistence, 101
buying, 108
definition, 89, 101
identifying, 106
metrics, 174, 193
skill requirements, 256
business domain classes, 88
business domain experts (BDEs), 14
business entity pattern, 128
and contact point, 129
and Shipping/Billing, 130
business objects
myths of, 108
business rules
and testing, 385
documentation, 239

C

C++
accessors, 229
adoption of, 205
features, 202
hybrid language, 202
learnability, 203, 206

maintainability, 203
memory leaks, 398
method size, 185
metrics, 176, 185
naming attributes, 228
simple code, 203
callback methods, 253
    definition, 96, 254
C-APIs, 348
    skills, 356
cardinality
    definition, 11
    notation, 40
CASE, 54, 101
    object-oriented, 216
centralized mainframes, 141
checklists, technical reviews, 376
class
    contracts, 151
    definition, 15
    messages, 38
class aggregation
    definition, 39
class attributes
    definition, 35
    implications, 37
    inheritance, 37
    metrics, 184
    notation, 34
class diagrams
    Ambler vs. UML, 69
    and collaboration diagrams, 38
    and CRC modeling, 26
    and data models, 79
    definition, 25
    metrics, 179
    notation, 56
    steps, 25
class hierarchy, 9
class-integration testing, 396
    definition, 396
class libraries
    definition, 217
    reuse, 216
class methods
    definition, 36

implications, 37
inheritance, 37
notation, 36
class normalization, 303
    and cohesion, 305
    and patterns, 127
    definition, 310
class relationships
    definition, 39
class testing, 392
    and state diagrams, 393
    definition, 393
class-type architecture
    advantages, 114
    and two-tier C/S, 145
    and use cases, 97
    and wrapping, 356
    construction, 255
    definition, 86
    development implications, 110
    disadvantages, 114
    five-layer, 97
    four-layer, 93
    project-management implications,
    109
    two-layer, 89
class types
    metrics, 193
classes
    abstract, 9
    and class types, 86
    application-specific, 180, 182
    as global variables, 231
    business, 88
    classification, 106
    client, 154
    client/server, 154
    concrete, 9
    definition, 5
    finding, 18, 30
    getters, 231
    interface, 75, 88, 98
    leaf class, 182
    maintainability, 247
    naming conventions, 247
    persistence, 91, 102

classes (*continued*)
 reuse, 247
 root, 9
 root class, 182
 router, 159
 server, 154
 subclasses, 9
 superclasses, 9
 system, 94, 105
 testing, 392
 tips, 258
 wrappers, 344
classes per developer metric, 175
clear-box testing, 384
client classes
 definition, 155
 identifying, 156
client/server
 and object-orientation, 149
 definition, 142
 fat client, 144
 features, 143
 thin client, 144
 three-tier, 146
 two-tier, 144
client/server classes
 definition, 155
 identifying, 156
clients
 definition, 142
 features, 143
code
 documentation, 239
 paragraphing, 241
code quality
 methods, 237
 metrics, 185–186, 190
code reviews, 382
 vs. code testing, 382
code testing, 380
 black box, 383
 boundary value, 385
 class-integration testing, 396
 class testing, 392
 clear box, 384

comparison of techniques, 402
coverage testing, 386
inheritance-regression testing, 394
method testing, 389
new techniques, 388
path testing, 386
process, 401
reviews, 382
traditional methods, 383
vs. code reviews, 382
white box, 384
cohesion
 and class normalization, 305
 and subsystems, 154
 definition, 12
collaboration
 defining, 31
 definition, 12
 example, 12
collaboration diagrams, 38, 50
 definition, 69
 drawing, 69
 when to draw, 70
collaborator
 defining, 18
 definition, 16
color usage, 275
comments
 and maintainability, 239
 metrics, 186–187, 190
component
 assemblers, 109
 builders, 109
 definition, 218
 reuse, 216
concrete class, 9
concurrency
 CORBA, 164
 definition, 293
conferences, 421
consensus, 378
consistency. 267
 and mental models, 270
 and naming conventions, 226
 and patterns, 134

and UI design, 273
constants
    getters, 230
construction
    and class-types, 255
    metrics, 185
constructors, 36
    definition, 235
contact point pattern, 128
    and Shipping/Billing, 130
context-sensitive menus, 277
contracts
    class, 151
    definition, 152
    subsystem, 158
contrast rule, 275
CORBA, 163
    and persistence, 165
    and security, 166
    concurrency, 164
    definition, 167, 355
    IDL, 163, 354
    services, 163
    skills, 356
    wrapping, 354
cost/benefit analysis, 30
costs
    of testing, 365
coupling, 199
    and accessors, 236
    and normalization, 316
    and wrapping, 348
    between class types, 89
    definition, 12
coverage testing, 386
    definition, 388
cowboy programmers, 223
CRC cards
    definition, 15
    moving, 19
CRC modeling, 14
    advantages/disadvantages, 20
    and class diagrams, 26
    and metrics, 174
    and use cases, 22
    definition, 15

metrics, 179
steps, 17
testing, 370
crossing lines, 51
CRUD, 90
    definition, 293
cursory reviews, 374

D

data dictionaries
    and mapping objects, 330
    contents, 331
    definition, 295
data entity
    definitions, 77
data flow, 71
data flow diagrams, 71
data justification, 276
data models, 50
    and class diagrams, 79
    definition, 77, 299
    drawing, 78
    when to draw, 79
data normalization, 300
    and coupling, 316
    definition, 304
    ease of data access, 316
    speed of data access, 316
data store, 71
data warehouse
    definition, 321
databases
    data models, 79
database proxies
    definition, 293
debugging
    wrapper classes, 350
deliverables, 50
design
    and message flow, 92
    and testing, 379, 398
    intelligent error messages, 112
    metrics, 180
    of interface objects, 281
    technical reviews, 372

design (*continued*)
  testing, 372
design issues
  class methods, 36
design patterns
  definition, 118
  Proxy, 120
  Roles Played, 122
  Singleton, 119
  state, 122
design testing, 372
  and sequence diagrams, 63
  requirement-verification matrices, 379
desktop
  vs. applications, 279
desktop metaphors, 271
destructors, 36
development
  incremental, 225
  small steps, 225
development/maintenance trade-off, 224
DFD. *See* Data flow diagrams
diagramming
  avoid cluttering, 53
  avoid crossing lines, 51
  avoid curved lines, 52
  avoid diagonal lines, 52
  bubble size, 53
  how it fits together, 80
  on white boards, 74
  simplify, 51
distributed applications
  history of, 140
distributed classes, 148
  applets, 160
  definition, 148
  disadvantages, 161
  Java, 161, 215
  vs. distributed objects, 215
distributed databases, 337
distributed objects, 161
  definition, 162
  vs. distributed classes, 215
distribution plans, 406

do/ (keyword), 68
documentation, 32
  internal to code, 239
  maintainability, 236
  of accessors, 236
  of attributes, 236
  of business rules, 239
  of interface objects, 284
  of methods, 237
  of prototypes, 283
  operations, 407
  standards, 407
  tips, 241
  user, 406
drag and drop, 264
DSL. *See* Dynamic shared libraries
dumb terminals, 141
dynamic-link libraries (DLLs), 280
dynamic models. *See* State diagrams
dynamic shared libraries, 326, 348
  definition, 328, 350
  skills, 356
dynamic SQL
  definition, 330
  vs. static, 329
dynamic typing
  definition, 202

E

e-cash. *See* Electronic cash
e-commerce. *See* Electronic commerce
80/20 rule, 189
electronic cash, 211
electronic commerce, 207
  and Java, 208
  architecture, 209
  definition, 210
  development checklist, 214
  international issues, 211
  payment processing, 210
  shipping and customs, 212
  taxes, 212
  virtual products, 212
encapsulation
  and languages, 200

and wrapping, 345
definition, 6
enforcement, 199
example, 7
English descriptors, 227
entity-relationship diagrams. *See* Data models
ER diagrams. *See* Data models
error handling, 251
estimating projects, 173
throughout the lifecycle, 174
evaluating prototypes, 283
extensibility
and wrapping, 358
definition, 86
external entity
and actor classes, 71
definition, 71

F

fat-client approach, 144
feature points, 177
field alignment, 276
final state
definition, 64
firewalls, 209, 213
1NF. *See* First normal form
first normal form, 300
and 1ONF, 306
definition, 304
1ONF. *See* First object normal form
first object normal form, 304
and 1NF, 306
definition, 310
flat files, 295
definition, 295
implementing, 296
random access, 297
sequential access, 297
FLOOT. *See* Full life-cycle object-oriented testing
foreign key, 301
definition, 304, 324
implementing relationships, 324
font usage, 275

forward engineering, 218
frameworks
definition, 218
reusability, 217
full life-cycle object-oriented testing, 364, 414
steps of, 368
function points, 177, 180
function testing, 404
and UAT, 404, 408
and use cases, 404
definitions, 404

G

garbage collection, 198
control of, 201
definition, 202
getter methods, 229
definition, 230
documentation, 236
for booleans, 232
for classes, 231
for constants, 230
testing, 390
global usage metric, 183
global variables
and class attributes, 184
and classes, 231
and Singletons, 183
graying out, 276

H

hacking
and evaluating code, 185
vs. incremental development, 223
vs. iterative development, 113, 223
human–computer interaction (HCI) boundary, 97
human factors, 269
definition, 272
Hungarian notation, 228
hybrid languages
C++, 202
definition, 202
vs. pure, 201

I

IDL. *See* Interface definition language
ignored methods
  definition, 184
  metric, 184
impedance mismatch, 299, 311
  definition, 311
implementation, 33
incremental development, 33, 225
  and testing, 369
  vs. hacking, 223
index cards, 14
information hiding, 229
  definition, 7
  example, 7
inheritance
  and interface objects, 263
  and languages, 200
  and mapping objects, 315
  and state diagraming, 65
  and testing, 394
  applicability, 31
  class hierarchy, 9
  defining, 31
  definition, 8
  example, 8
  implementing in relational DBs,
    317
  of class attributes, 37
  of class methods, 37
  metrics, 181–183
  multiple, 9, 124
  pure, 65, 184
  simplifying hierarchies, 152
  single, 9
  tree depth, 182
inheritance regression testing, 394
  definition, 395
  test cases, 399
inheritance tree depth metric, 182
initial state
  definition, 64
installation testing, 406
  definition, 406
instance attributes

definition, 35
instance methods
  definition, 36
instance relationships
  and data models, 77
  definition, 10
  example, 10
  implementing, 322
  vs. aggregation, 322
instances. *See* Objects
instantiate
  definition, 5
integration testing
  of classes, 396
  vs. class testing, 392
interface classes, 88
  and applets, 160
  and business logic, 100
  and clients, 151
  and screen scraping, 356
  and use cases, 100
  buying, 107
  definitions, 75, 89
  developing, 112
  example, 98
  identifying, 106
  metrics, 193
  skill requirements, 255
  supporting multiple language, 211
interface definition language (IDL),
    163
  definition, 167, 355
interface-flow diagrams
  and prototyping, 74
  definition, 75
  drawing, 75
  for OOUIs, 281
  when to draw, 76
interface layer
  advantages, 99
interface objects
  and inheritance, 263
  and polymorphism, 263
  definition, 75, 264
  design, 281
  documenting, 284

international commerce, 209
Internet
   definition, 210
   development, 203
   electronic commerce, 207
   newsgroups, 421
Intranet, 208
   definition, 210
"is-a" relationships, 8
"is-like" relationships, 8
ISO 9000, 410
ISO 9001, 410
   definition, 411
ISO 9003, 410
   definition, 411
Item-Item description pattern, 126
   and contact point, 129
   and Place, 132
iterative development, 27
   modeling, 80
   testing, 415
   vs. hacking, 113, 223

J

Java, 203
   and electronic commerce, 208, 213
   and ObjectCOBOL, 215
   and Smalltalk, 215
   applets, 160, 203, 280
   distributed classes, 215
   features, 203
   future of, 204, 215
   naming attributes, 228
   sample code, 204
   virtual memory, 204

K

key
   definitions, 77, 294
   foreign, 301
   vs. object identifiers, 312
keystrokes, simulating, 352

L

languages
   attribute naming conventions, 227
   comparison of, 207
   features, 198
   hybrid, 199
   pure vs. hybrid, 201
   purity, 199
Law of Demeter, 247
layer
   definition, 86
lazy initialization, 234, 390
   definition, 235
learning curve, 420
legacy applications
   and electronic commerce, 216
   definition, 87, 351
   reuse of, 357
   tips, 352
   wrapping, 347, 351
legacy code
   wrapping, 345, 348
lines of code
   metric, 188
LOC. *See* lines of code
locks
   definition, 293

M

maintainability
   and accessors, 229
   and C++, 203
   and comments, 239
   and paragraphing, 241
   and parenthesis, 245
   definition, 86
   factors, 224
   of attributes, 229
   of classes, 247
   of documentation, 236
   of methods, 244
   30-second rule, 245
maintenance
   and wrapping, 357

maintenance *(continued)*
  costs, 224
many-to-many relationships, 250
many-to-one relationships, 250
mapping objects
  and data dictionaries, 330
  and inheritance, 315
  seven commandments, 332
  to flat files, 296
  to relational databases, 326
master test plan, 364, 413
  definition, 414
member function. *See* Methods
memory leaks, 200, 398
  definition, 202
memory management, 198
memory management
  and C-APIs, 349
mental models, 269
  definition, 272
mentoring, 420
mentors, 421
menus, pop-up, 277
message dispatcher, 253
  definition, 96, 255
message flow
  between class types, 94
  restricting, 89, 92
message-invocation box
  definition, 60
messages
  definition, 12
  dispatcher, 96, 253
  Law of Demeter, 247
  metrics, 186–187
  testing, 397
  to classes, 38
messaging
  definition, 12
metaphors, 271
  definition, 272
  desktop, 271
method count metric, 180
method response metric, 186
method size metric, 185

method testing, 389
  definition, 389
  tips, 392
methodology, 54
methods
  accessors, 229
  and transitions, 65
  callback, 96, 253
  class, 35
  comments, 186
  definition, 6
  documentation, 237
  finding, 31
  getters, 229
  ignored, 184
  instance, 35
  maintainability, 244
  metrics, 180, 184–187, 190
  naming conventions, 237
  overriding, 184
  quality, 237
  refactoring, 243
  setters, 229
  should do one thing, 243
  should do something, 242
  size, 185
  testing, 389
  tips, 257
metrics
  and C++, 176
  and class types, 193
  and Smalltalk, 176
  automation of, 192
  classes per developer, 175
  collection of, 192
  comments per method, 186, 190
  definition, 172
  feature points, 177
  for analysis, 179
  for business classes, 193
  for C++, 185
  for construction, 185
  for design, 180
  for estimating projects, 173
  for improving development, 178

for improving your development
  approach, 191
for interface classes, 193
for persistence classes, 193
for Smalltalk, 185, 187
for source code, 185
for system classes, 193
for testing, 189
for tool selection, 190
function points, 177, 180
global usage, 183
inheritance tree depth, 182
lines of code, 188
method count, 180
method response, 186
method size, 185
number of children, 183
number of class attributes, 184
number of ignored methods, 184
number of instance attributes, 181
number of key classes, 174
number of reused classes, 176
number of use cases, 179
percentage of commented methods, 187, 190
percentage of key classes, 179
percentage of tested use-case scenarios, 189
person days per class, 174
printout height, 188
problem reports per class, 189
strings of message sends, 187
success factors, 191
use cases, 189
uses, 173
middleware
  definition, 142
  object request brokers, 161
mindset change, 421
MIS (management information system), 295
multi-platform support, 99
multiple inheritance, 9
  and C++, 202
  and OODBMS, 337
  and Roles Played pattern, 124

simulating, 124

N

naming conventions
  attributes, 226
  for accessors, 234
  for methods, 237
  Hungarian notation, 228
nested logicals, 246
networks
  features, 143
normalization, 299
  data, 300
not-invented-here (NIH) syndrome,
  135
notation
  class diagramming, 56
  comparison, 56
  definition, 54
number of children metrics, 183
number of class attributes metric,
  184
number of ignored methods metric,
  184
number of instance attributes metrics, 181
number of key classes metric, 174
number of reused classes metric, 176
number of use cases metric, 179

O

object adapter
  definition, 294
Object Database Management
  Group
  and CORBA, 165
object diagramming. See Collaboration diagrams
object identifiers
  and business meaning, 312
  and polymorphism, 315
  assigning, 316
  definition, 121, 292
  implementing, 312
  strategies, 313
  uniqueness, 314

object identifiers (*continued*)
  vs. keys, 312
object linking and embedding, 93
Object Management Group, 163, 167, 354
  definition, 355
object-message diagrams. *See* Collaboration diagrams
object modeling technique, 55
object models. *See* Class diagrams
object-orientation
  adoption of, 205
  and client/server, 149
object-oriented client/server, 149
  steps of, 150
object-oriented databases. *See* OODBMS
object-oriented user interface, 262
  and wrapping, 346
  definition, 264
  differences, 268
  example, 265
  features of, 262
  modeling, 281
  vs. standard GUI, 268
object/relational databases, 339
  definition, 340
object request brokers, 161
  and TP monitors, 161
  definition, 162
object streaming, 167
ObjectCOBOL
  adoption of, 205
  and electronic commerce, 213
  and Java, 215
  features, 205
  naming attributes, 228
  sample code, 205
objects
  definition, 5
  interface, 262
  versioning, 337
ODBC. *See* Open database connectivity
ODMG, 294
OID. *See* Object identifiers

OLE. *See* Object linking and embedding
OMG. *See* Object management group
OMT. *See* Object modeling technique
one-to-one relationships, 251
OOCRUD, 90, 104, 328
  and CORBA, 164
  definition, 293
OODBMS, 334
  definition, 335
  features, 335
  myths, 338
  scalability, 338
  13 golden rules, 335
OOCS. *See* Object-oriented client/server
OOSDLC, 27
OOUI. *See* Object-oriented user interface
open database connectivity (ODBC)
  definition, 328
OpenDoc, 93
operations testing, 407
  definition, 407
optimistic locking
  definition, 294
optionality
  definition, 11
  notation, 40
OQL
  definition, 91, 294
ORB. *See* object request brokers
override
  definition, 9, 184
overload. *See* Override

P

paragraphing, 241
  definition, 242
parenthesis, 245
Pareto's rule. *See* 80/20 rule
partitioning classes, 113
path testing, 386
  definition, 388

patterns
  advantages, 134
  analysis, 118
  and reuse, 134
  as a buzzword, 136
  business entity, 128
  contact point, 128
  definition, 118
  design, 118
  disadvantages, 135
  discovery, 133
  effective use, 132
  Item-Item description, 126
  list of, 136
  Place, 131
  Proxy, 120
  Roles Played, 122
  Shipping/Billing, 130
  Singleton, 119
  state, 122
  using them together, 129
payment processing, 210
peer-to-peer architecture, 149
  definition, 150
peer-to-peer wrapping, 353
  definition, 354
  skills, 356
percentage of commented methods
    metric, 187
percentage of key classes metric, 179
percentage of tested use-case scenar-
    ios metric, 189
persistence
  and CORBA, 164
  and data models, 79
  and proxies, 122
  classes, 102
  definition, 9, 292
  persistent memory, 10
  persistent objects, 10
  transitory objects, 10
persistence classes, 111
  and C-APIs, 356
  and DSLs, 356
  buying, 108

definition, 91, 102
development, 111
identifying, 107
metrics, 193
skill requirements, 256
persistence layer, 90
  advantages, 103
  and OOCRUD, 104
  definition, 292
  implementing, 93
persistence mechanism
  definition, 91, 292
  flat files, 295
  object/relational databases, 339
  OODBMS, 334
  relational databases, 298, 311, 326
  security, 337
persistent memory
  definition, 10
persistent objects
  definition, 10
  example, 10
person days per class metric, 174
pessimistic locking
  definition, 293
pilot testing, 409
  definition, 409
pinball SDLC, 27, 414
Place pattern, 131
polymorphic
  definition, 13
polymorphism
  and case statements, 246
  and interface objects, 263
  and languages, 200
  and OIDs, 315
  and testing, 397
  definition, 13
  example, 13
pop-up menus, 277
portability
  and Java, 203
  definition, 86
pre/ (keyword), 68
printout height metric, 188

problem reports per class metric, 189
process models
  and DFDs, 72
  definition, 71
  drawing, 72
  tips, 74
  when to draw, 74
productivity
  and patterns, 134
program code
  root of all evil, 107
programming, 32
project
  initiation, 30
  teams, 109
project estimating
  difficulties, 175
  tips, 178
project management
  and class-type architecture, 109
prototype walkthroughs, 370
  definition, 371
prototypes
  definition, 371
prototyping, 19, 112
  and interface-flow diagrams, 74
  and testing, 370
  definition, 283
  documentation, 283
prototyping
  OOUIs, 281
  steps of, 282
  tips and techniques, 284
  tools, 286
  types of, 286
proxy
  database, 293
proxy pattern, 120
pure inheritance, 65
pure languages
  definition, 202
  vs. hybrid, 201

Q

QA. *See* Software quality assurance

R

read lock
  definition, 293
recursive transition
  definition, 64
refactoring, 243
  definition, 244
regression testing
  definition, 367
  inheritance, 394
  test cases, 369
relational databases, 298
  reasons for using, 298
relationships
  aggregation, 11
  and CORBA, 166
  and foreign keys, 324
  cardinality, 11
  class, 39
  finding, 31
  implementing, 249, 322
  in data models, 77
  instance, 10
  "is-a," 8
  "is-like," 8
  "is-part-of," 11
  many-to-many, 250, 325
  many-to-one, 250
  one-to-many, 324
  one-to-one, 251, 324
  optionality, 11
  navigation direction, 41
  "uses," 58
repositories
  definition, 218
requirement-verification matrices,
    379
  example, 380
responsibility, 15
  finding, 18
reuse
  and inheritance, 183
  and patterns, 134
  and wrapping, 357
  class libraries, 216

components, 216
frameworks, 217
metrics, 176
of classes, 247
of legacy code, 357
of test cases, 399
of use cases, 59
three times rule, 176
reuse engineering, 218
reviews
advantages, 378
checklists, 376
code, 382
cursory, 374
design, 372
of test plans, 401
participants, 375, 378
planning, 375
process, 373
prototype walkthroughs, 370
technical, 372
tips, 377
user requirements, 371
Roles Played pattern, 122
root
definition, 9
router classes, 159
definition, 160

S

scaffolding, 347
definition, 348
scalability
OODBMS, 338
scheduling
and prototypes, 286
Scott's Soapboxes
automatic garbage collection, 200
coverage and path testing aren't as
important anymore, 387
don't hardcore SQL, 327
estimating is tough, 175
future of Java, 204, 215
good C/S implementation, 143
is history repeating itself?, 205

ISO 9000 says nothing about qual
ity, 411
iterative vs. hacking, 223
lines of code, 188
mapping objects to RDBs, 333
persistence mechanism market, 340
pure vs. hybrid debate, 201
UI standards are a must, 270
when is a language OO?, 200
your UI isn't OO ..., 269
screen navigation, 274
screen scraping, 351
advantages, 352
and thin-client approach, 145, 351
definition, 353
disadvantages, 352
skills, 356
scribes, 23
SDLC, 27
second normal form, 301
and 2ONF, 307
definition, 304
second object normal form, 306
and 2NF, 307
and 3NF, 307
definition, 311
security, 166, 337
sequence diagrams
and use cases, 60
definition, 60
drawing, 62
example, 61
when to draw, 63
serial development
testing, 415
server classes
and subsystems, 158
definition, 155
identifying, 156
servers
application, 146
definition, 142
features, 143
setter methods, 229
definition, 230

setter methods (*continued*)
  testing, 390
Shipping/Billing pattern, 130
single inheritance, 9
Singleton pattern, 119
  and globals, 183
skill requirements
  business classes, 256
  interface classes, 255
  persistence classes, 256
  system classes, 256
skills transfer, 420
Smalltalk, 280
  accessors, 229
  and electronic commerce, 213
  and Java, 215
  execution speed, 207
  features, 207
  for learning C++, 206
  method size, 185
  metrics, 176, 185, 187
  naming attributes, 228
  sample code, 207
  testing, 392
2NF. *See* Second normal form
software quality assurance, 410
  definition, 411
2ONF. *See* Second object normal form
SQA. *See* Software quality assurance
SQA departments, 411
SQL
  definition, 91, 294
  dynamic, 329
  static, 329
standards
  abbreviations, 227
  for UI design, 270, 273
  Hungarian notation, 228
state diagrams
  and testing, 393
  definition, 64
  drawing, 66
  hints, 67
  inheritance of, 65
  when to draw, 68
states

and attributes, 64
  definition, 64
  final, 64
  initial, 64
  substate, 67
  superstate, 67
state-transition diagrams. *See* State
  diagrams
static binding
  definition, 202
static SQL
  definition, 330
  vs. dynamic, 329
stress test plan, 405
  definition, 406
stress testing, 405
  definition, 406
strings of messge sends metric, 187
subclasses
  definition, 9
substate
  definition, 67
subsystem contracts
  definition, 158
subsystems
  and router classes, 159
  and server classes, 158
  definition, 155
  identifying, 150, 154
  implementing, 159
success factors, 191
superclasses
  definition, 9
superstate
  definition, 67
system classes
  and C-APIs, 356
  and DSLs, 356
  buying, 109
  definition, 94, 105
  developing, 110
  identifying, 107
  metrics, 193
  skill requirements, 256
system integration, 346
system testing, 403

definition, 403
function testing, 404
installation testing, 406
operations testing, 407
stress testing, 405
tips, 404
volume testing, 405
systems programming, 202

T

team development, 217
technical-design reviews, 372
advantages, 378
definition, 373
planning, 375
process, 373
what to review, 373
technical review checklists, 376
technical review plans, 375
definition, 376
test cases
and regression testing, 369
built-in, 399
definition, 364
implementing, 398
separate hierarchy, 399
test plans, 401
definition, 364
review of, 401
stress test, 405
UAT, 408
test scripts, 400
testing, 32
alpha testing, 409
analysis testing, 369
and good design, 379, 398
and incremental development, 369
and ISO 9000, 410
and polymorphism, 397
and QA, 410
and state diagrams, 393
application testing, 403
beta testing, 409
black box, 383
boundary value, 385

class-integration testing, 396
class testing, 392
clear box, 384
code testing, 380
costs of, 365
coverage testing, 386
definition, 364
design testing, 63, 372
FLOOT, 364
FLOOT overview, 414
function testing, 404
in the large, 403, 414
in the small, 414
inheritance-regression testing, 394
installation testing, 406
issues in, 21
messages, 397
method testing, 389
metrics, 189
OO vs. structured, 367, 388
operations testing, 407
paradigm, 388
path testing, 386
pilot testing, 409
process, 401
realities of, 365
regression testing, 367
requirement-verification matrices,
379
Smalltalk code, 392
stress testing, 405
subclasses, 400
system testing, 403
test cases, 364
test logs, 364
test object sets, 388
test plans, 364
test scripts, 364
tips, 412
tools, 217
traditional methods, 383
training in, 412
troughout the SDLC, 364
use-case scenario testing, 20, 22
user-acceptance testing, 407
user interface, 76

testing (*continued*)
volume testing, 405
white box, 384
testing in the large, 414
definition, 415
testing in the small, 414
definition, 415
test-procedure scripts
definition, 364
thin-client approach, 144
third normal form, 302
and 3ONF, 307
definition, 304
third object normal form, 307
definition, 311
13 golden rules of OODBMS, 335
30-second rule, 185, 245
three-tier client/server, 146
advantages, 147
definition, 148
tips
achieving the benefits of distribution, 148
analysis patterns, 125
application should be self-updat-
ing, 146
assign legacy screens unique IDs,
352
assigning people to classes, 189
be proactive with beta testers, 410
tips
combine test cases, 394
coding standards we input to code
reviews, 382
concentrate on typical situations
when testing another's code,
386
diagramming, 52
document interface objects once
they're stable, 284
drawing state diagrams, 67
effective documentation, 241
error handling, 253
errors are usually in your new
code, 383

establishing your priorities, 190
estimating, 178
for accessors, 258
for attributes, 257
for classes, 258
for methods, 257
for metrics, 191
for OO development, 256
for system testing, 404
for 2ONF, 306
get someone who can draw, 281
get the design right first, 379
good designs require less testing,
398
how to remember the rules of 3NF,
303
inheritance and relational DBs,
316
lazy initialization and persistence,
235
look at subsets of behavior, 308
look to past problems to create
checklists, 377
maintenance of methods, 244
method testing, 392
naming conventions, 226
naming loop counters, 227
people first, 242
performing reviews, 377
placing class types, 141
process modeling, 74
prototyping, 284
put classes into 3ONF only when
it makes sense, 310
return intelligent errors, 112
reuse existing classes, 247
set naming conventions for methods, 13
stabilize your code before testing
it, 381
test for inheritance, 396
testing, 412
timestamps vs. datetimestamps,
123
use a spreadsheet for requirement-
verification matrices, 380

use data warehouses for reporting, 321
user interface design, 273, 287
when to use the Roles Played pattern, 125
your prototype must be doable, 283
3NF. *See* Third normal form
3ONF. *See* Third object normal form
tool selection
metrics, 190
training and education
C++, 206
ObjectCOBOL, 206
training courses, 420
training plans, 406
transaction
definition, 293
transaction processing (TP) monitors, 161
transient objects. *See* Transitory objects
transitions
and methods, 65
definition, 64
recursive, 64
transitory objects
definition, 10
example, 10
two-tier client/server
definition, 144
typing, 198

U

UAT. *See* User acceptance testing
UML. *See* Unified modeling language
unified modeling language, 34
definition, 35
simplified class diagramming notation, 42
unit testing
definition, 389
vs. class testing, 392
vs. method testing, 389
use-case diagrams

definition, 58
drawing, 58
example, 57
when to use, 59
use-case scenario testing, 370
definition, 371
use cases
and class-type architecture, 97
and function testing, 404
and interface classes, 100
and sequence diagrams, 60
and user acceptance test planning, 23
creating, 30
defining, 19
definition, 20, 25, 58
metrics, 179, 189
reuse, 59
scenario testing, 20, 22, 25
scenarios, 20–21, 23
user acceptance test plan
and use cases, 23
user-acceptance testing, 407
and function testing, 404, 408
definition, 408
user interface design
and metaphors, 271
and standards, 270
color usage, 275
consistency, 267
field alignment, 276
fonts, 275
grouping widgets, 277
screen density, 277
screen navigation, 274
testing, 370
tips, 273, 287
wording messages, 274
user interfaces
and database access, 100
and interface-flow diagrams, 74
implementing, 98
user-interface specialists, 99
user requirement reviews
definition, 371

user requirements
  reviews, 371
users
  and testing, 366
  working with, 226

V

versioning, 337
virtual machinee, 204
  definition, 204
virtual products, 212
volume testing, 405
  definition, 406

W

walkthroughs
  prototype, 370
whitespace, 239
  definition, 240
whiteboards, 74
white-box testing, 384
  definition, 385
widgets, 274
  grouping, 277
World Wide Web (WWW), 203
  definition, 210
wrapper class, 344
  definition, 345
wrappers, 344
  database, 328
  definition, 345
wrapping, 344

advantages, 357
and coupling, 348
and electronic commerce, 216
and extensibility, 358
and maintenance, 357
wrapping
  and system integration, 346
  approaches, 346
  C-APIs, 348
  comparisons, 355
  CORBA, 354
  database access, 91
  debugging issues, 350
  definition, 91
  disadvantages, 357
  don't, 347
  dynamic shared libraries, 348
  hardware, 347
  legacy applications, 347, 351
  legacy code, 345
  operating systems, 347
  peer-to-peer, 353
  reasons for, 344
  screen scraping, 351
  skills, 356
  technologies, 348
  the system layer, 94
write lock
  definition, 293
WWW.AmbySoft.Com, 421
WWW. *See* World Wide Web